WOMEN IN
PRISON

WOMEN IN PRISON

Inside the Concrete Womb

REVISED EDITION

Kathryn Watterson

Northeastern University Press : Boston

Northeastern University Press

Library of Congress Cataloging-in-Publication Data
Watterson, Kathryn, 1942–
    Women in prison : inside the concrete womb / Kathryn Watterson.—
Rev. ed.
        p.   cm.
    Includes bibliographical references.
    ISBN 1-55553-237-3 (alk. paper).—ISBN 1-55553-238-1 (pbk. :
alk. paper)
        1. Female offenders—United States—Case studies.   2. Women
prisoners—United States—Case studies.   3. Reformatories for women—
United States.   I. Title.
HV9471.W37   1996
365'.43'0973—dc20   95-31968

Designed by David Ford

Composed in Times Roman by Coghill Composition, Richmond, Virginia.
Printed and bound by Edwards Brothers, Inc., Ann Arbor, Michigan. The
paper is Glatfelter Offset, an acid-free stock.

MANUFACTURED IN THE UNITED STATES OF AMERICA
00   99   98   97   96   5   4   3   2   1

FOR JOHN, MOM, AND ALICE

And for all of us trying to build lives
free from inner and outer tyrannies—
who want to hear, not just listen;
see, not just watch;
live, not merely survive.

CONTENTS

ACKNOWLEDGMENTS

I take this space once again to thank friends and colleagues who helped me with this book the first time around. They are Marie Stoner, Kitty Caparella, John Ware, David Rudovsky, Naomi Burns, Claude Lewis, Fletcher Clarke, Donald Nathanson, Carol Nathanson, James H. Neely, Julius Lester, Terry Derry, Julie Oshana, Sue Walton, Ellen McLaughlin, Ford Burkhart, Donna Calame, Rochelle Jones, Emiko Tonooka, and my ''Hamilton Street Mafia'' of Leslie, Charity, Lauren, Lisa, and Nini, who have become grownups with children of their own since the first publication of this book.

For this edition, I am grateful to Leigh Bienen, its rightful godmother; Scott Brassart, my editor, Ann Twombly and Larry Hamberlin at Northeastern University Press; and my agent, Ellen Levine. I also am grateful to Susan Danoff, who helped me reconceptualize chapter titles and the sequence of chapters and stories for this new edition; Lee Gruzen, my eyes for news on this subject, who listened with patience to my outpourings over the material; Gerry Boswell, who gave me legal updates; Marie Stoner, who went over old territory with me once again; and Jane Nakashima and Phillip Higgs, for their help. I'm particularly grateful to Meda Chesney-Lind, Rhea Schnaeman, Patricia Scholes, Barbara Bloom, Barbara Owen, Ellen Barry, Nicole Hahn Rafter, and the many others whose important research efforts over the past twenty years have documented so much of what I believed but couldn't prove to be patterns in the experiences of women in prison. Their work is illuminating and inspiring, as is that of women and men who have worked inside and outside prisons as social workers, drug treatment specialists, teachers, advocates, and volunteers for change.

PREFACE TO THE 1996 EDITION

More than twenty-three years ago I was talking with a group of women in the kitchen of Ohio's state prison for women at Marysville, when a prisoner started shouting from across the room, "Why are you talking to her? What good's it gonna do? She ain't gonna do nothing!"

She leaned on her mop, angry and unconvinced when the women I was talking to hollered back that I was writing a book that would "tell it like it is."

"Well, even if she does write it like it is, people ain't gonna do nothing about it," she said. "They'll just say, 'Ain't that a shame,' and nothing will change. It'll be the same. It was the same twenty years ago as it is now. Twenty years from now it'll still be the same. We'll still be here. And it'll be just the same."

Not long after that, a prison administrator in California sat back in his office chair, twirled his pencil, and talked about changes in the air that might affect the accuracy of *Women in Prison* when it was published. But then he reflected that while some regulations might change, "Jails will always be the same, so your book will still be valid, even ten years from now or as long as jails exist, I guess."

I knew he was right: even though new technology might be introduced or certain rules might change, the basic reality of prisons and jails would never change. But in those days, I was optimistic. I believed that when the public learned the truth—that the warehousing of human beings has nothing to do with alleviating crime—things would change.

I thought the facts would become self-evident. But it's clear that the public still doesn't understand how prisons really work. Everybody feels safer when bad guys are arrested and sent to prison. Naturally, we are concerned about public safety and crimes of violence, but we have a distorted notion about how these problems are dealt with and solved.

We still seem to think prisons lock up the killers who scare us out of our wits. But the reality is that most of the people in prison are nonviolent and that the really dangerous people are only a fraction of the prison population. The media's sensational focus on terrible cases blurs our senses until we can't see that these incidents, horrible as they are, represent only a tiny minority of the cases that clog our criminal justice system.

Our rage at child molesters, killers, and true psychotics blinds us to the reality that the vast majority of men and women in prison are locked in for years for petty property crimes, drug addiction, vagrancy, bad checks. Killer movies, violent television, and political hot air about "getting tough" on crime create heat and smoke that obscure the fact that prisons warehouse and destroy the lives of our most poverty-stricken Americans— people who would never spend a day in jail for the same crimes if they had economic resources.

I believed when I wrote the first edition of this book that the public would see that prisons have failed from the beginning, that they don't stop crime, that if anything, they *create* crime by keeping people locked in a repressive environment that drives them crazy before they're dumped back out on the streets. It was obvious in 1973 that we had more than enough prison cells to keep society safe from the small fraction (5 to 20 percent) of prisoners who were a danger to the community.

I also thought politicians would realize that to stop crime, we had to pursue workable alternatives to prison such as intensive probation and intervention with high-risk juveniles and adults, drug education and treatment, schools, job training, parenting programs, literacy programs, and counseling—programs that cost a fraction as much per person per year as prison and that are many times more effective.

I thought we might get smart. But I was wrong. And my observer at Marysville was right. I wrote the book, but it didn't change anything. In fact, not only are things the same, but they are worse.

The number of prisoners today is more than five times larger than it was twenty-five years ago. During the first six months of 1994, fifteen hundred new prisoners a week were ushered into America's prisons and jails. This ghastly increase—which brings the total prison population in the United States to over one million people in 1995—is almost incomprehensible. The number of people we have in prison would populate the ninth largest city in the United States. Today we lock up 519 out of every 100,000 people in this country, a per capita rate topped only by Russia. We have run amok with greater absolute numbers of prison inmates locked up for longer periods of time than any other nation on earth. In addition to the million people in state and federal prisons, there are about half a million people in jails, about six hundred thousand on parole, about three million on probation, and about a hundred thousand in juvenile facilities.

It might seem astonishing, but the numbers of women in prison have escalated more rapidly than any other segment of the prison population. When I wrote the first edition of *Women in Prison,* there were 7,730 women in city and county jails around the country and 15,000 women in state and federal prisons. Now more than 108,000 women fill our prisons and jails. Of those, some 48,879 women sit in small sections of city or county jails around the country, where they are awaiting trial, serving misdemeanor sentences of one year or less, or waiting to be transferred to a state prison where they'll serve longer sentences for felony convictions. (Some have been returned to jail for violating probation or parole, and others have returned from prisons where they are serving time to await a court date on an appeal for a new trial.) Some 59,237 women are locked into state and federal prisons—where they'll spend from two years to the rest of their lives for their crimes. (There are 53,102 women in state prisons and 6,135 in federal prisons, according to American Correctional Association statistics from June 1994.) Today the criminal justice system is more inclined than ever before to sentence women to prison and keep them there for longer periods of time. From 1980 to 1990, for instance, the number of women in prison increased by 256 percent, compared with a 140 percent increase in male prisoners.

Far from rejecting the prison system over the past twenty years, we've poured billions of dollars into it. In 1995, at a time the public is adamant about cutting governmental costs—when we are slashing public school budgets, medicare, and aid to dependent children, and when we don't have enough money for Headstart programs, job training for teenagers, college loans, housing subsidies, art, or urban renewal—we are spending millions of dollars a day to give ourselves the *illusion* that we will be safer in our communities if we pay the costs of imprisonment, no matter how high that cost goes.

Right before I sent in the final page proofs for this new edition of *Women in Prison,* I called the National Institute of Corrections to check the current cost of imprisonment per prisoner per year. I thought it was a simple question. But by the time I had followed that one question through many tangled paths, I had learned some shocking facts. First I learned that, based on a survey of corrections budgets from the fifty states, the federal prison system, and the District of Columbia Department of Corrections, the Criminal Justice Institute's 1995 *Corrections Yearbook* calculated that corrections agencies spend an average of $53.24 per adult prisoner per day in operating costs. As of June 30, 1994, 980,513 adults were confined in state and federal prisons, according to the 1995 American Correctional Associations Directory. That means we are paying more than $52 million dollars a day just to keep adult prisoners locked and fed in our state and federal prisons.

What's more, we also are spending more than $23 million dollars a day in operating costs to keep people imprisoned in American jails—and this is a conservative estimate. (According to the 1995 *Criminal Justice Yearbook,* among 127 jail systems the average cost of maintaining a prisoner in 1994 was $46.97 per day. In June 1994, according to the Bureau of Justice Statistics *Bulletin,* 490,442 adult men and women were in jail, which means bare bones operating costs are $23 million a day.)

It may be hard to believe that $75 million dollars a day is not the full amount of what we pay to keep people incarcerated, but it isn't. The actual operating costs of prisons and jails are unknown. That's because there are no uniform accounting methods by which each state, city, or county keeps track of its expenditures, measures its budget, calculates its incarceration rates, or reports its findings. Some standard costs integral to running prisons and jails are systematically excluded from figures many correctional systems provide to surveying agencies. For instance, retirement accounts for corrections officers and pension fund contributions are rarely included.[1] Even items such as electricity and heat for an institution, and prisoner transportation, and hospitalization often are not included in projections of a prison's annual operating costs.

Several studies have found that if these costs were added in, they would significantly increase the reported operating costs of imprisonment. Douglas C. McDonald, a political economist who has closely examined the costs of corrections, says that across the nation, it's "not unreasonable to expect" that audited and reported costs equal about 60 to 75 percent of total direct costs, which makes "the actual cost of operating public correctional programs about 33 to 66 percent higher than is actually reported."[2] Since state, federal, and local systems *report* that they spend an average of $75 million a day in operating costs, then adding the hidden costs of 33 to 66 percent means that we are spending from $100 to $125 million per day simply to house and feed adult prisoners in America—$36 to $45 billion annually simply to keep adult men and women locked up in America's prisons and jails.

This $36 to $45 billion does not include the additional expenses of

1. Douglas C. McDonald, "The Cost of Corrections: In Search of the Bottom Line," *Research in Corrections* 2, issue 1 (February 1989).
2. Ibid.

locking up teenagers and maintaining juvenile reformatories, nor does it account for probation or parole, or for the enormous capital expenditures of building new prisons, renovating old prisons, and transforming other facilities to hold prisoners. (Those expenditures boost correctional costs to more than $85 billion annually, up from $10 billion twenty years ago.)

What all of this means is that on a daily basis, we are pouring many millions of our tax dollars into a prison system that performs only one function in a crime prevention system: it keeps some perpetrators off the streets for a limited time. Unfortunately, during their imprisonment, prisoners learn nothing to help them change their behavior, and they become further isolated, embittered, and alienated from the society to which they will return. Instead, for a fraction of the cost of imprisonment, many prisoners could be leading productive lives in intensive supervision programs within the community. (In these programs—which do successfully reduce crime—probation officers see their probationers five to seven days a week, keep tabs on their daily work routines, and make sure they stay in counseling and drug treatment programs. Under these and other alternative community programs, people can take responsibility for their crimes, pay restitution and court costs, get treatment for substance abuse, become productively employed, pay taxes, and take care of their children.)

But instead of developing cheaper and more effective alternatives, we're simply building more prisons. During the 1970s we opened seventeen new prisons for women, and in the 1980s we doubled that number. In the 1990s women are imprisoned in seventy state prisons for women and women's units in twenty-nine men's prisons (these are referred to as co-ed facilities), three federal women's prisons, and nine women's units in federal prisons for men, according to the 1994 American Correctional Association Directory. Women also are locked up in several separate jails for women and in segregated sections of other local jails—which numbered 3,316 when they were last counted in 1988.

The expense of providing separate prison housing for women often is said to be higher than average, but even if we use the figures provided by the 1995 *Corrections Yearbook* and the 1995 *Criminal Justice Yearbook* for all prisoners, then we are paying operating costs of more than $5.5 million per day simply to lock up adult women prisoners in America. When hidden costs add another 33 to 66 percent, this means that we actually are spending from $7 million to $9 million every day to keep adult women locked in prisons and jails in this country. That adds up to expenditures of $2.5 to $3.5 billion a year for their imprisonment.

In the 1990s, despite crippling costs and recidivism, we're still scrambling to find more prison space for women prisoners by constructing more jails and prisons (at the cost of $100,000 per cell to build), renovating existing space, and moving women into quarters previously occupied by men. "One of the ways the prison systems have dealt with overcrowding is to take a unit in men's prisons and put women there," one corrections official told me. "Usually this is a big problem, because women are much more restricted in their movement when they're confined to only one section of a facility."

As I point out in chapter 4, we are putting so many more women in prison today and treating them so much more harshly because we *think* they're more dangerous. But government statistics show that while the public perception is that there has been an increase in violence and drug use among women, there has in fact been either no change or a decrease in violent crimes committed by women.[3] Between 1986 and 1991, for instance, Bureau of Justice statistics show that the proportion of women serving time for violent offenses fell from 41 percent to 32 percent. Similarly, the rates of drug use for women—while perceived as wildly increasing—have either remained the same or decreased. In 1993, for instance, government figures showed that female arrestees showed a decline in the rates of cocaine use—and unchanged or lower rates of marijuana and opiate use. The rate of cocaine use among fifteen- to twenty-year-old arrestees was lower than the rate for older female arrestees.[4]

Nevertheless, the increases in the number of women imprisoned for drug offenses are responsible for dramatic overuse and overcrowding of prisons. In 1991 some 12,600 women were imprisoned for drug offenses, representing a 432 percent increase since 1986. And despite this enormous influx of women into jails and prisons for drug possession and drug-related crimes, we still have almost no drug counselors or programs in our prisons and jails. Those that do exist are extremely limited in the numbers they can serve and must operate within the restrictions of prison security, the first and foremost concern of the prison.

When I look at the trends of putting more and more drug-addicted and alcoholic women in prison, which means breaking up their families—and damaging the home life, stability, and school achievement of their children—I'm discouraged. These women need help—and their children need attention. But by locking up the mothers, we're creating a self-fulfilling prophecy for these children who already are at high risk of joining the

3. Russ Immarigeon and Meda Chesney-Lind, *Women's Prisons: Overcrowded and Overused* (National Council on Crime and Delinquency), 1992.
4. "Drug Use Forecasting," 1993 Annual Report on Adult Arrestees: Drugs and Crime in America's Cities, National Institute of Justice, November 1994.

cycle of substance abuse and crime that continues from generation to generation.

Perhaps that prisoner was right, and nothing ever will change. As the children of baby boomers enter their most violence-prone years, as the new federal crime bill encourages states to adopt tougher mandatory minimum sentences and a raft of new federal crimes require long mandatory sentences, positive change doesn't look promising. Nevertheless, I am grateful that Northeastern University Press is giving *Women in Prison* a chance to be in print again and to find new readers. The women who speak from these pages speak timeless words, and it never has been more urgent for us to listen and respond to them.

Returning to this text after so many years has offered me the unusual opportunity to look at my own work in a more objective way. When I wrote *Women in Prison,* which was my first book, I was trying to show the reality of the prison experience through the stories of the women in prison. I had more women's stories than I could reasonably use, but I was determined that they be heard, and so I included at least one or two of them in front of and behind every chapter. They made for a dense and wonderful immersion somewhat reflective of the chaos of prison lives, but they didn't allow the reader a focused structure. I now have moved most of these personal stories to chapter 9, "Snapshots: Women's Stories, Women's Lives." I also have moved some of the lists of rules that I had woven in around chapters to an appendix at the back of the book. For comparison—to show how little things have changed inside—I've also added a list of prison rules and regulations from a 1994 prison "Handbook on Discipline."

The stylistic changes I have made include eliminating repetition, clarifying a few ideas, changing my sometimes arbitrary and wacky punctuation, and modernizing some of my 1970s slang. I have reordered and retitled chapters to reflect a more precise sense of the contents and to help readers have a clearer idea of where they are heading when they begin a chapter. Chapters 10 ("A Look at the History of Women's Prisons in America") and 11 ("Locked Out: The Concrete Wall between Women and Their Children") were formerly combined into one (very long) chapter ("One Step Forward, Two Steps Back") in the first edition. Likewise, I have divided the chapter on health care into two; the first ("Medical Treatment: Band-Aids over Broken Bones") focuses on medical conditions, the second ("Crime or Mental Illness? Shrinks, Drugs, and Therapy") on psychiatry and therapy in prison.

For this revision I visited the New Jersey prison for women, spoke with administrator Pat Christy, and also talked with many people who have observed changes that have taken place over the past twenty years. I have used that new information in chapter 4, "Facing Facts," and elsewhere throughout the book when it seemed germane. Where statistics or facts have changed dramatically, as they have regarding disparate sentencing laws for women, I have inserted 1990s figures and new information in a way that is self-evident, or I've put the new information into brackets or added footnotes. I can't do justice to all the wonderful research that has been conducted over the past twenty years, but I've done my best to match current information with what's preceded it.[5]

The women and men prisoners, the prison guards, the prison administrators, corrections personnel, attorneys, and advocates who speak from these pages have been frozen in time—in their ages, their states, their status, and their official titles. Many of them have gone on to other occupations, locations, and opinions, but in this book, they still are speaking from where they stood in 1973. For instance, the woman I identify as "Superintendent of the Women's Detention Center in Washington, D.C." *was* the superintendent when this book first was published. Despite the fact that someone else has stepped into her administrative post, however, her words are startlingly applicable to prison life in 1996. Similarly, Georgia Walton's description of "reception" into jail is as accurate today as it was then, even though information is put into computers, not just on paper. The echoes of prison conditions reverberate daily: Susan Moss's miscarriage in jail was duplicated recently when Angela H., a twenty-year-old Californian who was five months' pregnant, was jailed for possession and sale of marijuana. (Like Susan, Angela began to complain of vaginal bleeding, cramping, and severe pain, but didn't get to see a doctor for more than three weeks. When she did see the jail's doctor, he diagnosed her, without an exam, as having a vaginal infection and gave her Flagyl, a drug that induced premature labor. Her infant son lived only two hours.)

Certainly, some circumstances and rules have changed, but in today's severely overcrowded prisons and jails, the demands for security and control are even more stringent than they were in the 1970s. And while thousands and thousands of other women have filled most of the cells the women in these pages once occupied—and wear men's uniforms, not the prison dresses they often wore in the 1970s—the women in these pages still speak the truth about experiences and conditions that are as relevant and true today as they were then, and, unfortunately, as they probably still

5. The updated bibliography in the back should prove a good guide for anyone wishing to further explore any of the issues in this book.

will be twenty or even fifty years from now in jails and prisons throughout the country.

I still hope for change. I still hope that, if for no other reason than alarm over the horrendous waste of public funds, Americans will come to their senses, stop building prisons, and invest in the available alternatives. Not long ago, Jean Harris, who spent twelve years in Bedford Hills for homicide, wrote in her fine book *Marking Time:* "In here, God knows, life is not a rose garden. . . . Nothing lovely flourishes here. Little that is good is nourished here. What grows here is hypocrisy, obscenity, illness, illegality, ignorance, confusion, waste, hopelessness. Life in prison is a garden of dross, cultivated by those who never check to see what their crop is."

I hope this book will help you think more deeply about our gardens of dross and the crops produced by them. If you can understand through the compilation of stories in *Women in Prison* that prisons have little to do with stopping crime or achieving justice, and that the women in prison are not the criminals you thought they were, then something will have been gained. If you are motivated to stay informed, to reach out to women or children in need, to confront the problems of poverty, illiteracy, racism, and family violence within our communities, or to lobby for community treatment *instead of* imprisonment, then those efforts may become seeds for real change and growth.

FOREWORD

When Kathryn Watterson's groundbreaking *Women in Prison* first was published in 1973, it brought national attention to the reality of prison for a generation that had little thought of prison and even less thought for the women who were in prison. Watterson went into uncharted territory in search of a comprehensive mapping of women's experience in prison, and in the process she shed light on issues that until then had remained hidden from public scrutiny. To her credit, she didn't set out to examine one small corner of this story. She set out to explore it all, and in that process, she identified areas of much-needed research, which have been addressed by scholars in subsequent years.

When we first read this compelling and ambitious book, it left many of us wondering why the hundreds of women Watterson interviewed needed to be incarcerated. Yet since then, the number of women in U.S. prisons and jails has soared. Since 1980 alone, there's been a fivefold increase of the numbers of women locked in prison. This huge change makes reading the updated version of *Women in Prison* a must for anyone concerned about women, victimization, and imprisonment.

Women in Prison was the first book to show us the gritty day-to-day reality of incarceration for women. It allowed us to experience not only the terror but also the petty tyranny of prison life. Watterson takes us into solitary confinement cells where food is pushed between the bottom of the door and the unwashed floor, as are sanitary napkins if the woman is menstruating. She introduces us to the startled woman who watched a guard throw away her cereal because she had dared to put a spoonful of sugar on it. As the guard told her: if you want a spoonful of sugar in your coffee, you can't have one on your cereal. In prison, Watterson shows us, you have to choose.

To do the research for this comprehensive exposé, Watterson interviewed hundreds of women in prison—guards as well as inmates—in dozens of states. She also talked to girls in "training schools" throughout the country. The stories she tells are strikingly up to date—from the women incarcerated for decades for killing abusive husbands, to the women with terrible drug problems, to the runaway girls forced into prostitution after escaping abusive homes. Their stories are today at once the same and different. In those days, only the most ''serious'' women offenders went to prison. Today, the proportion of women doing time for violent crime has dropped dramatically, as the war on drugs has become a war on women. But as Watterson shows, the stories of women's crime is the story of women's place, and most particularly the rarely told story of black, native, and poor women's lives. So the stories Watterson tells do not frighten so much as illuminate. Ultimately, it is hard to imagine, after hearing the voices of these women, how prison could ever improve their lot—or ours.

Sadly, since *Women in Prison* first made us aware of the enormous problems of imprisonment for women and their children, the only major public policy response has been sharply to increase the numbers of imprisoned women. And today, as correctional leaders scramble to find places to incarcerate (or simply to warehouse) the thousands of women going to prison, Watterson's classic work has become all the more timely.

Reading this startling and instructive book again forces us to ask why these women are in prison and why there has been no public discussion or debate about imprisoning more, rather than fewer, women offenders. The answer to this question is not simple, but much of it lies in the evil of incarceration and the continuing secrecy of modern punishment. Watterson's quest was daring and unusual, and it went into areas where few have tread. Prisons are not places most of us look at, and even the citizens of towns that house the largest of these institutions tend to look the other way when they drive by.

As a result, silence shrouds those the prisons hold. As Watterson shows, most of the people we arrest, jail, try, and imprison are poor, and because they are poor, they are without a voice. Such silence particularly attends the jailing of women, since women are supposed to be ''good'' and not ''bad.'' Their tragedies, their suffering, and their pain are not news, and most of us want to believe that whatever suffering they do endure is simply their due, just as we want to believe that the ''system'' that processes them is fair and just.

Indeed, if today's public generally gives any thought to crime and punishment, it is to complain that the system fails to protect us from crime and is too soft on vicious criminals—whom we imagine to be male, violent, and very much like ordinary people. Little in our ordinary lives challenges that construction. Every night we are bombarded with images of egregious and senseless violence, and virtually every face of those shown as having committing these senseless acts is young, black, and male. What are we to make of these frightening images of anger and violence out of control in our cities?

The first and most important point to make about these constructions is that they are grossly *untrue*. Crime is down, not up, in American society. A recent study by the American Bar Association found that with reference to rates of violent crime, "in no instance is the rate higher than 20 years ago, and in most categories it is now substantially lower."* Murder rates, for example, were higher in 1933 than in 1992.

But how can this be true when the media are so full of violence? The sad fact is that our media and our moviemakers have discovered that violence, unlike humor or drama, travels well in the international market and comes cheaper than other forms of entertainment. The more images of violence our children watch, the more they (and we) come to believe that the scary, mean world they see on the screen exists outside their doors.

The notion of a mean society is also abetted by lazy local news, which finds that "if it bleeds, it leads" journalism takes far less energy than doing the real work of explaining the complex sources of crime and social problems—which is what Watterson has attempted to do in *Women in Prison*.

Also, politicians have discovered the fear of crime and its root cause—unarticulated racism—and they have no qualms about turning this fear and racism to their advantage. *Crime* has become a code word for race, and being tough on crime has become almost a prerequisite for election.

In their rush to "outcrime" their opponents and appear tough on crime, our leaders have dramatically increased the penalties on virtually every offense in the books, particularly drug offenses. This has caused the prison population to explode, not with new, more vicious criminals, but with the very same petty offenders who used to receive probation for their deeds. And the most invisible of these offenders are women.

As we prepare to leave the twentieth century, our nation has the dubious distinction of the second highest incarceration rate in the world. Corrections is the fastest growing item in virtually every state budget and is robbing money from education, housing, and social services. This mindless spending is fueled not by an increase in crime but by cynical political forces that have exploited the unresolved racial and economic inequities in U.S. society.

*American Bar Foundation, "Reducing Crime by Increasing Incarceration: Does This Policy Make Sense?" *Researching Law* 6, no. 1 (Winter 1995): 4.

How do we begin to challenge the correctional industrial complex that is rapidly emerging around and feeding off of our fear of crime and criminals? First and foremost, we must break through the stereotypes and meet the prisoner as a person and listen to her stories as she speaks about her life and her experiences in prison. We must see the human faces and know the human beings who all too often are portrayed only in mind-numbing, depersonalized statistics.

This is what Watterson does as she brings us this updated edition of *Women in Prison*. She takes us into the hearts and minds and lives of women in prison and lets us know them as individuals, as human beings who deserve our attention. Their stories and the lessons they teach us are timeless. It is to our shame that we need to read this book again. But reading it again should make us resolve to spend money that ends violence against girls and women, should help us learn to live together rather than apart, and should inspire us to end the grinding poverty that is destroying many neighborhoods and families, instead of punishing the clearest victims of these forces. Our silence about the crime of their punishment costs us far more than dollars. In this silence, Watterson reminds us, we begin to deny our own humanity as well as the humanity of those we imprison.

University of Hawaii at Manoa   MEDA CHESNEY-LIND

WOMEN IN PRISON

1   A SEPARATE SOCIETY

Inside the Concrete Womb

The horn cuts through the quiet of the valley and echoes loudly down the halls of the state prison for women in southern California. It sounds like a foghorn—jarring the senses, interrupting activity. It's an air raid warning, an alarm, an emergency. At the California Institution for Women, in Frontera, it blares its demands five times a day, informing even the uninitiated to be in their rooms for "count." The response is monotonous hysteria. Women scramble and run to their rooms. The horn signals the routine counting of bodies, which occurs from five to six times a day in almost every prison in the country. The count is a security check against escape.

Minutes after the foghorn sounds and each prisoner is sitting on her own bed, short, loud, popping sounds, like staccato cannons, go off one after another, inundating even the quietest mind. The doors are being locked. This particular prison is automated; there's no need for a guard to turn the key manually in every door. The matron sitting in the control room merely pulls switches that close and lock all the doors.

From your vantage point inside the cell, you see a guard walking by the narrow wicket in your locked door. She looks in, sees you on your bed, and checks your number off her list; you haven't escaped. This procedure is somehow reminiscent of kindergarten when teacher calls your name and you say, "Present." But the check mark here goes on the paper beside Number 8811, Number 7286, Number 7384 . . .

When her count is complete, the matron goes to the control center and calls in the number present from her unit. "Latham B: fifty-eight," she says over the public address system to the guard writing down the numbers in the Administration Building's control center. "Latham B: fifty-eight, okay," he repeats and confirms. When he has taken count from every living unit, the hospital, work areas, and administration, his voice booms back over the PA into the living unit: "Count clear." "Count clear," the matron echoes down the hall. The staccato sounds of cannon fire start again. The doors are popped open.

After count, women move back into the TV room or walk up and down the halls. Some women stay in their rooms to read or write letters. If you have a pass, you can sit in the "rec room," which is located between two living units, and play cards for the next two or three hours.

This particular night, on this particular hall in Latham B, the women are sitting lookout—alert and ready to stop one psychotic woman, Helen, from hurting one of her sister prisoners. Helen pulled the wires from the television last night. During the last week, she put shit in the showers and went into two or three rooms to smear lipstick on the curtains. She has started several fights.

It's now on the grapevine that she's going to kill Nancy. She has stolen scissors to do the job. Early tonight she watched, sullen but with wild terror in her eyes, from the corner as Nancy worked to fix the television— rewiring with care and skill the connections ripped out the night before. When Nancy switches the set back on and it works, a cheer goes up from the women who hope to see a TV special with Bill Cosby. Nancy bows to an appreciative audience and heads back to her room.

Meanwhile, Helen looks like a cornered, ravenous, wild child. She's whispering to herself, "I'm gonna get that bitch. I'm gonna get that bitch."

"Helen's a dangerous, sick woman," Marguerite tells me as we sit in her room, aware of the tension in the hall. "But it's not something we can go to the staff with—not yet. They don't have any idea who tore apart the television—and they don't know who put the shit in the showers. The code here is you don't go to the police—you handle the problems your-selves. Usually we do pretty well.

"But people are petrified . . . And we're not playing with somebody you can sit down and talk to. She's the kind who will jump out and get Nancy from behind—just slash, slash, poke. Nobody is going to let Nancy get hurt. The girls want to handle it, but they aren't capable of dealing with this one. Most of the law and order around here is done woman to woman, but there just aren't enough women to handle her. I think on this one I might have to break the code. It's so serious. She had wanted Nancy for a friend; now she wants to kill her.

"I have to think about it. It's a big thing to break the code. If I make the move, I'll be willing to accept the consequences. I have to be responsible for my decisions—but I believe that in this case, it's a matter of life and death."

Marguerite adjusts herself on her bed—the only place in her room to sit. "You know, this is a sick society," she says. "Women who should righteously be in PTU [Psychiatric Treatment Unit] are walking around on the grounds. If they actually let us run this place legally—which in reality we do anyway—things would be different."

She shows me her macramé and some baby sweaters she has knit for the children of her prison friends. "In many ways this is a true communistic system, living here. You know what? We are all convicts. We don't have money. We barter for the things from the free world—barter for dope, pills, food, cigarettes. Cigarettes are the biggest bartering commodity in this community. We are just like a small community except we don't have any men. So there are women who take the place of men. And how many housewives go further than the market, the church, and the school? We have fifty acres here. We don't pay any taxes—except in labor.

"There are some people who want power—and struggle for identification with the powers that be. There are also some sick women here who love chaos—house against house, woman against woman. But we deal with them, with the problems, collectively.

"This is a whole different world. It's a world I only glimpsed before. I lived in such a sheltered world. You know, I have learned so much from these women. It's something you learned naturally; it's something I've had to learn the hard way. People from the established society could learn so much from these women; they have so much to teach, so much to tell. I only wish people would listen.

"For me, prison hasn't been the end of the world. It's been a beginning—a chance to stand aside and look. When I tell you I've grown in the seven months I've been here, I mean it. Not because of any programs—there aren't any. But because of the people I've lived with and the bed I've slept on. And I'm beginning to live with myself and accept myself. I know I'm more of a woman, a valuable soul, than I ever would have been if I hadn't come here.

"If six hundred women can each say, 'Hey, I'm a woman,' regardless of being called homosexuals or convicts or being neglected and hurt and made to live under ridiculous rules and ridiculous pressures and mental brutality and heartbreak—they have something to teach the world. It was a mindblower to me to see the strength, the tenderness, and courage of these women and to find out, hey, I'm a woman, too. I'd just never had the chance.''

2 A PERSONAL JOURNEY

The Genesis of This Book

Many people have asked me how I developed an interest in writing about prisons. Recently at a meeting of the Philadelphia Bar Association, the chancellor of the bar asked how I "got into this business" when I have written about so many other things. His question, though asked many times before, startled me. "I fell in through a trap door," I told him. "I was just walking along and then wham, there I was." This was a facetious answer, but there was truth in it.

Although people I knew and loved had been arrested and gone to jail, in my mind they just "went away" and "came home." It was traumatic, but being in trouble with the law was "normal"—just like alcoholism or violent, erratic behavior. I was oblivious to the quality of life inside jail, the reality of it, just as I was oblivious to the qualities and substance of my own life. I didn't examine the dimension of my own experience any more than I examined what particular experiences were doing to the lives of others. I just struggled in my own way with the enormity of life around me in isolated, noncommunicative patterns and formulas for existence that gave me some sense of stability and cohesion, unaware of trying to envision that which was not visible.

It was only when realities I normally didn't see were forced in front of my eyes through someone else's perspective that I responded to what was there—whether it was classical music, racism, poverty, art, death from bombs in Indochina, prison life, or the effects of my own actions. I guess you could say there was a great gap between worlds, between experience and cognition. My sensibilities had to be shattered, along with my delusions, before I could begin picking up the pieces to examine them and gain a new perspective.

Imprisonment was one of those nebulous, unexamined areas that went unquestioned until I was jolted into a new awareness through another person's experiences.

I had never been inside a jail or prison until 1969, when I came back to this country from two and a half years in Asia. I had been teaching, studying Mandarin, and living in a Chinese community in Kuala Lumpur, Malaysia, where I also edited a small magazine for Peace Corps volunteers. Coming back to the United States was a shock. I had been so thoroughly immersed in the Malaysian-Chinese culture that I had trouble readjusting to the English language, to American spaces, sights, smells, and people. It was as though I was experiencing for the first time what I had thought familiar.

After traveling across the country from California, I returned to a newspaper in Florida, where I had worked previously, to do some special in-depth articles. Among my assignments was a series on rape. I worked with another reporter on the series, who took the victim's perspective. I took the "criminal" aspects as my task.

Among other things, I wanted to interview rapists and try to understand their perspective. It didn't seem fair to write about rape without getting more than one side of the story. At the time, however, I was told there was only one convicted rapist at the Broward county jail. Others had been charged with rape, but they were only in jail because they had been denied bail and were awaiting trial. The man who had been found guilty agreed to the interview and so did the county sheriff.

As I sat waiting for the interview in a small, barren detective's room at the jail, I realized how absurd I was. Why did I think a convicted rapist would tell me why he had raped somebody? Here again, I was in a situation where I was totally naïve, using only nerve and ignorance as a protective cover. I was sitting there feeling ridiculous when the door opened and in walked a heavyset young man with puffy cheeks and brown skin so dry that it created the impression of an ashen gray shadow across his face. He wore a blue prison shirt and overalls. A jailhouse aura seemed to surround him. He sat down, looking somewhat shocked and frightened. I felt frightened, too. We were both nervous, and I became increasingly aware of the detective in the back of the room cracking his knuckles.

I was the first outsider—and certainly the first woman—this prisoner had talked with face to face in months. He was the first "known rapist" I'd met. He was twenty-one years old. He had just been found guilty of raping a seventeen-year-old high school senior, a virgin, who was black. That's all I knew. Partway through the first hour of the interview I started feeling uncomfortable about all the details I didn't know. By the end of four hours—and a shift from his helpful speculations on "why rapists do what they do" into his personal case—a lot of question marks had replaced the periods in my brain concerning this convicted rapist, whom I'll call "Trevor Jones." The labels had slipped from their slots.

In the days to follow, Trevor Jones's story unraveled itself slowly, painfully—dislodging with small explosions whatever remaining myths of equal law and justice lay neatly hidden in my unconscious. I concluded that Trevor Jones, who turned out to be a community worker, youth recreation leader, and chairman of a grassroots black unity movement in Miami, was not guilty of the rape for which he had been convicted. Prior to his arrest he was enrolled in a local junior college. With painstaking research and backtracking, I could substantiate none of the facts established at the trial except Trevor Jones's claim of innocence and his dedication to improving conditions in the black community. He had been arrested only once before and that was when, in response to a policeman's request for identification, he said his name was "Black, Blacker, Blackest."

Jones said he had made one mistake—the only action he was sorry for. He said he slept with someone he didn't know—a friend of a friend, the young woman he was later accused of raping. That young woman later admitted she had been carrying around a newspaper clipping with Trevor's picture for several weeks before she met him. She admitted she had been "trying to meet him." She wouldn't say who had given her his picture, but word had gotten around that the police had given her the picture of Trevor Jones. After their meeting, and after Jones's arrest, the young woman tried to withdraw the charges she had placed against him. But something or someone pressured her to change her mind. She testified. And Jones, who claimed innocence from the beginning, was jailed without bail, tried, and sentenced to eighteen years on reduced charges of assault with intent to commit rape. The jury apparently had some doubts, because finding him guilty of rape could have meant the death penalty.

Jones had been in solitary confinement for more than nine months when I met him—most of that time awaiting trial. He was not allowed reading materials, exercise, recreation, or a full diet. He was isolated from other prisoners because he was considered a "leader"—a "black militant who would put ideas into the heads of other prisoners if he had contact," according to the sheriff.

It was as though the layers of my defenses against knowing what really goes on as a matter of daily course in the criminal justice system and in jail were torn away one by one. They were shredded by the white detectives who sat around their headquarters and talked freely of the "rabbit nigger coon" Jones and graphically of how they would like to "cut out his balls." They swore this was "the first case" of a black woman being raped in their town and that, they laughed, was real "equality." Black men always had been convicted for raping white women; cases involving the rape of black women by white or black men had traditionally been ignored, as if black women needed no such protection.

The detectives talked gleefully about circumstantial evidence they had against Jones and then went into what seemed to be euphoric reminiscing about the times they had dressed up as women in blond wigs and cruised the streets in unmarked cars with two cops hidden in the back seat until they "got some coons followin' us around lickin' their chops to make a white woman."

"We'd idle our engine at a red light and tell the coons if they wanted to fuck to follow us . . . and then we'd lead 'em out to a dark country road," said one big-bellied white cop whose neck grew purple with laughter. "You shoulda seen the shock on them coon faces when we'd get out with our rifles." The men who had been entrapped by the hoax would be charged with attempted rape and sent off "where they oughta be buried."

From one person to the next, all of whom were essential to establishing the state's case against Trevor Jones, the flimsy "evidence" continued to be revealed, including the attitude of the medical examiner who had sworn in trial that the "victim" had been a virgin—a major aspect of the prosecution's case.

"How'd I know?" he said to me in a telephone interview. "You can just tell those things. Of course it's not certain, but you got a good idea. She was tight, you know."

Another main point of evidence for the prosecution was the prosecution's claim that the young woman had been badly bruised and beaten by Jones and several other young men who were allegedly involved but not prosecuted. The medical examiner said he had not seen any bruises on the woman's body, but said she was "probably bruised." He told me he had personally not seen the bruises because "niggers don't bruise. If she was bruised, I couldn't a seen it anyway."

The face-to-face reality of racism and political prejudice in the criminal justice system was devastating. I realized that Trevor Jones had talked to me just to get out of confinement, just to see a face other than the one that shoved food under his door twice a day. He hadn't expected that I could change anything for him or prove his innocence. He was right: I tried, but I couldn't. His highly paid black lawyer didn't seem able to use any of the contradictory statements I had collected. The newspaper wasn't about to publish information they considered potentially libelous; it was only my word against the sheriff's, the detective's, the medical examiner's. Nobody I contacted seemed to have the power to right this injustice, and no one seemed to care—except Trevor Jones, his fiancée, his family, his friends, and now me. [At the time, I suspected that J. Edgar Hoover's FBI had set up this situation with the cooperation of local police to break up Trevor Jones's effective leadership in the black community. I believed the FBI was behind this prosecution, and I still believe it. Today evidence is abundant that the FBI Cointel's program, in fact, infiltrated and aimed to disrupt and divide members of the Black Panther Party and other black nationalist groups in the late 1960s and early 1970s. I believe Trevor Jones's case was one of their early "successes." Because his was a "black-on-black" crime, and he was represented by a black lawyer, it would have been hard to charge racial bias. My guess is that Jones's victim also was coerced to give evidence against him. When I recently tracked down Trevor Jones, I found out he had graduated from college while in prison; somehow he had the internal strength to make the best out of a terrible situation.]

My inability to do anything about what I saw and heard was shattering. Before I left Florida, however, I decided to spend some time in the women's section of the Broward County Jail. I asked to go in as an inmate but was allowed in only as a reporter for one day. ("If you want to go in as an inmate, you'll have to break a law in front of us," the sheriff said. "You'll have to go to court and be tried. The process will take you about two years.")

I chose one day—and that day was enough. I was led in through five locked doors to a small inner sanctum. I became less determined about my assignment and more terrified as the key turned in each lock behind me. I was even more shaken by the grim, hard faces of the black and white women I saw packed together in crusting, crowded cells—some sixty women in two cell blocks seemingly not big enough for twenty.

It was only after I was put inside the cell block that the receptiveness of the individual women melted my fear. They were eager to talk about the conditions they lived in and were amazed that I had gotten in. They were like women I have known all my life. Just folks. They put me at ease, and I became increasingly comfortable with them. The heat was the only overbearing factor. There was no air circulation. We sat talking and sweating. I was aware of the confinement but oblivious to how quickly I became absorbed into this deadly still, all-enveloping environment.

When I walked out of the jail that evening I was numb. I was overwhelmed with seeing the sky, touching a palm tree, breathing fresh air. I sat down in the grass outside the courthouse, awed by the earth. It was only then I realized what a totally isolated and controlled world I had just been in—how there had been no windows, no trace of the outside world inside those concrete walls. I was so overwhelmed that I never wrote an article about the experience. I was too confused, too angry to make sense out of it all.

When I moved to Philadelphia later that summer and began writing for the *Philadelphia Evening Bulletin,* I still felt the urgency of needing to do something and get involved personally somehow in changing what I had been oblivious to for so long. After hearing the superintendent of Philadelphia prisons say that ''community involvement'' would be welcomed in the prisons, I told him I'd like to start a writer's workshop for women or juveniles. He said if I wanted to conduct such a workshop, it would have to be at Holmesburg Prison, a maximum-security facility for men, most of whom were awaiting trial. [That was in 1969; I led the workshop for the next four years.] Over time, I became involved in the legal aspects of various individuals' cases and in attempts to change conditions both in the community and in the jail. Eventually this personal commitment carried over into my writing about the local and state systems. That, in essence, is how I ''fell through the trap door.''

I never intended to write this book. I would prefer to write a children's book, a comedy, or a novel. My best argument against writing it was that I hadn't done time myself; women prisoners are the only experts on women's prisons. They should write their own books about their own experiences. But friends I met in jail—and friends on the outside who had experienced jail—urged me to do it. They would write their own books, but I had access to more than one jail, more than one prison. As one older woman said, ''Baby, you gotta be the voice for us, 'cause according to society, we ain't got no voices. Numbers can't talk—everybody knows that. Besides that, we get so used to this whole thing we can't even see a lot of it. It's too close. You got some perspective.''

The women I met seemed to feel I could do their stories justice. They told me openly and freely about their experiences—their fears, their failures, their hopes. ''Usually the women treat anyone who comes in with silence; they don't trust them—so they treat them like pigs," Marguerite Ferrante told me. "But they know you're different; they know you're one of them. It's so apparent."

"We haven't never had the chance to tell our side of the story," another jail-weary woman said. "We get processed in here and when anything's ever in the paper about our case, it only quotes the DA. They don't never ask us nothing. I always thought I'd try to write a book about all this but I never got past the title: *Jail Ain't Shit.*"

After I became involved in the book, I realized some of the reasons I had resisted writing it. Like a lot of women, I didn't really like women. I didn't like myself. I didn't want to excavate the caverns of my life. I couldn't write about women in prison without looking at their reality and my reality. I didn't want to try to see past my own biases and limits at what was really happening, or struggle each day to use words that could never fully capture the pathos and actualities of our human condition. But I was already committed to the process of focusing in on that which had been oblivion. I was beginning to understand myself and, likewise, understand women.

Many of the prisoners I met said they never had been asked to evaluate the conditions they live in; and I believe they are the greatest overlooked source for examination and change of the system that governs their lives. Also, people who have been convicted of crimes have untapped insights on how to stop crime. But just how often are they consulted?

In this book, I try to give women prisoners a chance to speak for themselves—to tell their stories and to evaluate the effectiveness of the criminal justice system. I have tried to relate whatever they say without distortion or bias. Where I do make comments, my views and sentiments clearly are my own.

Because life in prison has been structured by reformists, theoreticians, and administrators, there is often a great gap between theories and their effects on individuals. I try to examine those differences and look at realities as opposed to myths—no matter how upsetting or disconcerting they may be.

I have also tried to look at what effect imprisonment has on crime; what kind of dent the system makes in alleviating crime. I am not blind to the fears people have of being hurt. I have been robbed and mugged, and my apartment has been burglarized. Two dear friends of mine have been murdered by strangers. Like anyone who has been poor or lived in inner cities, where crime rates are highest, I know the realities and horrors of crime on a personal, day-to-day basis. It has not been uncommon for me to step outside my door and see someone bleeding from a gunshot wound or to let someone in my house who has just been robbed or stabbed. When I was beaten by muggers one afternoon, I found myself driving around the next day looking for them, wanting to run them down.

So I am as concerned as anyone else about stopping crime, about curbing senseless activities, about making our communities safe. But I also recognize that to make our communities safe, we must treat each other with respect and *see* each other as human beings—even the most troubled and violent among us.

My basic research has come from visits to twenty-one jails and prisons for women, sixteen county and city jails (thirteen housing both men and women and three exclusively for women), five state prisons for women, and one federal prison for women.[1] In addition, I visited five state prisons for men, three county jails exclusively for men, and five juvenile jails. Two of the juvenile facilities included separate housing for incarcerated girls. I have received correspondence from women in several prisons I didn't personally visit and talked with women who have been jailed in Massachusetts, Connecticut, Tennessee, Louisiana, Texas, Oregon, Kansas, and other states.

I have interviewed some four hundred women in depth and talked at random with perhaps five hundred more, both in and out of prison. They are as old as eighty-nine and as young as fourteen; they come from diverse racial and ethnic backgrounds, have various religious and political beliefs. Some were incarcerated, some were on probation or parole, and others were out on bail awaiting trial. Some have finished parole but still have many memories and opinions to relate. I talked with women in criminal courtrooms in Philadelphia and New York and met others at drug rehabilitation centers and in community organizations for ex-cons. I've also spent many hours on the telephone and in the homes of women on parole, talking with them and their families.

1. The women's facilities included Arizona State Prison; Sybil Brand Institute for Women in Los Angeles; California Institution for Women at Frontera; San Bruno County Jail; North County Holding Facility in Palo Alto; Broward County Jail in Fort Lauderdale; Cook County Jail and the House of Correction in Chicago; Iowa Reformatory for Women; Camden County Jail; New York City Correctional Institution for Women; Erie County Jail and Erie County Penitentiary in Buffalo, N.Y.; Ohio Reformatory for Women at Marysville; State Correctional Institution for Women in Muncy, Pa.; York County Jail (Pa.); House of Correction in Philadelphia; Allegheny County Jail in Pittsburgh; Chambersburg County Jail (Pa.); Women's Detention Center in Washington, D.C.; and the Federal Reformatory for Women in Alderson, W.Va.

The juvenile facilities that housed younger offenders were the Youth Studies Center in Philadelphia and the John F. Kennedy Youth Correctional Center in West Virginia. It should be noted that juveniles were also incarcerated with adult women in most of the county jails visited. Male prisons I visited were all in Pennsylvania. They included Graterford, Western, Dallas, Huntingdon, and Eastern penitentiaries; Holmesburg Prison; the New Detention Center; and the House of Correction.

At first I wondered if my random sampling would be biased. The women I was instinctively drawn to tended to be labeled "aggressive" or "troublesome" by prison officials. They were for the most part fairly independent women who have "paid their dues," who are from the street and carry the humor and perspective of a woman, "S.A.P.," who wrote:

> I've played the blues and I've paid my dues
> And my race is almost run.
> I did Satan's task and I haven't asked
> If I showed, if I placed, or won.
>
> Now I'm past my prime and I've served my
>   time
> And I've been what I could be.
> So when you get to hell and ring that bell
> That old whore on the door will be me.

S.A.P. is the kind of woman I enjoyed talking with the most—not apologetic or withdrawn. But the more I let myself talk to women I wouldn't normally approach, the more I felt the sample was representative of the human interweaving of people in prison.

"Pick your girls at random and you'll get it all together," a middle-aged woman who had done a lot of time told me. "The consensus is the same, but people look at it different ways. Me, I do a lot of work up there in the administration. I keep records, type, and take dictation. I make six dollars a month, and they don't bother me because I don't make trouble. But there's a lot wrong here—a lot. I've learned a lot I don't want to know. But I'm just keeping myself busy. I gotta earn my way outta here. And Lord knows, I want to just maintain myself—at least ninety percent of what I was when I came in."

The majority of women in this book are not women you've read about in newspapers. They're the women who are listed as police and court statistics. Occasionally they have been mentioned by name in a paper— "Mary Smith Charged with Homicide" or "Police Make Morals Raid on Locust Street" or "Three Suspects Rounded Up in Drug Bust." That is the last you usually hear of them, if you hear of them at all.

Because I feel what people have to say is so important, I try to quote them exactly. Outside prison I usually used a tape recorder for interviews; but inside the prisons I tried to take verbatim notes. I did this because I didn't want to risk my tapes being confiscated or the women being punished for what they had confided to me. If my handwritten notes were seized by prison officials, they would be much more difficult to decipher. I regret that I have not been able to include information from every woman who shared her time with me, but each insight contributed immeasurably to the shaping of this book.

In these pages, each woman stands as herself, saying what she alone said, even when she is not quoted by name. Perhaps it would be less wordy to paraphrase, but I do not do this. People speak for themselves, with their own meanings, their own interpretations, their own raw, unadulterated expressions. Thus the lack of concision, the repetition and contradiction.

Along with interviewing prisoners, I've talked with administrators of prisons, heads of bureaus of correction, more than 250 guards and prison employees, correctional counselors, deputy sheriffs, police, lawyers, judges, parole and probation officers, and criminologists. These people are an essential part of any perspective on the whole system. Prison employees and administrators are particularly significant because they, through quirks of fate in their own lives, have ended up in positions of power over people incarcerated in this system.

I must confess that long before I first entered prisons, I was very biased against guards and matrons. Because they wore uniforms, I saw them as nonhuman and brutal. In my early and longstanding disdain for cops, I lumped police and guards into an authoritarian "enemy force." I have discovered, however, that guards and matrons are just human beings, too. It sounds simplistic and it is. I stereotyped them as I felt I had been stereotyped, copying a mind-set I deplored. It is true that guards and matrons are in positions of control over other people, but they also live under stringent rules and regulations that often imprison and brutalize them as well. They face a lot of hostility and are often expected to do jobs for which they are untrained and poorly paid. Some of them say they feel they also are being punished when they're asked to enforce rules they don't believe in. When they go out of their way to exercise understanding and humanity in the daily course of their work, they sometimes risk losing their jobs.

"All our work in the institution is so restrictive," one young guard told me. "We have to follow all these rules and we're told we can't get too friendly with the inmates. All our time seems to be spent solving little problems—like keeping count or who wants to move where or who broke this or that rule. We don't ever get to the big problems or to things that will really help somebody. We never know what happens to the women when they go out unless they violate [parole] and come back."

I have tried to treat guards and administrators with the respect they deserve as human beings. This does not make the meaning of some of their actions less malignant or assume that their positions of power are not often detrimental to the best interests of human freedom, healing, or growth. But exposing "bad" or "evil" guards or administrators is not going to change the process or the power of the criminal justice system any more than exposure of "bad" or "evil" prisoners has in the past. My purpose is not to revile wrongdoers but to examine the institutional system, to see what effect that system has on crime and on the lives of the individuals involved.

Most of the people I interviewed asked me to use their actual names. Women in prison wanted to be credited with what they say, what they believe. Mary "Doats" Sullivan, in the Montgomery County Jail, spoke for a lot of prisoners when she said: "Make sure to use my whole name. And my age—twenty-eight. I'm not ashamed of being in prison. I think they should be ashamed to put us here." Some names and locations have been altered at the request of prisoners who believe that what they say could damage their parole status or at the request of some guards or other prison employees who fear losing their jobs or a promotion. [I've indicated name changes by putting quotation marks around the name when it's first introduced.] Additionally, I've used only a first name or changed a name at my discretion when I determined an individual needed protection.

Some prisoners and some guards never had an opportunity to decide whether to have their names in print because they never had a chance to say anything at all. At the Camden County Jail in Camden, New Jersey, for instance, Sheriff Martin Segal explained: "The ground rules here are no photographs and no interviews.

"The public has the right to know," he said, "but you can't talk to prisoners. They may not be telling the truth. I like to be accurate and exact in my remarks. People have a right to know, but they should know the truth. There will be no talking to anyone but me. We can give you all the facts and information, but we want it to be correct. Don't talk to the guards either. You can't know if what they're saying is true. I'll tell you anything you want to know."

Some people may say that many of the prisoners quoted in this book are exaggerating, projecting, or distorting. The same may be said of administrators and guards. They are, and they aren't. This is the way they see it—and it's adding all these pieces together that gives us a fuller picture of what's going on. No single person has a full measure of truth. There are distortions and biases in everyone—but it's sorting them out and putting them all together that gives us clearer vision to melt myths.

I've had to leave a great deal of material out of the book. As a friend of mine said, "We are all like the tips of icebergs—we show most other people only the top five percent." Perhaps this book is like the top five percent or less. There's a whole iceberg, or mountain of human reality, underneath it.

For everything that shows, there's always more. For one person's perspective, there are a thousand more who see it another way, or experience it differently. Everyone has a separate reality, influenced by their own experiences, consciousness, and limitations. Nothing is cut-and-dried fact, even when it appears that way. Everything is true, and at the same time, everything is false. Memories are abstractions, just as words are abstractions to communicate real feelings and emotions and smells and sounds and tastes and sights. So this book is only a beginning, an attempt to document and draw the relevant and the authentic from the total of *What Is* in women's prisons and jails—as in the human experience to which we are all so inexplicably bound.

3   INJUSTICES IN THE JUSTICE SYSTEM

Does the Punishment Fit the Crime?

> Money talks, bullshit walks. If you're a Kennedy and you get busted for dope, you never do no time. If you're the president of the United States, you can murder millions of people in Asia, you never do no time. If you're a politician, you can cheat and conspire and steal money, you never do no time. I've watched about seventeen women go out of here after serving time for snuffing their babies, while hypes [drug addicts] still sit here. Society condones guns, but not addicts. I'm here for selling two nickel bags, yet the government is giving GIs whites to keep 'em up and reds to put 'em to sleep and getting 'em addicted so they can keep fighting. And the Army and the government ain't never taken to court or locked up. There's a lot of contradictions—you know, a double standard. If you're a corporation, you can fix prices and rip folks off every day, you never do no time. Me, I'm a hype. I sold two nickel bags and I'm doing life, baby, a day at a time. I already been here three years. And you know, that's like three lifetimes of psychological warfare. They call me a criminal. I ain't no corporation, so I'm a criminal! I'd like to ask, just where are the real criminals?
>
> —Mary, an inmate at the California Institution for Women

When we talk about crime in America, and when we talk about prisons, we are talking about power and powerlessness. We are talking about hopelessness and helplessness.

Crime makes most of us so angry that we don't want to think about the people committing crimes as human beings with problems. We don't want

1 9

to imagine their lives, we want solutions to our own feelings of helplessness in the face of crime. It's of little comfort to know that crime—and fear of crime—is nothing new. It's of little comfort to know that several centuries before Christ, Ezekiel said, "The land is full of bloody crimes, and the city is full of violence." We simply want to strike back at the people who rob us or hurt us. We want to beat them up, lock them up, throw them away.

The problem with this approach, however, is that it doesn't work. It relieves our anger, but it doesn't make us safer. In the long run, prisons not only fail to solve the problems that plague our communities, but create more crime.

You may wonder how this can be. For years, in our efforts to feel safe, we have looked to the criminal justice system to do the short-term and the long-term work of dealing with crime in our communities. We have depended upon the criminal justice system—with its layers of police, prosecutors, defense attorneys, grand juries, courts of law, diversion programs, probation departments, prisons and parole systems—to create justice and maintain order.

Increasingly, we've relied upon the most expensive and anonymous part of the criminal justice system—our prisons—as the preferred method for stopping crime and violence. Legislators, who respond to our concerns and outrage over specific heinous and highly publicized crimes, call for locking up "the animals" and throwing away the keys. They call for harsher measures against criminals, longer prison sentences, and more prisons. At the same time our legislators are cutting back funds for school programs, special education, transportation, and health and social services, they are eager to allot enormous amounts of money for new prison construction.

We support their effort and encourage it. We are willing to spend billions of dollars to maintain our old prisons and build new ones—we're willing to trade the quality of our schools for new prisons—because we believe the myth that prisons work. We believe the myth that prisons will protect us and keep us safe while they punish and reform criminals and solve the problems of crime in our communities.

We lock people in our jails and prisons for years and plan for increased incarceration of men, women, and juveniles *despite* the mountains of evidence that refute the effectiveness of prisons, *despite* the very plain words of thousands of individuals and organizations that have conducted dozens and dozens of studies, including the President's Commission on Law Enforcement and the Administration of Justice. Uniformly, these studies show that prisons do not reduce crime. With the exception of giving quarantine to a small percentage of predatory, violent criminals, they don't protect the public.

Despite our anger, the expansion of our prison systems over the past two decades has had no impact on crime rates—except, perhaps, to destroy lives and to create more crime by producing more hardened criminals.

The one thing prisons do—and they do it well—is to punish prisoners. Prisons strip them of their dignity, their health, and whatever self-esteem they once might have had. Prisons also punish the children and families of prisoners. But they don't stop crime. Most particularly, they don't stop the big crimes that skew our economy and threaten our security.

Detailed reports show that business and white-collar crimes cause more financial loss, injury, and death than any other crimes in America. In one year, for instance, price-fixing by twenty-nine electrical companies alone cost the public more than was reported stolen by burglars throughout the entire country in that same year. In 1994, Prudential Securities, the fourth largest brokerage firm in the United States, admitted it had illegally sold some seven hundred partnerships to more than 120,000 people. Only thirty-five of those partnerships involved the fraud of nearly one and a half *billion* dollars. Violations of safety laws and housing codes, as well as food and drugs sold in violation of the Pure Food and Drug Act, cause hundreds of thousands of deaths each year. Yet these crimes are rarely dealt with using the full force of criminal sanctions. Standards of right and wrong are less clear when they are committed in the course of big business transactions and production.

According to the President's Commission on crime, organized crime is the "most sinister kind of crime in America." It says "organized racketeers, big criminals, pursue their conspiracy unmolested in open and continuous defiance of the law—stimulating corruption among police, prosecutors, judges and public officials." It supplies goods and services wanted by people but prohibited by the law: cash loans, narcotics, prostitutes, gambling.

Because the various police agencies aren't organized to halt complex business crime or organized crime, single agencies continue to deal with simpler, individual crimes that have a frightening but much less damaging effect on our total society. Police, the courts, and the prisons focus on people who commit individual street crimes—not on organized criminals or investment bankers or others involved in fraud, who sit in secure, comfortable places and cause the greatest harm.

And just as it is difficult for police to focus on complicated systems of organized or corporate crime, it is difficult for us to focus our anger on a corporation or an illegal, interwoven web of activity we don't understand or can't really see. But because we want to feel safe and believe that something is being done about crime, we stubbornly maintain that criminals are caught and go to prison. In fact, some really bad people are caught and do go to prison, but they are a minority.

The vast majority of criminals do not go to prison.

People who do go to prison are a minute number of the lawbreakers—less than 2 percent in the entire country. Statistics compiled by the National Council on Crime and Delinquency show that Americans report millions of crimes to police annually. More than twice as many crimes presumably go unreported. Yet police make arrests on only 12 percent of all reported crimes. Of the number arrested, only half are found guilty. After suspended sentences, probation, and other alternatives to prison are used up, slightly more than 1.5 percent of all reported lawbreakers are sentenced to prison.

This minority of lawbreakers constitutes our prison population. Most of the public think this bunch must be the worst of criminals, fully deserving dreadful punishment. We imagine most prisoners to be psychopaths who would assault our children, rape us, kill us, cut us into little pieces if they had the chance. But only a tiny proportion of the people in prison have committed the atrocious, violent crimes that frighten us and make us want revenge.

The vast majority of men and women sentenced to prison are *not* violent or predatory. Murderers—the people we fear the most—make up a minority of the prison population, and most of them have killed a mate, not a stranger. Our fear of death from strangers, in fact, is exaggerated. Eighty-four percent of all known murders in this country are committed by someone known intimately to the victim, usually a family member.[1] Likewise, most of the sexual predators who molest and threaten our children are trusted authorities, "friends" of the family, or the fathers, stepfathers, uncles, or brothers of the child; most don't go to prison—and those who do constitute an even smaller portion of the prison population.

Surprising as it may seem, most of the people in this country who wear prison uniforms, are locked in cells, and answer to a number, not a name, have been convicted of nonviolent crimes. They are not who we imagine them to be. They have broken the law and many of them have cheated, lied, and done unethical and despicable things, but they haven't used

1. Fred P. Graham, writing for the U.S. National Commission on the Causes and Prevention of Violence, pointed out that rather than the FBI's publicizing the fact that a person is murdered each forty-eight minutes, it could be telling the public the average person's chance of becoming a homicide victim on a given day is about one in two million. His chance of being a victim of violent crime is once in four hundred years.

weapons or physical violence against others. The vast majority of prisoners are not in prison because they are a danger to the community; they're in prison because of sporadic or habitual crimes basically against themselves—such as prostitution, vagrancy, and illegal drug possession—or for property crimes against others such as shoplifting (larceny), fraud (bad-check writers), or theft. Some are mentally ill. Substance abuse and drug problems, which drive the lion's share of their crimes, could have been and still should be treated medically.

For the most part, the people who populate our prisons are people who have few saleable skills and are not good at making money. In 1989, 55.7 percent of the women in jail reported that prior to being arrested, they'd earned less than $500 a month, according to Bureau of Justice statistics. Their petty economic crimes produce equally insubstantial sums.

Most of America's prisoners are economically impoverished, poorly educated people who need to learn how to solve their problems—which usually are medical and economic, including addiction, poor physical health, lack of education, and lack of job skills, literacy, or psychological balance—within the community. They are employees or would-be employees, not employers, and we send them away to repressive, hostile, and unhealthy places far from home, where security is the first and foremost priority, and where they get no treatment, no counseling, and no training—no help with their problems. Being locked up hastens the breakdown of their relationships with their families and communities, further damages the fragile balance of their lives, removes them from their responsibility for their behavior, and then returns them ill-equipped to live a normal, crime-free life.

Mother Jones, a labor organizer in the early 1900s, made a startling statement that still holds true today when it comes to the prison experience in America. She said, "I asked a man in prison once how he happened to be there, and he said he had stolen a pair of shoes. I told him if he had stolen a railroad, he would be a United States Senator."

Despite changes in sentencing guidelines, and despite efforts to make the system more equitable, it seems clear to me there are two separate systems of criminal justice in America: a system for "intellectual" crimes and a system for "physical" crimes.

As I sat in many courtrooms and watched chaotic proceedings during trials of accused shoplifters, prostitutes, burglars, purse snatchers, I was always startled at the contrast when a "professional" (usually a white, middle-class male) came to trial for embezzlement, fraud, or bribery. A calm dignity would fall over the courtroom. The prosecution and defense would always be thoroughly prepared. Witnesses would be present. The judge would seem to be more focused, more thoughtful.

At first I attributed the difference in approach solely to the economic status of the defendants. The process seemed like an administrative rather than a criminal proceeding for white-collar criminals, middle- or upper middle-class defendants. Sentences were always much lighter, even for people who had embezzled huge sums of money. A person who robbed someone of twenty dollars usually got more prison time than someone who had extorted more than two hundred thousand dollars.

What I finally realized is that discretion seems to operate according to unconscious criteria as well. When a crime is unsophisticated and "primitive," the punishment is primitive. The more primitive the crime, the more primitive the punishment. Crime in America is equated with primitive physical actions. The more intellectual synthesis, abstraction, and creativity in a crime, the less it is perceived as crime and the more it interests lawyers, prosecutors, and judges—who basically live by the intellect, rather than by action. The same is true of the general public, who condemn a crime of violent action before an intellectual crime that results in an equal or greater harm to the victim.

Looking at these two standards of justice explains a lot of things that probably work on an unconscious, cross-cultural level. It can be "fascinating" when a banker, an executive, or a high-profile celebrity has been arrested for having embezzled money through an intricate mental process. It is a challenge for the judge to dissect and understand the highly specialized case and its motivations. He can unravel and empathize with the pressures that drove a privileged person to commit a crime—even a violent crime. Likewise, a judge can understand how the arrest and the attendant publicity affects the reputation of a person like himself and how the defendant is already being punished by the shame of exposure, loss of status, loss of income, or loss of employment.

On the other hand, when an indigent person who has robbed someone, snatched a purse, or offered to sell her body to a stranger comes before the bench, there is no basis for empathy from the legal profession. The judge usually doesn't understand the culture or class realities of the economically powerless person standing before him. Even the writing of a bad check reflects a "lack of control." The mental or emotional duress of an indigent person driven to committing a crime is not easily comprehended and thus she is condemned. The judge can see that this person of little status has probably been arrested before; she has a chaotic lifestyle, a lack of discipline, and she hasn't seemed to learn that crime doesn't pay.

He considers her hopeless. He doesn't understand her world, and he tries to "make the punishment fit the crime."

The varying standards lead to discretion readily interpreted as discrimination: one person gets out on bail; the other is locked up before trial. [While the purpose of bail reform in many states over the past twenty years has been to try to categorize crime at the earliest possible dates to get minor violators out of jail and put serious violators in, it doesn't always work that way. For instance, the son of a Chase Manhattan bank official was under "house arrest" while he awaited trial for the stabbing death of two doctors who were strangers to him, while the son of a local maintenance man was locked in jail for the same period of time awaiting trial for burglary. This kind of difference is the rule, not the exception.]

The same thing happens when it comes to prosecution and sentencing: one woman gets five years' probation for her part in a $750,000 hoax that was basically an intellectual game, while another woman is sentenced to ten years in prison for her part in a robbery that netted $56.43. A society woman driven to the point of shooting her cruel and abusive husband is acquitted for justifiable homicide because of the mental torture she endured. The court orders private psychiatric treatment. Her less prestigious counterpart, who stabbed her cruel and abusive husband to death following one of his many beatings, is sentenced to life imprisonment without parole.

Two crimes might be quite similar, quite brutal; the mental duress of each person involved might be equally severe—but after the arrest, public and judicial response differs. For illustration, look at the cases of two young women charged with murder: Heidi Fletcher, a twenty-one-year-old white woman, was arrested for killing a policeman in the process of robbing a savings and loan association in Washington, D.C. She pled guilty to first-degree murder, armed robbery, robbery, and illegal possession of dangerous weapons.

Before her trial, Heidi was released without bail for four and a half months in the custody of a high District of Columbia official with the stipulation she get a job and be in by 10 P.M. every night. The official was a friend of her father's, Thomas W. Fletcher, former deputy mayor of the District. A week before her twenty-second birthday, Heidi was sentenced to a maximum of nine years in prison, with the possibility of release any time before then. Her defense attorney said she was "starved for love." The judge ordered that she serve her sentence in California so she could be closer to her mother and father, who was the city manager of San Jose.

On the other hand, Rose Marie Dinkins, a twenty-three-year-old black woman, was arrested for killing two policemen in the process of attempting to rob a grocery store in Pittsburgh, Pennsylvania. She pled guilty to two counts of first-degree murder in a Pittsburgh court. The mother of four children, Rose was held in the Allegheny County Jail, without bail, awaiting trial. She had no money. When the judge sentenced Rose Marie Dinkins to two concurrent life terms in prison, he didn't make any stipulation for her to get to live close to her four children so she could see them. Rose probably won't get out of prison for twenty years or more. There's a good possibility she'll never get out. Was her crime worse? Couldn't she also have been "starved for love?" Was she more of a "threat" than Heidi Fletcher?

It seems we are slow to condemn a productive person of high status— even when he or she is arrested or convicted for committing a violent crime. We are shocked when an intellectual or a bureaucrat is sentenced to prison, but pay little attention when a have-not is locked up. No one would have been so shocked by Angela Davis's arrest and detention, for instance, had she not been a professor from the University of California at Los Angeles. Thousands of uneducated, indigent women are arrested every day and no one winks an eye; their arrest is "normal."

Racism, sexism, and class discrimination also play major roles in who is arrested and who goes to prison. When a law has been broken, the stereotypical suspect is African American or Hispanic. Poor people of every color are stereotyped as "criminals" simply because they lack economic power, but blacks bear the brunt of this prejudice. Disproportionate numbers of African Americans are arrested, detained, and imprisoned throughout this country. But this does not mean that there are, in fact, more black criminals than white criminals. Nor does it mean that blacks are more likely to commit crimes than whites, as some people choose to believe. It only means what many studies have shown: police focus harsher attention on black neighborhoods; prosecutors are not as apt to drop charges against blacks or agree to plea bargains; judges are less likely to grant bail that black defendants can meet and are more apt to sentence a black person convicted of a crime to prison instead of to an alternative program. Once imprisoned, blacks spend longer periods of time behind bars before being granted parole.

When immigrants from Europe came to America in the 1800s and lived in ghettos under the same meager conditions that still exist for the urban poor today, they were arrested and imprisoned at the same disproportionate rates as today's African Americans. The problem is that discrimination has continued against African Americans. While there has been some progress, blacks have not been granted the same assimilation; they can't just "lose the accent." Because of their indelible appearance and the persistence of racism, even African Americans of high economic status are still looked upon suspiciously by white strangers, as though all blacks are still in the same desperate state of need as poverty-stricken inner-city residents. The stigma of slavery, of the ghetto, remains in the unconscious mind, and the assumption follows that because of poverty and resentment, almost any black person is likely to commit a violent crime at any moment. This discriminatory attitude has not changed in the 1990s; college professors, doctors, lawyers, and authors are often stopped by police in their own neighborhoods for "driving too slowly" or harassed in other ways simply because of the color of their skin.

Upper- and middle-class black people also are subject to arbitrary arrests because they look "suspicious" to white policemen who have been trained to look for anything "unusual." A black person with economic or social power can usually clear up the "misunderstanding," be released on the arraignment level, or prove his case. But it is indigent black people living in crowded and deteriorated conditions who experience the harshest effects of prejudice on a sustained basis because they haven't the economic or political power to defend themselves effectively.

In Washington, D.C., for instance, administrators say that every class of woman is arrested—white, black, rich, poor. But after the initial hearings, the destitute woman, usually black, is held in jail. As an example, let's look at two women caught for shoplifting and charged with larceny and petty theft. Bail is set at ten thousand dollars, and the white woman with economic means is out of custody within hours. The destitute black woman spends months in jail awaiting trial. Statistics back up this scenario: black women have a one-and-a-half times greater chance of being returned to jail after their initial hearing than white women.[2]

Another study in forty-one counties in Pennsylvania determined that bail and fines tended to be higher and sentences longer for black women than for white women on similar charges. One exception was that the courts seemed to be more offended when white women practiced prostitution, and thus set their bail higher than that of their black counterparts.[3]

Does this mean the judge is racist? Is criminal law racist? Or is society racist? The intention of individuals involved may not be consciously racist, but the process is, the effective reality is. Our adversary system is an

2. Colleen Barros, Andrea Slavin, Virginia McArthur, and Stuart Adams, *Movement and Characteristics of Women's Detention Center Admissions, 1969,* Research Report no. 39, District of Columbia Department of Corrections, May 1971.

3. Margery L. Velimesis, *Report on the Survey of 41 County Court and Correctional Services for Women and Girl Offenders, Jan. 1, 1965–Dec. 31, 1966,* American Association of University Women, Pennsylvania Division, January 1969.

unequal contest, and indigent whites and blacks lose because they don't have the economic or social power to compete. Wealthy people are funneled out of the system. Poor people remain. As one observer in the 1990s said, "Rich women have the Betty Ford clinic; poor women have prison."

Prison administrators see and comment themselves on the gross inequities in our criminal justice system. Former San Mateo County Sheriff Richard Hongisto put it simply: "We can't talk about jails unless we talk about the inequitable distribution of wealth in society, the haves and the have-nots. We have to look at the emotional and cultural patterns that evolve out of the conditions of poverty.

"We have to remember that people in jail are inevitably the poor and the powerless. They don't have the power to change the system by themselves or they wouldn't be in jail. We have to change that balance of power through responsiveness and responsibility in the communities. . . .

"Jail sentences do not stop alcoholics from being alcoholics, prostitutes from being prostitutes, or heroin addicts from being heroin addicts," Hongisto said. "It never has and it never will. Jailing people as a way to solve social problems is very expensive, ineffective, and inhumane. We've had rotten, stinking miserable jails for years and years, and the crime rate has gone up and up. They're counterproductive.

"Stopping crime is keeping families together, building better schools, better housing, distributing the wealth. If we encourage loving families to stay together, we discourage crime. If people feel useful and constructive, they'll *be* useful and constructive. Day after day, change after change, little things can be done in the jails to make the quality of life better and relieve tensions, but the real work has to be done out here."

Hongisto made a lot of "little changes" in San Bruno's county jails, as have prison administrators in other parts of the country. But the injustices of greater proportion continue. Jails and prisons remain basically unchanged, as does the process that carries people to them.

The courts deal daily with people police have brought them from the streets—people alienated from mainstream economy and production, people who are breaking the rules but who often are abusing themselves more than they have abused others. Concerned judges often feel as powerless as anyone else to change what they see as a cyclical process. Sometimes they are frustrated by people who show no willingness to help themselves or to take advantage of other options.

"What can I do?" said Philadelphia Municipal Court Judge Paul A. Dandridge after sentencing a woman to six months in the House of Correction. "This woman is brought in the first time for a robbery and she's on heroin. I know her chief problem is drugs, so I give her probation and arrange for her to get into a drug program. She messes up that program and is brought back here before the court for violation of probation. I decide that what she needs is to go to Phoenix House in New York—something she wants to do, too. But she goes to New York and blows that program and comes back here and gets arrested again for something else—still having a fifteen-bag-a-day habit. What can I do?

"I've put her in programs and she's violated probation three times. She's out there in the street hurting herself and doesn't have any place to stay or any people to go to. So I give her six months at the House of Correction. There aren't any other alternatives. And I'm sending her there only because there's nothing for her in the community. At least in there she's safe—at least being there gives her a chance to dry out and a safe place to sleep. I know it stinks, but I don't know what else to do."

Dandridge was a rare judge to be aware of the kinds of problems the woman faces. He is black; he grew up in the city. And unlike the majority of judges in this country, he had visited all the jails and prisons to which he sentenced people. He saw that imprisonment is ineffective and tried to use constructive alternatives. But the available alternatives are limited. Sensitive people in the criminal justice system are aware that they're dealing with people who reflect the problems and effects of social disorder, racism, poor housing, poor education, poor health care. They know alternative programs within our communities need to be developed.

"Society dumps all their problems in our lap," says the warden of the Women's Detention Center in Washington, D.C., Pat Taylor. "The community wants us to do in six months what society hasn't done in the entire lives of these women. We're supposed to be undoing what they did to them for eighteen or nineteen or twenty-seven years. We didn't create these people. We didn't throw them out of the community, either. We don't have magic pills. We didn't create their attitudes and hostilities, but we become the object of them."

Pat Taylor is superintendent of a jail that books, processes, and incarcerates all the women arrested in Washington, D.C. More than 75 percent of her prisoners are awaiting trial. The rest are serving sentences, including two doing life. Eighty percent of the women are drug addicts. She estimates 3 percent of the population are "seriously emotionally disturbed." She says that 80 percent of the women are kept on some kind of medication such as Thorazine or Librium—tranquilizers that make them easier to control in the overcrowded, physically deteriorating jail.

On Taylor's desk is a sign: NOTICE: DUE TO LACK OF INTEREST, TOMORROW WILL BE POSTPONED.

"Look, there's an emotional need to attain money in our society," she says. ''There is nothing more important. We're all money oriented. Television, magazines, billboards—they all advertise *things*. We see the perfect family as having one or two cars at least, color televisions, pretty clothes, perfume, jewelry, money, and carpets on their floors.

''All of a sudden we're supposed to tell these women, 'Don't grasp for money. Money isn't as important as high moral values. Be a square.' It's a bunch of bull! Earning money as a prostitute, a booster, or a hustler, there are no taxes, no schedules, no time cards to punch. You expect a woman who can make up her own schedule and earn enough money to survive to take a factory job for a dollar sixty-five an hour or look forward to working over an industrial sewing machine?

''Society's taught that everyone has a right to have things—and that everyone should have nice things. They don't give these women any respectable way to get them, and then when they go out and get them the best way they know, we're telling them it's wrong. The community has just got to make up its mind what it wants. They're punishing these women for the very values they taught them.''

When police, lawyers, judges, and prison administrators—people in positions of power—feel frustrated, angry, and even helpless about the criminal justice system and its effects, you can begin to imagine how defendants feel.

One day when I was sitting outside a criminal courtroom in New York City, I met a woman who was awaiting trial on a forgery charge. She was in her midforties, and her enormous sighs as she talked about her case, one of many, reflected the powerlessness of her life.

''For me it was just like gettin' on an assembly line, baby,'' she said, patting my hand for comfort. ''It all started when I was about fifteen years old. I was living on my own and they busted me for hanging around a bar. Shit, it was nice there. I could hear good music. The broads was good to me. But the officers said I'd been truant from school and I was promiscuous or something like that. They made me feel like a regular whore—a sho'-nuff down-and-out little nobody. That first time I got busted, the cop made me blow him and his partner on the way to the station. I guess they would have made me fuck 'em if there'd a been more time. That really got me, that really did me in. . . .

''I'll never forget 'em. I was so scared. I didn't know what to do. The next thing I knowed, I was in jail. And I been here mostly on and off ever since. For drinking or hustling mostly, you know.

''Shit, girl, I been to court so many times, I never could count 'em. Who knows what the fuck goes on in there? They got their own language all hooked up—it might as well be French to me. They got all their people hooked up, too, including their public defenders. I never be knowing what they're saying. All I knows is I got a subpoena and another charge. They be tellin' me, 'You been bad again. What we gonna do with you?' And they preach at me some more about mendin' my ways. What ways? Shit, the only worse thing I did was come out my momma's womb. Yeah, that's where it all started, me just bein' born, period. I'd like to think if she'd a known what was waiting for me, she never would a done it.''

4   F A C I N G   F A C T S

Who Gets Punished? What Are Their Crimes?

I remember when I was thirteen and I was sitting on the front steps of my
grandmother's house. My father said, "Put on your shoes, I'm going
to take you downtown with me."
We got into the car and we went to the police station and I kept asking him,
"What are we doing here?"
He told me to hush, he had business to take care of. Then one of the
policemen took me and told me to wait in this little room. I was waiting in this little room for my father to finish his business and then I
looked out the window and I saw my father walking towards the car.
I screamed at him, Where was he going? Why was he leaving me? He never
turned around. He just kept walking to the car and then he got into
the car and drove off.
He never told me I was an "incorrigible" child . . . and Lord knows, at that
age I didn't know I had any problems or what they were. I just knew
he left me there. From there I was sent to the Youth Studies Center
and from there to Slaten Farms, and later on to all the rest of the
joints.
I never saw my mother. I still don't know who she is. All I know about her
is that she was real young when she had me, about seventeen or
something, and that she left home shortly after I was born. Nobody
will tell me about her or who she is. She's a big family secret in my
house. They know—Lord, with a family as big as mine, they know
everything. They just won't talk about it.
You know, for a while I tried to deny my past. When I got out of Muncy, I
wanted to be totally new and all that. But then I told myself, "Look,
girl, you've done all these things, they're part of your past." I'm not
wearing it all as a badge of honor, but then who should go to jail? Me
at thirteen? Huh-uh, baby; not me or nobody else.

—Theresa Derry, ex-inmate

What kind of women commit crimes? What kind of crimes? What are women "criminals" *really* like?

Although these questions have been asked often, the only women in crime we know anything about are the women arrested, tried, convicted, or sentenced to probation or prison. And we know very little about them. In 1972, three of every hundred prisoners were women, and they didn't merit even a footnote in volumes of discussions on the criminal justice system. Today the number of imprisoned women is five times greater than it was then. Six percent of state prisoners are women, as are 7 percent of all federal prisoners and 10 percent of the jail population. But despite this influx of women, there is still a dearth of information about them. Even fewer facts are known about their children, who are high-risk candidates for trouble themselves because of the trauma they experience from their mothers' imprisonment.

Stereotypes about women in prison run on a circular track from tough broads to whores to killers vicious to each other and a menace to society. Often people ask me, "Doesn't it *scare* you to talk to these women?" When I say, "No," I often find out they've gotten their impressions from movies with titles such as *Women in Chains,* which portray incarcerated women as amazons or bull dykes, crude nymphomaniacs, or psychopaths waiting to stab their unsuspecting victims.

In reading literature about women in conflict with the law during their time—whether they were abolitionists, suffragists, prostitutes, or pro-union women speaking in public places—I've found they are usually condemned as "wild," "loose," "immoral," or "fallen." The general public seemed more upset and distracted by a "general breakdown of inhibitions" than by the issues involved. In 1840 the *Public Ledger* in Philadelphia reported that the wives of poor workingmen in the Kensington section of the city stopped a railroad from being built through the heart of their community. To do this, the women apparently towed away wagons full of rails and tore up the foundations where the rails were to be laid. In an editorial entitled "The Mob," the *Ledger* wrote:

> A singular and most disgraceful feature of the disturbances was the active participation of women. The most efficacious leaders of the rioters were females. Unsexing themselves for the occasion, these Amazons led on their forces, and both by precept and example incited them to mischief. They prompted the destruction of property, they assailed with blows the officers who attempted to restrain them, they gave life and impulse and energy to the whole proceedings.
>
> It was a sign of evil times when they thus forget what is due to their sex and station, and rush into the turmoil and conflict of lawless strife. It is

a sign of evil times, also, when their husbands and fathers tolerate such misconduct.

Another *Ledger* editorial on the same event warned:

> Once cut loose from the gentle restraints of sex, and taught by experience that when united they are not only formidable but irresistible, what shall hinder them hereafter from renewing and repeating upon every provocation, real or imagined, the turbulence, which, once tasted, to ferocious natures never loses its relish.

Women in prison today feel they still bear the brunt of stereotypical 1840s standards for "immoral" women. As representatives for all female lawbreakers, they are considered the sample population for most projections about "criminal women." They say they are being punished for breaking not only social laws but also unwritten moral laws. They often report that prior to incarceration, they were treated by judges, lawyers, and others in the criminal justice system with contempt, as if they were "tramps" or cheap women—basically "anti-mothers"—for stepping out of place and threatening the status quo.

"Women in prison are less than a criminal in society's mind," said one woman with a laugh. "They think of us as summertime whores who don't have phone numbers."

"Most people have exaggerated ideas about people in prison," said another. "Most of us are judged as a whole—not as individuals. We're as different from each other as anyone anywhere is. I know I had exaggerated fears myself before coming here—but I've met a lot of really beautiful sisters. Of course we do have some people here for Grand Stupidity, but that's the way things go. People just forget that everybody in here is somebody's daughter, or somebody's wife, or somebody's sister. We're not no more bad or dangerous than anybody else. We just carry the stigma, that's all."

Who are these women in prison? It often surprises people to learn that very few of them have been locked up for big crimes or for crimes of violence. Martha Wheeler, the former superintendent of the Ohio Reformatory for Women, points out that the vast majority of women in prison are not real criminals. "There are a relatively small percentage here who are involved in criminal behavior," she said. "Most of the women who are involved in criminal behavior we never see. Every now and then we get some people who have been involved with shoplifting or narcotics rings on a big scale, but it's rare.

"The other women, the women who end up here, are acting out of their inadequacies as individuals—not with criminal rings or real criminal intentions. They have two or three kids and nobody to help them, so they write checks. Most of our homicides come out of long-standing volatile situations—a person who had meaning to the woman and the situation blew up. It's a personal interaction kind of thing—very often a drunk and abusive man, a husband, boyfriend, next-door neighbor who's been picking on the kids. . . .

"A woman who gets into trouble with a supportive family who has money will get sent to a shrink or to live with Aunt Susie and the court approves. She can be diverted from incarceration. Incarceration is for women without resources—financial and human. If she has economic support, she doesn't end up in an institution. This is not always true, but it's true for the majority. In this state, some nine thousand women are arrested in a year, but only three hundred are incarcerated here. There are all kinds of diversionary things going on for women.

"For the most part, courts are good at sorting out crimes where a woman is actually stealing bread for her children. But I have seen a lot of cases where it's directly the reason for the crime."

Today, in 1995, more than 108,000 women fill our jails and prisons: more than 59,000 women sit in our state and federal prisons, and more than 48,000 women are locked in city and county jails. The numbers are growing daily.

The women who go to prison are young—on the average, they're between twenty-five and thirty years old—and a large portion of them are parents. According to a Department of Justice study completed in March 1994, more than three fourths of them are mothers. Although nobody keeps track of all the children of prisoners or the numbers of parents who are separated from their young children, the studies that have been done indicate that four out of five of the mothers in prison have at least one child under the age of eighteen. Bureau of Justice Statistics indicate that 85 percent of the mothers in prison had legal custody of their children before entering prison and that they lived with their children at that time. While no one has a precise count, it's thought that on any given day in America, more than one and a half million children are separated from a parent who is in prison. At least sixty thousand of them have mothers who are locked away in adult prisons and jails. Nobody has kept track of all these children, but through no fault of their own, they suffer immeasurably. Their families, and their childhoods, have been disrupted by imprisonment—a fact not lost on the 85 percent of incarcerated mothers who intend to resume custody of their children after their release from prison.[1]

Twenty years ago, and still today, the great majority of women in prison are impoverished and were unemployed or underemployed at the time of their arrests. As single heads of households, they earned, on average, three thousand to ten thousand dollars a year.

When I wrote the first edition of *Women in Prison,* I was astonished at the number of women I met who had been physically or sexually abused. New research in the 1980s and 1990s has confirmed that, in fact, an enormous proportion of women in prison have been victims of abuse. In a survey published in 1990, the American Correctional Association found that over half of the women it surveyed had been physically abused and 36 percent had been sexually abused.[2] Women in prison say the figures are far greater than that, and a study in Massachusetts confirmed their perceptions. It showed that 88 percent of the women inside prison in that state had experienced traumatic episodes of violence—childhood sexual or physical abuse, or adult rape or battering—before their first arrest.[3]

Rhea Schaenman, the director of the Women's Prison Project of the Correctional Association of New York, told me that when she recently asked one prison drug counselor how many of his forty clients had been abused, he said, "Rhea, it would be easier to tell you how many weren't abused. Out of these forty women, I can tell you how many weren't abused. *Five* of them *weren't* abused."

Abuse is what kicked off alcohol or drug addiction in many of these women; it's what made them run away from home and get into trouble with the law in the first place when they were juveniles; it's what has made so many of them attempt suicide; it's what has kept their self-esteem at a low ebb; and it's what has kept them in trouble with the law as grown women who bear the label of "criminal."

Until the publication of Otto Pollack's book *The Criminality of Women* in 1950, there had been no thorough examination of the concept of women involved in criminal activity. Pollack emphasized the "masked character" of female crime—showing that instances of shoplifting, prostitution, theft, abortion, perjury, and disturbance were infrequently reported. He also

1. Philip M. Genty, "Procedural Due Process Rights of Incarcerated Parents in Termination of Parental Rights Proceedings: A Fifty-State Analysis," *Journal of Family Law* 30, no. 4 (1991–92).

2. American Correctional Association, *The Female Offender: What Does the Future Hold?* (Washington, D.C.: St. Mary's Press, 1990).

3. Mary E. Gilfus, "Seasoned by Violence/Tempered by Law: A Qualitative Study of Women and Crime" (Ph.D. dissertation, Brandeis University, 1988).

concluded that homosexual contact and exhibitionism in women were rarely reported, and that the roles of women as mothers inclined them to use different methods of homicide. His theory was that women's "devious methods" were misleading to law enforcement personnel. "At least in our culture," he noted, "women are particularly protected against the detection of criminal behavior on the one hand and exposed to a wealth of irritations, temptations and opportunities which may lead them to criminal behavior on the other."

Pollack and others pointed out how many more men than women are arrested, prosecuted, and sentenced to prison. Today, although the gap has narrowed considerably, men still are discriminated against with proportionately higher arrests and prosecutions because they are *considered* to be more dangerous, whether or not they *are* more dangerous. And once they are sentenced, men are more than four times as likely to be classified as high-security than women, according to a Federal Bureau of Prisons report in 1991.

In an unpublished paper for the President's Commission on Law Enforcement and the Administration of Justice in 1967, Walter C. Reckless and Barbara Ann Kay groped for the reason behind differential selection of women for prosecution and imprisonment and came up with the "chivalry factor": "A large part of the infrequent officially acted upon involvement of women in crime can be traced to the masking effect of women's roles, effective practice on the part of women of deceit and indirection, their instigation of men to commit their crimes (the Lady Macbeth factor), the willingness of men to 'cover up' for them and the unwillingness of the public and the law enforcement personnel to hold women accountable for their deeds (the chivalry factor)."

Chivalry has always been dead, however, when it comes to Bad Girls. Bad Girls have never received chivalrous treatment. And Bad Girls can be black or brown or red or beige or white—as long as they are also poor, aggressive, drug addicted, or selling sexual favors. Chivalry has been reserved for people who are able to sidestep the criminal justice system altogether.

To the extent that there is still a "chivalry factor," it may be that law enforcement personnel, prosecutors, and judges are reticent about hurting women, especially privileged, "respectable" women who could be their mothers.[4] Women who appear to be moral or "normal" by conventional standards, especially white women who seem proper, warm, dependent,

4. This could explain some of the favoritism shown white women by white judges, discussed in chapter 2. It could also explain their added outrage at white women being prostitutes.

and in compliance with traditional sex-role expectations, can and do get away with behavior men serve time for. When these Good Girls are arrested, they are protected by being sent on a different path from the Bad Girls.

On the other hand, unmarried women, minority women, women with substance-abuse problems, and women on welfare who have stepped far enough out of line to be arrested and who appear to have nontraditional, less "respectable" roles or shabby moral codes are no longer protected by stereotypes. Bad Girls are punished, not protected. In a 1985 study of differences in the courts' response to men and women defendants, Irene H. Nagel found "a strong adverse effect for females charged with personal crimes as compared with property crimes, and marital status—a variable not significant among male defendants—had a strong effect on the probability of women being sentenced to prison, with married women receiving preferential treatment."[5]

And when women appear to be living chaotic, disintegrated lives or violating their roles as "ladies" or mothers, prosecutors and judges seem to think they *deserve* punishment. In fact, indigent women—black and brown and white—who've stepped out of line often are subject to harsher treatment and additional disdain and abuse based on angry moral judgments. Bail is higher for them, indictments are more severe, sentences are longer, parole more often is denied. Stereotypes work both ways.

Of the Bad Girls, black women have always been treated the most harshly by the criminal justice system. Nicole Hahn Rafter writes in *Partial Justice: Women in State Prisons, 1800–1935,* of how black women prisoners never gained any advantages from being women; following the Civil War they were locked up in large numbers and leased out for longer periods than white women to work in the fields and on chain gangs. Today patterns of discrimination continue: black women are seven times more likely than white women to be sentenced to prison for the same kinds of crimes. Thirteen percent of the women in America are black, but they make up 44 percent of the female prison population. Black women are more apt to be jailed for victimless crimes, to be denied bail, and to be returned to prison for parole violation.

Despite facts to the contrary, a perception of women as increasingly violent and vicious has been growing over the past twenty-five years. This trend linking women's independence with increased crime began in June 1971, when the Federal Bureau of Investigation's uniform crime statistics

5. Meda Chesney-Lind, "Women and Crime: The Female Offender," *Signs* 12, no. 1 (1986).

reported a "drastic rise" in the female crime rate and front-page headlines broadcast the news that women were committing more violent crimes. FBI figures showed that from 1960 to 1969 arrests for major crimes rose 61.3 percent for males and 156.2 percent for females.[6]

Many of the newspaper stories reporting these statistics concluded the "increase of violent crime" among women was linked directly to the growing emancipation of women. The *New York Times* quoted Sheriff Peter Pitchess of Los Angeles to that effect: "As women emerge from their traditional roles as housewife and mother, entering the political and business fields previously dominated by males, there is no reason to believe that women will also not approach equality with men in the criminal field."[7] Law enforcement personnel, sociologists, criminologists, and other students of crime whom I interviewed at the time didn't always name the women's movement, but they attributed the "rise of crime among women" to three broad causes: the changing attitudes of society, the women themselves, and police willingness to arrest women. Usually their thoughts were as divergent as their biases:

- There's a general breakdown of inhibitions among women. They are committing more crimes because they aren't tied to the home like they used to be. They want to do everything a man does, even crime.
- Women aren't committing more crimes, they're just being arrested more. Women have always gotten away with murder before now.
- Women are getting younger. When I first came here, in April, the average age of the inmates was between thirty-one and thirty-four, and it's been slipping down since then. One factor is the increasing mobility of youth. They're coming out from the home at a much earlier age.
- Women are becoming more violent, but so is the whole society. It's observable in all parts of society—not just in the criminal element.
- It's true the women we get today are much more hostile, aggressive, and more dangerous than they used to be. It always amazes me that people think incarcerated women are like Sunday school teachers. They're not! Every woman here is capable of aggressive, assaultive behavior. Any time a tour goes through, we have to think who's on the floor—and what danger they represent.

Upon closer examination these "drastic increases" in crimes committed by women could be seriously questioned. Were women committing more violent crimes or just being arrested more often? How were both the

---

6. U.S. Federal Bureau of Investigation, *Uniform Crime Reports* (Washington, D.C.: U.S. Government Printing Office, 1969).

7. In contrast to this theory, Italian writer Gino Faustini reports that the gradual emancipation of women in Italy has resulted in a steady *decline* of female crime—particularly the more serious offenses.

male and female percentages affected by the different crime reporting processes, which varied from city to city during those years? Hadn't the uniform crime reports made a vast difference in the frequency of reported crimes and in the way statistics had been manipulated and tabulated? And what about the population increase in the age group of people traditionally arrested for major crimes?

Over time, it became evident that while a small number of women certainly did perpetrate horrible and harmful crimes against others, it was not at all conclusive that there ever was an actual increase in crime among women—and if there was, whether it was at all significant, proportionate to the increase in population or in the variation of crime statistics historically. Nor was there evidence that women were committing more violent crimes than they had previously.

Nevertheless, since that time, the myths have persisted. In the 1990s similar headlines have announced increases in women's crimes. Certainly the huge jump in the numbers of women sentenced to prison have made many people assume that women of the 1990s are committing more crimes and more violent crimes. What else could explain the fact that the female prison population increased from 13,420 women in 1980 to 50,409 in 1992—a jump of approximately 375 percent for women, compared to a growth rate of 160 percent for men?[8] Why are more than 108,000 women now crowded into our city and county jails and our state and federal prisons?

And why, even though only six or seven of every hundred prisoners sentenced to state and federal prisons are women, is the criminal justice system more inclined than ever to sentence women to prison? Why did the growth rate for the female jail population outstrip that for the male jail population between 1983 and 1991?[9] And why have we opened so many new prisons for women, and planned to build more?

Wouldn't these facts prove that women are getting more violent and committing more crimes? Why else would we put so many more women in prison today and treat them so much more harshly?

Politicians—particularly those with an interest in having new prisons built in their constituents' territories—still are suggesting that we need more jails and prisons for women because women are becoming more dangerous. They would have us think that women are being locked up more often because they're committing more serious and violent crimes.

8. Lawrence A. Greenfield and Stephanie Minor-Harper, *Women in Prison,* Bureau of Justice Statistics, Special Report, March 1991.

9. Louis W. Janowski, "Jail Inmates 1991," Bureau of Justice Bulletin, June 1992.

It's a logical assumption, but it is not true. The truth is that women's share of arrests for violent crime, according to Bureau of Justice and FBI statistics, has been remarkably stable for many years. Women's proportional share of violent crime has stood at roughly 10 percent for many years. Criminologist Meda Chesney-Lind, who has examined the national data on the characteristics of women in state prisons, maintains that the numbers state-to-state also support the assertion that women are not being imprisoned because of a jump in the seriousness of their offenses. Not only do women commit far fewer violent offenses than men, she says, but the number of women imprisoned for violent crimes has actually declined in the past ten years.[10] Three of every four women imprisoned for crimes involving violence are there for having committed a first-time offense directed against an abusive partner or husband.

According to Bureau of Justice Statistics, women in prison for violent offenses included about 3 in 10 female inmates in 1991, down from 4 in 10 in 1986—a decline in the proportion of violence.[11] New York City police also reported that while women were accused of committing a third more felonies in 1993 than in 1975, when it came to murder, only 59 women were arrested in 1993, compared to 120 women in 1975. (This may in part be the result of the establishment of more women's shelters, which provide previously unavailable options for battered women.)

What kind of crimes have most of the women in prisons and jails actually committed? The vast majority of women in prison have been convicted of nonviolent crimes—mostly property crimes and drug possession. According to Chesney-Lind, "Careful analysis of both unofficial and official data fails to support the notion that women have been committing more serious crimes during the last two decades."[12] In fact, she says, "one is struck by the fact that the female contribution to serious crime is minuscule."

There does seem to be a slight increase in arrests of women for larceny, fraud, forgery, and vagrancy. Apparently, the increase in these categories is due as much to the willingness to prosecute women for shoplifting, bad checks, and other petty crimes as it is to increased poverty among young single mothers. The increase in "vagrancy" among women reflects widespread use of vagrancy laws to arrest prostitutes. Juvenile girls, as always, still are arrested primarily for petty crimes, mainly shoplifting, and for

10. Meda Chesney-Lind, "Patriarchy, Prisons, and Jails: A Critical Look at Trends in Women's Incarceration." *Prison Journal* 71, no. 1 (Spring–Summer 1991).

11. Greenfield and Minor-Harper, *Women in Prison.*

12. Chesney-Lind, "Women and Crime."

status offenses (noncriminal charges for which only minors can be arrested) such as running away from home, truancy, and being "incorrigible."

Also, many of the women and teenage girls who are incarcerated for crimes that fall into the "violent crime" category are not dangerous to the community. In some states, for instance, burglary is included as a "violent crime," even though it doesn't involve violence. Burglary is unacceptable, of course, but more effective sanctions could be adjudicated that involve restitution for victims and a refocusing of the offender's energies into a productive line of work.

Unfortunately, while female crime rates have reflected little or no change, the number of women sentenced to jails and prisons continues to skyrocket. The fact that women are being arrested and locked up in greater numbers is due to punitive laws and practices, as well as shifts in law enforcement policies, not because of significant changes in their behavior.

Law enforcement's new willingness to prosecute, punish, and imprison women may be part of a societal backlash against women, or it just may be a mindless side effect of our rage against the Willie Hortons of the world. That rage has created the mandatory sentencing laws and other more severe sentencing policies throughout the country, along with a greater drive to sentence women to prison instead of to probation or other alternatives. Additionally, more women are being sent or returned to prison owing to greater enforcement of probation and parole violations.

Most likely, these increased sanctions have to do with an increased perception of violence and an increased perception of drug use, even though in both areas there has been, when change has been registered, a *decrease*. Nevertheless, these perceptions have influenced prosecutors and judges, who, after decades of imposing lighter sentences, now are treating "wayward women" more harshly, whether they are first-time offenders, thieves, drug addicts, or women who fight back against abusive husbands or boyfriends. As Chesney-Lind says, "It's as if the criminal justice system is saying, 'If you want equality, baby, we'll given you equality.' "

Twenty years ago, for instance, nearly 66 percent of women convicted of federal felonies were placed on probation, but in 1991 only 28 percent received similar treatment. Today prosecutors are accepting fewer plea bargains and increasing the seriousness of charges. Many offenses that were misdemeanors in previous times now are charged as felonies. Judges, who have a limited range of options under mandatory sentencing laws, are giving more prison sentences—and longer ones—to women now than ever before. The harshness of the sentences isn't diminished by whether the women are nonviolent first-time offenders, whether they have been charged with shoplifting or writing bad checks, or defending themselves from physical abuse from their husbands or boyfriends.

Women who kill are treated with even more vengeance. Even though most of these defendants have killed an abusive partner, have no prior record, and have very little likelihood of committing another crime, they're given higher bail or refused bail, prosecuted on more serious charges, and sentenced to longer terms in prison than ever before. Studies show that 90 percent of the women imprisoned for killing men in New York State had been battered by those men. Currently there are some two thousand battered women in America serving prison time for defending their lives against batterers.[13]

It's interesting to note that corrections officials and researchers have found that murderers—particularly those who have killed a spouse or partner—make the most trustworthy prisoners. When murderers get out of prison, they rarely come back. They have the lowest recidivism rates because their crime was a one-time thing. For the most part, these people do not have a pattern of committing crimes. One incident changed their lives. There's substantial evidence that the vast majority of women who have killed an abusive husband are no danger to society.

Nevertheless, it is as if these women are being punished for daring to fight back. According to the National Coalition Against Domestic Violence, data show that abusive men who kill their partners serve an average of two to six years in prison, whereas women who kill their partners and claim self-defense serve an average of fifteen years. It has been suggested that women serve longer for these crimes than men because they use lethal weapons—guns and knives—to kill their mates, whereas men more often use only their bare hands—the same weapons they used in the past for battering. I wonder, however, if the discrepancy of sentences doesn't have more to do with the legal rights and ownership men traditionally have had over their wives—and with the tendency male judges have to empathize with male vs. female violence. The devaluation of women also means that the death of a woman usually won't be considered as important as the loss of a "valuable" man.

Recent sentencing laws for drug offenses are the single biggest contributor to the increase in our prison population. In 1991, according to the Bureau of Justice Statistics, women being locked up in state prisons for drug offenses represented a 436 percent increase since 1986.

13. "Information regarding how many battered women are in prison for killing partners," National Clearinghouse for the Defense of Battered Women, Statistics 1992.

Under mandatory sentencing laws, judges are *required* to give minimum mandatory prison terms for various drug offenses. Under federal guidelines, for instance, possession of as little as five grams of crack cocaine—less than the weight of two pennies' worth—mandates *five years* in prison. This means a judge cannot take into account individual circumstances such as minor children, steady employment records, or other factors that might otherwise recommend effective alternatives to imprisonment. The result is that instead of treating addicts and helping reduce the constant demand for drugs, we are filling our already overcrowded prisons with them. Most shocking, perhaps, is that a full 91 percent of these mandatory drug sentences are imposed on men and women who are *nonviolent, first-time offenders.*

From the perspective of fairness, justice, or simple common sense, America's War on Drugs is a monstrous travesty. All the billions of dollars spent on drug enforcement haven't stopped addiction. And while the rich get richer on the sale and trafficking of drugs, poor people who become users—often enticed by "freebies" until they're hooked—pay the price in prison. "I see these women in here who were caught selling nickel bags," said Pat Christie, an assistant superintendent at the Edna Mahan Correctional Facility in Clinton, New Jersey, during a recent interview. "And I wonder, why do they notice all the nickel bags but ignore the bales coming into the country?

"We have to stop it coming in—right when it comes in," said Christie. "The majority of women here are in prison because of drug-related crimes. You're never going to eliminate criminality, but you could eliminate drug addiction if you could stop it from coming in. That would do more good than all the intervention programs."

As is the case on the outside, women in prison who want to break their addictions have a hard time finding help. Very few programs are geared to women addicts. Women who have suffered physical and sexual abuse need programs geared toward building trust, connections, and understanding. They need to be empowered as women and as mothers. Very few programs like this exist, and those that do are full. Women sign up on waiting lists and then they wait, sometimes indefinitely. At the Edna Mahon prison, there is one major drug treatment program, which treats only fifty women over a six- to seven-month period. But a chance for treatment for fifty of 1,100 inmates per year beats the odds on the outside, where America's 7.5 million hard-core addicts can find treatment in only about twelve thousand long-term residential drug-treatment centers.[14]

14. Mike Tidwell, *In the Shadow of the White House: Drugs, Death and Redemption on the Streets of the Nation's Capital* (Rocklin, Calif.: Prima, 1992).

While the expanding population of women serving sentences for drug offenses accounts for *more than half of the total growth of women in prison,* women's overall drug use actually has gone *down.* Figures from the National Institute of Justice in 1993 show there has been a slight decline in rates of cocaine use, largely unchanged rates of marijuana and opiate use, and a very slight increase in the percentage of women who tested positive for two or more drugs.

It doesn't make sense, but that doesn't change the reality for women inside—or for their children and families outside.

Legislation of morality is not unique to twentieth-century America. Throughout history women have gone to trial and heard lectures on their demeanor, the violation of their traditional roles, and what they have done that is unbefitting their sex and their station in the church.

Today the government has in many ways replaced the church as the ultimate source of authority over human behavior. Most of us trust the state's authority to punish violations of its laws as if divine command were still the rule of the law. The definition of crime depends on the interpretation of the group that has sufficient power to make its beliefs part of the social order. The thin line between what is considered normal and what constitutes harmful misconduct sometimes is so vague that it blurs our conceptions of ''crime'' and our notions of appropriate punishment. Since each state jurisdiction in the United States has its own penal code, for instance, what is criminal in one state may not be outlawed in another. In one state, for example, fornication can be punished with up to five years' imprisonment, but in another it is not a crime. In more than one state, sodomy can bring imprisonment, while in other states it is not a crime. Similarly inconsistent is the division of offenses into misdemeanors and felonies. What is a misdemeanor or a petty offense in one state may be a felony, or presumably a serious crime, in another.[15] In Ohio and several other states, for instance, a second conviction on prostitution charges becomes a felony offense for which women are sent to the state prison for one or more years.

Certainly, as we experience variations in the power structure and moral climate over time and place, we see differences in what is considered ''criminal.'' The national experiment in the prohibition of alcohol dramatized this lesson of change, as did the revision of abortion as an illegal act. What are crimes today may not be defined as crimes twenty or thirty years

15. Marvin E. Wolfgang and Bernard Cohen, *Crime and Race: Conceptions and Misconceptions* (New York: Institute of Human Relations Press, 1970).

from now. By making the use or possession of certain drugs illegal, we have created an enormous category of crimes. I believe that our drug laws and mandatory prison sentences for drug offenses in the 1980s and 1990s will someday be understood to have been a tragic misplacement of priorities.

Dr. Seymour L. Halleck, professor of psychiatry at the University of North Carolina and formerly a chief psychiatric consultant for the Wisconsin Division of Corrections, argues that what the public normally calls criminal behavior is more likely than not an individual's desperate effort to try to alter an internal state of helplessness. "I think all crimes are really either efforts to change oppression that is real or to change perceived oppression," he said at a psychiatric conference on crime and violence. "Of course, in some crimes it is perfectly clear that the effort to do something about a social system such as family or community is obvious. In other crimes people are reacting to more oppression in a situation than actually exists; they are acting from their internalized sense of oppression. But certainly much of this internalized pressure is related to real external oppression they have experienced previously.

"For the most part those people—not criminals—who get sent to prison are people who have been sorely oppressed by the society, who lack skills, who are inadequate in almost every conceivable way. They generally lack the capacity to make it as criminals. I would argue that perhaps over 90 percent of those people you'd find in our institutions are not violent, they're not greedy, not enemies of society, they are just very, very unfortunate losers."

Halleck said that one of the things he likes to do periodically when he goes into the prisons is sit down and pull a hundred prisoners' charts at random. "It is extremely rare to find anybody," Halleck said, "who has ever earned as much as a thousand dollars in a criminal career. And these are people who have committed many, many crimes and may have spent years and years in prison. It is extremely rare to find anybody who has any kind of decent hourly wage for his criminal activities when you gauge it against the risks entailed."

Halleck said that in his experience it is most common to run into people who do "life on the installment plan" for small crimes like cashing bad checks for fifty dollars or less.

"If you look at the behavior of offenders during a criminal act, it becomes even more disturbing to see how few precautions most of these people take to avoid being apprehended," he said. "You know the stories about robbing places next door to a police station and things like that. But I think one of the more startling statistics has got to do with the use of alcohol. Various studies indicate that up to 72 percent of felons at the time of arrest are in a state of inebriation.

"Now, I would hold that if one wants to commit a crime and get away with it, he should not try to commit a crime when he's drunk. It would be as ridiculous as trying to be a successful surgeon while operating while inebriated.

"What this suggests is that what we call criminal behavior is more likely than not a desperate effort to try to alter an internal state of helplessness, lack of autonomy, and hopelessness. The criminal act is a way of trying to adapt and change that circumstance."

From her personal experience, Jeanette Spenser confirmed Dr. Halleck's assessment. "I was drunk to start with—and I was even drinking during the robbery—right there in the laundry," she told me long after she was out of prison and off parole in New York City. "But I don't know why I wore that purple coat. I should have known. All they said was, 'She was wearing a bright purple coat.' Now, how many people wear a bright purple coat to pull off a robbery?

"They had me picked up in five minutes.

"I guess I was screaming to get caught. I guess I was screaming for help. And that purple coat helped me scream. Lord knows, I needed help. I was drinking so bad. I had lost my husband. I had lost my baby. I had really hit the bottom of the barrel."

5 FOUND GUILTY

Courtroom Theater and Women without Scripts

> The King turned pale, and shut his note-book hastily.
> "Consider your verdict," he said to the jury, in a low, trembling voice.
> "There's more evidence to come yet, please your Majesty," said the White Rabbit, jumping up in a great hurry: "this paper has just been picked up."
> "What's in it?" said the Queen.
> "I haven't opened it yet," said the White Rabbit, "but it seems to be a letter written by the prisoner to—to somebody. . . ."
> "Who is it directed to?" said one of the jurymen.
> "It isn't directed at all," said the White Rabbit; "in fact, there's nothing written on the outside." He unfolded the paper as he spoke, and added, "It isn't a letter, after all: it's a set of verses."
> "Are they in the prisoner's handwriting?" asked another of the jurymen.
> "No, they're not," said the White Rabbit, "and that's the queerest thing about it. . . ."
> "He must have imitated somebody else's hand," said the King. (The jury all brightened up again.)
> "Please your Majesty," said the Knave, "I didn't write it, and they can't prove I did: there's no name signed at the end."
> "If you didn't sign it," said the King, "that only makes the matter worse. You must have meant some mischief, or else you'd have signed your name like an honest man. . . ."
> "That proves his guilt," said the Queen.
>
> —Lewis Carroll, "Alice's Evidence," in *Alice's Adventures in Wonderland*

The courtroom is clean, dignified, almost pompous. Brass railings divide spectators from actors; they reflect off the shining mahogany surface of the judge's bench. Some forty people sit in folding chairs facing the judicial stage. For the most part they are a bedraggled, restless audience, seemingly oblivious to the decorum of the theater. Some of the women have come with rollers in their hair, dresses hanging unevenly, slips showing. Some men wear baggy pants, ill-fitting shirts untucked in the back. A few are neat, trim. Spectators include plainclothes detectives and men wearing blue police uniforms and silver badges.

A young black woman comes in, wearing a white knit dress and coat, holding hands with her sister's two small children. The children sit down beside her and then crawl up on their knees to hang over their seats, staring with curiosity at the people behind them. ''Hush, sit down. Mommy's not here yet.'' Their mother, Beatrice, will be brought down from the jail for sentencing today. She has been in jail thirteen months. Three months ago she pled guilty to possessing narcotics and being involved in a burglary. This will be the second time her children have seen her in more than a year. They are not allowed to visit her in the county jail.[1]

This is a tired, anxious audience before curtain time. But there is no curtain. Actors prepare in full view of the audience. The supporting cast warms up. Stenographers in designated seats check over their machines, straighten skirts, wait to begin. Stage managers carry papers to the proper tables. District attorneys and defense attorneys officiously thumb through their thick legal files and make stylized gestures indicating readiness for performance. They rehearse lines quietly. Occasionally one actor struts over to another decorously, whispering in low tones about the first scene. Court crier and bailiffs stand at attention at the corners of the stage, surveying the audience as they seat themselves. This is participatory theater. The audience will partake, but they don't know their cues.

It is a controlled setting. Those who come to this theater regularly know the performance will be monotonously the same. Yet there is always some variation, some detail or pathos, some outrageous person or crime or sentence to make it different. Rarely is there laughter; rarer still, spontaneity. The only constants are the tense, repressed anger, anxiety, and curiosity emanating from actors and spectators alike.

Suddenly it is curtain time. The court crier, an old regular named Sam McGhee, steps forward and cries: ''ALL RISE. OYEZ, OYEZ, OYEZ. ALL PERSONS BOUND BY RECOGNIZANCE HAVING TO DO WITH THE HONORABLE JUDGES OF THE COURT OF COMMON PLEAS IN THE FIRST JUDICIAL DISTRICT OF PENNSYLVANIA

---

1. Today, in the 1990s, many jails still do not have provisions for children to visit their mothers. Some jails will not allow infants or children under sixteen to visit, whereas others have rules that make the visit difficult because they don't allow bottles, diapers, or baby food.

HOLDING HERE THIS DAY WILL NOW APPEAR AND THEY SHALL BE HEARD. GOD SAVE THE COMMONWEALTH AND THIS HONORABLE COURT. BE SEATED PLEAZZE.''

His lines have been repeated so many times, for so many years, that now they are only a loud flow, a commanding tone, the words indistinguishable except at the beginning and the end. The repeated OYEZ is close to music, a chant, a rhythm that could be sung to the backdrop of drums pounding while people dance to the beat. But in this theater, the chant becomes a drone announcing that you *must* stand, or suffer consequences: contempt of court.

Black robes swish, there is a flurry of actions that have been repeated thousands of times—and then the judge is seated. He folds his arms in front of him, clasps his hands, and reads briefs and bills and psychiatric reports conscientiously, carefully, his brow wrinkled in serious effect. Like a god, he sits in front of the large bronze seal of the state. Supporting cast members confer with him briefly and then the play begins— simultaneously falling apart with confusion.

"The point is, I don't have a bill of 368," the judge tells the district attorney. "No, your honor, that's the photo number, Judge. The bill is 370 and 371."

"I see. Yes. I have bill 371. We can proceed."

"William Bradley, number six," the crier demands. "ALL PARTIES AND WITNESSES IN THE BRADLEY CASE COME FORWARD." A small black man, with wrinkled brown tweed coat too large, shuffles toward the brass railing. "DO YOU SWEAR WHAT YOU TELL THIS COURT OF THE COMMONWEALTH OF PENNSYLVANIA WILL BE THE TRUTH, THE WHOLE TRUTH, AND NOTHING BUT THE TRUTH SO HELP YOU GOD? KEEP YOUR VOICE UP. KEEP YOUR VOICE UP SO THE JUDGE CAN HEAR YOU!"

"Where's the police witness? Where's the police witness?" the judge asks. "Is Detective Zucker here? Is Detective Zucker here? You're taking a lot of time, Mr. District Attorney." Detective Zucker is not in the room—or if he is, he's hiding. The district attorney offers to find out where he is, why he didn't show. The case is postponed. The crier reads Bradley's name again, stating the case will be continued until June 6. William Bradley shuffles out with two guards.

I have come to this courtroom to see Jeanne Hardy be tried. She faces two charges of prostitution and one charge of trying to cash an American Express traveler's check at Thirtieth Street train station in Philadelphia.

"ALL PARTIES CONNECTED TO JEANNE HARDY PLEASE COME FORWARD." Jeanne stands tall, in black dress, black heels, and purse. She looks dignified, calm. But she is alone and frightened. This is the fourth time she has come to court. Today will be the trial, and her life for the next six months or next six years will surely be resolved one way or another. But the case is not decided. The district attorney explains he is not ready to proceed with the case; he and Jeanne's defense attorney are trying to "work something out." Jeanne's case is continued until July 8. The teller who has come to testify against Jeanne shakes his head; this is his fourth time in court, too.

Charges against another defendant are read. Andrew Moore, charged with violation of parole. Three counts: failure to report, failure to notify change of address, and refusal to undergo psychiatric treatment. In a matter of minutes, the judge surveys the report and orders that Moore be returned to the state prison to complete a five-year sentence inside the walls. He has committed no new crime, but he has violated parole conditions. I wonder if he has any children. I wonder how old he was when he first went to jail.

Finally the children in front of me spot their mother. She is now sitting in the front row between two matrons. Now standing in front of the bench, inside the brass railings, beside her lawyer. The two women sitting beside me—the defendant's mother and grandmother—put their arms around each other, hold their breath. The judge studies the reports in front of him, clears his throat. He tells Beatrice Connor that she has committed a very serious offense, does she realize this?

Her answer is inaudible, but she nods her head up and down, like a child being scolded. A young probation officer tells the judge that he has made arrangements for Beatrice to enter a drug rehabilitation program in the Kensington section of Philadelphia. The judge listens to the details of the program. More silence. Then he tells Beatrice Connor that he is going to give her a break: ten years' probation.

She will be transferred directly from the House of Correction to the drug center, where she will remain for ninety days. Following her drug treatment she will be expected to meet all the conditions of probation and have the opportunity to prove that she can be an upright citizen and a worthy mother. If at any time she violates the conditions of probation, she will be brought back before this bench and sentenced to a prison term of no less than five years. If she serves the conditions of probation satisfactorily for five years, she can appeal to him at that time to have the remainder of her sentence suspended.

The confused drama proceeds. Expected pauses, expected noise, with only some of the characters fumbling their lines. Some props are not available, some actors missing. It is confused tension—an emotional circus—controlled by legal syllables and statutes. Everyone plays his or her part with control. Defendants stand in front of the bar stoically, yet seeming to seethe inside. I think if someone moved too quickly or unexpectedly, shouted, laughed, or jumped up and started dancing, letting go of the dignity expected, the courtroom itself would explode or perhaps disappear in smoke. I feel like singing in a loud voice.

The bailiff is the only person who shouts when he feels like it or moves unexpectedly. He steps forward occasionally, seemingly on cue to break the tension, and hollers, "Keep it quiet back there." Earlier he has walked up to me to say I am not allowed to take notes in the courtroom. Now a man dares to wear a hat into the room. The bailiff seems outraged; his face reddens. "Take off that hat! Take off that hat!" He steps out threateningly; the man retreats, takes off his hat, sits down. I notice that "the man" is a woman.

Usually what goes on in the courtroom is unintelligible even to someone used to this scene listening carefully from the spectators' section. It is like hearing the lines from an ancient play read in a scramble without feeling; memorized lines or makeshift phrases in a language known only to the actors—words that have lost the essence, the clarity of their real meaning or original intent. The formality, the lack of warmth and awareness settles down like a fog and rocks defendants and observers alike into a maze, a daze of legal words.[2]

I walk outside the courtroom for air, an attempt to break the fog. Standing there, I hear an odd sound and realize the noise is coming from handcuffs clicking off and on defendants on their way to or from jail as they stand in the corridor outside the courtroom. I notice a small, dark-skinned woman in blue stretch pants and an orange sweater as she puts her hands out together in front of her. A matron and a policewoman lock the handcuffs to each wrist. A haunting look of humiliation makes her small-boned face sag as the wrist shackles are secured and she walks tight-lipped and drawn down the long hall between two guards, holding her head high.

The weight of those handcuffs on her wrists, the headache-inducing tension in the courtroom, the sleepless nights awaiting trial must feel like a nightmare. In pieces, women later recall their anger, the fear, the sense of not knowing what's going to happen to their lives and the lives of their children. It seems the play is almost over.

2. Until June 12, 1972, an indigent defendant faced the prologue to this kind of circus alone—without a lawyer. Then the Supreme Court ruled that every poor person is entitled to a publicly funded lawyer for even the most minor offense that involves a potential jail sentence. Only nine years before, in the 1963 Gideon ruling by the court, it was held only that any needy defendant accused of a serious crime must be offered the services of a lawyer. Before those decisions, defendants could be sentenced to months, years, or life in prison without a pretense of defense.

"What happened? What'd I get?" she asks her court-appointed lawyer or public defender. Her confusion mixes with anger at her defense attorney and the district attorney. Often the anger turns back on herself for not knowing her rights; wondering how things might have been different if she had only known the script, the rules of the game.

"I was so dumb when I went to court," Doris Jordan said as she sat in the Iowa Reformatory for Women. "I got a court-appointed lawyer and I didn't know I could choose anyone. I'd never been in trouble with the law before. He told me I should cop a plea. Then when we were in the courtroom, the lawyer—*my* lawyer—said, 'She's got two mixed kids by [her husband] and he's just been sent to the penitentiary for narcotics.' I couldn't believe it! What do my kids have to do with my case? What does it have to do with my guilt or innocence or time that my husband was black? What does his sentence have to do with my case? We'd been separated for five years! I was so stupid it's pitiful.

"We was in the judge's chambers and they told me if you plead guilty to this one charge, we'll drop the rest. So I pled guilty to one check for $44.33. I had written thirty-six of them, though, and they had me. They had my picture and my signature, so I figured I was lucky. But if I'd had any people or known anything, I probably could have gotten probation.

"I didn't have any education or vocational training, and it was my first offense. They gave me ten years—which is a long time to get educated with a GED [high school equivalency diploma]. When I heard the judge say ten years, I couldn't believe it.

"All I could think about was my kids. It was like they was slipping out of my hands, falling away, and I couldn't hold on to them or keep them safe. It was like everything I knew in the world was suddenly gone. Just gone. I couldn't even think of going to prison. And ten years? The only way I can be hurt is through the children. When I talk about them, I have to fight back the tears. . . . The court took my kids when I was in jail. I was on ADC [Aid to Dependent Children], and the welfare department said I was an unfit mother because the light and gas bill had got to be two hundred dollars. My kids are my life; I could never be an unfit mother. When I get out I have to get myself together for me—and I only have to prove it to me. But to get my kids back I have to prove it to the court."

It is hard to imagine Doris Jordan as a threat to the community or someone who belongs behind bars. Her crime didn't warrant it; she posed no danger to the community. She doesn't fit the stereotype of a rough, hardtalking con. Her hair is long, black and shiny. Her deep brown eyes and smooth, olive-colored skin would make her a wholesome-looking candidate for the cover of *Seventeen* magazine or *Good Housekeeping*. Doris was tried by a judge, not by a jury. She was arrested, prosecuted, defended, tried, and sentenced by policemen, prosecutors, public defenders, and judges with backgrounds far different from her own. Their annual incomes total more money than she is likely to accumulate in her entire lifetime.

Like Doris, few of the women in prison have had jury trials. Very few men have either, because a jury trial is an expensive, time-consuming rarity. In Philadelphia alone, there were only 260 jury trials out of more than 30,000 criminal court cases in 1971.[3]

The majority of defendants sentenced to prison have big chunks of their lifetimes auctioned off in plea bargaining—a legal exchange that encourages the defendant to plead guilty to a lesser charge for a reduced sentence, getting maybe five to ten years instead of eight to twenty. Some embittered lawyers refer to it as "flesh peddling"—a gambling game between prosecutors and defense attorneys. ("You give me ten years for Green's case and I'll give you twenty instead of life for Saunders.") Off-the-record agreements are made with the judge. The process is said to speed up court efficiency and save time and energy for judges and attorneys. A defendant who refuses to plead guilty is told he will be risking the wrath of the judge and will probably wind up doing more time if found guilty.

Few people sentenced to prison have had the money to hire skilled criminal lawyers to defend their innocence or plead their case. In 1971 more than 85 percent of the cases in Philadelphia's municipal court were referred to public defenders, who are allowed to represent only indigent clients. These same clients, for the most part, were jailed awaiting trial because they couldn't afford bail.

The law of our land says that any person charged with a crime is innocent until proven guilty. But arrest and incarceration usually define guilt in a more pragmatic sense.

3. Even when a jury trial is conducted, it is rarely a trial by peers of the defendant—"having the same legal status in society as that which he [the defendant] holds." In 1879, when the Supreme Court ruled the exclusion of blacks from state juries unconstitutional, it added: "A state may prescribe the qualifications of its jurors. . . . It may confine the selection to males, to freeholders." In 1972, in "Juror Selection: The Law, a Mathematical Method of Analysis, and a Case Study," David Kairys pointed out that the process or method by which jurors are selected is invalid and discriminatory. His analysis of jury selection quite clearly revealed that juries were representative of the white, middle-aged, suburban and rural middle class. Black, poor, and young people—the groups most often charged with crimes and who most often have their lives placed in the hands of jurors, find virtually no peers on the juries. Kairys concluded that "the one institution through which the framers of the Constitution sought to guarantee that the voice of the community would be heard in the courtroom has been undermined. The courts have done little to implement the constitutional mandate of cross-sectional juries." Today it is unconstitutional for jurors to be excluded because of race or gender, and much effort has been made to equalize representation. Nevertheless, it still seems that black, poor, and young people often are underrepresented.

The person who comes to court from jail has a feeling of confinement about her, an aura. She has been treated as guilty during the days or months of incarceration. She has been subjected to the humiliation of jail life, to strip searches, daily counts, and arbitrary rules. Even if she is acquitted, what is the difference between being in jail six months following a verdict and having been in jail for six months prior to the verdict?

Sometimes, the longer a defendant stays in jail before trial, the less chance she has for acquittal. From jail, it is difficult to prepare an adequate defense—while, on the other hand, a person who can make bail usually is able to search for a lawyer, round up witnesses, secure a job, and make a good case for herself in court. This also means, then, that women with any economic power have a better chance for acquittal or probation.

In her notes for arguments in court on the issue of self-representation, Angela Davis wrote, in part:

I begin by directing the court's attention to the fact that as the accused in this case, I find myself at an enormous disadvantage. As a Black woman, I must view my own case in the historical framework of the fate which has usually been reserved for my people in America's halls of justice.

. . . In a courtroom situation, the white prosecutor, white witnesses, especially white policemen, are given far more credence by the jury—usually overwhelmingly white—than the Black defendant. In the event that the Black defendant has been previously convicted of a crime, his chances of acquittal are virtually non-existent. . . .

I repeat, as a Black woman, accused of three capital crimes, I am at an enormous disadvantage. The prosecutor, representative of forces which have continually upheld this institutional racism, has enormous advantages. The history of America is on his side. There can be no doubt we are unequal adversaries.

This inequality expresses itself not only in broad, historical terms but is also quite tangible. No one can deny that the immeasurable resources available to the prosecutor, indeed the entire state apparatus of California cannot in any sense compare to the resources available to me. His financial resources are virtually limitless—the state did not for a moment hesitate to extradite me from New York by the unprecedented means of a special military guard. I, on the other hand, must rely on the donations of concerned citizens, many of whom have had to make tremendous sacrifices in order to contribute small sums.

On another level, the prosecutor's superior position has been buttressed by the widespread publicity in his favor. I place particular emphasis on Nixon's gratuitous and unwarranted remark when he congratulated J. Edgar Hoover for capturing "one who engages in terrorist acts." It would seem that the overwhelming advantages enjoyed by the prosecutor would call into question the basic presumption of the innocence of the defendant. I contend that the circumstances are a priori balanced in favor of the prosecutor.[4]

4. Angela Y. Davis et al., *If They Come in the Morning* (New York: Signet, 1971).

Few women awaiting trial have the publicity or excellent legal defense Angela Davis had against the prosecution's case, even though the odds were stacked against her. The odds against an average prisoner's winning an acquittal are just as tremendous, if not more so, because the average defendant has no means of preparing a defense that challenges the prosecution's evidence.

For the most part, defendants meet their public defenders for the first time when they come into the courtroom for trial. Another public defender has interviewed them, and still another has investigated the case or talked to alibi witnesses or prepared pretrial motions. The defendant's lawyer—often fresh out of law school—receives the defendant's file, along with five to fifteen other files, the night before the trial, or the day of the trial. He has just read over the notes taken on the case and has had no time to talk with witnesses, search out evidence, or prepare motions that could effectively challenge the arrest procedure or prosecution evidence.

To say that public defenders are poorly paid and greatly overburdened by case loads is an understatement. Often their files are incomplete, lacking interviews or pretrial motions. In this circumstance, the lawyer can ask for a continuance—and the defendant is sent back to jail, often only to meet a different lawyer and a new continuance the next time she is brought down to court. Sometimes the public defender, who may be handling as many as fifteen to twenty cases the same day, proceeds with the trial without further information. [In many states this extreme disorganization no longer is true in the 1990s; public defenders have made and still are making a big effort to provide defendants with "vertical" representation from preliminary hearings through the trial. Many public defenders are highly skilled and dedicated, and they do an excellent job of representing their clients. Some do more professional and exemplary work than their private attorney colleagues.]

Although the Gideon ruling provided that indigent defendants should have representation in the court, no standards are set for the quality of representation. Some young public defenders are often as overwhelmed by the courtroom scenes as defendants. Their personal commitment to winning a case can be nullified by the frantic pace they maintain. Ultimately, this overload can result in slipshod and often meaningless representation for women and men without economic means. The interests, the lives of defendants and their families can go almost unnoticed, neglected. Mothers are separated from their children; fathers are separated from their families. Terrible mistakes are made and remain undiscovered.

Nevertheless, aspects of the human experiences in many of America's twentieth-century courtrooms can be compared to some of the human auctions held during the eighteenth and early nineteenth centuries. On the slave block, in that moment of sudden realization that all known reality, all present time, affections, activity, warmth, and routine were slipping away, fading into an unknown, fearsome world, the persons who were sold as slaves experienced powerlessness—a feeling that has been shared by millions of indigent Americans in the twentieth century sentenced to enter the unknown gates of the prison world. Prisoners go into a world the public knows little about. And just as slave mothers were separated from their children, the majority of women in prison today are cut off from their children by a word, a bargain, a gentlemen's agreement.

If it weren't for the power the police and courts wield over people's lives, the courtroom scenes could be called tragic satires. The state of Pennsylvania, for instance, spent thousands of dollars to bring a woman to trial for attempting to steal her neighbor's pig to feed to her children. She didn't even get to kill or cook the pig before she was arrested. This could be funny—but the woman was sentenced to *twenty years* in prison. What will happen to her children without her?

Rebecca Cross was in the Federal Reformatory for Women in Alderson, West Virginia, for twenty years without parole on her first offense—*possession* of fifty-five dollars' worth of dope. Her two children in St. Louis were left without a mother when she was sent to prison. It was nine years before their first visit with her, because the trip from St. Louis to West Virginia cost more money than she had. Of course, Rebecca shouldn't have had the dope. But does imprisoning her and turning her children over to the welfare system stop crime? At one tenth the cost of her imprisonment, Rebecca could have kept her children with her, gotten drug treatment and job training, and learned to be a productive member of her community.

These cases don't seem real. But they happen every day. Defendants come forward, carrying with them from the streets burdens and pressures of poverty and racism not evident in this setting or in statistics on forty million poor Americans. "Do you plead guilty or not guilty to violation of section 174, title 21 . . . possession of narcotics?" If what you have to say fits into the slots prepared by decades of jurisprudence, you can, perhaps, say it. But there is no slot, no space, for your feelings as a person. There is just the law—you broke it or you didn't.

It didn't occur to Doris Jordan to tell the court about her life. And if it had occurred to her, what process would the court have to deal with the information? To Doris it was all a part of growing up: In an orphanage when she was seven years old. Always alone. Rejected first by her own mother, who, because she didn't know how to guide or get along with her little girl, called Doris "incorrigible." Transferred when she was thirteen to a juvenile home, where she lived until she was seventeen. Never given an education, never given anything but neglect. Out on her own at seventeen. Yes, she did get desperate. Yes, she did break the law by writing bad checks. But should she be sentenced to ten years in prison?

"The only reason I really had such a bad time and got so much time is 'cause I didn't have no people," Doris said. "I don't get too close to people very easily."

It's amazing how many people are told they are eight-year-old "incorrigibles" or thirteen-year-old "failures." It shouldn't be surprising that they get into a process that carries them from one institution to another. It's an A-B-C process. From being in a prison of no alternatives as a child to Juvenile Hall. From Eighteenth and Diamond streets to jail. From the teacher yelling at you in school to getting bad grades to having your parent yelling at you to running away. Getting arrested at age twelve or fourteen for being a truant or a runaway and being taken to juvenile court. From the Indian reservation to the city to the Federal Reformatory for Women in Alderson, West Virginia. From the first taste of escaping oppression to the first taste of heroin to the first taste of jail. From a foster home or juvenile hall to jail to prison. A-B-C.

If you're a girl and you're a runaway, there's always the fear that you've been "promiscuous." So you're locked up in a juvenile jail for your own protection. You experience the effects of sexual and racial discrimination at a very early age—not knowing the history of this kind of discrimination, only being told that you're bad.

Many women in prisons have backgrounds similar to Doris's. And while each has had experiences unique to herself, the demolition process worked on each human being seems to be a pattern of abuse repeated a thousand times over. The personal histories fit a pattern:

• Gwen, who ran away from home when her stepfather began forcing her at fourteen to submit to sexual intercourse.

• India, who ran away from home at thirteen after being locked in the house every day when she came home from school and beaten with a belt strap for "talking back."

• Dorothy, a sixteen-year-old with festering scars on the inside of her arms. She attempted suicide to get attention—to get her mother to notice her.

• Susan, locked up for being "promiscuous" when her only crime was being a white girl with a black boyfriend.

• Sarah, locked up in the same place for being black and having a white boyfriend.

• Ellen, one of six children of a family living on two hundred welfare dollars a month. At eleven she was still sucking her thumb. At twelve, she began hanging around waterfront bars in her hometown, sexually servicing sailors—just as her uncle had taught her to do—for five or ten dollars a trick.

Some instinct to survive makes these young women run away or try to break out of a destructive environment. They are crying for help. But the "help" they get is all too often impersonal institutionalization. They are sent to foster homes, reform schools, and juvenile jails for truancy, running away, nebulous "incorrigibility" or "uncontrollable behavior"— actions that would never be considered crimes in an adult court. Yet these girls are labeled "juvenile delinquents."

If their actions in the reformatory don't conform to rules, they often wind up in solitary confinement. I have seen children locked in maximum security cells indefinitely because they are "extremely emotionally deprived." In many cases when young women have run away from a juvenile institution repeatedly, they have been sent to the state prison for women on criminal charges of "prison breach"—thus the first criminal offense on a sixteen-year-old's police record.

The President's Commission on Law Enforcement and the Administration of Justice found that more than half the girls in juvenile court are referred for general behavioral problems that do not amount to crime. Only one fifth of the boys are brought in for noncriminal behavior. And even though their offenses are not as serious as boys', girls are committed to institutions with proportionately the same frequency as boys.

Furthermore, their sentences are significantly longer. In "Equal Protection for Juvenile Girls in Need of Supervision in New York State," Sally Gold reported in 1970 that girls average twelve months in New York training schools; boys, nine months and three weeks. Some of the people she interviewed felt that parents were more threatened by and less tolerant of their daughters' "acting out" than of their sons'. While girls in their teens are labeled promiscuous if they become sexually involved with boys, teenage boys are thought to be "just experimenting" or "sowing wild oats."

"I was classified as promiscuous when I was fourteen because I had run away," one woman at a state prison said. "They classify you as that whether you've balled a guy or not. I was a virgin until I was twenty. But they figure you have to do something sexual to support yourself if you run away, since they think you can't make it on your own. But that's their own hang-up. They definitely play the psychological thing that you are a dependent person because you are female."

The same moral standards often follow women into adulthood, when one out of almost every five women arrested is brought in for prostitution or "commercialized vice," a label for minor sex offenses. It's estimated that as many as 80 percent of juvenile women are incarcerated for sexual reasons or sex-related offenses. David Ward and Gene Kassenbaum found that 68 percent of the women at the California Institution for Women had at some time in their past been officially reported for prostitution or promiscuity. The vast majority of these women also were sexually or physically abused when they were young. Most of them got their start in the cycle of imprisonment as children.

I heard about "Sheila" when she was in the Camden County Children's Shelter for being a runaway. She was fourteen years old, the daughter of a woman convicted repeatedly on charges of prostitution. Sheila had grown up in small rooms, dark, scary places. When she was five her mother went to jail and she was put into a foster home with a younger sister. An older sister and brother were in the same foster family for a while. Her oldest brother was in jail for armed robbery and for being AWOL from the navy. Steve Cohen, working as a psychologist at the children's shelter, was Sheila's caseworker.

"The staff at the shelter feels that these children are criminals and have to be treated as such," says Cohen. "Mail is censored, and there is no teacher, so they get behind in school. They never get exercise except for their work cleaning and scrubbing the place and setting tables. The punishment is arbitrary."

After Sheila ran away from the shelter, they locked her in solitary confinement for two weeks, with only a thin mattress for sleeping on the concrete slab. No windows, mirrors, visitors, mail, books, or toys. Her uniform was taken away; she could keep on only her underwear.

"They wouldn't let me talk to her," Cohen said. "The assistant superintendent of the shelter told me I couldn't see her because she was on 'indefinite restriction.' The superintendent told me, 'No, she is being punished and is not allowed to have any visitors, not even therapy.'"

Cohen said he tried to explain that therapy is *treatment,* not something that should be withdrawn for punishment any more than insulin should be taken away from a diabetic for punishment. But the final word came from the chairman of the board of trustees for the shelter, who was also chairman of the board of the Society for the Prevention of Cruelty to Children: "No one is to see Sheila. She has to be punished. These kids are in the shelter for punishment, and they are going to get it." Finally, by calling a judge and getting a court order, Cohen was able to visit Sheila. He was later reprimanded by his boss for not using proper channels of authority and told he had overstepped his authority by calling a judge. He was placed on probation and eventually resigned from his job.

Sheila's situation is not atypical. And Sheila, like many others, carries her bitter scars with uncanny sensitivity and acceptance. Sometimes the acceptance is frightening. Women who have been in trouble with the law for the major portion of their lives rattle off stories of physical violence, sexual abuse, and violence to the psyche that could make the most hardened person shudder.

Yet it is clear that for many of the women in prison, going to prison is just a traumatic if not unexpected transition from one confining and oppressive society to another. The one on the outside often meant not knowing when you could get enough money together to get your baby a new pair of shoes; it meant figuring out how to get groceries or carfare or how to get away from the pimp you were working for when you didn't even have enough money of your own to go downtown.

For many people, the planet Earth includes the liquor store, pimping, prostitution, welfare, stealing, buying any clothes you wear ''hot,'' hiding the television when the welfare detectives come to look around for signs of a man, a television, or a telephone. It's having the toilet get clogged up and not being able to flush it or get it fixed. It's having the hot water go off, not replacing the light in the bedroom that's been burned out for three years, and never being able to get the heat in your apartment higher than fifty degrees in the wintertime. It's sleeping with your coat on and childhood nightmares that still haunt you when you're almost thirty-four. It's never thinking of going to a dentist when you have a toothache or to the doctor when you hurt. It's trying not to believe a promise but believing it anyway and then being disappointed again.

It's knowing you're on your own, you're grown. Knowing you had to grow up fast—but you never really grew up because you never were a child, not really. You never had anyone love you and take care of you like it's supposed to be when you're a child. You were responsible for your own survival when you were still a baby. But now you've got children of your own.

Prisons on the outside are made of neglect and knowing that no one knows or cares. It's a prison of no limits, so everything's limiting. Perhaps the most horrible thing about these prisons on the outside is that you often don't realize you're imprisoned. And you don't have the motivation to change what's happening to you in any significant way, because this life is normal. It's the world; it's the only reality you know. It's so normal that you wouldn't begin to think about what to do to change it on a realistic level, because to you it's not unusual.

Jail and prison are a part of this reality. And although imprisonment is an intrinsic threat to middle-class people, it seems to become just another "thing"—a minor evil—to indigent people who have become enmeshed in the prison culture. It often, in fact, becomes a relief after the initial fear is over.

"The first time I was in juvie, I was twelve," Pat Halloran remembers. "Mom and Pop Moriana was there. I really loved them. Like they were my parents, you know. I really dug it.

"Oh, I can remember the first night I went in, though. I was in a room by myself. And they had a window in the door. And the next morning—this is when I was twelve—they'd go walking by, the old-timers, and they'd be lookin' in the window. They'd go, 'Umm, nice in there. How are you, baby?' The other inmates would always do this to new girls. But see, that's how they scare you. I was so scared after being searched and everything. You don't know what the fuck's going on, but these are older people telling you what to do, so you just get right in there and take off your clothes and whatever. So you sleep it through, and then you wake up and all's you see is these faces in the door, you know, yelling at you and telling you, 'You better watch it, bitch.' I was thinking, 'They're going to kill me. What did I do? I don't know anybody. They're going to kill me.' So when I came out of my room, I was high-stepping, hanging on the wall. How funny it is we become adjusted so fast . . . because two days later, I was looking in someone else's window: 'Hey, bitch.'

"I didn't go through no court process to get there. They just pick you up and you go to juvie, period. See, what happened was that I was supposed to go to a football game, and I was in high school. I was twelve years old in freshman year and I wouldn't be thirteen until February. So I was supposed to graduate when I was sixteen. And my parents wanted me to have all the responsibilities of being a high school kid, but they didn't want me having the privileges.

"This one night they said I couldn't go to this football game. I was really pissed, so I took a walk. Well, my mother overpanicked. She called the pigs and says, 'My daughter ran away, go look for her.' Of course I had ran away before. But this time I was just out taking a walk. When I goes back into the house my mother goes, 'What were you doing?' And I says, 'I was out walking around.' 'Sure you were, sure you were. What were you doing?' I said, 'None of your business.'

"So I went up to my room and she called the pigs and she said, 'Well, she's back, but I don't know what she's been doing. I don't know where she's been.' So they came right out and they came in and my mother comes upstairs and she says, 'Get dressed.' I said, 'What for?' She says,

'The police are here.' I said, 'What for? What happened?' 'They've come to arrest you. You ran away.' ''

Pat got dressed and was taken in a police car to juvenile hall. Scared, she told the police she hadn't done anything wrong. But like many other young women, under the law she was a runaway; she was taken to jail.

"I was so scared at first," she said. "But within a week or two, by the time it took to take me to court, I liked it there so much I didn't want to go nowhere." When she met with the probation officer, she was recommended for a foster home. Her mother didn't protest, nor did her father.

"I wanted to stay at juvenile hall, I didn't want to be in a foster home," Pat said. "They put me in a foster home, and I didn't like it. I had a little problem with the foster father; most foster kids do. And even later, when I didn't, it's a good excuse. I told 'em and they put me in another foster home, and I ran away from it. I really fucked up bad. But after I ran away from the foster homes, they'd put me back in juvenile hall. I was in and out of there. I think I held the record for a long time. It was something like forty-six arrests and times in juvenile hall in six years. For runaway.

"It's good when you sit back and reminisce. 'Cause like we brought out a good point. I didn't know . . . It's funny, I was always afraid to admit that I really liked coming back. You know, when you get there you always say, 'Oh fuck, I don't want to stay here. Let me out of here.' And all the time, you know, you're staying there. It's that security. It's that instant gratification, coming back and having everybody holler and say, 'Look, Pat's back,' all happy to see you."

Pat didn't stop going back into juvenile hall or into other jails until she was nearly twenty-four years old, when she was charged with a crime she hadn't committed. She said she was sitting in jail awaiting trial on an arson charge and was talking with another inmate about seeing her at the state prison. "All of a sudden I had this flash. I realized, hey, I didn't do anything. Why should I go to prison? I must be crazy, just accepting going like this. It really blew my mind. I was sitting there and I knew for once that I wasn't guilty—but I was talking about going to prison and just accepting it. Like, well, that's the next step."

Pat managed to get out, raise money for a lawyer, and beat the charge. She moved to San Francisco and worked with an organization called Connections, which serves as a link to people inside prison, assisting in their problems and working with their families. If it hadn't been for her "flash" of questioning why she should be in prison for something she didn't do, Pat might never have broken free.

The "normality" of going to prison and the security of a concrete womb after a lifetime of abuse and oppression lull many people into never asking why. The idea of changing that life is as alien as going to Mars. They don't know about or understand any real options. "Treatment" or "rehabilitation" are just words; a matter of lip service. Jail has become just a part of the bigger world—an extension of "the life," a reinforcement of natural self-destruction learned during formative childhood years from models who never asked why either. Abuse for many people is a way of life. It's the world.

6 WELCOME TO THE CONCRETE WOMB

Leave Your Dignity at the Door

> Being in jail is harder on a woman than a man. Men are always together. They grow up taking showers together, sleeping together. They've been in the army with other men and are used to being around each other naked or dressed. Women are taught to undress in private and be modest. They don't like to undress in front of other people. Women have stall showers, men have one big shower room . . . so think how much harder that would be on a woman. She comes in here and we undress her and tell her to "bend over, lady," to look for contraband. We make her bathe in front of everyone. Right off that gives them mental problems that are hard to handle. The initial shock is the toughest thing. That sort of thing can break your spirit.
>
> —Male warden

The word *reception* is usually associated with a friendly, hospitable event. Wedding receptions, welcome-home receptions, and ''warm'' receptions call to mind an entirely different image from the receptions women receive after arrest when they are processed into jail. When they are stripped and searched. When they become the name on whatever identification they carried at the time of arrest and are given a prison number. When they hear the sounds of doors closing and the turn of the key for the first time.

The popular euphemism for a woman's initial orientation to jail or prison is ''reception,'' but it doesn't ease the initial shock of confinement. In state prisons, women are confined to a cell block for two to six weeks for ''reception and orientation'' while they are examined medically, given tests, interviewed, and assigned jobs before they are put in with the general prison population. Prisoners in county jails are given a shorter reception before entering their new homes.

Deputy Sheriff Georgia Walton at Los Angeles County's jail for women explained the reception process in straightforward terms from her own perspective as a guard who had helped to process more than thirty thousand women into that jail at the time we spoke. We began at the point where women are escorted in handcuffs or waist chains into the jail from police districts.

"For a new booking," Deputy Walton explained, "the officer types up a booking slip while another officer has the inmate in custody. She gives her a number and then goes through her purse to search for contraband. After everything is complete, the inmate is sent through number three gate and delivered to a female deputy, still in full view of the control center and hall leading to the administrative offices. At that time the deputy gives her a pat search. She removes her wig, rings, shoes, and socks. Anything such as a leather belt, drugs, or medication is taken. She can keep up to ten dollars, but no more than two dollars in change. More than two dollars in change is not allowed because it could be put into a sock and used as a weapon.

"This is where I am generally assigned. The pat search means I also look in your ears, your nose, and mouth. I search your bra and around your waist and look up your pants legs. If they have dentures I ask them to remove the denture and look at this for contraband possibly being concealed under it. Then we put them into one of the two holding tanks."

The three walls of the two holding tanks were bare except for names, messages, and telephone numbers scratched into the concrete. The wall facing the hallway was half glass, which allows the deputies to keep constant observation on the women inside. One of the tanks had two pay telephones and no toilet. The other had one pay telephone and an open toilet bowl and sink exposed to full view from inside and outside. Thin aluminum benches lined two of the walls. Officer Walton noted that they are too narrow and "women fall off of them all the time."

"They're kept out here approximately two hours," she said. "They can make telephone calls because this is run just like a police station. If they don't have any money, I give them a dime and tell them to call collect. Before I put them in, I tell them what they're charged with and how much their bail is—whether it's a misdemeanor or not. We take new bookings right off the street, and women are sent here from other jails. If someone is intoxicated and can't stand up, we put her in a reception observation room."

The reception observation rooms were two tiny padded square holes seemingly dug out of concrete blocks. "You see the walls are padded but not spongy," Deputy Walton said. "The floor is the same—and it's softer than the cement in the holding room. It's for their safe being we put them in here. Before they're placed in this room they are seen by a nurse to make sure she is drunk and not having a seizure. Then the officer checks on them through this little glass window every fifteen minutes to get some form of response. They're kept in here a maximum of four hours, and then if they're sobered up they can come out and make their calls or whatever before they continue the processing.

"We also put inmates in here who are combative—someone who doesn't want to be here. If in the process of searching her she is swinging, kicking, or biting, she is put in the observation room until she settles down. She is also checked on by the officer. When she's ready to behave she can come out and make her calls in the holding tank.

"Some say they don't want to call anybody, they don't want anybody to know they're here. Then we make a notation of call declined or uncompleted. After I have that response, they are taken out of the holding tank and into the reception room.

"Everybody that is arrested is given a bath. They are instructed to remove all of their clothing, including their underwear. Then we give a narco search. Do you know what that is? Well, I'll explain. I would have a flashlight, and I would feel through her hair and use the flashlight to look inside her ears, behind her ears, in her nose, in her nostrils and her mouth. I would look between her fingers, both sides of her hands, under her arms, and around her breast area. If her breasts are so heavy, I would have her lift them up—sometimes they tape things under them. I'd have her spread her toes apart. Then I'd have her turn around and do the same thing down her back—hair, arms, and all.

"Then I would have her spread her legs and bend over and I would look up into her vagina area to search for weapons, contraband, or narcotics. The only area I touch is her hair. I can see into her vagina because her legs and buttocks are spread and I use the flashlight. I don't touch her. I couldn't say I look into her rectum—I look into her buttocks area. I have her lift her feet and check the bottom of her feet. That's a complete narcotics search.

"Then she is instructed to get into the bathtub. Then I take the tray and search her clothing—the seams, the shoes themselves, and the soles. She may have her underwear returned along with her comb and lipstick. If the shoes are similar to tennis shoes, I would return them to her—as long as they have no metal buckles—along with the money she had. Everyone that comes through has a clothing bag, along with a clothes tag that lists her name and everything she has. Jewelry, money, and license go to the cashier for safekeeping.

"After she has completed her bath, she's instructed to get out and clean the bathtub. Then she is sprayed with Kwell lotion." She points out a large tank of parasiticide with a spray nozzle on the end of the hose. "She is sprayed under her arms, under her breasts, and in her pubic area to get rid of any body bugs she may have.

"Some people come in and appear to be very clean and I don't suppose they have body bugs, but everyone has to be sprayed. It would be terrible to have bugs spread around the institution. If an inmate has lice in her hair she is given Kwell shampoo and instructed to shampoo her hair. It works the same way as Kwell lotion—it kills the bugs. If somebody comes in with a cast on, we make an exception about the bath, but she'll still be sprayed. After they have been sprayed, they are taken back and given their underwear, a jail dress, thongs, and a sweater. If an inmate comes in with a dress that needs laundering, we do it. If they come in in a nightgown or a bathing suit, we wouldn't send them to court in it. We would provide a dress."

As Officer Walton talked, I remembered what Connie Powers said she felt about her reception into prison life: "What really happens is that when you come in they search you and poke you. They give you fourteen needles, pull what teeth they think need pulling, dump you in the shower with your mouth full of blood, shave all your pubic hair, and dump a lye disinfectant over your head."

"They try to strip you from the very first minute," another woman said. "They try to strip you of any dignity or self-respect you have as a woman. When they brought me in county jail, the first thing they did was take my wedding ring and my earrings. Then they stripped me stark naked and made me jump up and down on the floor in a squat position—while they all stood around watching. They have to forget we're human beings to treat us that way."

Officer Walton proceeded to walk me through the process. "After they are fingerprinted and photographed, they go up to see the nurse," she said. "The nurse asks questions, ranging from 'Are you pregnant?' to 'Have you ever had seizures, heart problems, diabetes?' and a number of questions. If it's confirmed, we would give her medication. If an inmate is booked with medication on her, we cannot use her medication, even if we confirm that she needs it. We must use our own medicine prescribed by our medical department. If she's an epileptic, the nurse at her own discretion would give medication or have the doctor check it. We just can't take the word of an inmate. If you were coming in and say you're an epileptic, you might just want your medicine—but we don't know what's in that medicine you have.'' (Women at the Sybil Brand Institute for Women in Los Angeles had told me they didn't get medical attention for the first week or two weeks after arrest—and some said that although they put in requests, they never saw the doctor. Those who needed medication said that after it was confiscated, if it was replaced, it often was the wrong dosage or the wrong prescription.)

After leaving the photo and fingerprinting room, I walked with Deputy Walton down a long hall, passing another holding tank, where women wait to go to court. Across from the holding tank was the dressing room where women are given a search and change of clothes when they return from court. Beyond the ''court holding tank'' we walked out into an open area where some twenty-five mops were lined up parallel on an iron rack.

''The jail is divided into two halves,'' Officer Walton said. ''The left side is the minimum side—that's the sentenced inmates. The right side is maximum security—that's for unsentenced inmates. This is the mop area. Trustees are assigned to wring out the mops and deliver them to the housing areas. They are required to work from seven to three each day in the laundry, or on the freight and trash crew—going around and picking up trash and dumping it. The laundry does all the washing and ironing for the whole institution—dresses, sheets, towels, officers' white blouses. Tank trustees wash the personal underwear of all the inmates in their block, sweep and mop the area. Others work in the kitchen or in the sewing industry.''

We walked down two long halls and through three electrically monitored gates, past the dorms for sentenced inmates—sixty women to one dorm. Attached to the front of each dormitory was the officer's watch station, separated from the room by a glass cubicle. From the watch station you could see all areas of the dormitory, the bathroom, and a connected dayroom, which is open to the women from 12 noon to 2:30 P.M. daily and for two to three hours during the evening. The dayroom contained one television set, one table, and several benches secured to the floor. Women said later that each dorm is allowed to watch one television station only. They are not allowed to turn the dial to a different station. According to prison staff, this reduces the possibility for friction over what program to watch and reduces the chances of the women breaking the television sets.

It was about 11:30 A.M. when we were walking through one of the maximum security dormitories on our way to the dining hall, but no one else was in the area. ''Everybody goes out for lunch, because the officer doesn't want to leave them unsupervised,'' Georgia Walton said. ''The officer goes with them to eat. She doesn't eat with them. She watches them.

"They're moved by ramps, not by stairs, because we're moving large numbers. They walk two by two. There's no talking after they leave the cell block. There's no talking in the maximum-side dining room. Yes, these are all unsentenced or untried inmates. There's no talking returning to their housing area. They come through the dining room door single file and they get a tray and a spoon. They slide the tray along the line and food is placed on the tray. There are no forks or knives and no pepper. They could throw pepper in an officer's eye.

"If someone was talking in the dining room, I'd say, 'Stop talking.' If they did it habitually or didn't stop when I told them, then an incident card is written on her and it's up to the lieutenant what to do with her. If somebody burps, we set her at the diet table. ["Oh, you wrote that down—make it belches, not burps," she said.] We have her sit up here so she won't be offensive to the other inmates who are trying to eat."

I asked why no talking was allowed in the dining room. "For security reasons," she said. "You have approximately two hundred and fifty-one people in here at one time for approximately twenty minutes. We feed approximately four hundred and fifty people during one hour. It's basically because of the number of people in the dining room. You cannot talk quietly. You cannot talk at all. You have people who have just been booked—and here she is sitting worried about her case. If someone even said, 'You touched my toe,' she might get belligerent. Or if two people were booked in the same case and the arresting agency wanted them separated before court, we would try to comply. If they could talk, they might holler back and forth and it would be disrupting. The same would be true of old friends or people from the same neighborhood.

"On the minimum side, the sentenced inmates are permitted to talk when they leave the housing areas or while they are eating as long as it is quiet. They can also talk quietly when returning to the cell block. Sentenced inmates are assigned to jobs they are physically capable of doing. They get knives, forks, spoons, and pepper. They know they have got a certain amount of time, and they are stable; they're adjusted to being here."

Georgia Walton kept walking. She pointed out the dining rooms, the kitchen, the garment shop. In the large industrial sewing room, a sign with the letters of each word penciled carefully in large block letters was taped to a desk with masking tape. It said: "IN THE DUNGEON OF YOUR MIND, WHO IS CHAINED TO THE WALL?"

Finally we stopped for a cigarette in an empty control room. From the room we could see through glass and screen into every nook of a large dormitory. The women's beds were divided only by small foot lockers. Each bed had an army blanket covering it, tucked in smoothly in military style. Bunk beds lined the back wall of the dormitory. ("We would not assign an epileptic or a pregnant woman to a top bunk bed," my guide noted.) Only two women were in the large dormitory; the others were at lunch or on job assignments. The two remaining were "day workers" who scrubbed the toilets and floors and did laundry for the other women. There was no music, no sound in the area. "An officer is not permitted in that dormitory unless there is another officer in the officer's station," Deputy Walton said. "That's for the officer's security.

"If two inmates are fighting, I cannot just go in there," she said. "I have to call for help. I can give orders from here to break up the fight, but I am not allowed to go in by myself."

I asked Georgia Walton what her feelings were about punishment for rule infractions. "If I instructed an inmate to do something and for absolutely no reason she used profanity on me, I would have to report it to the lieutenant and a disciplinary would be written up. Say I instruct an inmate to get out of bed and report for duty. If she said, 'Oh shoot,' I wouldn't report it. But if she was more profane towards me personally, I would have to report it. I'd have no choice.

"Another reason someone can go to discipline [solitary confinement cells] is if she refused to work. If she asks to go to the cell, in essence, she's refusing to work. If she refuses to work, she's asking to go to the cell. If she's in disciplinary, she's not allowed to smoke and can have no reading material, no writing material, no candy, and no cigarettes. She is given exactly the same food as other inmates with the exception she does not get dessert.

"Before each meal her bed must be made and she must be dressed—in her jail dress, not her nightgown. She's required to clean her cell three times a day—sweep and mop it and clean the toilet and sink or washbasin after each meal. In a regular cell for exclusions and in disciplinary, I would pass the broom and the dustpan through the bars and she would use it. If she needed cleanser, I would pass it through. I would pass the mop through the door and she would use it and return it, the same.

"She does not leave the cell with the exception of going to court or seeing an attorney. They are not allowed to receive or write mail. But quite a few of them are quite ingenious. They might go to court and get a pencil and make playing cards on toilet paper. They also try to write letters on toilet paper if they can get a pencil.

"They do not necessarily stay down there long. Lieutenant Hess goes down with a sergeant and does board. She talks to the inmate, and depending on the case, they get more or less time. Each circumstance is different. But we do have rules and regulations they must abide by.''

Policies vary slightly from one prison or jail to the next, but they all share a similar focus, which prisoners learn by heart. The first page of rules and regulations for inmates at the Cook County Jail in Chicago includes the following mandates:[1]

1. Address all correctional officers as ''OFFICER.''
2. DO NOT use slang in addressing an officer.
3. NEVER argue with an officer.
4. Obey all orders given to you by an officer or civilian personnel immediately. If you feel you have a legitimate complaint, you may put in a request to the person's superior only after you have done what you were ordered.
5. You cannot give anything to other inmates without permission.
6. Report all threats, acts of violence or pressures to an officer immediately.
7. Clothing, like everything else, is County property. Take care of it. Destruction of ANY County property may get you more time.
8. You will not have cash in your possession at any time.
9. You cannot transfer money to another inmate at any time.
10. No gambling of any kind is permitted.
11. No food, tobacco, stamps, stamped envelopes, or medication can be brought in or sent to you.
12. Turn in all outgoing letters to officer in housing unit. Letters being written to Attorney, Judges, Court of legal nature may be given to the officer sealed by you.
13. Only books which have been approved are permitted.
14. When moving from one place to another, you will go straight to destination always with an officer or a runner.
15. When in a line, always move quietly, in an orderly manner.

1. This is only the first of several pages of rules and regulations for the Cook County Jail. I have included three sets of rules in the appendix to illustrate typical regulations for prisoners. Although inmates do not always receive copies of these rules, they are expected to obey them. These rules have not changed significantly over the past twenty years.

7   FORCED DEPENDENCY

The Prison As Abusive Parent

You start losing your identity when you get locked up. You stop seeking
things, you stop doing things for yourself, you stop looking for things.
You feel nothing's gonna be all right again. . . . You can dress only
one way, you can adjust your uniform only so far, you can wear shoes
only so high and so much makeup. When you start doing jobs that
are a man's jobs, you start having female problems and that breaks
down your feeling about yourself. The attire does a lot. I still feel like
a woman, but I can't have what I want and I want these things.

You do the same things day in and day out. You lose a sense of what day
it is, what date. The most difficult thing to adjust to is not being able
to be who I want to be at certain times, not being able to do certain
little things I want to do when I want to do them, not being able to do
anything without pressure.

The pressure starts in the morning. You get in line the first thing in the
morning for breakfast. if you're one minute early, they say, "Wait a
minute, wait a minute." You want to knock 'em down, but you know
you can't. The hardest thing for me is not being able to say what I
want to say. Like why should she be called Miss or Mrs. and me be
called Betty? Why should she be over me? Why can't I say the things
to her she can say to me as far as defending herself and saying what
she thinks?

You just can't let out emotion. If you laugh or halfway try to enjoy yourself,
you're called silly. The other night we were laughing and the matron
called us fools. She told us to be quiet or we'd be sent to bed—just
like children. A lot of times it's only because we're getting on their
nerves or they can't cope with the situation, so we get three days'

lock-up. The officers bring their family problems in here and go off at us for them. A lot of them talk about inmates, not only with each other, but with other inmates.

—Mary Jo, Betty, and Tiki, during an interview at the Ohio Reformatory for Women

I know it is not logical to treat anyone who is grown as an infant. But as a way of examining reality from a different perspective, I'd like for you to try to imagine for a moment that you are a very young child.

First of all, you are taken away from your real home and led into a big place with concrete walls and locks on all the doors. You are told you have been taken here because you are a bad, naughty girl and this place will help you learn how to be good. You are immediately probed and examined to make sure you are not carrying any toys or food on you.

Children about your own age have been put in charge of you. Your new parents have apparently ordered that these strange children in neat, clean uniforms and shiny shoes look into your vagina and rectum and make you stand naked in front of them. They handle you roughly and tell each other jokes. They take everything you brought with you away from you. They whisper to each other about you.

Next they make you take a bath in front of them, spray you for lice, and give you a set of ugly clothes. The clothes they give you are hand-me-downs; they're not made for you. They're either too big or too small.

You then are given a number written on paper enclosed in a plastic bracelet to identify you. You are told that this number is your new name and you are never to take off the bracelet or destroy it. "We have to have a way of identifying you," the strange children say. "There are a lot of other girls here, so there's no other way we can keep track of who you are. Only this number will identify you, so don't forget it—because any time we want to talk to you we will call out your number."

Now you are led into a cage or large dormitory, where you see other children wearing ugly old clothes exactly like yours. They are your new siblings. They also wear plastic bracelets and some even have numbers stamped on their clothes to identify them. This is your new home. You have to go to the bathroom in front of all of the other girls and you never can find a place to hide when you want to be alone.

After a few days, you find out that the strange children who poked you and ordered you around are actually members of a military gang. You find out that you might never get to meet your new parents—you are not even sure who they are. The gang members are your parents' favorite children, so you have to follow their orders or be punished. They say they take orders from the parents, and even though they aren't any older than you, they're in charge. You can't say anything disrespectful to them. You're supposed to act like they're adults, but you know they're just the same as you, and it doesn't seem fair.

Nevertheless, you must follow their rules—even though each of them plays by different rules. They tell you the rules are equally enforced for all number children, but you see other number children getting away with behavior you are punished for, so you resent them. You find out that if you want to do something fun, you have to sneak. If you want extra food, you're punished for asking, so you have to steal it. You also know that if a military gang member asks you to "tell the truth: did you do it?" and you say yes, you'll be punished anyway. Honesty doesn't help. So you learn to lie, because lying may help you get away with it.

If you are good, you are awakened every morning, fed, and put to bed each night. During the day, you scrub the floor and make it shine. If you never ask for anything, object to a rule, laugh too loud, or cry or throw anything, you're being good, and the gang members will usually leave you alone and not bother you too much. But if you do anything they think is naughty, or if you feel sick and don't go to work, you are put to bed early three nights in a row or you're locked in a dark closet—the bad girls' closet—where you don't get to talk to anybody and somebody pushes a bowl of food under a six-inch crack in the door a couple of times a day.

While you're locked in the closet, you can't ever come out to play, and you can't have any crayons. If you ask why, they tell you it's because they don't want you to hurt yourself. They say you're being punished, so you can't talk to anyone either. And you don't get dessert. Sometimes you see rats and roaches staring at you. If you scream or cry to get out of the closet, you will be locked in the closet for at least an extra week. If you bang your head against the wall, they might leave you there forever.

Pretty soon you've forgotten even what you're being punished for. A lot of times you're cold and you want an extra blanket or you're hot and want to make the air cool—but there's nothing you can do. If you get sick and want to be taken care of, a gang member just tells you to be quiet and says, "If you hadn't been a bad girl, you wouldn't be here in the first place."

In this new home you cannot play with boys. And if they are ever around, you are not allowed to look at them, laugh with them, or talk to them. If you do, you will be locked in the closet again. You are not allowed boyfriends—you can only stay by yourself. The gang members can have friends—girlfriends and boyfriends—but you can't.

So you are left to play with the sisters who look like you in their ugly clothes. You laugh with them and you love them. They have to scrub the floor, just like you. But you also hate them and fight with them. They're the only ones you're allowed to holler at when you feel like hollering at somebody. You smell them and understand them. Since you don't get to hug a parent, you only can reach out to your sisters for warmth and comfort and love.

But then you are told by the gang members that this is against the rules, too. You are not allowed to touch or hug your favorite sister-friends. If you are caught on your little sister's bed combing her hair or bandaging her knee, you will be punished severely. If she is sick and you want to take care of her, you are told to go to your room and be quiet. If you are ever caught playing doctor or kissing, you will be locked in the closet again. So you are very careful not to let anyone see that you like your sister or want to hold hands with her, because then you might be separated from her forever or locked into the bad girls' closet indefinitely. Some bad girls never get out of the closet.

The parents don't stop gang members from being friends or holding hands, but they stop you. The parents don't want their favorite children to be friends with you. They tell the military gang members that it is against the rules for them to do you any favors and that they will be punished if they ever treat you differently from anyone else.

You can tell that your parents don't like you. If they did, they would understand. They would let you be friends with people. They would also protect you from other number children who are bigger than you and who bully you. But your parents don't care what happens to you. They just want you to work and keep their house clean. They never talk to you and they don't give you comfort or protection. They won't even let you play or have fun. They don't know how it feels, and they don't care enough to find out. They make you and their favorite children do everything, and they don't even know what happens to you.

Since you're all left alone so much, you start playing cops and robbers. You use a lot of your energy seeing what you can get away with. The gang members play the cops and you play the robbers. They sneak around trying to catch you, so you always have to be on guard. The object of the game is not to get caught. Sometimes when you figure out ways to get extra food and they don't catch you, it's great fun. Especially when you know they know, but they weren't as fast as you were. They get mad when they know you've fooled them, but they can't be mean to you unless they catch you, so you learn how to fool them. You and your sisters fight them, and when you stick together, you can almost always outfox them. It's a problem sometimes, though, because they will often take some members of your gang aside and give them extra food or toys to tell on you, so you can't really even tell your own gang everything.

Some of your sisters try to act tough and order you around because they want to be like the military gang. And if they don't like what you're doing, they'll hit you. You've always got to watch out for people who hit.

Pretty soon you start to realize that your parents never want you to grow up. They won't let you make any decisions on your own. They won't let you find any new playmates or see any boys or encourage you to grow or to take responsibility. They make you feel silly and dumb—and even if you know your're not the names they call you, you begin to wonder if they're right.

After you've gotten really used to your new home, your parents open the door at midnight and say, "Okay, you can leave now." They tell you to leave, even though you don't know if you want to. They tell you to go out and take care of yourself. "You're grown up now. Now you're an adult, so you can leave. You said you wanted to leave, what are you waiting for?" They give you a dollar to take with you, but no food or toys. The gang members stand around and whisper and joke with each other. They laugh and declare: "You'll be back. That's a big world out there—you won't be able to take care of yourself. You'll be back to see us 'cause you need us. We'll still be here when you get back." You get to turn in your number now and take off your paper bracelet. They tell you to use your real name out in the world, not your number. They say you can't play cops and robbers anymore because now you don't have anybody to play with. They tell you to be friends with boys again, but you've forgotten what boys look like, and you don't think you will know how to act with them. You don't know what to expect. You don't know what it will be like out there and you're afraid.

Strange as it may seem, this analogy touches at the core of much of what is going on in prisons today. I had often heard prison officials say that women prisoners were "babied" compared with men. It was obvious to me that women prisoners were not coddled, but I kept being baffled by statements to that effect. For instance:

- Lieutenant Archibald at Riker's Island in New York City: "They're grown up, but they act like they're in kindergarten." Pointing out one forty-year-old woman who was quarreling with another inmate over a seat in the auditorium, the lieutenant said, "She's my problem child."
- The superintendent of Riker's Island, Ms. Essie Murph: "We're a lot like a family here. This is home for most of them. I was captain for ten years before becoming a deputy, so we've sort of grown up together, you

could say. Most of these women I've known off and on for years. I even know some mother and daughter and grandmother sets.''

• Marjorie T. Ward, director of the women's division at the Arizona State Prison: "They don't have that much time to lollygag around. They're generally busy. We keep them busy, plus we're constantly watching them.''

• Another officer: "When they act like children, we treat them like children. When they want attention, they break out the windows or throw temper tantrums just like two-year-olds.''

Inmates had repeatedly told me, "They treat us just like children. They think we're four years old. They think we can't think for ourselves. They call us girls, but we're women.''

In a letter to Ericka Huggins, Angela Davis wrote of her experiences in the Women's House of Detention in New York: "I have often heard the rumor that as compared to men's prisons, women's institutions are humanely benign, the gravest problems being the tendency to baby the women captives. This is a myth which must be immediately smashed.''

She said the "notion of mildness in the midst of coercion is a blatant misrepresentation.'' It is obvious that babies are not locked up in cells, put in isolation, forced to work, disciplined for laughing out loud, or neglected when they are sick. But the myth bothered and baffled me every time I heard administrators talk about "feedings'' and "controlling the girls,'' who acted "just like babies.'' I knew there was some piece of reality in the misperception, but I couldn't put my finger on it.

Then one day I was talking to Missouri Beckton, an older woman who had spent time in the State Correctional Institution for Women at Muncy, Pennsylvania. Missouri had gone up for parole one year and been denied. The next year she was supposed to go before the board, but they wouldn't see her. They had given her a one-year setback for having had a bad record. She said the setback came from an incident in which she had been punished for "talking impudent to a matron.''

"The main thing I think kept me in Muncy so long was they was trying to rehabilitate me down to be a two-year-old. I refused to be retarded,'' she said. "I'm grown. I'm forty-nine years old. They can't make me be a two-year-old.''

The same day I talked to Missouri, I got a letter from Bernard Orr at Graterford Prison, outside Philadelphia. Bernard was writing me about a newspaper he and some other men had started at that institution: "At present, subscriptions for 'outsiders' are out—so say the omnipotent administrators. Because we are only in the infant stage, I think it's a question of watching the baby's feeding. But as soon as they find out how silly the games they play are and do what should have been done in the first place, I'll send you a copy of our first edition.''

I remembered the other conversations: "You can dress only one way; you can adjust your uniform only so far." "You have to eat everything on your plate. You can't even decide for yourself what you want to eat."

The simple truth to the "mystery of the myth" I was probing is that total institutionalization is synonymous with forced dependency. The controls of prison that attempt to regulate lives, attitudes, and behavior are synonymous with those used during infancy.

The only other time we know of in life where nearly every moment is dictated for us by other people is infancy. Children are told when to get up, what to eat, where to go, how to spend their time—in short, what to do and what not to do. Parents dress their infants, set feeding times, make decisions, reward and punish behavior. If they are wise they are delighted when their child begins to make decisions for herself that don't hurt her. They are delighted to see her grow, change, take new steps, and use initiative.

Good parents are not arbitrary or irrational but observe their child's response to the world, encourage her to explore it, and watch her development with love and care. They know she will make mistakes, because they know mistakes are part of learning. If she plays with matches and burns herself, they won't punish her further or hurt her for hurting herself. If she is sick, they won't punish her for being sick.

Institutions that control the lives of people confined in them have accepted the role of parents. People confined in these institutions are forced into childlike status by the fact of their incarceration and isolation. Thus, the role of the prison system to the prisoner becomes that of parent to child. Authorities have total power over the lives of the people they govern. And the more isolated the institution from public view, the more helpless inmates are to defend themselves.

We would call parents who treated their children in the manner described above as cruel and abusive, and we would refer to their children as neglected and battered. We would not wonder why their children might have problems adjusting to the world. Prisons have this same kind of power over prisoners. And what we have in our prisons today is treatment that by its very nature is abusive and battering.

Forced dependency also is illogical, especially when we expect people to come out of prison as independent, law-abiding, responsible citizens. Our prison system strips people of responsibility, independence, human contact, and dignity. It is a punitive system that traps many people into roles and fosters crime. Even progressive and humane administrators who want to encourage growth and responsibility are pressured or coerced themselves by a structure that negates creativity and growth.

How can you deal with large numbers of people in a constructive manner when your chief responsibility is to regulate and control their actions? What good does it do to offer counseling or education to help a woman become self-sufficient when she still has to get up by a bell, eat at a prescribed time, walk a certain way, and be locked into a cell at night? How helpful is it to encourage people to be responsible and independent when the majority of their decisions are made for them and they are punished for initiative?

In jails and prisons that adhere to the old methods of strict custody, prisoners are ordered what to wear, what to eat, how much to eat, how to work, where to work, what to read, whom to see, whom to write, when to write, when to talk, and what to say. Prisoners are made to do everything at the same time, the same way, every day.

Even in more progressive institutions where administrators believe in an emphasis on treatment rather than strict custody, and on reintegration into the community rather than retribution, there is still a basic conflict, which is summed up in the *Manual of Correctional Standards,* issued by the American Correctional Association: "The fundamental responsibility of prison management is the secure custody and control of prisoners. This is universally prescribed by custom and public opinion. Although at times such a concept may seem at variance with attempts to introduce rehabilitative services, it is doubtful that any correctional program which ignores this reality will long endure."

In a progressive institution that has made a humane effort to individualize treatment of the inmates, women may be allowed to choose what to wear each day, wear their own street clothes, and choose how to fix their hair. They may be able to hang pictures on the walls of their rooms and be allowed the choice of whether to eat certain meals or participate in certain education or self-improvement classes. But even with these possibilities for self-expression, authorities and the controls of prison life still dictate a prisoner's degree of contact with the outside world. A woman's choice of friends and her expression of beliefs are still monitored and censored. Her life is still regulated and dictated by the limits of the institution, and the majority of her choices are determined for her, not by her.

Principle 20 in the *Declaration of Principles* of the American Correctional Association states, "Moral forces, organized persuasion and scientific treatment should be relied upon in the control and management of offenders, with as little dependence upon physical force as possible."

What a woman should be, as opposed to what she is, is dictated by the standards of proper behavior set by the institution, according to its needs, rules, and expectations. Staff members often are unaware or disdainful of the different culture a woman comes from or the different interests and problems she has.

Prisoners are placed in a double bind. If they accept custody and allow other people to make their decisions and set up all the rules, they will try to play the game properly. They will repress their anger, never talk back to an officer, obey all the rules, and follow all instructions without complaint. They will then be rewarded with positive staff reports, which will make it more likely for them to be released on parole before the expiration of their sentence. But this reward has a high price; with it comes the erosion of their self-determination, independence, and sense of responsibility in making decisions.

Prisoners who refuse to bow to all the rules and restrictions on their words and actions get into trouble but have a better chance of maintaining a sense of autonomy over their own decisions. If they express themselves, they may argue over a rule they consider stupid, laugh when they feel like it, or otherwise behave in the manner they would if they were free. Even if they don't fight the system but simply ignore the regulations laid down to govern their behavior, they are considered "problem prisoners" and are apt to spend a lot of time getting demerits or being locked in "close custody" or segregation. At the least, they are viewed as uncooperative by staff and maintain a poor institutional record. They are often denied parole for the behavior that ironically might allow them to adjust more quickly to society than their less independent counterparts. These women often stay in prison until expiration of sentence.

Seymour L. Halleck, a former psychiatric consultant for the Wisconsin Division of Corrections, suggests one way of looking at the whole issue of incarceration: "If one had systematically and diabolically tried to create mental illness and tried to create situations in which there were no alternatives, he could probably have constructed no better system than the American prison system.

"If you think about what qualities one could define as being conducive to mental health and then take a look at what actually exists in prisons," Halleck says, "the argument that the prison is there to create mental illness is well put.

"We all agree that to be mentally healthy, we have to be able to feel intimate toward others and others toward us. As you know, any kind of intimate expressions in prison are repressed. Certainly contact with the opposite sex is not available. Contacts with the same sex are looked upon as homosexual and are punished. Contacts with the officers—real camaraderie and all sense of sharing—are absent.

"Also, to be healthy one has to express a certain amount of aggression. Now, I'm not talking about violence. I'm talking about being able to use one's aggressive impulse to argue verbally, to gain mastery over the situation. Any kind of aggression in a prison situation is punished—not thwarted, punished.

"Also, to be mentally healthy one must have a certain sense of autonomy. One must have a sense of dignity. One must have a sense that there is hope. That he is not totally helpless and dependent. Obviously these things are gradually stripped away from prisoners.

"Also, to be mentally healthy one must have a sense of responsibility. One must feel that he is accountable for what he does. That he is not totally dependent. And that he is master of his own destiny. Again, the prison system systematically strips inmates of these kinds of very, very basic needs essential for mental health."

Halleck says there are few things a prisoner can do to change this situation. But there are several kinds of adjustments to it. One is saying to oneself, "Well, I will change something about my own physiology or my own attitudes so I can live with this situation." And indeed, some inmates do. They blame themselves. They work hard. Religion helps enormously if they believe in an afterlife or in a time when things will be better.

The most useful kind of adjustment, according to Halleck, would be "organized, legitimate-within-the-system grievance, i.e., legitimate efforts to change the society, the prison society in this case. These efforts are what have been used in reforming other institutions. But these outlets are simply not available to the prisoner. There are very few inside prison organizations or inmate councils which have much influence on the authorities. There is very little power that prisoners have, ultimately.

"What's left for prisoners are some other kinds of adjustments," according to Halleck. "When other legitimate outlets are closed off, another type of adjustment is simply to attack the prevailing community. So far this has not been used excessively, but I think now there is greater awareness of the possibility of using it. Now that there are more riots in more prisons, we are probably going to face more of this direct attack upon the institutional system."

Principle 29 in the American Correctional Association's *Declaration of Principles* states, "No law, procedure or system of correction should deprive any offender of the hope and the possibility of his ultimate return to full, responsible membership in society."

Some percentage of the people in prison obviously do need or want to be controlled by others. Some are psychotic and out of control, while others have committed certain crimes in order to put themselves in bondage, in order to feel safe or to have security. This happens both inside and outside prison. They are people who want to have most major and minor decisions made for them. They are the people who literally need forced dependency as a way of life—maybe because they are emotionally or mentally unable to grow up. Or maybe it is because they have been so warped and stretched out of shape by life that they have gone beyond the elastic point of return to a natural, healthy shape. They are dependent on care; whether it's adequate or inadequate, they need outside direction and support. But these people are easily identifiable. As a minority of the prison population, they are mainly neglected or locked up in solitary confinement for being emotionally disturbed.

What is tragic is that the regimentation molded for protection against these very few dangerous, violent, or psychotic women prisoners—who are estimated by administrators to be 3 percent or less of the total prison population—dictates the controls on all the women in an institution.

Mary Vangi, a small, blue-eyed woman with blond, pixie-style hair, wrote about this problem in *The Clarion,* the convict newspaper at the California Institution for Women, a relatively progressive institution with an emphasis on therapy. "The fact is that some convicts are violent and dangerous," Mary wrote. "The fact is that no or little provision is made once they are in prison to get them adequate psychiatric care. There is not enough money in the budget, we are told, and the State Mental Hospitals refuse most convicts treatment while they are doing time. None the less, patients deemed unmanageable by the Mental Institutions of this state are sent, without being convicted of a felony, to the state prison for control. None of this is publicized. The fact that most convicts just want to do their own time and get the hell out of prison is not often made public."

Mary was responding directly to an eleven-part series on the California Institution for Women that was being run on local television. The series, called "Ladies in Waiting," depicted the surface realities of the prison in a manner Mary believed was akin to creating a fairy tale leading people to believe it was "comfortable, constructive and cozy here." Since the green prison yards of Frontera look much like a college campus, prisoners felt the public would mistakenly believe that curtains on windows and rugs on floors indicated a relaxed freedom and a setting for constructive growth and dignity in contradiction to what they felt was a degrading, confining, and infantile reality.

Mary wrote:

It begins to seem that the public is more interested in sensationalism than in reality. The society out there is not interested in how their tax dollars that go to support prisons and pay salaries of people who work in prisons and related fields are spent. They are not interested in whether or not there is anything worth salvaging from the warehouse called prison. They are more interested in getting the thrill of seeing what the inside of the prison looks like—room, curtains, rugs, food—not the need for or the lack of reality within the gates to prepare the convict for returning to the community.

This, though, is a typical sociological phenomena of the Amerikan [*sic*] society. We have been programmed to reject reality. Perhaps because the realities that make this country a great world power are so very ugly. I recently read an article by a man on death row that suggested that all executions be televised, so that the public that screams for convictions, for blood, may see their work realized. I think it's a good idea. If we cannot face the truth then we should change it so that it is acceptable to us, instead of trying to build fairy tales around it.

I would like to suggest that the woman who is doing this eleven part television series voluntarily commit herself to the prison for one week. In the booking-in process, instead of staff who might try to treat her like a human being for the public opinion that will come of it, convicts should book her in, search her just like they were searched on their arrival. All of the very real things that happen to us should be allowed to happen to her: lost mail, disciplinary measures for things like ''silent disrespect,'' visits with male friends denied until she chooses just one of them . . . all of it. Perhaps then she would be well versed enough in loneliness, indignation, hunger, alienation and desolation to tell the truth.

We are not physically abused, we are demoralized drop by drop, that's all. We are not physically uncomfortable, we are involved in a psychological war about ten out of every twenty-four hours, that's all. We are not starving to death from self-inflicted and other kinds of pain we live with; we are not cold from lack of proper clothing or heating. We are freezing from the cold, icy reality that even though we've done time for a crime, we will pay for it for the rest of our lives.

From infancy.

8 SECURITY AND DISCIPLINE

Springs Wound Too Tightly

The way the criminal justice system is run now leaves no alternative to failure. A fundamental issue here applies as long as we use punishment to control human behavior. It's axiomatic that if you use punishment to control behavior and want to have any effect, you have to punish a person immediately following the behavior.

In this system, the use of punishment just can't work. Not only do you have to wait before arrest, but by the time a person gets to court a year or two later, the behavior itself is totally forgotten. It's so long ago it doesn't even seem related and it seems you're being persecuted for something you didn't do. That's when people start feeling victimized by the system rather than being called to account for what they did.

One other crux just as illogical is that our corrections rehabilitates people so they can adjust better to the community when they get out. Impossible! It's just impossible and illogical that you take a person away from normal society and put them in an abnormal society and expect them to adjust to the community. You just can't live inside the way we live outside.

—Bennett Cooper, Ohio Commissioner of Corrections

Whenever you have exaggerated repression, you have exaggerated response. A spring wound too tightly will recoil with extra force. A child who has no natural, direct outlet for his anger will throw a temper tantrum. A people who have been held down too long and denied alternatives will explode in anger—over a police brutality incident in the inner city, over a prison guard insulting an inmate in a crowded cafeteria. We often call such a response a "riot."

A woman brutalized by her male partner over a long period of time sometimes will "riot" just as unexpectedly, striking back with a blind fury that ends the life of her mate. Individuals turn to drugs or release pent-up hatred by striking out over seemingly small incidents that sometimes appear only casually related to the suffocating oppression he or she has experienced for years. The overwhelming nature of disasters also can cause delayed reactions. After a death, a hurricane, a horrible train crash, a tornado or flood, for instance, people often protect themselves unconsciously from the terrifying experience by mentally putting it away and not thinking about it. When the response finally does come out, it's devastating, particularly when it seems random and no one realizes its source.

Going to jail or prison, in and of itself, is an emotional and mental disaster. You are separated from everyone and everything you know, and you must adjust to the rules and regulations and terrible reality of prison life. The punishment and humiliation of imprisonment itself is larger than most of us can imagine. Further, the judgments and punishment that continue once imprisoned create terrible repression.

The response, the outlet, is manifested in broken windows, senseless fights. Although the occasional news we hear about prison rebellions would give the impression that only male prisoners stage uprisings, women also rebel. Women also strike, they negotiate, they boycott. They also escape. At the California Institution for Women alone, one fifth of the population successfully escaped in 1971, one or two at a time. [Since that time, armed guards and barbed wire around the perimeter of CIW have been installed to prevent escape.]

The same pressures that lead women to escape often result in "riots" or disruptions in prison routine. Sometimes the incident sparking prisoner response seems minuscule. But the reaction is one that has been pent up from day-in-and-day-out pressures, coercion, and anxiety.

It may be sparked by the fact that a woman's father died and the administrative staff delayed its decision on her pleas to go home to his funeral—even though she was sick and collapsing with grief, even though her prison friends wanted to pool their funds to pay the required expenses of a guard escort and transportation, even though time was running out. The administration's casual disregard ignited a "riot" in the administrative building at Muncy, Pennsylvania, in a case like this, when women who went to protest were confronted by locked doors, male guards, and maintenance men.

Another incident was reported by the *Philadelphia Inquirer* in a front-page article, "Women Riot, Attack Guards at Jail Here," on February 19, 1973:

> A band of women inmates stormed the Philadelphia House of Correction dispensary, apparently in search of drugs, touching off the second of two disturbances here Sunday.
>
> No one was injured in the first melee, which erupted about 9 A.M. in the G-2 cellblock and took about 30 minutes to quell. But four male guards, a matron, and an inmate were injured in the second disturbance, which broke out shortly after 11 A.M. It involved 50 women—half of the 92 held in the prison—who wielded broomsticks, kitchen utensils, and legs pulled from chairs.[1]

What's missing in this account is that the purpose of the attempted break into the dispensary was to get medication for two very ill women after legitimate avenues for medical help had been exhausted.

A minor "riot" can happen because a woman with hepatitis is not getting medical attention. This happened at Bedford Hills in New York. "Full investigations" can be launched, but they rarely focus on the pent-up frustration of no change after agonizing conditions have been ignored by "proper channels" even when women have gone about expressing their grievances in a reasonable way.

"What people fail to realize is that being locked up at all is punishment enough," said Barbara Collins, now out on parole after four years in a state prison. "They think you come to prison to be punished, and so you're punished in all kinds of ways while you're there.

"But there are times you can get pushed too far and you just can't keep your mouth shut. You can't lose your pride one more time without giving up some part of yourself, and that's the only thing you have."

The response of prison administrators to disruptions is a microcosm of the way we as a society behave when we condone or ignore the violence of racism, poverty, and imprisonment, and then condemn the violence of spontaneous resistance or reaction to the years of oppression and abuse.

We denounce riots, but we fail to equate them with daily violence perpetrated in more subtle ways. Women at the House of Correction hurt four male guards and a matron. But how closely do we consider how badly they have been hurt—especially the seventy-seven out of the ninety-two women there who were locked up awaiting trial? Those women were presumed innocent but, mainly because of finances, were separated from their

---

1. Notice the incendiary language used in reporting this incident. Women "riot"; they "stormed" the dispensary; it was a "melee" that had to be "quelled." The article does not mention what weapons the guards used against the women, nor does it attempt to track or understand the conditions that led to this confrontation.

children and locked up. Further, how adequate are the social welfare services in providing for the children of these women? What role does the trauma and anxiety the mothers experience play in such an incident?

When we witness any violent outburst, we seem to forget that this kind of predicament doesn't happen in a vacuum, that it is a response. To examine the crisis alone is myopic and sensational. We must probe more deeply for the real causes—otherwise we continue blindly and blandly to place Band-Aids on cancerous sores.

The origin of most prison outbursts is woven into the day-to-day fabric of prison life. Women being punished for breaking the law enter a new social order in prison, with its own picayune system of discipline, where crime and punishment revolve around behavior issues that never could be "taken to court" in the larger society. Central to the system is the notion that prisoners have privileges, not rights. A sign in the dining room of the women's House of Correction in Chicago expresses the limits quite well:

> Words were made to be spoken
> Voices were made to be used
> If you speak lightly, and also politely,
> This privilege will not be abused.

In jail and prison, whether or not you are guilty of your crime, speaking is a privilege, not a right. Visitors are a privilege. The smallest things we take for granted on the outside become a matter of rewards to be allowed or withheld: showers, mail, laughing out loud, touching, walking slowly, running, dancing, smoking, eating. Even the quantity of sugar or milk in coffee is of consequence.

"I went to get sugar for my oatmeal," Marlene Riffert says. "I took a spoonful and then the matron came up and took my bowl away and threw the cereal in the garbage. I was so shocked, I didn't say anything, I just looked at her. She said, 'You know you already used sugar in your coffee.' I was given three nights' early bed."

Marlene had violated a sacrosanct rule at the House of Correction in Philadelphia: she attempted to use sugar in her coffee and on her cereal at breakfast. Her option was one or the other, not both.

Marlene told this story when she was testifying about conditions at the House of Correction for a Philadelphia court. Inmates from three male institutions and the women's section of the House had filed a class action suing the city for violation of the Fourteenth Amendment—cruel and unusual punishment.[2]

2. In *Bryant v. Hendrick* (444 Pa. 83, 1971) the court found that conditions at the three jails constituted cruel and unusual punishment.

She sat dwarfed in the witness box and explained her history: She ran away from home at age sixteen, was declared "incorrigible" by the state, and was locked up at the House of Correction. That was 1962. She was there again in 1963, 1970, and 1971. She is in detention this time for possession of narcotics. Her voice is small and shaky as she talks about her unresolved drug problem, her husband at Graterford Prison, and their two-year-old son. She says she is testifying because she thinks "things should change" for the women who will follow her into the jail.

Marlene tells the judge that when she finishes her testimony and goes back to the jail, she is scheduled to go into solitary confinement for another infraction of rules at breakfast. "Men work back in the kitchen," she says. "They're from over on the men's side. . . . I was on the line getting my food. Well, the men were bringing the food in from the outside and the door opened and I looked at one of the men. I didn't wave or call him or nothing. I just looked at him. When I got to the end of the line the matron said, 'Marlene, you're going to get lockup when you get back from court.' I said, 'What for? For looking at the men?' She said, 'Yes.' "

Bizarre as it may seem, this kind of infraction is not uncommon in institutions that hold both men and women in separate sections of the same jail. At the Cook County Jail in Chicago, which the warden, Winston E. Moore, describes as "one of the best-run jails in the country," women are put in lockup for talking through the window in sign language to men in other sections of the massive jail complex. Passing "kites" (notes) is an automatic lockup.

More rarely prisoners are disciplined for "talking on the wall" to the men on the floors below them. By getting down on the floor and putting your ear to the wall, you can hear voices from the other floors through the air vents. Men and women signal each other with specified numbers of knocks on the wall and sometimes carry on long, intimate conversations throughout the day and night. Since it's almost impossible to stop the conversations, inmates and guards have established a truce; matrons usually tolerate such an exchange as long as they don't personally witness it. Women shout, "Respect," when a matron's coming, and conversations cease as the women stand at attention for the matron passing their cells. ("The time goes fast when you're down on that cold floor talking on the wall," Toni says. "You get tired of talking to women all the time. Man, on Saturday nights those walls be steamin'.")

The only opportunity male and female prisoners have to see one another close up at the Cook County Jail is when they go to the co-ed concerts that Winston Moore instituted after he became warden. When Lou Rawls, Joan Baez, Dick Gregory, and other artists perform at Cook County, the women are ushered to the front of the prison yard and seated. Then the male inmates file in and sit down. Women inmates are not allowed to turn their heads, wave, nod, or look at the men. After the performance, the women walk out single file. "Heads forward, girls." Any woman who looks to the right or left, acknowledges someone with her eyes, or turns around is banned from future concerts and subject to lockup. ("They seem to think we're going to take our clothes off and lay right down," one inmate said. "They treat us like we're a bunch of nymphomaniacs, not just normal women who like to look at a man every now and then. The whole thing is in their heads. It doesn't have shit to do with what's really going on.")

"Women here are locked in for 'silent insolence' if they raise their eyebrows at an officer or refuse to answer a stupid question," said a case-worker at one prison. "They are never allowed to let go except when they're watching television or having a dance. Even then they're told to keep it down. Sometimes I feel as if I were living in the middle of a nightmare; I don't know how long I'll be able to take it. I've been here one year, and it's the incredible intelligence and sensitivity of the women that's made me stay this long. They need someone to talk to. But I'm just overwhelmed by the needs they have—and my inability to meet them.

"There's no way the unexpected can be incorporated into the living situation here. Custody depends on a known and strict schedule so that the unexpected cannot happen and harm 'security.' No matter what rhetoric they have here about treatment and rehabilitation, any disruption of the schedule or the routine is a security risk. And any woman who does any-thing she is not supposed to do—even like talk while she's eating—means that she's a 'security risk' and must be locked up or disciplined."

In many county jails there is no pretense of a disciplinary hearing for women sentenced to solitary confinement. The women are just locked up, period. If there is a disciplinary hearing, it comes sometimes four or five days after the punishment. In June 1971, when women at the Detroit House of Correction refused to work in protest of humiliating search procedures and abhorrent prison conditions, participating strikers were locked in their rooms for several days, some up to two weeks. Before they had been locked up, they sent letters to the mayor, city council, and prison board listing their grievances. In answer to a city investigation of the incidents that followed, the superintendent, W. H. Bannon, said that "each girl was interviewed to get the facts on how this started." He admitted that they were locked in their rooms before they were interviewed, but maintained that "after a period of six or seven days we released each of them without any punishment whatsoever."

In state prisons, disciplinary hearings are more common—but if I were to describe them, I would call them "pretend trials," with the concept of "proving" guilt only make-believe. Although the disciplinary hearings are often called "tribunals," "behavior clinics," or "adjustment hearings," the process is not impartial, nor is guilt or innocence the issue. Guilt is an a priori assumption. As one administrator bluntly put it: *"The process used for determining punishment* [my emphasis] includes a hearing with a senior correctional officer, a senior counselor, the warden, and a psychologist when he can attend.

"Theoretically a woman can have an attorney present if she wishes, but think of it logically. With court processes so slow and lawyers with so many clients, how many would even consider taking time to come here for a disciplinary hearing? And even if a woman could get a lawyer, how would she pay him?

"A woman can speak on her own behalf and try to convince us she's telling the truth, *but we know what really happened* [my emphasis]."

Inmates say the process normally is one-sided. A matron or guard does a "write-up" or a "blue slip," which is a summons to come to a disciplinary hearing. Sometimes offenders are put into solitary confinement before the hearing. If not, they usually receive no prior written notice until they are called to behavior clinic or the hearing. The woman is not allowed to call witnesses in her behalf, and the disciplinary board is not required to give a decision based on evidence. [In most states in the 1990s, disciplinary sheets state the charge, and inmates are entitled to receive this notice twenty-four hours before the hearing. They are entitled to a lawyer, but this rarely happens. In some circumstances, an inmate can call a witness.]

"It's your word against hers," said one woman who had been in solitary confinement for a week when I met her. "She's always going to win because they're her people, they're going to listen to her. You're just a number or a blank space in their minds. You go in and sit in front of that board and you know you don't have a chance in heaven to get out of going to solitary.

"I got nine days here because Miss Brown in Central Food Service said I refused to drop a pan and clean the grill. She was just upset about her husband being sick and she was taking it out on me. She told me to quit what I was doing and I said, 'Just let me finish this pan first.' She just went off on me—started hollering about my 'insolence'—and then she wrote me up. Of course she blew it up in front of the behavior clinic. They asked me to step into the hall, and about two minutes later I came back in and heard my sentence. Then the guards brought me up here."

Getting "locked up" is a common occurrence for women prisoners, as it is with men. All prisoners are familiar with the "bing," "hole," or "strip cell." In every jail and prison I've visited, these cells are windowless and bare. Some have one thin, dirty, and bloodstained mattress on the floor. Some have no mattress. Some jails provide blankets for the women confined, some do not. In some quarters, women locked in solitary are allowed to wear prison shifts; in others they are allowed to wear only their underwear or are stripped naked. Toilets are most often flushed from the outside, and women complain that on occasion, matrons play games with flushing the toilets, either flushing them repeatedly until they overflow or not flushing them at all for a day or more at a time. ("If the toilet backs up, there's nothing you can do about it but live with the stench.") Food is passed into the room two or three times a day between the bottom of the dusty door and the unwashed floor, as are sanitary napkins if the woman is menstruating.

"You can't even take a shower or comb your hair. Sometimes they'll remember to pass a comb in to you, or toilet paper, but sometimes they forget. And you can imagine what it feels like to use a dirty Kotex. Last winter I was in solitary for six weeks and they'd leave the windows open and I'd just freeze on that floor."

Women joke about the names used for solitary confinement. What originally was called "the hole" changes to "solitary," "max," "administrative segregation," "punitive segregation," "isolation," "the quiet room," "security cell," "control center," "reflection," "behavior center," or currently, among the satirists, "loss-of-privilege module." At the Cook County Jail, Lieutenant Dorothy Zeno explained, "We don't call this the hole or confinement, we call it the Blue Room." It was painted blue.

Although euphemisms may make isolation cells sound more palatable or comfortable to outsiders or administrators, the reality for prisoners in max is harsh and unchanging. Women often say they are afraid they will lose their minds or whatever sense they might have of who they are, where they are. Women with severe emotional difficulties sometimes try to slash their wrists with any sharp object they can find (such as a piece of metal from the window) or set a fire if they can get matches. Often they are kept even longer in solitary for having tried to hurt themselves. Some administrators say they have no other means of coping with such problems.

"You lose track of time, you start feeling crazy, even though you know you're not there for anything," one woman said. "It's hard enough if you're strong or you can direct your anger on the people who deserve it for putting you there. But some women are sick to start with and just plain need help. When you put them in there, they're going to go crazy. I'll never forget one night listening to an eighteen-year-old girl just crying and screaming. She kept saying, 'Please somebody talk to me. Please just talk to me. I think I'm losing my mind. Oh, God, help me.' Any one of us would have gladly gone down and talked to her, but we was locked up, too. It just made me cry to hear her. And you know the matrons weren't going to talk to her. Those two be sitting down there saying to each other, 'She'll get used to it. She gotta learn sometime.' "

Becky Careway, at the Ohio Reformatory for Women, said, "I guess it used to be a whole lot worse in here. Miss Riley, the warden before Miss Wheeler, would shave your head bald for walking on the grass and put you in maximum security for no less than six months."

Becky—with short blond hair and a cherub face that reminded me of the Campbell's Soup girls—said she had been in max several times for short periods: once for refusing an order from the matron while working in the kitchen and another time for stealing supplies from the storeroom. "They didn't have no evidence on me," she said. "My room was clean. But I went to max anyway. I usually go peacefully. But one night the matron, who's a drunk, told me I hadn't swept the floor good enough, and it *was* swept good enough. Besides, she had just been drinking and she was all loud and sloppy. I told her, 'Bitch, call the guards, 'cause you ain't taking me nowhere.' The motherfucker . . . If I didn't have two more years before parole, I would have liked to slam into her. She called the guards, though, and I went with them."

A constant source of tension for women is the disparity in the way the prison staff members enforce rules and hand out punishment. "You never get away from it—it's always different strokes for different folks," one inmate said. Often women involved in the same incident are dealt with in different ways, whether the infractions are serious or are just plain silly.

Sharon Wiggins, sentenced to life at the State Correctional Institution for Women at Muncy, Pennsylvania, for instance, was charged with possession of fifty cents—which is "contraband" on "campus." All official monetary exchanges at Muncy are supposed to be transacted on paper.

"I was sitting on the steps in front of Sproul Cottage, and Mrs. Spaulding and three guards and three maintenance men drove up and told us to come into the building. They didn't say what they wanted. She stripped us and searched us. She made me pull down my Kotex to look. She found fifty cents on me, so she wrote me up. The male guards and maintenance men were there in case we refused to be searched. But we didn't.

"I was charged with possession of fifty cents, but on the behavior sheet she wrote that she had searched us for narcotics and implied she knew we had it on us, but she didn't find it. At the time we asked her to take us down for urinalysis after she looked at our arms. We didn't have any narcotics and hadn't used any, so we wanted a urinalysis. She said she didn't have the authority. We asked, if she had the authority to search us, she could give us the urinalysis instead and that would be less humiliating—plus it would prove whether we were taking drugs or not.

"But we didn't have a chance to prove ourselves. When they searched me, they said they would have to have a hearing on the fifty cents, but they didn't say nothing about searching for dope. They just wrote it on the behavior sheet and read it out loud at the hearing.

"I spoke in my own defense at the hearing. I was guilty of fifty cents but I said it was not right to write stuff about drugs on my record when she flatly refused to give us a urinalysis, which I thought was my right. After the hearing I waited five minutes in the hall and when I went back in they told me what I had. I was locked in my room for three nights from six P.M. to six-thirty A.M. for the fifty cents. There's no way to appeal. None of the other three who were stripped and searched were charged with anything because they didn't have nothing on them."

Many prisoners have told me that addicts are discriminated against; at other times I have been told that Chicano women, black women, or white women are the ones who are more apt to be written up or called on the carpet for rule infractions. Occasionally I heard racial antagonisms from both black and white women. "They're always complaining about how they get the raw end of everything," one white woman said, referring to black women. "But I'm a living testimony to the fact that whites get fucked over just as bad. You can't tell me any different. If you ask me, they got more privileges than I ever had. I get tired of all their bellyaching. I got some black friends, but they're not into that bag all the time. If you lived here, you'd know what I mean. I just get tired of hearing black this and black that and black, black, black."

"We don't get shit around here," a black woman said. "Don't tell me no white girl has to do time like I have to do time. They get the best and they still be carrying that white thing around on their shoulders, signifying and strutting—like 'Ain't I somethin'!' You'll see it, they get away with all kinds of shit we get locked for."

Although some racial hostilities give vent to "disciplinary problems," most of the women in the prisons I visited maintained that racial tensions are created by the staff and staff policies, not by the women themselves. They say that the staff uses tactics to divide and rule.

"There's a lot of racial tension because there's the feeling that whites get treated better," Sharon Wiggins said. "They get the better job assignments and they don't get sentenced to Clinton [the maximum security "cottage"] as much. So they get parole sooner, too. If a white girl breaks a rule, she's more likely to get a warning than get written up. Inmates are ready to fight then because they say, 'Hey, I did the same thing but I got written up for it.' Then they take it out on the other women instead of the matron. There are fights, but nobody's been hospitalized.

"The guards and the officials are the problem. Some of them do it on purpose because they're very prejudiced. Others have just never been around blacks so it's a natural thing. The problems don't come from the white inmates, but from the officials. The administration has started a group for the staff to talk about things like that, and it has made a small difference." The staff at Muncy in 1972 included one African American guard and seven white guards, one black matron and sixty-three white matrons. All the administrators were white except the head of the school. The religious leaders, medical staff, and counseling staff were white. Before 1970 there had never been an African American on the staff. [In 1995 eight of Muncy's 210 corrections officers are African American; one drug and alcohol counselor is African American and one is Hispanic. Mary Leftridge Byrd, superintendent of Muncy, is African American and the only female prison warden in the state of Pennsylvania.]

"The general policies favor whites," Sharon said. "Fifty-three percent of the population is black and forty-seven percent is white. But there's only two black girls on the farm who have higher paying jobs, and I'm one of them. I make one dollar a day. All the other office positions—nine of them—are held by white girls.

At the Cook County Jail in Chicago, where 85 percent of the staff is black, women say that the policies and jobs and discipline favor blacks, who make up 80 percent of that population. "A girl from a southern state came in here, and three of the women were gonna beat her up," said Maria Fisher, an inmate in Cook County. "She was from Alabama or Mississippi or one of those states. It was three against one, and I told them, 'If you wanna fight one by one, that's okay. But three against one ain't fair.' I had just been sick and didn't feel too good, but I told them they were forcing me into it. 'She's a whitey, you gonna fight for a whitey?' I said, 'I don't care if she's a greenie, three to one ain't fair.' The officer was there, but she wasn't doing anything. She was just sitting at her desk pretending nothing was happening 'cause she wanted to see the white girl get licked, too. Anyway, it was really wild in here; I got hit in the chest with a waste-basket and hurt pretty bad.

"But I'm not gonna beat her just because she came from a southern state. She can't help where she comes from any more than anybody else can. The officer [who was black] locked her up after the fight and spit on her and threw water in her cell. I used to think it was whites against blacks in America, but in this jail it's blacks suppressing whites *and* blacks.''

Maria, thirty-four, had been in Chicago's House of Correction awaiting trial on a homicide charge for more than a year. She said she was maligned at the jail for having been previously associated with the Black Panther party: "They're just so afraid of revolution in here. I'm not with the Panthers anymore, but I'm a revolutionary. I been a revolutionary since I was born.

"One of the officers, she says to me, 'Look what they've been doing to us for four hundred years—it's about time they got theirs.' I told her, 'Hey, look, I'm not four hundred years old, but I know I'm black. You're just finding out. I was born in Jamaica, and when I first came to this country, black was the worse thing I could have called you. You're not black just because your skin is black. The way you use your power is just as bad as the way white people use it. It looks to me you're trying to be just the same.''

Despite their difficulties, imprisoned women I met had broken through prejudices and racial barriers in positive, if not remarkable, ways. "We all come out of the same bag, baby,'' one thirty-year-old black woman told me. "They can't put that old divide-and-conquer thing on us. We know where it's at. It's the same in the free world, really, but people don't dig it yet.''

Although women work through most problems themselves, the institutional effects of class and race prejudice still create personal strains. Latin and Chicano women, for instance, sometimes are not allowed to speak Spanish to each other. In spite of changes at some prisons, they often are not allowed to read or write letters in Spanish (because the censors can't read them), subscribe to Spanish-language newspapers or magazines, or converse in Spanish with visitors or friends.[3]

Lydia Amada, a Puerto Rican woman from New York, said that even though there was one Cuban, one South American, and two other Puerto Rican prisoners who didn't speak English "except for 'Yes, yes,' '' they were not allowed to speak Spanish to each other at Muncy. "One day another girl and I were talking, and an officer snuck up and yelled, 'No foreign languages can be spoken here on the farm,' '' Lydia said. "I told him, 'It's not a foreign language to me.' They make you feel you're a

3. It seems that in most prisons in the 1990s, Spanish-speaking inmates officially are allowed to send and receive correspondence in Spanish and also to speak their native tongue during visits. The same is true of most inmates whose first language is other than English.

foreigner because you can't speak English. I tell them, 'As far as I'm concerned, you're all foreigners.'

"It's not so bad for me since I speak some English, but I speak Spanish anyway when the matrons aren't around. My attitude here is, since you have to do time, why be miserable and get locked up in solitary? So I get along pretty good."

Although it may seem ludicrous that a woman is punished for speaking her native tongue, harboring fifty cents in change, or "insubordination" because she didn't clean the grill in a kitchen, what is put into a woman's file is serious business. A woman's "behavior record" can make or break her ability to get out on parole. Although the individuals are never allowed to hold or see their own files, staff members, parole board members, law enforcement officers, and commutation board members can see and use them. On the basis of what is in the file, institutional personnel write progress evaluations or recommendations for parole. On the basis of staff evaluations and their own brief contact with prisoners, parole board members determine when a woman can be released under supervision to the community. When "threat to an officer," "contraband," "fighting," or "assaultive behavior" is written on her record, it doesn't appear that a woman is working in her own interest and obeying rules or that she is "prepared to respect law and order in the community."

In addition to the nature and severity of her original crime, the intent of the sentence, and the prosecution's investment in whether or not a prisoner is released, the parole board depends on a prisoner's institutional record and her ability to convince them within fifteen minutes or less that she is "rehabilitated." A poor behavior record in prison almost guarantees extra time in prison—sometimes as much as five or ten more years. Of course most women count on getting paroled before their maximum possible sentence is served (some are serving twenty-five years or even sixty years for robbery alone), but the pressure of possibly "maxing out" still provides the feeling of trying to balance on a tightrope. Every woman is aware that her immediate behavior affects her future. Some women give up caring about when they will get out.

"I could have did a year," said a parolee from the Edna Manan Correctional Facility in Clinton, New Jersey. "But I did three 'cause I was a sho' nuff bitch. I had that attitude: 'You can throw me in here, but I'm gonna do my time my way.' Once I spent thirty-six days in the hole. It was the same day Kennedy was killed, and everybody was watching TV. Some of us wanted to put records on instead, but the matron said, 'This is your history in the making.' We said, 'Whose history? Ain't our history!' Anyway, somebody set fire in the cottage. I knew who set it. It wasn't me, but I wouldn't tell who did it and they knew I knew.

"This guard took me to the cell and he told me to take my clothes off. I told him I wasn't gonna take shit off in front of him, the honky white motherfucker. He snatched me and tore my clothes off. I kicked him and jumped him. I knew I wasn't gonna win 'cause he was too big, but I wasn't gonna strip in front of him. He beat the hell out of me and handcuffed me spread-eagle to the bed. The matron was out there in the corridor and she didn't do nothing. My bra and dress had been ripped off but my panties were intact. I lay spread-eagle like that for about six hours. Then another dude, he was pretty nice, he came in. He took me out of shackles and gave me salve for my face and a slip to wear. He told me he was sorry. Yeah, I was sorry, too. That motherfucker had closed my eye. Believe me, I called his mother every name in the book."

"Lois" said she figured she couldn't handle worrying about when she would get out and saw no alternatives to serving three years rather than one. Other times women say they just "go off"; they can't take it anymore. They say that the pleasure of asserting themselves is worth lockup—like the time Theresa Derry got nine months in solitary for taking a bath in a female officer's bathtub: "It was hot and I was tired of taking a shower standing on the bare concrete floor. So I went up to Miss Taylor's room in the administration building, filled the tub with water and bubble bath, and crawled in. The girl who was my lookout fell asleep, and the next thing I knew, Miss Taylor came up, opened the door and asked me, 'What do you think you're doing??!' 'What the fuck does it look like I'm doing? I'm taking a bath.'"

There also are peer rewards in being a rebel. "You live in a whole fantasized world of Miss Bad Girl," said Fran Christman, who did time in both New York and California. "And the badder you are, the more strength you have, because you're looked up to by the inmate population. Also, once you've established yourself, they don't mess with you so much. The guard who says she's not scared of the women is lying. She says, 'Move,' and you say, 'Make me.' That's why they have male guards put women in the hole. Some male guards can't believe what they see out there."

For the number of women who play "Miss Bad Girl" there is an equal number pushed to the opposite extreme of becoming excessively withdrawn and passive. But most women figure out ways to work around the power structure and do "easy time." Superficially, the threat of confinement and a poor behavior record contributes greatly to management and control of the institution. But in the long run, ironically, the repressive security considerations add to the development of all the qualities prison is supposed to erase, not promote: dishonesty, cheating, stealing, hustling, evasiveness. These attributes are necessary for prison survival and better chances at getting parole.

Honest or direct responses to the conditions—such as openly asking for extra food, refusing food, trading favors, discussing how to improve work conditions, telling a guard you want to visit a sick friend in another cell, sticking up for someone else, asserting your rights openly—mean punishment and a poor record. Another irony is that insignificant things, not big issues, more often than not give a woman the "bad" record that denies her parole or commutation.

When Evelyn Newman applied for commutation of her life sentence, for instance, she had had a good record at Muncy for ten years. She had been convicted of conspiring to murder her husband in 1959 following a three-day trial and a jury verdict that she says took less than three minutes to determine. Although this was her first offense and Evelyn maintained her innocence, she said she pled guilty under an intense threat from the district attorney: Don't plead and you'll get the electric chair. Do plead and you'll get life.

Under Pennsylvania law, someone doing a life sentence can apply for commutation when she has served nine years of the sentence. After ten long years in the mountains on the isolated Muncy farm, Evelyn was sure she would get commutation. During her time in prison she had worked every day and conducted herself well. For ten years she had been separated from her children, who were five, four, and sixteen months when she went to prison. Her four- and five-year-olds were put into foster homes and shuffled from one shelter to another. She gave her youngest son up for adoption. "I didn't want to do it," she said. "It broke my heart. I couldn't bring myself to sign the papers, but they kept pressuring me. I felt I just couldn't sign my baby away, but I finally realized I was being selfish. I realized I couldn't be mother and father to him with the time I had. So I signed the papers and adopted Charles out."

Despite the heartbreak, Evelyn hung on to the dream of getting out and being mother again to her two oldest children. And when the time came to apply, even her mother-in-law wrote a recommendation for her release to the state commutation board. "She knew how her son treated me, and she wrote a beautiful letter on my behalf," Evelyn said. "Everybody was for me, except the state." Evelyn was denied commutation—even though, had she gotten commutation, she would have been on lifetime parole. She was never given a reason. [In the 1990s prisoners have a federal constitutional right to know why their parole is being denied.]

Thinking about possible grounds for having been turned down, Evelyn decided it must have been because of demerits she had collected in prison. "Sure, I got a lot of demerits. There's no angels in jail. But mine were always for contraband—perfume, makeup, eyebrow pencils, earrings," she said. "I had my connections and always got busted for it. I couldn't never understand why—something that a woman wants and needs. But they wanted to strip you of your femininity." Evelyn's bitterness made her tremble as she sat in her cell telling me about it. "I mean, I thought ten years with a good record should mean something."

Evelyn hadn't been the only person looking forward to her release. "When my daughter found out I didn't get commutation, she got rebellious and ran away from home," Evelyn said. "I got bitter, too, and decided I'd leave this joint of my own accord. That's when I got the additional time [five years] for attempted prison breach—and we didn't even get out. I just had the screen off my window. But the whole thing had taken me out. My mother said my daughter asked her, 'What does it feel like to have a mother?' "

Just as Evelyn Newman eventually decided to try to make her own escape to freedom after having no explanation, no legitimate outlet for her despair, people otherwise seemingly oblivious to the pressure-cooker environment of prison end up exploding when they hit an internal boiling point.

Sometimes it happens in response to an affront; sometimes it's simply a delayed reaction. Because of the effect of everyday humiliations, tension among prisoners sits like dry kindling ready to burst into flame.

Whether or not outsiders hear about it, there's some kind of eruption in a jail or prison every week, every month. But as Sydney Shaw, at the California Institution for Women, said, "When they go too far with the women, there's bound to be an explosion. But if there's a riot and I'm killed, I don't want it to be over a sandwich."

In fact, a "taco search" at CIW was one such event that disrupted the delicate balance of emotions at the institution. Windows on buildings and a vehicle were smashed one day after all the women in the dining room had been "searched" for tacos as they left the cafeteria. Later the women referred to the incident as "The Great Taco Shake."

"It's a no-no to take food out of the dining room, but usually we can manage surreptitiously to stock up for midnight snacks," said Joanne (Friday) Fry. On this particular day women looked forward to Mexican food and the expectation of a snack before bed. ("Eat one, stash one.") But officers were waiting at each door, patting each woman down, checking pockets as women started to leave the dining room. ("Check that out! That police is chasing that woman halfway across the lawn to try to take her tacos. What a trip." "Hey, haven't they got anything better to do?"')

"It was a very tense situation," Friday wrote later in the inmate newspaper, *The Clarion.*

> As we said, it is against the rules to take food from the dining room. Perhaps this is one of the many small rules that needs looking into, changing. Obviously we can't have grocery stores or restaurants in our cells. Aside from the stench of spoiled food, the mass invasion of ants and other insects is discouraging. But why not a reasonable quantity of food for eating later?
> It is this kind of added frustrations and tensions that make tempers short. Short tempers lead to unnecessary violence. But these things can be avoided. Communication is important. So far we can't find anyone who will admit to ordering the "taco shake." We can't even ask why; we have no one to ask. When the line of communication is broken, all that is left is frustration. In a caged society like this, frustration can be a dangerous, deadly thing—when there is nowhere to go with it, no way to alleviate it.[4]

With no way to alleviate the anger or agony of different policies, sometimes the entire population at a prison will react collectively to an affront to personal dignity. A parolee from the California Institution for Women wrote to me in detail about a rebellion at that progressive prison while she was still incarcerated. I say "progressive" because, relatively speaking, CIW is very open-minded. Women wear their own clothes, have pre-parole furloughs, have contact visits with their families and children, keep birds and fish in their rooms, have an inmate advisory council and the inmate newspaper, *The Clarion,* which allows some degree of dissent.

I quote my friend's letter at length because these details tell us a great deal about "good" intentions designed to protect the women, about inmate-staff communication, about administrative steps used to alleviate or agitate an impending crisis, and about the truth of what is later called a prison riot. My parolee friend wrote:

> In early March, 1971, a woman was hospitalized for an overdose of narcotics, taken while in her cell at CIW. She was a Mexican woman. On the 11th of March, at approximately 1 P.M., a frozen count was called at the institution. A frozen count is a count taken when there is either evidence of an escape or when an inmate is missing from a designated area. Everyone, without exception, returns to her cell, locks in and gets counted. Frozen counts sometime last as long as three hours. . . . On this particular day, though, the frozen count was for another reason. We were told as we went to our cells to turn on our telexes for a special bulletin from the superintendent.
> Over the telex we were told that we had ten minutes to get rid of any

4. "Friday's Child," *The Clarion,* California Institution for Women, Frontera, Calif., January–February 1972.

contraband we might have, that at the end of ten minutes a room to room, person and room search would be made. The reason given was that there was an abundance of narcotics on the reservation, and that some people were in danger. Reference was made to the Mexican woman who had taken more than she could handle. There were no incidents, everyone—both inmates and staff—got over the search with as little discomfort as necessary.

Rooms were searched systematically and nothing was destroyed. But in their eagerness to gather contraband, personal, legally issued articles of clothing, jewelry, pottery, shoes and so on were taken in error. The search of the entire prison, every woman in it, took a little over three hours.

Women who had things of theirs taken as contraband, which were not in fact contraband, and could prove it, petitioned verbally to have these things returned. They were given excuse after excuse and very little was returned to them. After two weeks had passed, tensions were building due to the lack of positive response from administration in regard to the return of personal property, also due to the clumsy, uneducated efforts of staff to bust people using drugs. Even medication that was issued by the nurses became suspect. Because the woman who had almost overdosed was Mexican, the Mexican American Research Organization in the prison was told that they could not have outside guests until an investigation was made. Nor could any of the other groups, but the only group under suspicion was MARO.

Visitors were frequently, during this two weeks, searched, and turned away in some cases because some eager guard decided that some one's mother was a hype, and children were also asked to be searched. Women returning from visits were searched as well. They told us staff were also being searched, but this writer has well founded reason to believe this was a statement made to pacify the tense convicts. In fact, the main source of drugs, a staff member, continued all during this time to supply those women who had cash money with drugs.

A chart, circa 1959, was placed in each control area, describing the symptoms of various drugs and their effects. This was a guideline, supposedly for staff to use in case of suspicion.

On about the 26th of March, thirty-five state employees were called together and told to go to one of the living units and search it thoroughly for drugs. These thirty-five people held various jobs in the prison. Some were cooks, nurses, typists, clerks and some were off-duty custodial staff. But the fact that most of them were not taught how to search, nor were they given any instructions as to what to look for added to the outcome in a disastrous way. Nurses, cooks, clerks and typists are not paid by the state to search convicts or their cells. They are not, in fact, supposed to participate in this kind of thing because of their ignorance of the ways to do it.

At about 1:00 P.M. on the 26th, everyone living in the unit to be searched were locked out of their rooms. If they were in the cottage, they were locked in the recreation room that separates the two sides of the unit. The search ended about 4:00 P.M. Behind them these thirty-five people left torn up photographs of children and loved ones, disheveled linens and in some cases footprints on sheets, plants un-potted, gravel in fish tanks torn up, fish dead, parakeets hysterical from being searched, coffee spilled out of jars, makeup dug out of jars, creams probed—and in general a total disrespect for the personal propriety of the convicts that lived there. They were unnecessarily destructive of things that in many cases hold the sentimental value such as children's photos. Things were taken in the guise of being contraband—again that were not in fact contraband. Jewelry, wigs, dentures, toilet paper, Bibles and even a bowl or two of guppies were taken as "contraband."

Dinner that night was tense, uptight, angry and ready to explode. I thought that night was awful, but the next day I was to learn what it feels like to be in the midst of a human explosion.

The next day, at 1:00 P.M., thirty-five employees at the prison descended en masse on the unit in which I was housed. I was at work. The women in the unit across the path came and got me. They were angry, upset and demanding that we do something to stop this madness. I went illegally—out of bounds—to the superintendent's office. She had the associate superintendent and the chief of institutional police (a WCS IV) with her. . . . I demanded that they go at once to the unit I lived in and stop the destruction taking place there. They said they couldn't do that, that it was a necessary precaution against drug use in the prison.

I then told them in blunt, hostile words that unless they stopped the pigs in the unit, I was going to incite a riot that was already well on its way to becoming. They told me I was too smart to do that. . . . They then proceeded at a very slow pace to go to the unit and survey the holocaust that their subordinates had created under the title of searching. The administrators did not stop the search, they did not request that the staff be more careful not to destroy, they in fact merely looked on for over an hour.

At four that day, the yard was a bubbling boiling sea of indignation. It was decided by some of the women who are usually looked to for leadership by the rest of the population, that the next day no one would go to work nor would we lock in. We would lay out on the grass and refuse to move until our requests were met, our property returned or paid for by the state, and a guarantee given that this kind of thing would never happen again.

The cooperation of some six hundred women did not come until they were pushed so far up the wall by the staff they had no choice. Women with parole dates were ready to forfeit their freedom for this cause, others who intimated they would not cooperate were told in vague terms what their station within the prison would be if they didn't. It is not easy to be told by the forty women you live with that none will ever speak to you again if you do not join with them.

By that night the feelings in the units were that we shouldn't wait until tomorrow, we should sit down in the TV rooms, refuse to be counted at ten or to go to our cells until our things were returned. Since tear gas had been used on three women not too many weeks prior, this idea had its dangers and most of the constructive women in the prison wanted to avoid any physical violence that the pigs might incite by their attitudes and/or actions.

At this point, this writer and several other women were called to a special meeting with the associate superintendent as representatives from each living unit. . . . His offer (broadcast at ten over the telex): by eight the next morning every article of contraband would be returned, and a meeting would be held with every counselor present and representatives from the convict body as well as the Inmate Advisory Council. Everyone locked in by ten-thirty that night, with the agreement that if at 8 the next morning things were not returned, the prisoners would not go to work but would proceed to the original protest plan. The only ones exempt from this were hospital workers. . . .

At the meeting the next day, the only agreement we could reach was that the superintendent should have a face to face confrontation with the entire campus as soon as possible. At eight that morning, almost everything was returned, but the women had not been given any assurance that this would not happen again. . . . So as we ended the meeting, we were told that the lawn was covered with convicts, that they refused to eat, work or move. We were asked to go out and tell them that the superintendent would meet with them and hear them out at 2 P.M. in the auditorium. We were also asked to keep things under control, which we refused to do. We felt that we were all together on this, and none of us could make a commitment or decision for all of us.

I told the women in my unit that I was with them, if they decided not to listen, or if they felt they were not being given honest commitments from the prison, we would all go to the rack together. That if one of them got into it, all of us were in it. This same thing was said in every unit that day.

At 2:00 P.M., the auditorium was packed. There were four men, in suits, whom we had never seen before, escorted by staff and seated at the back of the room. Earlier that day, myself and another convict had heard the WCS IV [guard] telephone one of the men's prisons nearby and request support, extra guards, etc. Thus, the four men were in fact armed with guns of some kind, and were not merely observing. We'd been told they were reporters, but when I asked one where he was from he said CIM [California Institution for Men].

The confrontation went on and on, not only the searches, but many grievances were aired. Nothing much was accomplished, unless you consider a promise made by a cornered prison administrator an accomplishment. We were told: we would not be abused in this way again; the clothing and property cards would be brought up to date; staff would continue to search but would be required to leave things as she found them and to have the women called to the unit before the search. Staff would also have a form to fill out with room number and convict's name and a complete list of anything staff removed from the room on it.

Two things that came out of the confrontation that had more of an effect than the searches did: One, a woman who had spoken out in the auditorium was given a 115 [a write-up] later that day for a minor thing, and the Parole Board prolonged her release date for thirty days. The other thing was that certain convicts were labeled leaders, inciters, agitators, militants and several other words that the staff evidently didn't know the meaning of. And these labels are still stuck on us. Our mail was read thoroughly, we were watched, baited, and verbally attacked by several staff.

The fact that we could have blown the prison apart with not only a loss of staff lives, but our own, was never recognized. It still is not recognized.

When one of those "leaders" or "militants" asks for anything that is usually granted to other convicts, they are denied—but in such a way that there is no recourse for them. I recently received a relatively short time by the Parole Board for parole consideration. This was because they know that to keep me here can only bring my boiling point down lower, that they have not been successful by any of their tactics in trying to force change upon me, and that there is no real reason to keep me here that could be justified in a courtroom.

Prisoners—like citizens in larger communities—seem to respond to exploitation not because of political theories but because of a sense of themselves as human beings. It seems remarkable that although these women were putting their lives on the line, the aim and the effect of their resistance was only to change degrading institutional procedures. The most obvious achievement of their work stoppage was the promise of more sophisticated and respectful search procedures—not abolition of them. The outburst subsided pretty quickly after it began—as most prison "riots" do—and the prison structure remained intact. For staff to label any protesting woman a "revolutionary" was, as the writer said, a misnomer.

For prisoners to rebel at extreme jeopardy to themselves is the exception, not the rule. As the inmate writer said, "The cooperation of some six hundred women did not come until they were pushed so far up the wall by the staff they had no choice." Every day in prison, inmates exhibit noncooperation, "malingering," disdain for the structure, and resentment of authority. But these small acts of resistance differ from conscious attempts to overthrow the criminal justice system or the prison itself. A lot of people theorize that if they lived under a totalitarian regime, they would fight back relentlessly, would take up arms and lay their lives on the line. In theory this sounds fine, but in actuality a totalitarian society has its system of rewards, incentives, punishments, and coercion to keep people in line—just like the society of prison.

Prisoners accept certain standards of fair treatment within the system that controls their lives. Only those willing to risk death or indefinite confinement will consistently revolt in an open manner. No one in the "Free World" should doubt that he or she would behave much differently under the same system.

Another interesting aspect of this story is what it suggests about inmate loyalty. Women who "intimated they would not cooperate were told in vague terms what their station within the prison would be if they didn't." Inmate loyalty is part of the unspoken prison code. But as we have seen before, extra privileges, honor status, parole, and other considerations serve to break down solidarity on a day-to-day basis. The result is the individual's need to create personal strategies for accommodation and survival that will still meet the basic requirements of the code.

Balancing individual survival with peer pressure can be a delicate matter. At times the peer pressure can be stifling and exacerbate tensions within the prison. Sometimes it's self-destructive. James Ward, a young black correctional counselor at CIW, for instance, said that because of peer pressure on inmates, he had been "ineffective" in one cottage, despite his belief that the prisoners were desperately in need of change.

"I felt my approach was pretty much rejected," he said. "I assumed the women would appreciate a new concept, and as a result I made a lot of mistakes in dealing with this population at its own level. One thing that hurt me more than anything else was I felt that some of the women would like to do what I'd suggest. But the culture is so strong that if they're accepting the staff, the person is automatically interpreted as rejecting her peers and culture.

"It's hard to work with a group that's rejecting you outright or sitting silently while others do—or to have women come into the office afterwards and tell you what they really feel but not say it in front of the group. Some of the women would be one person in the group and another in my office. This was hard for me to accept."

Sometimes peer pressure is used for democratic purposes and results in petitions, grievances, or peaceful revolts. It seems that inmates are becoming increasingly aware of their rights and taking more risks. Administrators say they're getting "more militant." Women and men in prisons all over the country are more and more questioning why they are in prison while so many other criminals—particularly upper-class criminals—are walking free.

As a result of the jailing of civil rights and antiwar demonstrators, prisoners otherwise isolated have been exposed to the politics of civil disobedience, as well as to white, brown, and black militants. These middle- and upper-class newcomers also have been exposed to and shed light on the conditions inside jails and prisons in America. They have addressed many conditions that longtime prisoners previously saw as a way of life, "normal" for prison.

Increasing numbers of prisoners are beginning to look beyond immediate conditions to the system in broader terms. A demonstration at the Federal Reformatory for Women in Alderson, West Virginia, that began on September 14, 1971, reflected the increasing sophistication of demands affecting the entire system. On that date the women at Alderson held a memorial service for the twenty-nine inmates and ten guards who had been killed by the indiscriminate gunfire of state policemen and prison guards at Attica Prison in New York the previous day. Following the service and a march around prison grounds, which was approved by the administration, some of the women gathered to sleep in the prison yard. Earlier in the summer three hundred women had signed a petition urging clarification and reform of parole procedures. It was part of a petition campaign in many federal prisons. Nothing had been done about it, and there had been a growing dissatisfaction with the lack of results.

About 130 black, white, and Latina women then occupied the old garment factory on the prison grounds and drew up forty-two demands to present to the administration. Representatives from various cottages sat in on the sessions, and after the first day, some 500 women out of the 600-inmate population stopped work and school for four days in support of the demands. Prison officials, along with a lawyer from the Federal Bureau of Prisons, agreed to a number of changes but said that many of the others were "out of our jurisdiction." They told the grievance committee that the demands agreed to would need to be rewritten in "legal language" and then would be implemented. The women said they would wait to see how the agreements were written up.

On Saturday, September 18, male guards wearing gas masks and carrying sticks were called into the prison. The women left the building to avoid a violent confrontation. Prison officials announced the incident was over and that agreements about grievances had been negotiated successfully.

But women in various cottages were still talking about continuing the work stoppage until demands were implemented. On Monday, September 20, about forty guards from neighboring correctional institutions came on "campus" with gas masks and sticks. A Greyhound bus was parked nearby. One of the men called out names of prisoners through a bullhorn, and sixty-six women were ordered without warning to board the bus. When some resisted, they were maced and dragged aboard. The women were transferred to the Federal Youth Center at Ashland, Kentucky. About ten days later, fifty-nine were flown to the federal penitentiary at Seagoville, Texas, and the others were returned to Alderson. Their families and lawyers were not informed of the move.[5]

Some of the women from Alderson said they'd like to know what programs could have been set up at Alderson with the money the Federal Bureau of Prisons used to finance the flight to Texas alone. The women's demands had related directly to the prison itself, including the establish-

5. Several courts have held that transferring an inmate to another prison, either to the same or to a different security level, does not violate any rights of the prisoner (National Institute of Corrections, 1991).

ment of a work-release program, an open mail policy, more caseworkers, sufficient diet planning (pork-free, bland, low-salt, etc.), more complete commissary stock, and lower prices. They asked for a complete law library, as well as medical examinations as a prerequisite for job assignments and sufficient reasons for severe disciplinary punishment. Also related to institutional life were demands for the freedom to choose cottages and to have washers and dryers in the cottages.

The chief focus of the demands, however, was on larger issues. The women asked for contracts for halfway houses and for Congress to appropriate enough funds to enable educational rehabilitation programs to function properly. They also demanded that funds be appropriated for emergency furloughs, in cases such as critical illnesses, family deaths, and childbirth.

Much of the women's distress was directed at the parole system. They, along with federal prisoners in Danbury, Connecticut, and Springfield, Missouri, demanded these changes in the operation and effect of the U.S. Parole Board:

1. The Parole Board should recognize that prison is destructive of our personalities, our humanity, and our ability to cope well with society. Since this effect is contrary to the Bureau of Prisons' expressed aim of "rehabilitation," the board should adopt the policy of speedy release for all prisoners.

2. The Parole Board should be required to give reasons for its decisions.

3. Parole Answers for both hearings and write-ins should be given within two weeks.

4. A person should have access to all the material in the file that the Parole Board uses to judge her case.

5. There should be no parole restrictions that interfere with a person's freedom of association, freedom of travel, and freedom to participate in legal, political and social activities. Parole should not be revoked without a positive conviction on a new charge.

6. People released on mandatory release rather than parole should not be under restrictions.

7. There should be a party beyond the Parole Board to whom parole or mandatory release revocations and Parole Board decisions can be appealed.

8. The Bureau of Prisons should insure that there is institutional cooperation for prisoners who want help with their release plans (jobs, furloughs, contacting potential employers and community resources, etc.).

9. Lawyers should be made available to represent or advise people before and during their parole hearings, when this service is requested.

Women are still kept waiting in the isolated hills of West Virginia for eight to twelve weeks following their interviews before they hear whether they'll be granted or denied parole or commutation. Sometimes prisoners are given the results of hearings that have enormous impact on their lives in ways that seem unbelievably malicious. For instance, at Bedford Hills prison in New York, New Year's Eve is the time women hear the news of whether or not they have received clemency. Why begin any woman's new year that way? "Not one human being out of 54,000 worthy of compassion last year," Jean Harris wrote in *Marking Time*. "Not one human being out of 55,000 worthy of compassion this year. . . . Either the justice system must be infallible, or the prison system must be a total failure. I wonder why they don't just close the Clemency Bureau and give the money saved to the WIC Program or Head Start or some other place where the money wouldn't be wasted."

Ninety-eight percent of the women in prison will eventually get out, whether it's on parole or at the termination of their maximum sentence. Ninety-eight percent of all prisoners are eventually released. Will their voices be heard before they hit the street? And will anyone listen then?

9 SNAPSHOTS

Women's Stories, Women's Lives

> When you starts measuring somebody, measure him right, child, measure
> him right. Make sure you done taken into account what hills and val-
> leys he come through before he got to wherever he is.
>
> —Mama Younger's advice to her daughter, from Lorraine Hansberry's
> *A Raisin in the Sun*

Dealing with Death

"When I was here the first time," Patty Velasquez says, "my husband of five years died of an overdose. The next day a friend of ours came and broke the news to me. She'd read it in the obituaries in the paper and she brought me the little article. It was only about three paragraphs long. It was just a notice of death. It didn't explain anything. I had just moved on campus and at that time they were real strict here. I asked them for a phone call to call my brother-in-law to find out what happened.

"The correctional counselor told me I couldn't call him because he had a record, but that I could call my husband's parole officer. He couldn't tell me anything but that they were still investigating the cause and circumstances of his death.

"The police [prison staff member] called and asked for medication because I was quite upset. She asked for medication 'cause she was trying to help me. I was standing there as she was talking on the phone and I heard her say, 'I beg your pardon?' She held the phone out and I heard with my own ears: 'She is a drug addict and she is going to have to learn how to cope with tragedy without the aid of narcotics.' The staff started crying. She couldn't do anything for me.

"I was up three days and three nights. My friend went to the doctor and said, 'She's just sitting there reading the article over and over. She's blowing it; she won't talk to nobody.' The second day, they came and told me I was to go to work in the kitchen. I said I wasn't going anywhere. My friend went and asked to take my place, but they wouldn't let her. Finally about the fourth day I went over to the doctor and told him what the nurse had said. He blew up. He gave me the tranquilizers.

"That was probably the ugliest thing that's happened to me here. It may sound like a little thing to some people but when you're locked up . . . I could have blown it. Broads have hung themselves for less.

"They used to send inmates into the room when a broad had hung herself. The inmates had to photograph her and cut her down. I was here once when the broad that took photographs was told to go into fifty-seven. She wasn't told what she was going to photograph. She went in and saw the broad hanging there and just blew it. She really flipped out."

Patty Velasquez arrived at the California Institution for Women several years ago, when CIW was "rigid, strict control." Now that the prison had become more open and treatment oriented, it might seem that this sort of inhumane handling of a partner's death wouldn't happen. But what happened to Frances, a fifty-year-old first-time offender convicted of fraud, gave testimony to the rigidity of any prison system, no matter how open. Frances herself called it "a good example of the coldness here."

"I came in here last November," Frances said. "I had just been in here three days and I still didn't even know where I was. They took me out of noon count, which was an unusual thing. My counselor took me aside and just said, 'We just had a call that your husband is dead.' Just like that.

"I've never been down on my knees in my life but I was on my knees to Mr. Kehler. Wasn't there any way I could get out to make arrangements and to go to his funeral? There were only the two of us. I didn't get to go out. I didn't even know when he was buried. My husband laid in the mortuary for four days because I couldn't do anything. They did let me make a couple of phone calls and let somebody come to visit. But then to top it all, I was evaluated as 'emotionally passive' and they put me in the hospital because they thought I was suicidal. We'd been together more than twenty years. But like my counselor told me: *'It is awfully hard to get here.'*

"Even when that happened with my husband, I basically understood it. I was in custody and there are rules and regulations. You can't forget you did something wrong and you're in prison.

"The only thing I resent and resent deeply is that I was promised by my lawyer and the district attorney that if I copped a guilty plea I'd get probation. I waived all my rights before the court—they say, 'No one promised you anything, this or that'—and you swear to it. When I went to court for the sentencing, the judge sentenced me to prison, not to probation. I have cancer of the abdomen and need radium treatments. The judge stipulated I get whatever I need in here, but I haven't yet. The judge said he figured I had cancer when I committed the crime, so I should have considered it."

Pat Red Cloud

"Coming here to prison wasn't too much of an adjustment for me," Pat said. "It's a lot like Indian boarding school was. I was raised on a reservation and then they took me to boarding school on the same reservation when I was five and a half years old. I never left until I was thirteen. So for eight years I was confined to just that one area. The school was very confining, very strict."

The woman talking was "Pat Red Cloud," a member of the Blackfoot Indian tribe in Canada. A tall, exquisite woman with smooth umber skin, strong facial bones, and long, straight black hair, Pat guided me around the grounds of the California Institution for Women. She spoke in low tones, her words deliberate and sometimes spoken after long pauses of thought. We stopped repeatedly and in silence watched birds in flight, studied two fat goldfish in a small pond by the greenhouse, and looked up at the vast expanse of blue sky dotted with white clouds.

"We can have birds and fish in our rooms," she told me after pointing out where the lawn crew works and telling me of the job details women prisoners have as auto mechanics, electricians, plumbers, tractor drivers, and maintenance "men." "A man drives the dump truck, but women haul the trash and do all the work," she said. "They repair lamps and TVs and radios and do all the painting. The place is pretty well run by inmates themselves."

Pat had been at the prison at Frontera for eight months on a forgery conviction. It was her first offense. "I was lucky, though," she said. "They could have gotten me for a lot more checks than they did. I wrote more than I can even count now."

While pointing out blatant contradictions such as the green recreation yard being closed for the Southern California "winter" and opened for three "summer months," Pat said that in spite of the pressures, "I've learned a lot about myself here. In some ways it's been good, and now I just want to learn more about myself and how to better communicate with people, because that's my number one problem. It always has been.

"They say problems here develop because of lack of communication between staff and inmates. But it's not lack of communication between staff and inmates, it's lack of communication between staff and staff. That's what creates problems. We really run our own lives. For me the problem has always been lack of communication between me and other people, period.

"When I was thirteen, they closed down the boarding school I attended and sent me to a city about a hundred miles away from my home to junior high school. The adjustment was tremendous. There were three Indian students there. By the next year I was the only Indian there. I stayed there through the twelfth grade as the only Indian. A lot of the students there used to make cracks at me for being a 'savage.' The only Indian they had seen was the Hollywood Indian. They thought I was nonverbal and illiterate—only making little grunts and 'ughs' here and there. That's how Hollywood had portrayed Indians.

"I lived with five different foster parents, who were paid to house me from the ninth grade to the twelfth grade. All they were keeping me for was the money. They didn't take me in as their own. Some of them tried, but they didn't know how to communicate with me. I was backward and shy.

"A lot of times I was tempted to go back to the reservation and just live there. If it wasn't for the encouragement of my parents I probably would have gone back and still be there. I was just going through all sorts of turmoil. The only place I ever felt at home was in the Indian organization they had for Indian people that lived in the city. I felt they were the only people who understood what I was going through. No one seemed to have the interest or understanding about what I was going through except my fellow Indians. Somehow I managed to go through high school, but I wasn't a very good student. If I didn't have all those adjustments I probably could have been a better student. But it was lonely.

"Like many other Indians just coming from the reservation, I had that problem communicating with people. So many times I wanted to communicate my thoughts and feelings, but it didn't seem important enough. I was afraid no one would listen, because they never had; they never had gotten down to the core. I guess I just more or less withdrew into myself and I felt that no one really gave that much care, really.

"Then I wanted to keep on in school but I wasn't happy with that sort of life. I thought changing my environment might be better and people would be more understanding. So I enrolled in a church-oriented school in Provo, Utah, where I thought I might be able to help myself with the help of others. I felt I wouldn't be too far away from my people because I knew there were other Indian people there. And so I journeyed down there not knowing anyone or anything except the fact that I was getting away from this previous environment where I felt like a stranger, and knowing I did not want to return to the reservation, knowing I would never be happy staying the rest of my life on the reservation, and knowing I couldn't leave if I didn't get an education.

"So when I went to school in Utah, I got involved in Indian activities they had there at the time. It was a very beautiful experience. I was more at ease there. The Indian students were able to communicate with each other, and we could express our feelings to each other. The students were more open and accepted me so much better. There were about six or seven of us from Canada and all of us tremendously enjoyed that environment, free from the red tape we had to go through in Canada just because we were Indians from the reservation.

"I think those were two of the most beautiful years I had in my life. I felt so happy. I was starting to open up. Before, I'd been so afraid to talk to any stranger.

"I wanted to stay and finish school, but I didn't have the funds to finish my education. We had had a grant from Canada, but after two years they dropped it. They thought we could get educated in Canada as well as we could in the United States. I was quite indecisive in what I wanted to do. I was debating whether to go back to Canada, but the experiences there . . . there were too many bad memories. I wanted to investigate and kind of look around to see where I could find a place, so I came to California. I had heard about California and so many opportunities and I thought I could come to L.A. and possibly get into the modeling field. I guess I made a big mistake—coming unprepared, not knowing anyone.

"I was scared. I was lonely. The first people I met that made me feel accepted and at home were some black people who were into another way of life. I hung on to them as my friends. I guess they knew I was an easy person—I didn't know much about city life. They made their game sound very easy and very exciting. Their game was forgery.

"One thing I had in my mind was to get some money saved for going back to school to finish my education. So their game sounded very inviting. It sounded like easy money, and I thought this is one way I could get money to return to school.

"Before I knew it I seemed to get further and further into the mess. To tell you the truth—it was exciting. It was sort of fun to just walk into a bank and come out with all that money. It was a different way of life for me. I had never had a lot of money and so many pretty clothes and money in my pocket all the time. I'd never lived in a luxurious apartment and had a luxurious car. We had a 1970 Mark III. I guess I was very adept, and so I just kept on cashing those checks until I got busted."

The inevitability of Pat's getting busted made me laugh. Seeing her striking, unusually beautiful face and her regal Blackfoot carriage is really a memorable experience. She might easily be a movie star. And to think that she walked in and out of banks, oblivious to being identified, getting caught, or being remembered in black and white Los Angeles made us both laugh.

"After I got busted, I got out on bail. My old man even convinced me that money could buy my freedom. So after my first bust I even tried harder to get the money, but I knew then I would end up in some prison or jail. But it seemed the further I got into it, the worse it was to get out of it. I was into forgery for a year. But the deeper I got, I really didn't enjoy getting the money. It was a hassle. But the people I was working with counted on me. Plus by then I was paying lawyers and bail bondsmen. I felt it was my job. At the end I wasn't doing it for good times—I was doing it for necessity to set me free. But it didn't set me free. It just sent me to prison.

"The last time I got busted, the fourth and final time, all the holds popped up from all over. There were so many holds there was no way to get out of it. There were detainers from all over the place. It seemed like an endless thing—it seemed like I'd never get through all those court proceedings. I thought, 'Well, this is it.' I guess that was the moment I had been waiting for all the time. I knew this would happen, I might as well accept it. It was kind of a relief for me.

"I had fourteen counts of forgery. I had so many different names I can't even remember them. I went to the first county—the one I got popped in—and they sent me to prison for observation. I dreaded going to all the other fourteen counties. I went crazy in county jail. Every time they would take me out to court I would just look at everything I could see. A tree. The sky. It meant so much to me. It makes it much easier for me to do time when I can see life around me. Inside a jail with those bars and everything, you start to forget there's a world. You miss the earth.

"So anyway, the second county I went to, I said, 'Well, I give up. I don't want to go to all these other counties. Send me to prison, I may as well get started doing time in prison.' By some miracle they dropped all the other charges on me, so I'm here on one commitment. So here I am on another reservation, feeling lucky I didn't get more time.

"My old man's on the lam, so I can't see him or write him. One of the stipulations of my parole is that I can't see him. That's going to be hard, but maybe it's best, because I don't want to get back into that life. I love

him though, and I'm going to keep our baby. He's a beautiful child.''
Their son, almost a year old, was in a foster home while Pat was in prison.

"While I was in L.A. before, I wanted to go down to the Indian Center,
but I never got a chance to. I was too busy running in and out of banks.

"My greatest desire now is to possibly work in a city and help my
fellow Indians that are coming from the reservations, to help them in their
problems in adjusting to city life. One thing my brother Indians need is a
helping hand and a listening ear from someone who understands.

"It's hard for me even now. I guess I never really knew what I wanted
and I really didn't know what was being offered to me. I was just confused,
I guess. This experience sort of stopped my world and gave me time to
think. But now, just knowing what I do now and experiencing what I've
experienced, I think the biggest thing is to know me better and communicate with the world better. I still have my whole life ahead of me.''

Trinada

Trinada has been on heroin since she was a teenager. She has been in jail
off and on for short stays frequently in the last twenty years—"so many
times I can't even count 'em no more.'' I met her in county jail in California shortly after I had turned thirty and she had turned thirty-eight on the
same birthday—February 4. I was feeling young, as if my life were just
beginning, and she was feeling old and as if her life were almost over. "It
is old, if you think about it in terms of running around in the life,'' she
said.

Trinada had been found guilty of violating 11500.5 Health and Safety
Code: possession of narcotics with intent of sales. She got a one-year
sentence with a five-year parole. The six months she had spent in jail
awaiting trial were counted as ''dead time''—not counting toward her sentence. When we met, she had three more weeks before release. If she
violates parole anytime within the next five years, she will have an automatic two-to-twenty-year sentence to serve in the state penitentiary.

"When I got this sentence here, the court put me on methadone. So
when I get out with that help, and my own, I should stay drug free. I also
have Naline parole and probation for the next five years. Naline is a shot
they give you to test your eyes to tell if you have any trace of narcotics in
your system, period. They also give you a urinalysis test whenever they
want; it's up to your parole officer. That's why so many people are being
returned to jail.''

The jail Trinada was in was strictly regimented. There were no educational or vocational programs or drug therapy. The women just worked

manual jobs and slept. They were not allowed to dance or to laugh out loud in the dining hall. It was run by deputy sheriffs—the same as other county jails in California.

"A place like this, there's less chance of any type of drugs or alcohol getting into the institution. Here, it's discipline. You learn to control yourself. Your wants and your needs are inside yourself. And you can't do anything about it. Plus, you're doing short time so you can't sneak anything in. It's telling me, 'You can do without'—'You don't have to have'—so I guess it's good for me.

"But locking up addicts or alcoholics is not the answer. It's only good on a thirty-to-sixty-day basis to dry you out, 'cause your body can only take so much. But it really doesn't make sense. But then, neither does California Rehabilitation Center. I was there, and in my personal opinion, it's a farce. What can one dope fiend do for another? They're the same people you've shot drugs with all your life. What good's it do? Maybe it would be good for youngsters, fourteen- and fifteen-year-olds, but not for us. Besides, the staff are all these people who've learned from books and don't know shit.

"People who get jobs there should have knowledge of life, not books. Then maybe it could mean something. You have these fresh-face, naïve little things trying to find out what it's all about, and they can't begin to get to your problems. They're hung up with all the details on the way.

"I don't know why the state feel they're God Almighty and can tell you how to live your life. There's too many strikes against you. Society on the one side, the man on the other, parents on the other, and you jump right on in it.

"The first thing I'm gonna do after I get my first drink is go and see my new grandbaby and see my kids. I might have to go see the parole and probation officer before I get home, though. They say I must maintain employment. But at my age, I'm not thinking about it. I'll probably sit home and knit and crochet—there's good money in it to sell the stuff. At this stage of the game I don't want to spend the rest of my time behind somebody else's bars and gates and things.

"My man needs me, and my kids. I still got three at home. They're six, twelve, and eighteen years old and staying with their dad's family. I'm still with him. There's too many years and memories wrapped up in that—can't cut that loose. We can stay together and we will stay together, even though he's still a junkie. We always been together. They tried to keep us apart, but we went to court about that years ago. We fought it and won. They don't give us no trouble now.

"No, my main fear now is, Will I be able to maintain myself without getting involved in any things that are unnecessary? I have a real fear of getting busted and returned. And I don't wanna face no twenty years in the penitentiary. I don't wanna die in no penitentiary. So I'm gonna try. Just try and maintain myself. I know I can make it.''

Willie King

Willie King got busted on an 11721: being under the influence of narcotics. The judge told her 180 days, but when she got to jail, the papers said nine months. (Another nine-month scar in Willie's mangled thirty-nine years on earth.)

"I couldn't even count all the times I been here."

Willie's been going to jail since she was seventeen and busted for prostitution. Next she got three years for forgery, then petty theft with a prior conviction—which meant prison time. Next time, for parole violation. "In '52 I got me a public defender to send me to the penitentiary. PD, yeah, prison deliverer."

"All that time . . . Now, I could see it for robbery or killing, but not for misdemeanors. I'm always incarcerated."

Willie's a trustee in the jailhouse laundry. "Whatever officer is on tells you what you have to do. Today the officer she asked me to help on the mangle and folding gowns. I don't do no officer's blouses. If I did they wouldn't wear them."

Between trips to jail, Willie lives near her mother in Los Angeles. "The police out in the street dislike me. They try to proposition me and I go off on them. I just get out and they start coming around. They tell me when I get out, they'll send me back. They keep harassing me. They know me real well.

"My mother lives in the district, and I like to be close to her. But at this rate, I might as well move away. I'm always incarcerated.

"You know, I'm not going to let them rehabilitate me. I'm the only one who can rehabilitate me.

"If the police wouldn't harass me, I'd straighten up. I'd get off dope and try to get my children back and not commit no crimes. But as long as they try to keep me away from it and demand I don't do it, I'm gonna do it!''

Georgia Walton

Georgia Walton is the kind of all-American beauty you see in television advertisements and in *Better Homes and Gardens*. At twenty-seven, with teased blond hair, slightly lightened and bouffant, she still carries the self-assurance of a high school cheerleader going steady with the captain of the football team. She tells me she has been at the Sybil Brand Institute for Women for three years, four months, and four days, and there is no question in her posture: she is a deputy sheriff, a guard, not an inmate.

Georgia Walton is a wife, mother, and model of military discipline in the long, sanitized corridors of the Sybil Brand Institute. She turns keys and recites rules meticulously, almost automatically, with no need to pause for breath. She's a woman who loves her work. She's made for it, and it's made for her. She walks tall and proud in her deputy sheriff's military green skirt and regulation jacket. Her white blouse is spotless, neat, ironed with starch. Her flat regulation oxford shoes, polished to a spit shine, are the only police feature that make her look more like a deputy sheriff than an airline stewardess.

As we walk from the "heartbeat of the jail," the name she and other officers call the control center, Georgia Walton begins to explain the booking process, the "pat search," and the "narco search" in great detail. Her recitation seems automatic, chronicling each step of the process, but she is constantly alert, vigilant to inmate movement. On guard, in control. She has to be, she says. That's the way it is.

"After the inmate has been booked, given the pat search, the narco search, bathed, sprayed, and dressed, she is brought over here," she says, pointing out all the equipment in a small room. "Everyone is required to have fingerprints and a photograph. If her hand is burned, we put her on Identification Room Hold. If it heals while she is here, then the fingerprints are taken. If she's ready for release and her hand's not healed or is still in a cast or something, she is allowed to leave without having been fingerprinted. And then we are left with no fingerprints. That happens rarely, but it has happened."

This is one of the few exceptions to the rules that Georgia Walton pointed out. Generally, there are no exceptions. Security reasons don't allow them. She points out the security telephones. "These are all security phones, just like the one I showed you in the fingerprinting room. You can just pick up the phone. I don't even need to say where I am. The light on the main control board shows the exact location. The moment you take it off the hook, the light goes on in the control room and they send in reinforcements within seconds. It's a very effective system."

Georgia Walton understands her job and respects it. She is upset when she hears criticism of the training she got or the job she does. "Some people think that law enforcement officers are inhumane or uninteresting," she says. "Personally, if I became personally involved with every person sitting there crying, I couldn't function in my job. I'm not inhumane—I'm just removed from the emotion.

"If I became upset and showed it, I would lose my self-control and my control over the inmates. If someone has a bloody nose, I say, 'You've got a bloody nose. Sit down. I'll call the nurse.' I cannot lose my self-control. I cannot become emotionally involved. Even though I'm concerned sometimes, I cannot show it.

"I really love my work. This is the kind of work I always wanted to do. My father was a policeman. My husband is a policeman. Ever since I was a little girl I said I wanted to be a policewoman. Now I am one. Even though I'm called a deputy, it's the same thing really. It's just a different name."

Ms. Walton attributes her self-control and skill to her training for the job at the Sheriff's Academy, where she had a stringent sixteen-week training course. "Other people criticized it in an article in the L.A. *Times,*" she said, "but I really enjoyed it.

"It was wonderful training for me. I think the stress training was especially valuable. Every word out of your mouth began with 'Sir' or 'Ma'am.' We had tests every Monday—sometimes after no time off. We had to shoot with the men, run long distance with them, work out with them, everything just the same. If we were allowed to smoke, we could go get our cigarettes and smoke. But we had to go to our lockers or wherever we kept them. That's because we carried utility bags, not purses. All we could have in them was our handcuffs, revolver, and keys. Women weren't allowed to put lipstick or anything else in there. We couldn't carry cigarettes in our utility bags. If you were caught with cigarettes in your utility bag, you would be up for discipline and punishment. I never carried cigarettes in my utility bag.

"It really is a form of stress training. You have somebody screaming orders at you for sixteen weeks. It's just like the military training. And you get used to the screaming without getting upset. It really developed my self-control. I was yelled at and I had to follow instructions. Now if an inmate yells at me, I don't get upset.

"Classes were also stress. Although there were a couple nonstress. One time we were sitting there and there was a loud noise—like a boom—from behind. You can't turn around in class. Those who turned around had to write a paper on why they turned around. It was like a test to see how much self-control we had, but we didn't know it then. Oh, no, I didn't turn around—I really wondered what it was. But I wouldn't dare turn around."

Marta Fernandez

The petite Chicana deputy sheriff said good-night at the control center and walked with small, precise steps up to the entrance building to the country jail for women. She went to a small safe-deposit box, opened it with one of her ten keys, pulled out a small automatic revolver, and put it into a brown leather holster inside her small brown leather purse along with her badge. She punched her time card, told the two officers in the room good-night, and walked out to her small gray 1960 Porsche. She was wearing her sheriff's uniform—a tight green skirt, white blouse, and military green jacket.

"Marta Fernandez" was giving me a ride back to my hotel from the jail. She hadn't spoken to me from the time we had met until we started to drive down the winding road from the jail back toward the city. Still somewhat shaken at the sight of the gun and the knowledge that she always carries it with her, I commented on what a nice car she had.

"I keep a small car because I don't like to haul people around, and this gives me a good excuse," she said. "I can never fit more than one person in, so it's sort of a built-in safety valve."

She told me that she was single, which put her in a minority of the personnel at the jail. She said that more than half the deputies are married, and half of those are married to other sheriffs. It was 10:30 P.M., and the car was loud on the curving roads that led us into the lights and shadows of the metropolis.

"This work is more liberating than most jobs for women," she said. "We get equal pay all the way and equal opportunities. Less than one percent of the people in the department are women, but we get the same jobs and promotions the men do. We're very lucky. There are not that many jobs for women where you can get this kind of pay.

"But one thing about this job is that it makes social life difficult. The requirements here are more stringent for women than they are for men. They expect us to be more than the average woman. I have to be very careful. The public expects us to be superhuman—or not be human at all. Therefore the requirements are quite strict on our behavior. People will quickly fink on a policewoman. Personally, I don't like to tell people what my job is. If they really push me, I tell them I work for the county. People don't trust you if they know. They have so many attitudes.

"Most police officers associate with people in the same field. I personally don't. I find it too stifling. But unless they're very sensitive, it's hard to retain a friendship with people in other areas when they know what kind of work you do, because they don't approve or they don't trust you.

"The work is a real strain—it takes a lot out of you. It's heartbreaking sometimes. After work I really couldn't take it. I need a totally different environment. Even when I get together with girlfriends who are policewomen—and that's rare—we avoid talking about work. You've got to maintain your sanity."

We had arrived in front of the hotel, but Ms. Fernandez kept talking about her struggles with her work in controlled, carefully chosen words. "I don't expect to stay in this work for all my career. It takes too much out of me; it's just too draining. I'd like to go into an administrative position—maybe in corrections or in the adult authority, where I could have some effect on the decision-making process. You see, I have a little different background than many of the officers, so I have a little different attitude. I see the women and their problems and I think, There but for the grace of God go I. That's why I'd like to do work that's more involved with them. And that's why I'd like an administrative job where I could really effect some change.

"At the jail it's not our duty to become personally involved or to try to rehabilitate or counsel. We're not supposed to. And actually we're so busy booking, fingerprinting and all, there isn't time anyway. The women come in so upset. Some are crying. They think we're so callous and have no human emotion. But we're just so busy processing we don't even have time to get a drink of water half the time. The correctional officers for the state have more freedom. They're not chastised for becoming involved with the girls' problems and personal matters. We are chastised; we are not supposed to become involved in any way. Our duty is custody and security, and that's it. We're there to keep them safe.

"The girls don't think of us as human beings—or as people. Just the little questions they ask—like 'Do you dance?' or 'Would you wear that kind of dress?'—show it. They only see us as robots in green. They must think when we leave here we crawl into a little box. They don't think of us as people.

"And I guess I can understand why—but that doesn't make it any easier. A lot of it is because some of the deputies are in fact only working for the money. The money really attracts people. When I got my B.A. in fine arts, I had a hard time deciding where to go to work. I didn't want to teach in our schools—they're terrible—and this was one of the only good-paying jobs. I had worked as a student in the sheriff's office one summer, and I had a very negative attitude towards policemen. They really turned me off. When I was going to graduate, they said I should try it from the other side and learn what it's like. So I went into it as sort of an experiment. And I've been here three and a half years.

"The problem is that many officers go into the field just for the income, to help their husbands or pay for the mortgage. I think they can be more detached because they're only in it for the money. If they were screened more for interests in the work itself, they could have people be more sensitive. There has to be some kind of balance."

I was still trying to deal with the fact that Deputy Fernandez was an artist, a painter, working as a deputy sheriff, when it was time, finally, for me to get out of her car. I was thinking about my own early attitudes toward cops and her statement, "They must think when we leave here we crawl into a little box," when I got out. The pain in her face was clear, and it taught me a lesson I wouldn't forget.

Louise Bezie

Louise Bezie's face is round and beautiful. Her hair is white. Her eyes sparkle—with interest, with anger. She is seventy-one years old and she's been imprisoned at the California Institution for Women for nearly twenty years. She's been totally deaf for forty-five years.

Early in 1953 she was arrested and charged with second-degree murder. "I was accused of not being deaf from the time I was arrested," she said. "The women deputies at Los Angeles County Jail refused to call out for me. They said they would let me use the phone, but they would not use it for me to call two witnesses I had. They told me, 'You can hear as good as I can.' But if my life had depended on it I could not have called to save my own life.

"I wrote three letters to three doctors that I had gone to back in 1925, when I first lost my hearing after I had scarlet fever. They had given me tests and treatments, but the one doctor finally said I'd never hear again barring a miracle and not to pay out any more money to other doctors. He told me I'd never hear again because the auditory nerves were completely dead. Well, my letters were picked up, but the next A.M. I found them sticking right back between the bars. When breakfast came, I asked the woman deputy about it and she said, 'They could not go out.' When I asked why, she gave no answer, only her back."

Mrs. Bezie talks loudly, drawing deep breaths between statements. She pauses often to make sure I have written down exactly what she is saying. We are sitting on the bed in her room, which is in a CIW cottage for older and handicapped women. When I have a question, I write it down for her. She nods her head and thinks a minute, then answers in precise, loud words. There is an aura of the 1950s about her—as though somehow her world has changed into only a series of details in the last twenty years, leaving the essence of her prior life untouched.

She tells me she had to go to court without any witnesses because she had never been able to call them or get letters out to them. When she went to court she had an attorney, secured by her half sister, who was out of state—but she had never met him before the trial: "I did not see him until I went to court and he came up to me with a piece of paper on which was written, 'My name is Kenneth Lynch. Your sister sent me to defend you.' That was all. Then he walked over and sat on the other side of the courtroom with some court attachés. I was not allowed to have an interpreter."

Louise said "no one wrote" her anything concerning the trial. In other words, no one told her anything about what was going on. "It was my first felony, so I regret to state I was too ignorant to know about court procedures. After I'd been tried and found guilty, some inmate at county jail asked about my transcript, and when I told her I had none she became furious and said, 'You cannot hear that trial, you have been denied the stand, you've been denied a polygraph test, you've been denied a witness, you've been denied an interpreter. You make that crook give you your transcript when you go back for sentence.'"

Louise said that she did get transcripts after she was sentenced, but only after she got back to the jail and read the transcripts did she find out what had happened during the trial. "I had been lied on right there in front of me without me having any way of knowing what they were saying." She said she turned in the copies of her transcripts when she was admitted to CIW, but that they were never returned to her.

"I just lost all hope. No one told me anything about appeal, and I was not well versed in the law, not enough to know it was my privilege, and I am not denying that after reading my transcripts and having been denied every request, I tried my best to wreck this jail when I got here. I was so shocked to find justice a thing of the past in this country of my birth— which now I'm ashamed to admit. I was put in the padded cell in just a jail shift, and it was very cold in December, with only the stone floor and no cover.

"After the initial outrage of feeling I'd been lied to and deceived—as well as everyone thinking I was a fake—I began to do my work and go along the best I could. I worked here at housework—mopping, scrubbing, and cleaning windows—until I was forced into idleness and now I've been idle these past seven years! From this inactivity I contracted kidney trouble and arthritis from nothing but idleness and inactivity. I came to this place strong and healthy. The first year I was kept inactive I contracted both diseases."

"Have you asked to work again?" I wrote.

"I raved about it for several years, and they refused to give me anything to occupy my mind. It was the doctor—who left here in January, thank God—who wouldn't let me work."

In November 1970 Louise Bezie was given parole to a nursing home called the Beverly Manor, in Riverside, California. She was checked out of the institution after seventeen years with an official listing of all her worldly goods. She had saved the receipt. She carefully unfolded it from a collection of papers, to show it to me.

Property Receipt Release

I, Louise Bezie, No. 2004, hereby acknowledge receipt of:

Jewelry: 1 pr. of tweezers, 1 gold filling, 1 silver filling.

Personal Effects:	check	$1,931.00
	check	88.20
	check	20.40

The above property constitutes all jewelry and personal effects held for me by the officials of this institution.

Date *November 12, 1970*　　　　Signed *L. Bezie*
Witnessed *N. Weaver*　　　　　Institution *C.I.W.*
property clerk

"I left here with over two thousand dollars," Louise said. "It was the money from my husband's Social Security. I don't spend much. I had saved it. The home took it from me—and my sister will verify this. You can see the amount of money listed on the form. My parole officer kept my receipt. I asked to be transferred to another home. Instead, they brought me back here. My sister wrote her congressman about the home taking my money and the whole thing. He advised her to get the receipt from the parole officer. It's been fourteen months since then.

"When I left here for the home in Riverside, I was told by my correctional counselor and parole officer due to my deafness that I was going to a place where I would pay a hundred and forty-five dollars a month. When they got me in and the door locked on me, I was informed that I was paying five hundred dollars a month. And when I tried to contact the parole officer, the management at the home told me she had no name or telephone number. I had to smuggle a letter out to my sister giving her all this information what was being done to me. She wrote this administration with threats of having an attorney go to the home and tell my story. Then the superintendent contacted the parole officer to come for me. I lacked four days of being there two months and paid nine hundred and seventy dollars, and the parole officer still had my receipts for the money paid out.

"I had been told they had Medicare there. But you can't believe anything they say here. When I got there I had no Medicare. They were even more strict with their rules there than they are here. I couldn't have a radio in my room. I couldn't go out. They mainly kept me locked in my room. I could hardly breathe in that place. They sprayed almost continually, like we were a bunch of insects.

"The very first night there I had my shower and then went and pulled back the cover to retire. The bed was soaked—a big brown circle reached from one side of the bed to the other—with urine, and the stench almost knocked me down. I went out and said to the aide 'Look at this bed. We do not have to live like varmints even in jail.' Right then I wanted out of that place, my very first night. So we changed the bed.

"They did not even have a throw rug on the floor, which was shower tile. I have a parakeet, and there was not even a table to set his cage on and no library, no handwork in the rooms, no knitting needles or crochet hooks, not even my mother's picture. No face lotions or shampoo bottles or cold creams were allowed. They allowed nothing but a few clothes brought from storage. I said, 'Why, I'm shocked. I had small work scissors, knitting needles, hooks, etcetera, for seventeen years even in jail! I had jars, bottles, and in fact my own Gillette safety razor with removable blade all the time at CIW.' I said, 'This place is worse than jail!' All the mail had to be left open, and if it did not please them it was destroyed. All incoming mail was opened and checks and money removed. My Sis called long distance and wrote me about it later. The manager never let me know one thing about that call.

"Finally, when her letters kept asking me, 'Why don't you write?' I cultivated a maid and made her a promise to pay her, and then she smuggled letters in and out for me from general delivery at the post office. My sister and I wrote to the superintendent here asking her to transfer me to another home. Instead, the parole officer brought me back here January 1971 on a parole violation for 'refusing to cooperate with parole officer.'

"At CIW at least I can shop every week at the canteen—soft drinks, candy, cookies, nuts, canned meats—and our former superintendent [Ms. Carter] let me go to town with a friendly staff member I'd known for fifteen years who was very good here.

"Believe it or not, last year when I went to the parole board about my return from Beverly Manor, I wrote all the details out for them—over nine pages. I told them how I had no parole officer for six weeks when I wanted to appeal for a move. I told them how before I had checked in that all my money had to be left at the office to 'protect it for me' so that I could draw on it when I shopped once a week with a staff member. I also told them how that Christmas 1970 when I wanted twenty-five cents to get my Sis a Christmas card, they refused to give it to me. The parole officer had not left any name or phone number, so I was helpless and wrote to another state to my sister to get help out of there. Well, I handed the nine pages to the board member and he tossed it back to me without reading. Then they showed me what the PO had charged me with: 'refusing to sign checks.'

"My letter and testimony was ignored completely. They called it 'refusing to cooperate with parole officer,' and my God in heaven knows I had no parole officer to cooperate with. How they do lie on people in these places!

"Anyway, I was given two more years here by the parole board. This is paradise compared to that place. I have seen my parole officer only once since I came back from the Beverly Manor, and I ran up to her and asked, 'Where are my receipts? My sister and my congressman want them.' She did not even grunt; she just tossed her head and looked down her nose and brushed past me as if she were defiled. Miss Carlson would not even give me a chance to take it up with her—it's easier to get an interview with the U.S. Supreme Court. Miss Carter was trying to recover those receipts when she retired one year ago this month, but after she left, everything stopped.

"But they do not treat inmates who have families nearby or who are going back to the outside world like they do the ones they know will never go back, and if the truth as it is has been lived and breathed, as I have—you are sure in for the hard way. I tell them, 'You can do no more than kill me. You can't eat me.' I have kept right on talking.

"The problems here are with the staff, not the inmates. There was a television show and Dr. Drieser, a psychologist, said on the television, 'The inmates do not make the trouble here, it's the staff that makes trouble for us.' She speaks the truth. The whole campus was happy when she said that. She is in charge of the Psychiatric Treatment Unit and knows what she speaks of. She is a very brilliant woman and since her truthful statement on TV she is (like me) not so popular with administration and staff at large.

"I think it should be against the law where any totally deaf person is concerned for a psychiatrist to refuse to write out questions. That is not giving us a break. Reading a stranger's lips is very, very difficult. But before I was given my parole in 1970, I had to have an interview with the psychiatrist. I do not know one question he asked me. I just groped and floundered in an attempt to guess what he was asking me. I wanted to hurry and get away from that man, for I knew he thought he was talking to a hearing person, so I just answered at random, 'Yes, no, I don't know,' etcetera. How can one answer a question correctly if they do not know what the question is?

"I do not know his name, because he came from the outside. I do not even hear my own voice, so I do not even have the pleasure of talking to myself. I cannot hear what I have to say." She smiles.

"It is very hard being handicapped in a place like this. Here in CIW I was once put in solitary with not even a shift, not even panties, just like I came into the world, no water in the cell, no toilet, just a hole in the floor with a pipe. No towel, no mattress, just a stone floor and my bare skin. I was sixty-five years old at the time, seventy-one now. I was in there for three weeks' lockup over crackers. Just because I had a few illegal crackers that were given to me by a kitchen girl in my room. I was sent to PTU from Walker after three weeks' lockup.

"I'm in the same kind of spot that the Jackson boy was in San Quentin. He had given out the rotten truth and also told his attorney, friends, and parents that he would never leave there alive. I do not believe that boy was killed trying to escape. They—the guards—just knew it was the best opportunity they would ever have to get him. I have talked to any number of inmates here who have brothers, husbands, etcetera in that same prison and write all the lowdown direct from there. That boy was doomed and he knew it, for he kept right on putting out the truth regardless of the punishment, just as I have done and will continue to do until death stills my tongue and hand.

"I do not believe anyone is out to kill me. They have other plans for me and that's to keep me where I can never talk. You are the first outsider I've had a chance to talk with in private in eighteen years and I think the Good Lord must have sent you to me."

In August 1972 I got a letter from Louise that began:

DEAR BUDDY
. . . I will not put your name here until I'm out of this isolation for it might be lifted. An old wore out whore and bootlegger from Little Rock, Ark., told a lie on me and got me in deep trouble. Been locked for three days now and have had not one person stop from CC, adm, or committee even stop to ask me if I'm guilty or not. Been taking dope from clinic to knock myself out so I will not go crazy. No sound in the world and now nothing to see. . . .

Now I am lied on again and no way to prove it again. If only they had a polygraph here; they are dependable. I am not being punished for anything I did. But the more they punish me the more determined it makes me. . . .

I'm afraid I will never have the opportunity at my ghost writer or the book on this place I said I would write after I first was here. But I would gladly submit to a lie detector test, sodium pentothal, or any other truth medication known to medical science to prove every word I have told you where and when you visited me, is the truth. I have suffered and screamed but it has fell on deaf ears.

Constance Johnson

Constance, a young white social worker at the women's prison in Marysville, Ohio, accompanied me around the grounds one morning and watched me talk with prisoners. As we walked together that afternoon, she told me she had observed that I wasn't getting a "total random sampling of prisoners."

"You are talking to women who are aggressive enough to come up to you—and the ones you seem to pick are aggressive, too," she said. "You are missing a lot of more meek people who have good things to say. These are the ones who are good workers and good citizens. While you were in the sewing industry, for instance, they stayed at their jobs and kept working. The ones with poorer work records who need closer supervision felt freer to come up and talk to you. There are a lot of passive people here who were scared to death when they came in—and many of them feel that prison has helped them."

She then accompanied me to the infirmary, where she introduced me to another Constance—this one Constance Arlene Johnson—a very small, middle-aged black woman intently scrubbing and mopping the narrow hallway between the rows of tiny rooms for prisoners who are sick. Each of the dilapidated infirmary rooms contained a bed and a sink. Sick women walk to the end of the hallway to go to the bathroom, and I had heard complaints that you weren't allowed to walk to the toilet unless you had the nurse's approval. ("If you're not sick when you go to the hospital, you're bound to get sick while you're there," one inmate had said. "It's the most disgusting place in the institution outside max.")

Constance Johnson said she works in the hospital every day of the week. "Most of 'em here, they ain't sick the way they eat," Constance said, glancing up at me but never pausing from mopping the floor. "They mainly just don't want to go to work one day. But they get here, and they don't want to stay. This is less appealing than their rooms. Inmates are not allowed to run the hall here. If they're sick, they stay in their rooms the way they should."

Her small-boned face, graced with high cheekbones and a strong jaw, wore a hard and bitter expression. "Look, they'll tell you this place is terrible now. You'd think the world owes them something," she said. "But life is what you make it. If you make a hard bed for yourself, you sleep hard. If you make your bed soft, you sleep soft. I was here from '64 to '66, and I liked it better then. There were more experienced women.

"Now there are too many teenagers here. They be destructive, they be out to satisfy themselves. I know what people say about how it is here, but it ain't the truth. Inmates do their own dirt. If they would learn to cooperate it'd be different. It's not the officers riding the inmates, it's the inmates riding the inmates. Officials didn't put 'em here. They put their own selves here.

"The inmates making rules is hurting themselves—it ain't gonna hurt the officers. It ain't gonna get 'em nowhere. They're still in the penitentiary; they still have numbers. There's just a lot of talk going around that ain't real. No inmate council gonna do no good. They don't have no power, they can't change nothin'. Anyway, it ain't my way. If they tell me to get down on my hands and knees and scrub, I will. If they tell me, 'Mop the floor again, Connie,' I will—'cause it's *my* job to do it. I'm liable to be here six more months. I have four more months before I meet the board, and whatever they ask me to do, I do it, 'cause it's my job to do it. I made my own bed—I gotta sleep in it now."

Susan Moss

"Susan Moss" is a police statistic, a court statistic, a prison statistic. She is a murderer, by definition, an ex-con now on parole. One night after she got out from four and a half years in prison, we met for supper to talk about her specific prison experiences at the state correctional institution in Niantic, Connecticut. Sue had been in prison for killing her husband, "Marvin Moss"—a man she says she loved more than any other person in her life. With no urging on my part, she began to talk about the day she killed Marvin. She seemed to need to talk about it, to share the horror and finality of her act.

"When I was pregnant with Kit, we had a five-room apartment," Sue recalled. "I was working and Marvin was working and we had saved money and bought a beautiful home. We had got married and things were going really good.

"The day it happened, the twenty-eighth of June, Marv stayed home from work. He ran a filling station with two other guys. The week before we had celebrated our first anniversary. We went out to get some little things for the house and on the way home we got into a silly-assed argument.

"It started 'cause I told him I'd been sick in the mornings and for me that means only one thing. I was pregnant. He said, 'Oh, no.' I told him it would be okay, I'd get a job again and save up the money, just like I had done with Kit. Then he came out with, 'I'll tell you what. I'll give you a hundred dollars and you can get an abortion.' I came up with things like, 'I'm anemic,' and, 'Getting an abortion is laying my life on the line. Not only is there the danger of me bleeding to death, but the knife could be dirty or anything else.' I said, 'You want to kill the baby, but you're not thinking about me and my life.'

"I've blocked so much out now—I hate remembering it all. But I remember going back to the house and Marv's sister and her man were there. Her husband was in Vietnam. I remember feeding the baby and Vicki, my daughter from my second husband. Marvin was mad at me, and every time he was mad at me, he tends to take it out on Vicki. He was upset 'cause he just couldn't see spending five hundred dollars for another baby, plus an extra mouth to feed and all.

"Well, I guess Vicki sensed that something was wrong; she got to tearing up papers, and he went over and whipped her ass. I was always sensitive about his attitude to Vicki, because she's my child. Her father had died from a liver disease. Anyway, I told him if he was mad at me to take it out on me, not on Vicki. Then I took the children up and put them to bed.

"[Later] I was sitting on the couch, and he came into the living room and said, 'You're gonna listen to reason. You're going to have an abortion. It's not a life yet. You're not listening to reason, you're just talking from the heart.'

"I said, 'I'm not having an abortion and that's final. If you don't want the responsibility, I'll do it by myself and you can get out. But if you don't want it, you're not the man I thought you were.'

"He struck me across the face. I can't stand to be struck. I been struck too much. I said, 'You'll be sorry you did that.'

"I walked into the kitchen and started looking for the butcher knife. I looked everywhere but I couldn't find it in the drawer, on the wall, I couldn't find it anywhere. Finally I saw it, sitting right on the drain board over the sink. I walked back into the living room and he was putting an album on the hi-fi. I walked up and stabbed him. I didn't feel the impact of the knife going in—that's how angry I was.

"My sister-in-law was on the porch, and she came running in when she heard the thump of the body. She said later she saw it all happen, but she didn't.

"I think when I knew I had stabbed him I would have stabbed him again, but what actually saved me in court was that I saw the stain begin to spread on his shirt. He was wearing this white polo shirt I had given him. He pulled it up and said, 'Oh, Sue, look what you've done to me.'

"I don't know who called the police. But it took 'em five to six minutes to get there. I thought that if I gave him mouth-to-mouth resuscitation he might live. But the air wasn't coming back into my mouth from his. I knew he had died. I knew I had hit the heart.

"I was sitting there holding him when the cops came in. I kept asking them if he was dead, but I knew. Then I went off. The sergeant grabbed me and told me that they'd have to put me into restraints if I didn't settle down. I knew that I'd go crazy in restraints and I couldn't stand that. Then they took me out. They took me out barefoot in shorts and a see-through blouse. I left my kids in the house and my husband dead on the floor.

"They told me they were going to take me to the hospital for sedatives, but they took me to police headquarters and booked me for willful murder. By then I was more under control. I was numb. The detective lied on me on the stand. He said I was composed and that I wasn't hysterical and that you'd never know I had just killed somebody. He said I'd even ate and that wasn't true. I had only had a cup of coffee.

"I was fingerprinted and mugged and interrogated all night long in the homicide division, and then was taken downstairs to a holding cell about four or four-thirty A.M. I was taken up at about five o'clock in the morning, still barefooted and in my shorts, for the arraignment.

"The magistrate asked me if I knew why I was there and said that one Marvin Moss, thirty-two years of age, had died of a stab wound at approximately ten forty-five P.M. the night before. I had signed a confession in front of a detective the night before, and I gave a verbal confession into a tape recorder.

"After the arraignment I was taken to the House of Detention. I was numb—completely numb. I had no feelings, no emotion at that time. I felt very cold and very cut off. I felt like my life had ended. You must realize, Kitsi, that I had committed the act of murder.

"I didn't even think at that time. I wasn't thinking. I stopped right there. I didn't know where my kids were. I was going crazy about them. But I found out through the social worker at the prison a week later that they were at my mother-in-law's.

"At the House of Detention, I was pregnant and I knew it, but they wouldn't believe me. They wanted me down on my knees scrubbing the cell block. I was spotting and I told the nurse, but she said, 'That's nothing unusual. Everybody spots.' But I knew I didn't. I knew I was pregnant and they just didn't want to take me off my hands and knees on the con-

crete floor. Finally they gave me a rabbit test, and found out I was pregnant—but I was already spotting bad.

"Before I started bleeding bad, though, they took me down to a hearing
in the police paddy wagon with my hands handcuffed behind me. It's just
the bare paddy wagon, with no padding. I passed out with my arms behind
me and fell off the seat. The cops were pretty decent. They stopped the
wagon in the park and let me get out for air.

"When we got back from court I didn't feel very good and started
bleeding. For ten days I hemorrhaged in the cell—and then I aborted right
in the cell. I asked to see the doctor, but he told them to give me an ice
bag for my stomach. The girls took care of me. They brought me milk and
extra vitamins, but the vitamins didn't do any good then—I had already
lost the baby.

"When I passed the baby and called for the nurse, she wouldn't even
come down until the next day. They wouldn't take me to the hospital until
the end, and I was almost dying. Finally they took me to the hospital, but
they didn't want to leave me there because it was a holiday weekend, and
they didn't want to put a watch on me, since they were short on matrons.
Since I had a murder charge on me and a detainer, they wouldn't leave me
there without a matron to guard me. But the doctor at the hospital said I
would die if they let me go out and that if they sent me back to jail, the
hospital would take no responsibility.

"So they let me stay at the hospital. After they had given me a lot of
transfusions and built me up enough, they gave me a D and C to clean me
out. To be fair, I should tell you the doctor said I would have probably
aborted eventually anyway from shock and the initial aftermath of the
crime, even without the fall.

"Later, in the month of April, I had my trial. By that time, I had an
indictment for second-degree murder, voluntary manslaughter, and involuntary manslaughter. I pleaded not guilty to second-degree murder, so
naturally I had to plead not guilty on the other two. I guess they figured if
they didn't get me on one, they would get me on one of the other two. If
I'd had my choice, I would have pled guilty to involuntary manslaughter,
which carries a max of three years and you usually get probation on it.

"I was offered a plea of guilty on second-degree murder in exchange
for one to eight, and I refused it 'cause I didn't want no second-degree
murder for my record. I didn't feel I was guilty of second-degree murder,
not as the law defines it.

"I had a thousand dollars of my own money, so I paid my lawyers a
retainer and after that took the pauper's oath and the state paid for the rest
of it. They were pretty decent men.

"It was a two-week jury trial. I went through the whole bit again. My sister-in-law flew in from Albuquerque to testify against me. She did the most harm to me—she's the reason I got the guilty plea on voluntary manslaughter.

"I was put on the stand and had to go through the question-and-answer bit. The district attorney tried to make me out as a cold-blooded murderer, but said it didn't rise any higher than second-degree murder. After my sister-in-law testified, the DA said he thought they could justifiably charge me with first degree. My lawyer said, 'Now, just a minute. There was no intent involved.' He said I was guilty of murder, but I was motivated out of fear and anger. My psychiatrist from the Trouble Center testified for me too. He volunteered to come to court from the street. I'd had a nervous breakdown the year before and had gone to the Trouble Center at the hospital, where they deal with people having problems dealing with every-day life.

"It was a nightmare. I don't even like to remember it even now. It's too new."

Sue, who eventually was found guilty of voluntary manslaughter, served four and a half years in Niantic and now is serving the remainder of her ten-year sentence on parole. One of the conditions of her release is that she not establish any relationship with a man until she receives permission to do so from her parole officer.

Dessie Kuhn

Dessie Kuhn is sitting on the edge of a prison hospital bed in Marysville, Ohio. Her thin, short legs dangle limply above the bedside stool. She is a little white woman, extremely thin, with wispy, uncombed brown hair. She is a picture of misery in her hospital gown. Her small-boned face is nearly hidden by a huge bandage covering her nose and cheeks.

I ask her what happened to her and she tells me she has just had surgery to straighten her nasal passages. But she wants to tell me why she is in prison; she wants to know, Can I do anything about it? She has bigger concerns than surgery.

"I'm doing one to three years for fraud," she says. "I had food stamps from two counties, and it was my first offense. I offered to give them back or pay for them. They was a hundred and sixty dollars' worth, but they wouldn't let me turn them back in or pay for 'em. It was just a small hick town in Gallia County. It was the first time this judge had a chance to send someone to Marysville, so he sent me. He could have given me probation because I have no past record whatsoever.

"I have seven children and two stepchildren, plus over the years I've had five foster children. They're all with my husband now, but it's really hard for him working and taking care of them, too. I already been here nine months, and I could be here for another two years and three months.

"If I had ever had any idea that would happen . . . I regret having had those food stamps so many times. See, I signed up for food stamps in Meigs County, but that was before we moved to Gallia County. After we moved, I kept the food stamps from Meigs. So when they discovered in Gallia I still had food stamps from Meigs, they issued a warrant. I'd a gladly paid 'em back or done probation.

"This way breaks your home up. It's January now and I haven't seen my kids or husband since November. They tried driving up before Christmas, but the car broke down and now it's still broke down, so they have no way to come up.

"From a big city, I wouldn't have gone here for [what I did]. They wouldn't even notice it.

"I had a state-appointed lawyer. He told me if I dropped the jury trial and pled guilty, the judge would give me probation. All he done was prosecute me worse than the prosecutor. I got one to three for fraud because I done what he told me and pled guilty. I feel I was unjustly treated all the way through."[1]

Mary Lynne Wilkins

My legal name is Mary Lynne Wilkins,[2] aka Mary Johnson, I was born and raised in Detroit Michigan, May 20, 1931. The origin of my crime career started in 1949, when I started using dope. I was doing ninety days for prostitution, at the termination of the ninety-day sentence the Federal agents put a "Hold" on me for three counts: Mail theft; Breaking and Entering; and Forgery. I was sentenced by Judge Thornton for three counts; the sentence was 18 months, 18 months, 1 year (respectively) running concurrently

---

1. Stories like these haven't changed in the 1990s. We still spend from $30,000 to $60,000 a year to punish mothers who have cheated on welfare benefits or food stamps when they couldn't make it through the month. In *Marking Time* Jean Harris tells the story of Lila, who did two years at Bedford Hills for cashing a $167 welfare check. Lila refused a plea bargain because she said she was innocent. During two years in prison, she didn't learn a skill with which she could support her four children, nor did she improve her ability to read and write. Harris comments, "You and I both know someone who took a $200 income tax deduction at least once last week for a business lunch. Is there any more reason for the taxpayer to pay for that lunch than for Lila's welfare check? I simply pose the question."

2. This account was written by "Mary Lynne Wilkins" and is reproduced with her permission. She asked that her name be changed for her family's sake, and these are the pseudonyms she chose.

into 18 months, at Alderson West Virginia. I was denied parole, and maxed out in April, 1951.

In 1952, I had a son, he lives with my mother. In 1953, I was arrested and sentenced by the Federal agents for Interstate Commerce, transporting stolen money orders, across the state line. I received 2 years in Alderson, or two counts running concurrently into 2 Years. I was denied parole and maxed out in June 1955.

In 1956, I was arrested by the Feds. and pleaded guilty to Interstate Commerce and sentenced to 5 years in Lexington, Kentucky. In April 1960, I was released from Lexington, and around October violated my CR and was sent to Alderson, to max it out. I was released in November 1961.

In 1963, I was arrested for Grand Larceny and pleaded guilty to a lesser charge, attempted Grand Larceny, which is a 2-year maximum. I received a one-to-two year sentence. I was granted a parole in 9 months and the Michigan Parole Board made it clear to me that the only reason they was granting me a parole, was that in all my convictions, I had never had a parole. In 1964, I received my discharge from parole.

In 1965, December 26, I was arrested in Ohio for Grand larceny, and Narcotic Implements. I pleaded guilty to Arrangements on Information, and received 1–5 and 1–7 running concurrently into 1–7. The State appointed me an Attorney, by the name of Samuel Jones III, (if memory serves me correctly). On January 1966, I was admitted to Ohio Reformatory for Women. While in Isolation, I got some matches [contraband in isolation], was caught with them and spent 8 days in punishment.

After being released from Isolation, I was in School, Gospelettes (a gospel group that practices unsupervised), Choir, Drug Therapy, and had honor status. *But when I met the parole board in December, eleven months after entry, they gave me two additional years!* This place and its petty rules just made me sick, you cannot touch another inmate, can't comb each other's hair, the personnel talks hostile to you, you can't get medical attention over the weekends, because there is no nurse. If a relative expires, and you're from another state, you cannot attend the funeral services.

A couple of weeks [after the news from the parole board] I tried to run away, in fact I did get as far as town. I was returned and placed in a cell with a steel bunk, three dirty blankets, and not fed for 24 hours. I went to Disciplinary Court January 21, 1967, and was told that when I met the Parole Board in 1968, I would automatically be given two *additional* years for running away. This would have meant I had four more years to do.

Immediately, I started planning to run away. Successfully I went on a diet, and in July, 1967, I squeezed through the window and made a successful escape. I went to Los Angeles, California where I got a job at the Sunset Uniform Company. I worked under "Mary Ann Richmond" (I think). I left California and went to Detroit, Michigan and got a job under another alias. In 1968, I went to New York City, and worked under Betty Sue Prophet, at the Bevolry Dress Company; I am an experienced power machine operator, working for $1.65 per hour. This did not even pay my expenses, so I started cashing checks. I was caught at the Hanover Bank and Trust Company and while in the House of Detention in New York City, Ohio dropped a fugitive warrant on me. I did not fight extradition and was brought back and placed in a cell, for thirty days of punishment with another group of runaways (4 others), 3 in Maximum Security and another in Upper Isolation.

Finally all 5 of us were released in November, we was put in an Isolated area, called P.Q. [punishment quarters]. On November 28, 1968 a balmy Thanksgiving evening, we five got together and tied up the guard and matron, taking the keys off the matron, and escaped. Four of us were captured 3½ hours later, the 5th was captured about 12 hours later. We was held incommunicado for 28 days in Maximum Security, and for two months or more we went without a shower (once a week they would bring a face basin with warm water in it and set it outside the cells we were in). The cells are approximately 6 by 8 feet, with iron bars. We would have to sit down on the floor and stick our arms through the bars to touch the basin, in order to wash up. No one had told us what was going to happen to us or anything.

I had a meeting with the Parole Board in December, 1968, they came back to Max to speak to me, 5 days later the Superintendent told me the Parole Board would see me in 5 years, December 1973. Meanwhile back to Max. The 5 of us started banging and shouting we was tired of staying back there, not knowing when we was going to court. Miss Wheeler came back to Max and told us we was going to court January 9, 1969 (this was December 1968). On Monday, January 9, 1969, the snow was very deep and driving was hazardous, so we didn't go, in fact no one told us we was not going, other than one of the matrons insinuated that the snow was so bad that the Grand Jury probably couldn't get into Union County. In February we started making noise again, asking for a shower, three meals a day, and cigarettes. We got a shower once a week, and to smoke once a week too. We also got three meals a day.

February, about the second week we all went on a hungry strike, we refused to eat because we said we wanted to know when we were going to go to court. We fasted about seven days, and on or about the 17th of February, Miss Wheeler came and addressed us saying, ''You wanted to know when you were going to come out, well you are getting out today, you're going to Lima.''

February 17, 1969 two Penal Transportation guards came into Max with long chains. They put the chain around my waist, the chain was so long that it hung between my legs when I walked. Then they put hand-cuffs on my wrists, escorted me to a truck and drove us 4 to Lima State Hospital. Miss Wheeler had already sent one of us, named Wilma, to Lima, in December 1968.

Description of Lima: An isolated dirt road, leads to a paved road where there is a high tower about 100 ft. tall. A guard with what looks like a machine gun, but the nurse said that it was only a high powered rifle. (These women that work at Lima claim the title of nurse, although some are not even nurse-aids.)

The high towers also consist of huge flood lights. There is, about a ten foot fence, that is also bob-wired. This fence is also alleged to be charged. We were unshackled and lead to a dining room where you eat with only a spoon, and you are not allowed seconds on any food. You only receive two slices of bread. The food is placed on a sectional tray made of steel. After dinner we were assigned to wards. Two went to ward 22, and myself, and Norma, went to ward 23. Boy were we lucky to get ward 23, that's supposed to be the honor ward.

They fingerprint me and photograph me, now I'm sitting in a chair waiting to see the Doctor. The Dr. breezes through, and one of the officials tell him he has to see us. He says he haven't got time, he'll see us later.

When he sent for me, he asked me how many times I had been arrested. I told him about 25 times. [He] blew, in a whistle, then he asked me the date and the year. I explained that I have not seen a calendar in about three months, but I think it's Feb. 17, 1969. [He] then asked me why I was sent to Lima. I told him I did not know, that it must have been for disciplinary reasons, because I sure wasn't crazy for wanting to get out of Marysville. He said, "Well!" That's all. I then asked him how long would I have to be there? He said he did not know, that I was sent there for an indefinite period. I asked him how long was that, and he said *that depended on me. I could stay there five years, ten years, or maybe life*. This is verbatim and I get nervous every time I think about it. Can you imagine how I felt, knowing what I do about law, I know the first thing it takes some MONEY. I'm from an indigent family, I do not have any money saved, and I'm from out of State. I'm not asking for sympathy, I'm just telling it like it is.

Mrs [——]: From the moment she saw me she seemed to take an attitude towards me. (Hostile) She was the Head Nurse, passing medication and really her status was a citizen. However, I swallowed a many lump because, I knew that she wanted to put me on medication. I would find worms, bugs, and paper in the food, and never say anything, at least not to the officer.

If the nurse gets angry at you, she'll say, "You better be quiet, or I'll put you on medicine." And she had this authority, because if she told the Dr. that a patient needed medication, the Dr. did not question the nurse. And once you're on medication the patient must be off medication 4 to 6 months before he can meet Staff, which is like a parole. Sometimes the nurse would give the patients a stronger dosage so the patient would be dormant, and sleepy and not ask the nurse for different things, like toilet paper etc. All the nurse had to tell a patient was, you're too worrisome, and the patient knew what that meant. That if he or she kept doing what they were the nurse would either put them on medication, or have their dosage increased. Some of the nurses had a bad habit of kicking the patients, Mrs. [——] was one. She wouldn't kick them hard, but its the idea, of putting your feet on another human being.

At shower time approximately 2:30 they have a room where its something like a supply room, about 8 feet by 10 feet. As many as can goes into this room and undress, for your shower. Then you walk across the hall NUDE and there is another room about the same size. The only difference is it has three small shower faucets. With very little water dripping from them. There are as many women as can squeeze in this area. About 15 women crowd into this space, because the nurse wants them to hurry up and get through with their showers so that the nurse can sit back down. The nurse all of them do the same thing. They sit on a stool in the hall in front of the shower room and yells, to different patients that are staying under the water too long, "Alright Sally, Mary, etc. get away from that shower so someone else can use some water." "Move over so Mary can get wet." When you get soaped up, you are then allowed to get under the shower and rinse off. The nurse sitting on the stool holds a can of Right Guard, and you hold your arms up and she sprays them for you. Then the nurse puts some lotion in your hand, to lotion with.

There was an old Chezslovia [sic] woman named Frances with cataracts on her eyes who almost never said anything to anybody. She just sat, and stare. Now when Lima calls SHOWERS that means everybody. So one day this poor old lady didn't feel like taking a shower, because she had just told me how bad she was feeling. But the nurse insisted. And poor old Frances was trying to get to the Head Nurse, and ask permission to not take a shower. On her way to the office, she fell, and some 9 hrs. Later the lady was Dead. Now I agree that some patients needed to be reminded to take showers. But they never even stop to ask "WHY."

Another patient named Carrie Hayes, complained that she was sick and bleeding. Nobody paid her any attention, they just said that she was lazy. She was 56. They transferred her to the punishment ward, where they have no compassion at all for human lives. They put Carrie Hayes in a punishment cell, with a pissy smelly mattress on the floor and one blanket to serve as anything you want to share it for. Something like a sheet, a pillow, or just to cover yourself. They even take your shoes, and you have no toilet, no water, and Nothing else, unless they have changed it since I have been there. Carrie stayed down there and caught something and DIED, TOO. The day before we left, about the middle of March, [another woman] hung herself, because she was threatened to lose her cigarette smoking privilege for 6 months, and she just couldn't take it.

I feel these deaths might have been prevented, if someone had done something. That is why Lima was such a mental strain on me. I never was on medication the whole time I was at Lima. Lima really did something to me. I can never forget.

March, 1970, we five were released from Lima State Hospital, and turned over to the custody of Union county sheriff, Ameron. The sheriff drove us to Union County Jail, where he served us with one indictment Assault on a prison guard. We five women said we would fight the assault charge because we did not assault Mr. Redder, the guard, we only tied him up along with the matron, Mrs. Mary Mitchell. My court appointed attorney, Mrs Jeanne Dailey told me if we fought the assault, the prosecutor would serve us with another indictment, "Escape." I asked Mrs Dailey to show me the other indictment. She went to the court building and returned with the indictment. The proposition was that we plead guilty to assault, and the escape charge would be Nole Prosque. Although I have a carbon copy of the escape being Nole, the Parole Board Members have no knowledge of such a decision whereas the charge was nole.

April 1970 we five were sentenced to six months in the Dayton Workhouse, sentenced to run consecutively with our prior sentence.

May, 1970. The Sheriff, Mr. Ameron told us he was transferring us back to O.R.W. but that only four of us were going back to O.R.W. The fifth, Wilma, was to be returned back to Lima State Hospital, because she had not been "cleared" through staff. About 5 weeks later she was transferred to Ohio Reformatory for Women.

Now that I'm back here again, I have tried to comply with these petty rules, for instance now, if an inmate is disagreeing with the matron, the matron might tell the inmate, "To shut up," or the matron will just cut the inmate off and say, "You have three nights early bed." This place now has approximately 12 guards here, and two guard houses. The guards now harass the women, especially if the woman is not too popular at the "Front" where Miss Wheeler presides.

If you're at the clinic, and are caught asking a sick inmate, is she feeling better, even though you are whispering, you get 3 nights early bed, plus your hospital privileges are taken. The matrons have found pills on some inmates, so now to prevent the inmate from swinging with her medication, the medicine is crushed and put into a cup. Now, common sense tells anyone, that if an inmate wants to swing with her medication, she will. And the nurse makes you stick out your tongue. But let me add, where there's a will; you'll find the way.

The "only" reason I'm complaining about the crushed pills, and opened capsules is that the different medicines irritate your tongue, makes the inside of your mouth sore.

If a matron has a personal grievance with an inmate, she is in a position to send the inmate to punishment, any time she chooses, all the matron has to say is the inmate was insubordinate. After you have been in Max you go to disciplinary Court, to tell your side of the story. You can't talk to another inmate twice or you are branded as a homosexual. They think everyone is homosexual.

However, I managed "not" to get a punishment slip from December, 1968 to August, 1971.

May, 1971. The Grapevine said that the Governor was no longer assessing time, it would be a "continuance" since all assess time was either for hitting a personnel or running away. There were 17 of us runaways, and matron hitters. So in June 1971 Mr. Worley, the Review Parole Man, called me and told me since I had not been in any trouble since 1968, I was eligible to meet the Review Board in one half of my five years assessed time. My name was added to meet the Regular Parole Board in August. They acknowledged my very good work, I reminded them I am a power machine operator with 23 years experience. I am going out of state, I was discharged on the last parole I had. My old parole excepted me. I have a home placement, and a job waiting, as a housekeeper, and I intended to go to I.B.M. key-punch school at night.

But, you know, when the answer came back—I was continued for another year. I meet them in June, 1972. How much longer will the Ohio State Parole Board punish me? Why would they even put my name on the board if they were not going to let me go home?

Martha Wheeler

Turning left off of Route 411, about an hour's drive from Columbus, Ohio, you see a small sign that says, "Ohio Reformatory for Women, Marysville. Trespassers will be prosecuted." Driving up the long, winding road, you pass a small guard's office and see two- and three-story red brick buildings that remind you of a boarding school or a closely constructed sanitorium where old folks walked around in bathrobes in 1940s movies. More than 280 women are prisoners here in the middle of a cornfield, in the middle of the state: a small and isolated community not even served by a bus.

"It's a silly place to begin to get it all together when the root of many women's problems is with their families and loved ones in the city," said the institution's seasoned superintendent, Martha Wheeler, a dignified gray-haired woman in her fifties. Ms. Wheeler relaxed behind her desk and chain-smoked as we talked in her comfortable administrative office. "It's a big disadvantage for visitors to get to the institution without public transportation. You must have a car to get here, and since most of the families of the women are poor, few have this luxury or are able to get to Marysville easily."

Ms. Wheeler said she agrees with the trend toward community-based systems, as opposed to rural prisons. "These community-based centers would have fewer women. It's important we concentrate on building newer facilities much earlier, as near as possible to the community where most of the resources are, where the women are, and where the problems are. This way we can have realistic intervention on the first offense."

Martha Wheeler knew before she went to college she wanted to work in prisons and in the corrections field. Deliberately she charted her courses, studying criminology and social administration. She worked for eight and a half years at the state prison for women at Bedford Hills, New York, and then returned home to Ohio in 1958 to head up the women's prison at Marysville. Currently she is president of the American Correctional Association, which is no small achievement. She's the first woman elected to that office.

"There are relatively few in my generation who came into corrections on purpose," she said, surveying the neatly stacked papers on her desk. "But I had exposure at an early age. I've known Marysville girls since I was eight years old.

"My parents used to operate an honor camp for the Marysville girls about two hundred miles from here. They ran it from 1929 to 1956. It was an old-age home, a small institution for elderly women. Specifically, it was an honor institution for wives, widows, and mothers of military personnel.

"Trustees from Marysville served as attendants, cooks, and maids and looked after the patients. When I was little, they got me up in the morning, fed me my breakfast, and put me on the bus. They were older women, stable, and could handle the situation. They could make more money and feel useful. They lived in three dormitory sections, five women to a room. They were earning forty dollars a month when we phased out the program.

"We continued with that institution until a couple of years ago, but it had changed, housing retarded women and then being a halfway house for borderline mental defectives. As our programs here intensified, we hated to send them two hundred miles away to do laundry and clean. Also, the population was younger, so we didn't have the kind of women who were happy going there. It didn't have that much in it for them. It was giving the honor camp problems and not doing much for us. Plus sentences were shortened, so it no longer fed their needs or ours. So there's no more honor camp."

Some of the women who worked under the purview of Martha Wheeler's parents now have daughters serving time under the administrative eye of Martha Wheeler. Two elderly women prisoners at Marysville knew Martha as a little girl and still refer to her as "Captain Wheeler's daughter."

Now Ms. Wheeler's parents are retired and live on the prison grounds with Ms. Wheeler in a large brick house located next to the administration building. "Marysville girls" still take care of them, feeding them breakfast, cleaning the house, washing, ironing, brushing and feeding two dogs, and serving dinners to the family and their company.

Barbara Baker

"I'm twenty-eight, and it's too late for me to be rehabilitated," Barbara Baker says. "If I could get something out of this experience, I don't think I would mind. But it's not only the system that stops an effective experience, it's also the inmates. There's a lack of communication between the staff and inmates—but there's just as much a lack of communication between inmate and inmate. We gotta start with unity from the inmates. It's impossible for the staff to regroup themselves without us regrouping ourselves right here. This is where it's at.

"Unity to me is first regrouping yourself and then coming together with a group. If you can't accept yourself, you can never accept anyone else.

How can you talk about Janie's problems or deal with them without talking about yourself first—and really looking at yourself?

"It's gotta be something you do for yourself first; you have to examine yourself before you can see anyone else. Otherwise it's just like taking a mirror and looking at yourself—you never see the other person."

Barbara Baker knows a lot about people. A lot about institutions. A lot about people in institutions. She grew up in them. Before I got to the Ohio Reformatory for Women in Marysville, I had heard about Barbara Baker. Friends in Iowa at *Penal Digest International,* a paper put out by cons and ex-cons, had told me that Barbara was their prison correspondent and that she had been in prison for eight years on an armed robbery conviction. Within the first six hours after I arrived at Marysville, I heard Barbara's name mentioned by staff members three or four times. One staff member mentioned to the superintendent that Barbara had put in a request to see a friend from another cottage who was about to be released. Because a precedent already had been set, the staff member said she couldn't get away with denying Barbara's request even though she wanted to. "It would be a bigger headache than it's worth," she said.

When two other staff members exchanged passing comments about Barbara as a "troublemaker" and a "big mouth," the superintendent, Martha Wheeler, said, "She ought to put her head where her mouth is. She's got a faulty connection between her head and her mouth." They had no idea I was aware of the person they were talking about; but even if I hadn't already been looking for her, their comments would have intrigued me.

Finally, on my third evening at the reformatory, I got into Washington "cottage," where Barbara lived. The women were in the recreation room, talking to each other and playing cards before they would go back to their rooms and line up for showers, to be taken one at a time into tiny shower stalls. Bits of evening light were coming through the windows. As I started meeting the women and talking with them, I saw several women I'd met the day before in the garment factory. They introduced me to Becky Careway, a diminutive white woman with a lively expression and short red hair, and to Barbara Baker—a tall, urbane, and attractive black woman with a short black Afro, who shook hands firmly and directly. I gave her messages from her friends outside and we agreed to talk after showers. The matron blew her whistle and we started upstairs.

"Come on, girls," the matron said. "Step it up."

Later that evening, following long conversations I had with other women, Barbara and I sat down to talk. She had been in Marysville from 1962 to 1967, and she came back again in 1969 with a ten-to-twenty-five-year sentence for armed robbery.

"We've got a rotten system here," Barbara said. "Most people's dogs are treated better than the women in here. But the majority of the women don't carry themselves like women. If you want to be treated like a woman, you have to see: Where does womanhood begin but in yourself? How can you expect them to treat you like a woman when you act like a child?

"I don't like Martha Wheeler or Dorothy Urn. I don't like things they have done in the past. They don't do their jobs. But there are two sides to every story. Martha Wheeler has one of the greatest minds you could ever come across. The woman's brilliant. She has an education. Everyone needs it, but there are two classes of education: education with common sense and education with refusing to use common sense. This has happened to Martha Wheeler—she doesn't use common sense along with her education. She has let her mother and father and two dogs be the circle around her life. It's impossible to pull her from those walls and let her see each woman as an individual. She's walled herself up into a prison that's tighter and more binding than most of us are in.

"It's like I said—if you look, you see two sides to every story. When women first line up to go through that gate and go into isolation for orientation to the prison, the first thing the matrons try to do is stamp out womanhood and respect. They treat us like children.

"But many women continue that child thing in here because they are afraid. Where's their courage? They've stood up to society some way outside or they wouldn't be in here. If their husband smacked them down and they were afraid to leave, they tolerated it up to the point of taking a gun and blowing his head off. But you don't have to go to that extreme.

"Courage to stand up and speak is the beginning of your womanhood. You're going to be classified as a renegade, but who cares, when you're speaking the truth and fighting for everyone? Just because you have a number, why throw away your pride? I'm in prison night and day, but for twenty-four hours a day God has given me the courage to be a woman. When Martha Wheeler or someone says something I feel isn't right, I'm gonna stand up and let them know this. I'm not going to say, 'Yes, ma'am, you're right.' That's another ounce of pride from your womanhood. And that's basically all we have in here. I would rather go to room punishment or maximum security.

"But people sell their soul for artificial treasures," Barbara said, referring specifically to "honor" status—the reward system at the prison symbolized by "moving up from a plain blue uniform to a print dress of flowered material" made in shirtwaist style.

"You've got your 'prints' and that lousy JG [honor dorm]," she said.

"The majority of the women in this prison never wore a print on the streets. They didn't know what a print looked like until they entered this institution. As for JG, I can go to my room right here in Washington Cottage and roll my hair up at six o'clock. The only real difference is they can keep their doors open or closed when they want. It's like telling your child, 'Honey, I'll roll your hair up and you can come out and watch TV.' Yet there are so many women here who would lay down their lives to get into JG for those simple little things—doors open, hair up when they want it up. I often wonder who is the real dogs, people up front or people in here. I would not sell myself for such small, petty things. This is not human.

"I could run down this institution after eight years here—and I'm not institutionalized—but you have to look at the whole picture. Running the system down isn't gonna solve the problems.

"We gotta start here with the inmates. I don't mean to get up and rebel or carry signs saying we want this or that or rioting. This is silly. It would just prove to society that we're nothing but children. There's a way for a woman to do anything she wants. She can get anything she wants. Women get here in isolation and they forget women are blessed people. They are the gentle creatures, yet they are very shrewd. We know how to con from a little girl up, from the time we got up on our daddy's lap and got him to give a dime to go to the store.

"I believe each and every one of us is God. He created us in our own image. If we cast our womanhood aside, we are smacking our God aside, saying, 'We don't need it.' There are a few staff members here who are able to give some of themselves among the women. There are a few matrons who are open to people. And Mr. Kowalski, our psychologist, is open. For a long time I refused to talk to him or any of the rest of the staff. He was the first person I learned to trust after I learned to trust myself. Now I also rap with some of the matrons who are open. I found out if I tried to understand the world, the world would try to understand me.

"But there are many women in here who crave help but refuse help when it's offered to them. Mrs. King, the correctional officer who's our matron, is all for the girls. But some girls call her a bunch of names because she wants to help them. They cry out they want help—but it's a false cry for many of them, 'cause when someone comes in here to help, they try to destroy her. Maybe it's a question of jealousy of her freedom. But you gotta be able to stand up like a woman and see the truth, good or bad. You have to look at yourself as a human being and look at your oppressor as a human being.

"With the system here, if inmates and officials would learn to cast out the past and look at each other with new eyes, it would be very different. It weakens you to rely on the past. We have to keep our feet halfway through yesterday and move on into tomorrow. This is a new day. It's got to be a new beginning. All of us have faults because we refuse to come up to date with what is going on around us in this big, bad world.

"It's a drag sometimes, sure it's a drag. We each gotta do time. We're the ones doing it, so we know what it's like. But I wonder if there were some way we could all get together. I don't believe in sitting back to wait, because there's only now. We move forward but together to unite, to look out at the world and face the world and be the world—not with black power or white superiority, but with power for all, calling out unity among the people.

"In order to survive, I must look at my people—not just black people, but all people. There's good and bad in all people. We need understanding from them. But they need understanding from us, too, evil as they are. I don't care what crime a person has committed, there's still some good in him. We can sit back and condemn them and we can say we know the reason why, but what good does that do without looking at yourself? There's an old story about a woman named Mary Magdalene. People were ready to stone her for being a prostitute. But this man named Jesus came up on the scene and said, 'Ye who have not sinned cast the first stone'— and nobody was sinless. No one could cast that first stone.

"I don't like to come on in a psychedelic world of fantasy. I like to say, 'Hey, man, this is it.' No matter how many dreams I try to dream to make it better or worse, it comes out the same way. I'm still here, man. I'm still in the penitentiary. I know why I'm here. No matter where you run to, the reality is still there with you. If I get out, I get out. If I don't, I know I committed a crime. There's a reason for everything.

"I was automatically found guilty of robbery this time—even without evidence—just because of my record. There are probably reasons I came back here. I lay up there in isolation when I came back and said, 'Maybe there is a reason.' In the eyes of God all things are possible. But what the hell would that prove?

"But then things began to rolling. Censorship was lifted and I could write my man at Ohio Penitentiary. And then I got a visit from Reverend McCracken—my first visit in three years. When I talked to Reverend McCracken, I found a *people*. He was sixty-five years old, and I myself was twenty-seven. He was white. I am black. But we found no gaps. There is no gap. It took me all these years to realize there is no gap when your heart is reaching out. There is no gap when you are open to understanding."

Aletha Curtis

DEAR MOMMY,

I got me a job so I don't have to steal till you get home. Ronnie ran away again but otherwise, everything is fine. How are you?

I love you,
XXOOO,
VICKIE

Aletha Curtis, at the Ohio Reformatory for Women, is little and round, with a down-to-earth bawdiness that made me laugh in spite of the sense of sadness right under the surface of her humor, in spite of the apparent lack of options in her life. "They be callin' us girl all the time," Aletha said to me. "I ain't no girl. I got ten kids. That ain't no girl there."

Aletha Curtis could never be accused of trying to sugarcoat her story or make herself look like a Goody Two-shoes. "I be tellin' my kids, please go to school and get me a diploma," she said. "But nobody's in school. My oldest one's in jail for A and B [assault and battery].

"My one son, Johnny, who's next to the baby, is in the Industrial Home for running away from the foster home. I told him to stay in school, but he didn't. One is staying with my sister. The oldest ones go where they wanna go. My three youngest is in foster homes.

"I tell them, don't steal, 'cause it's the only thing I ever did. I been stealing ever since I was seventeen. I got a letter from my little girl. She wrote me, 'Mommy, I got me a job so I don't have to steal till you get home.'

"Me, I loves to steal.

"You can go out, and say you see something I want or would like. You think, I can sell this mink coat to her and get a couple bills. I didn't know how to do anything else but steal. I loves to do it. *I loves to do it!* I wanna go around the world and steal when I get out.

"I would rather be in a county jail where you can holler out the window and contact people than be here. In county you can sleep all day. You don't have to work and you don't get paid no way.

"I guess I been in jail about ten times. I was here before, too. I been in Cleveland jail, Akron jail, Wooster jail, and Toledo."

Kathleen Anderson

The ombudsman at the California Institution for Women is a woman who has spent her life asking, "Why?" Kathleen Anderson said that her "whys," in fact, are what got her into prison work in the first place.

She had been teaching in a school for the deaf in Riverside and during one vacation some twelve years ago came up to CIW in Frontera to take a tour of the institution. "I was just curious," she said. "But when I got here they told me the only way I could get in would be to take the test and come in as a line officer.

"At that time, they didn't let outsiders in, period. It wasn't just because I was black, it was just the rule. I didn't think it was right the way they treated outsiders wanting a tour. I figured if they treated adults like that— other state employees like myself—how were they treating the women inside? I wanted to know. I wanted to know what made them tick.

"I guess I've always been a nosy person. Anyway, I took the civil service examination and I accepted the job. When I quit my job, the people at the deaf school were upset at my leaving, so I figured if I didn't make it through the six-month probationary period I could always go back to the deaf school. I thought I might want to go back if I didn't like what I saw here.

"At that time they had an ethnic quota. They had two blacks and one Mexican American working here, and they couldn't see why they had to hire any more. I couldn't see why not, and I couldn't accept it. I wouldn't accept it until I got the job.

"I started out as a line staff. I worked in one of the cottages. After I had been here six months, a supervisor came up and asked me what was wrong—I had been here six months and I hadn't written out a disciplinary report. I told her I didn't see any reason to be writing disciplinaries when I was talking to the individuals and we were preventing the problems from happening. They just didn't understand at that time that the best method of control is to know and understand the individual.

"I made it through that six months and worked my way up through custody rank to program administrator. That's through five levels of supervision. It took me three years to make my first promotion—that has a lot of overtones!

"I have to admit I'm still biased against people in uniforms myself. Why do they need them? Are they a crutch?"

Ms. Anderson's job today is as ombudsman. That means she's a liaison between inmates and staff. She's also in charge of self-help groups at the institution and organizes volunteers and outside activities coming in. In addition, she sits in as an appeal officer at disciplinary hearings.

"The possibility of hiring an outside ombudsman was defeated by the legislature," she said. "Our position was that if you'd worked your way through the ranks, you could see more things that are needed than a person from the outside."

The programs Kathleen Anderson coordinates are centered around the community more than around corrections. "This is definitely positive," she says. "The problem isn't how to get along in the institution, but how to get along in the community you come from.

"There will always be prisons, because there will always be some people who need to be controlled. But there is another large group of women here who could go to community corrections centers, and if they couldn't make it, they could come back here.

"Forty-five percent of the women still here now could maintain themselves in the community if they had some kind of support.

"But then you have to talk about whether the community would accept them at all—and that's a whole different ball of wax altogether. Every person in prison was somebody's neighbor, somebody's child. That's the problem that should be looked at.

"We're working with society's rejects. You can get us to understand, but how do you get society to understand? We all have to deal with what society expects of a prison. And when you want to implement any changes, people tend to say no first, whether it's staff or inmates or the public. I don't know why, but people just tend to resist change."

Nevertheless, Ms. Anderson has followed through on a lot of changes since she came to Frontera. "When I came here twelve years ago, this was a holding center," she said, "and that's all. But now we really try to deal on a one-to-one basis. People from the community come in for programs and classes every day of the week, and if you look at the overall picture, you can see a lot of changes. Today our method of control is to know the individual.

"My main question here in every position I have been in is, 'Why do we do what we do, and what can I do to help it or make it a more positive experience?' My whole cause is for positivity.

"When I leave here at night, I become a mother. The girls expect me never to leave. They seem to think I should be here twenty-four hours a day. I ask them, 'What, do you want me to lose my husband?' He's in construction. He's a drywaller of inside walls.

"My three children are pretty self-sufficient. They're eight, nine, and fourteen. Plus my husband's an excellent cook—probably in self-defense, because I'm also still going to the University of Southern California for my master's degree in business administration."

Ana Lou Coelho

In the summer of 1970 Ana Lou Coelho and her four children left Oakland, California, to go camping on the Yuba River outside Grass Valley,

California. "It was so beautiful and we all loved being on the earth again. I asked them if they'd like to stay and they said yes, so after spending most of the summer there, we moved up permanently in September 1970.

"I had wanted to get out of Oakland and get the children out of the city, so it seemed like a very good thing. We were all really happy up there."

For Ana, who is three-fourths Apache and one-fourth Chicana, being in the open countryside again was realizing a dream. She had been city-bound in the Oakland-Alameda area since she was four, but had taken every opportunity to get outdoors from the time she was small. She had always gone camping with her parents, sister, ex-husband, and other relatives.

"Even with four children to raise, she's always managed to get outdoors every chance she got," her sister, Dora Canepa, says, "whether it was for swimming, picnicking, camping at Yosemite, hiking, or just cooking out at home or the park. She just plain loves the fun things of life. Ana and her children always just enjoy themselves. Just enjoy being alive."

One year after moving up to the idyllic Yuba River outside Grass Valley, life changed drastically for Ana and her children—Rhonda, fourteen; Linda, eleven; Sherri, ten; and Ronnie, seven. On September 25, 1971, Ana was charged with murder and held without bail in the Nevada County Jail. She was charged with killing a man she didn't know in a barroom brawl. The man had been stabbed to death. Ana had been wearing a hunting knife in the bar the night of his death.

Ana's children went back to Oakland to stay with their grandmother and her husband. Ana sat in the Nevada County Jail without bail while stories and pictures of her ran on the front pages of the Grass Valley newspaper. On December 6 her jury trial began. Thirty witnesses took the stand against her, and according to Ana, her lawyer, and court transcripts, they told thirty different stories, agreeing on only one fact: Ana was wearing Levis, a T-shirt, and a hunting knife when she came into Tip and Lindy's bar with her friends.

After fifteen minutes' deliberation on December 10, 1971, the jury found Ana guilty of second-degree murder.

Twenty-five days after she had been sentenced to five to twenty years, Ana and I met for the first time in the Reception and Guidance Center of the California Institution for Women. Ana was CIW Number 8811.

"You gotta talk to Ana," several different women had told me after I had been in the center for less than an hour. "She's here for something she didn't do. She's innocent—and that ain't no jive."

Contrary to popular conceptions, prisoners rarely claim their innocence outside the courts. They usually admit, matter-of-factly, "If you play, you gotta pay,'' or say, ''I don't object to having to pay for what I did. It's just that I object to being treated like this while I'm here.'' So I was curious, but I also should say I was skeptical, as well as exhausted from my traveling and my interviews. And if it hadn't been for the insistence of the other women, I might well have missed meeting five-foot-tall Ana, who looked about seventeen years old instead of thirty-two, with her shiny black hair tied in pigtails on each side of her small olive face.

Ana wore a prison uniform covered by a beige prison jacket about three times too big for her. We sat down in the hall to talk, then asked to have her door ''popped'' from the control center so we could talk in more privacy. Her cell, small and bare except for bed, toilet, sink, and desk, was decorated with pictures of her children. Letters from them covered her desk. It was obvious they were as much the emotional focus of her life there in that small barren room as they had been in their home on the Yuba River.

''I've never been in jail before, and to be plunked down in prison is so heavy,'' she said, her hands shaking as she fixed coffee for both of us in a small automatic pot. ''At times I get so close to losing my mind, I think I just can't take it.

''When I first got here, I didn't know anything. They just said, 'Here's your room.' Every time I asked a question, it was so stupid, I stopped asking anything. Like the first day I went back to my room and it was locked, so I went up to the control desk and asked if I could have a key to my door. She just looked at me and said, 'No, we don't give keys.' I said, 'Well, how do I get in?' 'Just tell us and we'll pop your door.' I didn't know anything. I didn't even know I could go out in the yard for a week. So I just stayed in my room and went so close to going out of my mind. I was dangerously close to it. I knew I couldn't keep staying in my room and thinking about everything. But then I got a copy of the rules and read them and knew more what was going on. Then I asked if I could go outside, and they said, 'Of course. All you have to do is open the door.'

''It's so hard to write to my kids. There's nothing to write about but bad things. All I can tell them is someday justice will be done.

''I'm here for a crime I didn't commit,'' she said. ''I guess if I wasn't innocent, it wouldn't be so hard. But I just can't accept that I'm really here for something I didn't do. All during the trial I was optimistic 'cause I didn't see how they could find me guilty of something I didn't do. My son Ronnie wrote, 'Those people must be mean to keep you there,' and I just told him, 'They can't help it—they're doing what the court ordered them to do.' It's hard for them to understand; I'm innocent, yet I'm still being punished for it. It's hard for me to understand too—and I guess I never will accept it."

Before we were able to talk any more, an officer came to Ana's room and said that we would have to go back to the dayroom to continue talking. "This is for your protection," she said to me. "We don't know what these girls might do. You could get physically attacked or propositioned, and we don't want to put you in any kind of embarrassing or compromising situation." The order seemed arbitrary, and the notion that I was in jeopardy seemed ludicrous, but we nevertheless moved back to the dayroom.

Ana then began to tell me about the night a man named Billy Ray Cook was murdered in Tip and Lindy's, a small Grass Valley barroom that features rock music and dancing. She had gone to Tip's with several friends to drink beer and dance. "It's quite dark in Tip's, and there was a band playing very loudly, making it impossible to talk and be heard without yelling. I may have been dancing wildly, whatever 'wildly' means— like they said in court—but I was only feeling pretty loose and having a good time. There were numerous altercations between people, but I wasn't involved in them, I was only aware of them.

"I had a hunting knife strapped to the side of me, and somebody took it from the sheath when a big fight broke out. It turned into a brawl—like a free-for-all—with about fifteen or twenty people involved. I was pushed up against the jukebox when the man was stabbed. I had never even seen him until the pictures of him were shown at the trial—I couldn't even see what was going on during the brawl. It was like a football huddle, only everyone was swinging, including myself, even though I was shoved back against the jukebox.

"During this brawl, a man I knew named Ralph handed me back the knife, led me by my arm towards the door, and told me to get rid of it and don't let anyone see me. I ran down the street and put it in the back of the truck. During this time I heard someone yell, 'Someone's been stabbed.'

"I didn't even know anyone had been stabbed until I heard that. At this point I panicked because I thought someone had seen me put the knife in the truck. I knew something bad had happened and that Ralph was involved in it, because there were a lot of people outside yelling and screaming about a stabbing. I was yelling, 'Where's my knife?' because I didn't want anyone to know what I'd done with it. I know this was wrong, but I was trying to protect Ralph and I was confused.

"The crowd had already dispersed and we were standing outside when the police came. I was standing near Ralph and some other people. Someone told the police officer, 'Arrest them two, because someone's been stabbed and either one of them did it.' The officer told me to get in the car, which I did.''

Ana said she was wearing the knife because she was going to join her children and another family on a camping trip when she left the bar. Ronnie, Rhonda, Linda, and Sherri had gone ahead to the camping site with the other family, carrying along their camping equipment, sleeping bags, extra clothes, and food.

"I always wore Levis, T-shirt, and a hunting knife on these camping trips,'' Ana said. "The knife I used primarily in the preparation of meals, making sandwiches, cutting watermelon or cantaloupe—just general camping uses. I used it to help skin a rattlesnake once, but had a hard time, as the knife isn't very sharp.''

Ana was charged with murder—her first offense—and two Nevada County public defenders were appointed to her case. "The first one was put on another case, and the second PD told me I should plead guilty,'' Ana said. "He told me it was a cut-and-dry case anyway and if I admitted to it I would get off easier—like manslaughter and probation or something. He said, 'If you don't plead, they'll make it hard on you.' But I didn't want to plead guilty because I wasn't guilty. So he refused to take the case. Then my parents got a private attorney from San Francisco to go all the way up there. I saw him three times before we went to trial.

"I asked him to get it moved out of Nevada County because the case had been widely publicized and my picture had been on the front page several times. He said he thought the jury would be fair and wouldn't find me guilty. But he was wrong.

"First of all, the witnesses were so hostile. I wasn't an active member of the community in Grass Valley. We lived three or four blocks out of town. We had made friends with a family with seven children and apparently the community didn't like them. I didn't even know how unpopular they were until the trial. But there was a lot of emphasis on them—the Salazar family—all through the trial, as though just because I was friends with them, it must mean I'm guilty of something. It was also against me that I've been divorced six years and I was on welfare—all kinds of negative points. It didn't matter that I had been past president of the PTA in Alameda or active with the drug abuse council and the Alameda City Council. None of those things were brought up at the trial. They just said I was on welfare, but they didn't say that I had been working with a social worker and he was putting me on job training. I wanted clerical or secretarial work, although I'd like to teach roller-skating.'' (Ana had taken third place in the National Roller-Skating Meet in 1956 in Richmond, Virginia, representing the Bay Area and California.)

"Witnesses also said they heard me arguing and saying things in Mexican or Spanish, but I speak neither Mexican or Spanish, so whatever I said was in English!"

Ethnic background, economic status, marital status, and association with an unpopular family seemed to be the chief determinates against Ana at her trial. Apparently the testimony of the pathologist who performed the autopsy on the victim, Billy Ray Cook, was either discounted or ignored. The pathologist testified it would take an incredible amount of strength to inflict such a wound, because the victim was slashed from his chest to his waist and the stab penetrated muscles and tendons, going deep enough to cut the man's backbone. Ana, who doesn't appear at all muscular, weighs less than a hundred pounds.

Another crucial point in the trial was testimony from an officer as to whether Ana's clothes and shoes had been sent to the lab for tests to see if there was any blood on them. The district attorney objected to admission of the report on the grounds that an officer could not read a laboratory report. The objection was sustained. Ana said that had the report been allowed into evidence, it would have proven she didn't murder the man, because there was no blood on any of her things.

"In court, when they showed me pictures of that place, the floor was covered with blood and there was blood all over the wall and post. There was only one person besides the victim with a lot of blood all over his pants, shoes, hands, shirt, and face. He was involved in the fight, he had the knife in his hand, and I know he did it and he's walking the streets, a free man." The "star witness" against Ana cleared the man who Ana believes really committed the murder.

"I think I could have done a better job defending myself," Ana says, "even though I don't know the law. But the jury was incredible. One woman was knitting all through the trial and another was addressing Christmas cards. Can you imagine being a member of a jury at a murder trial and knitting or addressing Christmas cards? It took them such a short time to reach the verdict after five days of testimony. They'd made up their minds ahead of time. But all during the trial I was optimistic anyway, because I didn't see how they could find me guilty."

Ana's feeling that her association with the Salazar family prejudiced her case was substantiated by reading the presentence report filed for the court by William L. Heafy, the chief probation officer of Nevada County. In the report, Heafy repeats word for word the district attorney's version of the offense. The second sentence of the report refers to the family—a fact that should be irrelevant:

"Ana Coelho has lived in Grass Valley Area with her children for more than a year. During that time she has been known to be associated with the Salazar family and some members of a loosely formed organization, 'The Misfits,' which is a kind of motorcycle club."

The district attorney's report also says: "According to a large number of witnesses who testified in generally consistent fashion, but each to only a portion of the activities of the evening, Ana Coelho wore her knife in the bar, acted rowdy, belligerent, insulting and threatening. Several people testified that she menaced Kenneth Haynes with her knife and engaged in a number of instances of disturbing the peace or fighting. At one point Ana Coelho menaced Kenneth Haynes with her knife; several persons saw this *although Mr. Haynes did not* [my emphasis]."

"At the trial, there were a number of minor inconsistencies," according to the DA, "and one major conflict. Ana Coelho claimed she did not stab Cook or anyone. The jury resolved that question by its verdict of murder."

Mr. Heafy's probation evaluation states:

> The court is presently concerned with an attractive, diminutive thirty-one-year-old female of Indian-Spanish extraction who has been convicted of second-degree murder in the knifing death of a twenty-seven-year-old man. . . .
>
> Mrs. Coelho has steadfastly maintained her innocence of the crime for which she has been convicted. During several interviews with the Probation Officer, she has been polite and respectful and appears intent on making a good impression. During interviews she appears to consider her responses very carefully and seems intent on measuring their effect on the Probation Officer. At no time during her incarceration or in her contacts with the Probation Officer has the defendant displayed the vulgarity, hostility or threatening attitude attributed to her.
>
> . . . Although it is contrary to the defendant's statement, there are numerous indications that the defendant becomes extremely hostile, belligerent, aggressive and profane particularly while under the influence of alcohol. Nearly every law enforcement report making reference to the defendant describes her as such and witnesses present in the bar, on the night of the offense, describe her as wearing a hunting knife in a sheath on her hip, and acting in a very wild and threatening manner.
>
> The defendant's impulsiveness, aggressiveness and potential for violence as demonstrated by the gravity of the offense for which she was convicted appears to necessitate that for the protection of society, future rehabilitative efforts be implemented in a secure, long term correctional facility.
>
> It is respectfully recommended that probation be denied and that the defendant be committed to the California Department of Corrections for imprisonment in the State Prison.

The day of her sentencing to five to twenty years, David Kogus, Ana's lawyer, filed an appeal. He says he made a grave mistake in not getting a change of venue. "The jury was unbelievable," Kogus said in a later telephone interview. "They were so hostile to her—it was apparent from the first. Ana was disliked in the area because she was close to people in a motorcycle gang who had moved up to Grass Valley and terrorized the people. It's a conservative, white, older community of people who moved out to Grass Valley to escape the cities themselves.

"I was used to San Francisco juries, and I didn't anticipate or see what a small-time jury would be like," he said. "Ana had asked me to get a change of venue and she was right. I should have listened to her. I've been living with this case now and it's really rough. Ana has beautiful children and comes from a fine family. I feel so strongly about it I don't think I'd go back to Nevada County for another trial.

"There were allegedly two eyewitnesses, but they didn't seem like much to me. And I don't think they're worth much, so I would expect that eventually we'll get her out. I'm confident we'll get her a new trial. I can't pick the county, but we will have a new trial. I just don't know whether they'll cut her loose or not. I don't know; I can only hope.

"I went to New York to talk to the guy who really did it, but he's scared. He's on parole and not willing to confess to anything, let alone open his mouth. So that's not much help."

Nothing has been much help for Ana. Her brief was filed in January and her appeal was submitted in March. In April the attorney general asked for an extension on his argument for denial of her appeal. In June he asked for still another extension and her appeal was scheduled to be heard in August. If she wins the right to a new trial, it could be another year or two before her case goes to court again.

Meanwhile, thoughts of freedom are on her mind. In April she wrote to me about being pulled out of CIW on a Superior Court subpoena to testify in a trial in Alameda County: "I was taken to Santa Rita Rehabilitation Center where I stayed until the end of March," she wrote.

What a horrible experience that was! Whew!!! While I was there, a girl kicked a hole in the wall and escaped. They still haven't caught her. It was a beautiful sight to see her leap over that fence to freedom. Being a few miles away from home myself, I was tempted to flee, too. I had the opportunity and I blew it. I hesitated because I felt that if I was to escape, it would be bad for my case. But if I could have escaped successfully, I'd be free. You just can't imagine what a hard decision it was that I made, to try and do this thing their way. But now I'm not so sure I made the right decision. . . .

At any rate, shortly after I returned here, I was moved from R.G.C. [Reception and Guidance Center] over here to the permanent prison side of this institution. They call it "campus," I call it "prison"! They call these buildings we live in "cottages" but they aren't. I call them "cell blocks."

The first day I was here they took me on what they call a "tour of the campus." What they did was show me the three work areas and the school building and that's all. The work areas include the laundry, industry and the kitchen. I have been over here for one week now and it's been a hectic week.

Ana spends her time now working in the kitchen of the California Institution for Women, scrubbing pots and pans. She's fixed up her room "so that it is comfortable to live in," with pictures of her children and letters from them still dominant among the decor, along with a Leo astrological poster. She has ten little guppies in a fish bowl and has acquired a drum, tambourine, and harmonica. She's secretary-treasurer for the United Indian Tribes, a self-help organization for Indian and non-Indian women at the prison. The group discusses Indian history and culture and is cultivating arts and crafts, learning weaving, beadwork, and leather tooling. She's going to school to take a high school equivalency test.

Ana might be considered a "model prisoner" getting "rehabilitated." But her personal turmoil would not be apparent to an outsider touring the prison "campus." She writes to her lawyer and to friends, going over and over the details of her case and the inconsistencies of testimony against her, hoping somehow to speed up the legal processes that may set her free.

"My hands are tied," she wrote in late June.

I'm so utterly helpless in here; I can do absolutely nothing. Where does a person turn for help?! And does help have to cost a lot of money? Is that what justice is, money?? There is no one here I can turn to for help, because in their eyes I am guilty because I have been found guilty. They don't know that in the eyes of everyone in Nevada County, the fact that I was arrested was enough to make them believe I was guilty, even before the trial. I keep calling it a trial—but it wasn't! You know that thing about innocent until proven guilty? Well, it's the complete opposite.

Yesterday I was told by one of my fellow inmates that we are only allowed to keep ten letters when we leave here. I've got scads and scads of letters. I don't know what I'm going to do with them, but I do know that I refuse to destroy any of the letters I have received from my little people. For the whole of last week, I was at my worst. I was nervous about the fact that my little people were out of school and I didn't know what they were going to do . . . as my mom and her husband both work. This plus the fact that my lawyer hasn't written to me and I haven't seen him since February. I was in such a bad frame of mind that the doctor prescribed some heavy tranquil medication and told me I was on the verge of a complete mental breakdown. Wow, it was super scary. I've never been there before, and I'm hoping and praying I'll never return there to that mental condition.

I work from 11 A.M. to 7 P.M. Some of those pots 'n pans are so huge I have to literally climb in them to get 'em clean. When I get back here to my room at night, I'm so completely exhausted I just fall out. I just don't know how much longer I can hold up to these terrific pressures both physically and especially mentally. I've been fighting very hard, with every ounce of strength I have, against becoming the kind of person you've got to be to exist here. And I feel my strength dwindling.

Twenty four hours a day, you're being subjected to brainwashing, and they're constantly trying to get you institutionalized. Oh, it's really ugly. When Ma and Frank and the kids came to visit me during Easter break, I tried real hard to give the impression that I was doing O.K. But I'm not. It's been a long time and I was so sad to see them leave. I just can't take all this, it's way too heavy. I can't sleep, think or function. And these thundering headaches are killing me. But they have enough to worry about, without worrying about me, too. I am so hurt, confused and lonely. And what's worse, I am learning how to hate. The hatred is building up in me every second of the long days and nights. My hatred is centered on the person who's responsible for the crime I'm in here for, but it doesn't stop there. It includes the D.A., the judge, the jury, the probation officer and those witnesses who were either bribed or made some kind of deal to get on the witness stand and lie. I really used to believe in justice. Now I know there isn't any.

God knows I am innocent—and if I can maintain my sanity, someday justice will be done. It has to be. I can't stand not being with my children.

Ana's Children

A letter from Linda, eleven years old, to her mother on January 9—the day after their visit in Nevada County Jail. Ana Lou Coelho had just been sentenced to five to twenty years in the state prison.

Dear A Beauitful [*sic*]
   Person,
Hi, I Love you,
I cryed all the
way home. I am
going to write
Ralph and tell him
what he is doing
to us, keeping us
apart for all this
time, and beg him
to go tell the
truth. Tell Dee I
said hi.
        (over)

I think I am going
to go crazy with-
out you. I love you
MOM more than
anyone else!
I'v got to eat break-

fast now, give me
your new address,
I love you forever
ever, ever, ever, ever,
 Love,
 LINDA

This letter was written two days before Rhonda's fourteenth birthday.

 Nov. 11, 1971
 8:00 p.m.

TO MY MOM
 I got your letter today. Thank you for the beautiful birthday card. It was poetic and sweet. I hope those people know they have made a sin putting you in "there"! Aunties house is nice. We went to Aunties house for dinner. Twart & and I were playing a game. When we went out in the kitchen to eat Laree told me that their going to have a skating party for me. She blew it. But their still having it for me even though I know. Peety died of distemper. Nothing is new at Better Way. Linda's Angel fish gets along with the other fish. She got them from "Doll." My rat "Persy" is so spoiled now by me and Grandma. She loves him. We don't even need a cage. Grandma lets him run around. She digs on him. She lets him climb on her.
 I'm watching Flip Wilson Show the same time I'm writing. Last week the Jackson 5 was on it. We were at Auntie's house. She put the [TV] up loud and everybody danced even "Grandma" ha-ha. Bet when you get out you will be so fat I won't know you. ha ha. Don't get too, fat. Sherri & Ronnie will write as soon as they get their ——— [censored] together. Well better go now have to feed my baby "Persy."

P.S. Persy says,   LOVE Rhonda   Love
"I Love Ya."   of course   Happness
P.S.S. I'll put Ronnie's   Miss   Peace
letter in here too, also.   America   Persy misses you
P.S.S. Kick out the Jam
 M.F.

A poem by Rhonda—which she wrote originally for Mother's Day when she was eleven, but sent to Ana again at CIW.

DEAR MOM,
 Deep in each heart, God puts the need of a love that is tender and strong. The need of one who can understand each sorrow and share each song. And to us all he grants one gift sweeter than any other, He grants us each a MOTHER,
 By: Rhonda
 of
 course

DEAR MOM,

We went trick-or-treating last night. It was fun. I was a witch. Linda was a hobo, Sherri an angel, Ronnie was a clown. Eddie had a fever so he couldn't go. Gloria was an Indian, Kathi was a hobo, Auntie had a pumpkin in the window with a peace symbol cut in it. This is Miss America speaking. I almost forgot the poem, I finished the poem and its time to go to school—
baaaaa
I wuv ya
this much_____

LOVE
Rhonda
of
course

From Sherri, ten years old.

DEAR MOM,
HI!!!
How are you   I am fine?
I wish you were here NOW.
But your wish will not come true.
It will come true for you—and me.
I better go and eat.

Love
alway
SHERRI
Loose

Another from Linda . . .

I will
kiss me please

Feb. 8, 1972

DEAR MOM,
Hi,
How are you? I hope
you have been feeling O.K.
Can Peggy and Joshua use our Washer & Dryer?
They really need them know that the
baby came. I saw Randy the baby's father.
He is tall and strong. He swung me all
around in peggy's front room. It was fun.
Grand ma already said Peggy could use the

W & Dryer. It is no fun when your there.
I don't feel like I'm living without you.
Time to go.

Love

LINDA

Loose

Peace   Love
I LOVE YOU
13,1110, 000, 000, 000, 000 more even!!!!

And from Ronnie, when he was six years old:

11/18/71

TO MOM,

    I Love you. I'm doing good in school. I don't have my school pictures yet. I miss you too also. I got my haircut ½ month ago. I hope you can get out for my birthday. Those people must be mean to keep you in there. Well time to go.

Love

RONNIE

After Ronnie's seventh birthday:

december 1971

DEAR MOM   I got some money for my birthday. We had cupcakes an brownies. I am 7 years old. I got a hat from Dorthy. I got a silly straw from Linda. I miss you. Will you be out for Christmas?

Love   Ronnie.

Father Charles

Father Charles Repole, a Capuchin priest and Franciscan monk, sits down in his little office, folding his floor-length brown robes around him. I had met him in the hallway of the women's jail on Riker's Island, and he cheerfully had welcomed me into his office to talk. Now he offers me a piece of peppermint candy and a cigarette and tells me he has worked at the women's New York City jail for six years.

"The girls here are eighty-five percent addicts and eighty percent prostitutes," he says. "They will open up to me because they know my lips are sealed.

"I've seen 'em all. I even had Angela Davis in for an interview. I wanted to see her even though she was not Catholic. I wanted to know what I could do."

Father Charles riffles through three-by-five cards in a little book that he says contains the names of the women he has interviewed along with his comments about them.

"I've seen Weathermen, Black Panthers, a doctor, a psychiatrist, a correctional officer from another institution, and a lot of Colombian girls. I call the consulate for them. I speak Spanish, so much of my work is bilingual. Twenty-five percent of the population is Spanish-speaking.

"Some of them are in here for bringing drugs into the country. All the heroin comes from Turkey to France to the U.S. Some comes in from Colombia. They get a poor farm girl and give her fifteen thousand pesos to come to America and all she has to do is bring this 'package.' In all my years, I had one gypsy, three Chinese, and three redskin Indians."

Some of Father Charles's other opinions and anecdotes included the following:

• "A girl tried to cut her wrist, she tried to commit suicide. It didn't work, and when she came in here, I said, 'Why'd ya do that? Why not come in and sit down and have a cigarette?' I always give the girls cigarettes free. You know, a little extra treat."

• "After the baby is born, a girl can give it to her parents or family or put it up for adoption. I leave it up to them. It's a hard thing for a lady to give up her own flesh and blood. But if they keep on drugs and are an unfit mother, I say, 'You can't take proper care of your baby. You should give it up for adoption.' "

• "I think pimps should be castrated and put up in front of firing squads and shot!"

• "In all my experience inside and outside, psychology notwithstanding, lesbians are made, not born. Homosexuals, yes, some are born that way."

• "Visits for children would not be very rewarding. Most of their children are placed with foster families. They can see them again when they get out."

• "Prisons are not as bad as people make them. It's a priori; they wouldn't be here if they hadn't done anything."

• "In the case of the death of their baby, the girls can go to the funeral if they get the proper papers from court. They can write to anybody they want, and they talk on the phone in case of serious sickness or death."

"I never divulge what they tell me," he said. "I meet with staff, but I never divulge unless it's public and I have their permission. Or unless it's something like an insurrection that would affect the institution. My role is different; instead of being in a parish on the street, my parish is here. I get them lawyers, I call their mothers, sometimes I let 'em talk on the phone to their kids. I keep candy and cigarettes in this drawer for them. See, look at all the candy. And in that file cabinet I have cards they can send out on special occasions.

"I am the link between the girls and the authorities and the outside world. When there was trouble here last year, they were going to take me and the Protestant chaplain as hostages. But I know they wouldn't have hurt us. They probably chose us because they knew we could speak to the administration for them."

Margaret Morris

The day I met Margaret Morris, she was sitting in the lobby at Marysville waiting for an appointment with the voluntary attorney to start the process of a divorce. Leaning forward on her cane, she called me over to talk with her. She was a short, extremely heavy white woman who appeared to be in her fifties.

Margaret told me she was graduated from a vocational high school in 1947. When she was arrested in 1970 she was charged with insufficient funds and intent to defraud. "I just signed the checks to get medical care. My husband wouldn't help me and I didn't have any other money. I wasn't getting proper medical care until I came here. There's a lot of things wrong with the hospital here, but at least I'm getting attention. I've had polio and don't have complete control.

"They've done a lot for me here. I weighed three hundred and five pounds when I came in and had had two mild nervous breakdowns due to medication. Now I've lost more than fifty pounds and I'm going to lose more. I weigh two hundred and forty-seven right now and it's because the nurse is giving me water pills. I'd been through the big hospital in Cleveland and they never gave me any water pills.

"Coming here has done me a lot of good. This was the best thing that could have happened to me 'cause now I have the chance to start a new life. People here have helped me. When I first came in here I was scared of my shadow. When I leave here I'm gonna start a new life to prove to the people here they've helped me."

Margaret Morris got tears in her eyes as she talked about how much she had been helped, and about how it was a big thing for her just to talk to me. Before, she said, she would have been afraid to open her mouth. The water pills were the main thing that had helped her, she said, and getting on a regular schedule that was helping her organize her life.

She said she worked in the sewing industry, making American flags. "I'm an official flag starter," she said. "I take the blue field and I dust this with a pattern, leaving point marks. You take a star and follow the pattern, but you have to be careful.''

Earlier that day, prisoners had told me how the flags are made: *You take a strip of red material and white material and sew them together. Then you sew thirteen stripes. Then you sew in the blue piece with stars. One woman sits and does nothing but draw stars all day. Somebody else cuts out the stars. Then you sew the lining on the back and then you put the band on the side and knock the holes in it. Then it's hemmed and ironed and starched and you have the national flag of the United States of America folded and ready for the public.*

Margaret smiled. ''When I leave,'' she said, ''I would like to work with people and help others, like I've been helped.''

Martha Moore

''I've been here since November,'' said ''Martha Moore,'' a correctional officer at a state prison. ''Before, I was a cosmetologist. I had my own shop. But now I have my shop up for sale. I thought this work would be easier; I've always worked with the public, plus my mother's a supervisor over at the prison hospital. She's been here ten years. I'm changing fields totally and I'm very happy about it. My mother always said I would like the work here.

''I work from seven to three, but I come in a half hour early. That's the way I do my job. I come in and check the log book to see what has happened before I came on. Very soon after I come in they start unlocking.

''I'm not teaching any cosmetology here. I'm mostly in supervision as a CO. I make sure to keep a schedule going: get the doors locked and unlocked on time, write reports, make sure the housekeeping's done. When the laundry comes in we supervise to make sure it's put away properly. The women come in and you check the pass for each woman. It has to be re-signed and marked with the time before she can leave the corridor.

''At lunch everyone comes back to the cottage. This is when food cards come back, and that's another roll call. We check them in, and after the food cards are checked and roll is taken, we make two calls and say we have everyone. They stay on the corridor during this time. No one goes to their rooms except under very rare circumstances. They have to stay here so we can supervise. Then when the whistle blows they all go back to work.

''I couldn't do anything with cosmetology training. Being responsible for fifty women at one time is enough. When the phone rings I know where they are. Each one of them. That's fifty people; that's a big responsibility.

"Today we have a cottage meeting and everyone has to be locked up—housekeeping and everything."

Anna Hardy

"I started to quit the first day I worked as a guard," Anna Hardy recalled. "I was taken into the mess hall, and every face I saw was sad. I was sick inside. I developed a migraine headache. I didn't think I could go back the next day and see all that sadness. But my brother, he was a policeman, told me I had to go back and face it; that I had made a decision and I should follow through on it. Well, I went back the next day, and the next, and then it got to be a day-to-day thing."

Anna Hardy "went to jail" after coming back to the United States from four years in Europe as a correspondence specialist for the U.S. Army. In Europe she supervised one of the army correspondence schools sponsored by the Department of Information and Education.

"After I came to Washington, D.C.," she said, "I went to jail, and I've been in jail ever since. I guess it would be nicer to say I hit the corrections field, and then the escalator moved me up." After Anna Hardy became a prison guard, she moved up through the ranks to become an assistant superintendent of a women's reformatory, chief administrator of the women in the District of Columbia Jail, and then administrator of the Women's Detention Center in Washington. Now she's the first woman to be a parole examiner for the Washington, D.C., Parole Board. Our interview was in her Parole Board office.

"The first year I was there I would cry," she said. "I would see mothers visiting their daughters and it would tear my heart strings up. I never got over it, but I learned to deal with it.

"There were many times I did things I did not personally believe in. I was not asked to violate the law or be inhumane, but in my time we had many difficult things. There were times persons were put into segregation for reasons I thought they shouldn't be segregated for. There were too many minor situations they used major solution tools for.

"For instance, I believe a person has the right to talk. It used to be that the officer would feel offended and call it 'back talk.' Too often action was taken because of personal feelings or because the officer was short-tempered. There are many other ways to deal with the situation.

"I guess I was a nuisance. I was always asking, 'Why?' It bothered me to see a person locked up for what I thought was minor. But I had to live with it. It used to bother me to take black coffee and a heel of bread for breakfast to a woman in a cell.

"Something else used to bother me. You'd have a woman in a control cell who was not allowed to take a bath. You wouldn't find it in the book—it was the exercise of power and authority that was overused. What could you do as a junior officer? You couldn't spare the time and sneak and give it. You had to live with that power and authority too.

"Among other things, what they were perpetuating was punishing the staff as well as the inmates. But I guess I stayed because I began to feel there was something about me that made me feel that I was somebody and there might be one of these somebodies who might want to be like me.

"I kept thinking: Someday, if it's possible, I'm going to be a supervisor. There were so many things I wanted to change. I didn't get to change all the things, but I think I made a difference. And I know I've changed. I used to be more of a hard-liner than I am now. I had been orientated to regimentation with the army to follow *do*s and *don't*s. Out of that, if I was expected to do something at a certain time, I did it. But a lot of what I had to do made me sick. I just kept telling myself that someday I might have a chance to change things. But it wasn't easy.

"When I came into corrections, I was black. I'm still black. In the beginning it didn't look like I could by competitive examination come through the uniform ranks.

"But if you put your mind to what you are doing and believe in what you are doing, it can work. I made up my mind that I would never allow my black skin to keep me from being in competition by not allowing myself to be part of that competition. I'm very efficient, and through efficiency, I did it my way.

"I remember, when it came time for the lieutenant exam, I had misgivings about it. I was afraid. Then another officer who was also taking the exam asked me why I was even bothering to take it. She was so sure she would get the promotion.

"I told her, 'There's only one way to lose the exam, and I'm not going to let it happen. You're the only other person taking it, and in education we're equal, so we'll score the same. In longevity, you've got it on me. In efficiency I'm better than you. There's only one way you can beat me out of it, and that's 'cause you're white, sweetie. That's why I have to get one hundred percent on that examination. And I'm gonna get one hundred percent.' I did get ninety-nine and a half percent right—and I got the promotion.

"I'm not ashamed to say I've been a competitor all my life. I was one of nine children. I was in the middle, and I didn't want my brothers or sisters to beat me.

"Things have changed a lot since I first began. And, like I said, I've changed a lot. I've learned a lot. It was during my time when we began to learn the really serious impact of drug abuse. I had seen some of the late stages of withdrawal, but when the policewomen's building was closed, we began to receive a woman directly from police on arrest. This means taking them through line-up, fingerprinting, and booking. We took over the precinct function for policewomen. Police started bringing us the women straight from arrest with no overnight in the district or a day in the court. We saw the whole works, straight from the street. I saw narcotics withdrawals that words do not describe—so pathetic that you couldn't look at it. It's total grief itself.

"We've had every kind of woman—women emotionally disturbed, women prone to go into catatonic state. Sometimes they're just one-shot situations; they come to jail just once. A number of fine people who just built up an emotional state—committed a crime once and not again.

"Then we've had some who are just bad. Not necessarily killers, but ones who just have no respect for their bodies or the law. And who show neglect in terms of children. Occasionally we get someone motivated some way and it's rewarding to see a change of face.

"I like the women. I'm not telling you we sat up in each other's living rooms. But I don't have any biases. I do understand what is happening with these women. I know their children and I know their mothers.

"All of them have problems to face. Additionally a woman has to face coming out of jail. Some have feelings about it; some could care less about going back again. Some know they're gonna do it again, whatever their crime was, so it's a calculated risk and they don't put up a big protest.

"Eighty-five percent of the women return. The figures kept creeping up—or maybe they didn't creep up. Statistics were not being kept for many years like they're being kept now.

"A considerable number of times there would be fairly affluent women eighteen and over arrested on a variety of charges. But once an affluent woman had gone to court we'd never see her again. I have every reason to believe her less affluent counterpart—on an identical charge—came back to jail. I can't vouch for what happened in court; I just know they didn't come back to jail.

"It's the same with prostitutes. There's no difference between one who prostitutes herself on the street and the one who lives in a luxurious apartment and pays for it in the same method. It's just that the ones in the luxurious apartments don't usually make it to jail.

"I'd personally like to see no woman arrested or prosecuted for prostitution. It would reduce the jail population considerably. We fill up the jails on prostitution charges. If there is to be a charge, it should be against both the male and the female. If you're not going to arrest the man, then it's not fair to just arrest the woman.

"And believe me, not every arrest stems from the agent. Like these rich big shots from out of town who come in and want to pay for some fun, and they end up charging the women. The poor innocent men have been led astray—tsk, tsk; no one thinks about what happens to the woman!

"So much of what brings about the prisoner comes from way back there in the community. There are serious ills that prevail in the early years that severely limit people from doing anything different. A lot has to do with family structure spread out into the immediate community and the schools. Not everybody is necessarily a victim in that sense, but so much of the responsibility for what brings people to jail lies in the general community frustration.

"So many of the women have been in juvenile facilities. What good's it do? Even if you're a hard-hearted Hannah, you gotta realize that.

"In my time I've been around women who were motivated and had good thoughts of making it. Sadly enough, I've never had time to follow through. I did have one woman who served a felony term, and some years later she went to a reformatory in Maryland and went to school there. She sent me a high school graduation invitation from the reformatory. I had two of her daughters under my purview at the time, and two of their brothers were in jail, too. But in spite of all the things that happened to them, you had to admire their family spirit and unity. If one of 'em got sent to jail, they'd write faithfully to them. And when it was time to get a box, they'd pack up a big box to send. In a way, you can compare it to another family when it's time for the kids to go off to college.

"These are the kinds of things that make people like me work in jail. I've gotten to know a lot of families—daughters, mothers, grandmothers. One family I knew for a long time. There were five sisters who came to jail at different times, and I'd met their mother first.

"I'll never forget one tiny kidnapper from Wisconsin who kidnapped a large man. I asked her how she did it. Her answer was, 'It was easy. He was scared. I wasn't.'

"There was one girl who escaped, and I felt a lot of personal involvement with her case. She was a beautiful girl with an IQ of a hundred and thirty-two. She was on trusted status and was attending American University. The psychologist took the girl to school, and I'd bring her back when I was coming on to the midnight shift. Well, one night I went and waited for her in the same spot and she didn't come. I went everywhere looking for her and left the car unlocked so if she'd gone off for a beer or something she would be able to get into the car. Finally I had to call the institution and report that she was missing. It was not as if I had been responsible for her or she had escaped from me—it was just the disappointment of it all.

"About four months later we got a call from New Mexico, where she'd been picked up on a drunk and disorderly charge. She was brought back, and we didn't prosecute her. She got out on parole and went back to American University. She graduated and married a fellow student. She's living a very successful life right now. If she walked in here right now, you'd never know her from anyone else.

"Another girl had a baby and no place for him to stay at the time. She didn't want to give him up, so he lived in the cottage for more than a year. You can imagine, the girls loved him to death. After he was a year old, we were afraid of overloving him, so he had to be placed in a foster home until she got out.

"When I had my first demonstrators out of the Pentagon, I had a whole new experience. I got accused of inhumane treatment, brutality, fantasies. The switchboard was flooded with calls. The complaints were made by white college-educated girls mostly, who had lived comfortable lives. Most of the persons arrested out of demonstrations are people either of very strong convictions or high academic qualifications. These are people you can't rehabilitate, and what are you gonna give them? After the first Pentagon arrests we had a lot of them for the first time. I felt so helpless then. It appeared to us nobody in the public wanted to believe we were other than inhuman.

"We established rapport with the demonstrators. They told us that part of their philosophy was that 'anytime we're in a situation we can't control, it's cruelty. We're in your jail and we don't have the key, so therefore this is a cruel situation.'

"During that time the contingent of women [prisoners] we had dealt with before were most cooperative with us. But often they got angry at the 'falling out' [passive resistance] and that sort of thing from the demonstrators. But I think after a while it was difficult for the demonstrators not to see us as monsters.

"Part of my orientation to jail had been that there could be no newsmen near the scene of any trouble. Throughout, the media was excluded; the idea was that newsmen make the situation worse. But then things started opening up. When we were getting all the calls after the Pentagon arrests, Walter Masterman from NBC came to interview me, and after people saw me on the camera, I think it changed things; it just wasn't what they expected. I think that's what stopped the calls. Usually more exposure is a good thing, but sometimes it backfires.

"We had one woman come in—a reporter—and opened everything up to her, let her stay overnight. I'd like to spit in her face. She did me a great injustice, and I'll never forget it. The things she wrote—the cold, bare-faced lies. She wrote and implied that I was responsible for the death of a girl at the institution I had known for years. Why she didn't ask me about it, I don't know. It would have only been fair. She said the girl, Willa Mae Johnson, died in jail, but that was a lie. She died in D.C. Hospital.

"Willa Mae Johnson was the kind of person I'd save her life, and I like to think I'm the kind of person she'd save my life. I'd known her for years and I never would have let her die. She came into the jail and was going through cold turkey. Eventually we sent her to the hospital, and she died in the hospital four days later of complications—not from the cold turkey.

"I can't tell you how that newspaper article affected me. I couldn't go to work the next day. I was really sick. I'm still bitter. But I just thought, 'What will my friends think, my neighbors?' I couldn't call everyone I knew to dispute the article; I just had to live through it. I didn't know if I could.

"We all knew it was an imperfect institution. Not one of us would have wanted to be an inmate there. I know what people go through in jail. I always keyed the officers up to 'It could have been your daughter, or it could have been your sisters.' But I also have empathy for prison adminis-trators.

"It's true—in jail a woman sleeps, eats, bathes by regulation. Every-thing she does is controlled, and everything she doesn't do is controlled. Her flexibility and our flexibility can expand only to the walls of the jail or within the confines of the walls.

"Basically by philosophy I'm the same individual, but now the atmo-sphere provides for more use of my talents. I'm given great leeway in making decisions. I no longer have to respond to *do*s and *don't*s.

"I've seen a lot of change in the corrections field. There are lots who'll never change until they die—some who are hard-nosed—but there are others who were hard-nosed who learned and are still changing. Even though I used to be so oriented to military thinking, I'm fully able to accept all kinds of programs the community has to offer for advancement of a person who needs it. I have no hang-up about a person serving a sentence to go to school or job training in the city.

"I think the Parole Board trusts me to use my judgment, and up to this time it's been pretty good. I give the full respect accorded to the board chairman, and it goes beyond this to the people I am examining and mak-ing recommendations on. I have the satisfaction of feeling I am doing a good job. I've reached what I want professionally; I don't want to go any higher. I want to retire eventually—probably within a few years.

"Probably the reason I can sleep at night is that at the end of the day I feel I have not done an unjust thing to someone. My husband [Kenneth Hardy, commissioner of corrections in D.C.] can worry, but if he does, he has to do that by himself. It's a big picture to me. Even if I have recommended against a man or woman getting parole, I have to believe it's a justifiable recommendation—leaving the possibility open that I may not have put all the little screws together right. So far my batting average has been very good."

Proud Mary

Proud Mary sold her soul for 50 grams of speed.
Then she sold her body,
To meet her hooked brain need.
She sold her brand new dress
Her only pair of shoes,
Now Mary haunts the street
Dressed only in her blues.
The vulture came and ate her veins
Until there was no trace
Now hungry Mary kept shooting dope
Between tears on her face
No one mourned Mary's passing
There was no one to bother
But I sold my tears to buy her grave
Proud Mary was my "mother."
                    —Ida Mae Tassin, Bedford Hills

Suzanne Williams

KW: Can you tell me about when you escaped from the federal penitentiary at Alderson?

Suzi: Oh, I'll never forget that whole scene. Whew. Well, my best friend had gotten himself into a jam in New York City. He had been arrested for the draft, and not too long before that he had a really horrible jail experience in Wyoming. He had been beaten up and had almost died, and had not been in too good shape as a result of the thing and sort of was putting his head back together. And shortly after that he was arrested. He's into a lot of noncooperating with jails; he feels pretty absolutely about right and wrong and stuff. And then he was picked up on his draft thing, and like I didn't know what sort of mental shape he was in, or how he was, or if he needed aid and comfort, or what. And I was unable to find out. They wouldn't let me call, so I figured, well, you know, I gotta find out. I was just very worried about him. So I split.

KW: How did you get out? Did you just walk out?

Suzi: It's a little harder than that. First of all, you really can't hitchhike anywhere in the area, because it's in the middle of nowhere, and everyone knows what's down the road, and any strange unidentified females will immediately be picked up on. And then this little matter of count. Because their physical security is not that great, they keep careful track of you, pretty much. They have nine counts within every twenty-four-hour period. So they count you up at eight-fifteen in the morning, and then at twelve-fifteen in the afternoon, and at four-fifteen in the afternoon. Then they count you an hour after you come back from supper. Then they count you when it becomes twilight. And then they count you at ten, and then at midnight, and then at three, and then at six.

Two of those were added while I was there on my '68 to '69 bit. We call the eight-fifteen one the "Nancy Memorial Count." She skipped right around then, and then they put in that count. And the midnight one is the "Jo Memorial Count." They caught Nancy after about three years of her being out, but I'm happy to say that Jo is still at liberty.

Besides that, like you have your work assignment, and several of those counts are counted on the job, or else you're counted in the unit if you have a day off or something. But just generally, if you're not on the job, they want to know where you are. And if you're supposed to be in the unit, you got to be there. If you go anywhere that isn't on your regular schedule, then they will call up and say, "Suzanne Williams is on her way to the clinic," and if I don't arrive within five or ten minutes, they try to track you down. And then they call back, you know, to my boss at work, "Suzanne Williams is on her way back from the clinic." So that most of your comings and goings are according to a set schedule, and things that are out of schedule, they will call you in and out.

There are ways to get around them. But generally they keep a close eye on people. And one thing which helps it a lot with the whole security thing is that women are generally trained that they can't do things, and to stay down and that kind of stuff. Plus most of the inmates there are from the big cities and don't have the vaguest idea of what they would do if they were out in the sticks in West Virginia, or which way is north, south, east, or west. So that's why they don't have more escapes than they do.

But what I did was, I went to the regular Saturday night movie, and I was dressed in warm clothes. In fact the cottage police remarked, "Oh, Suzanne, you're all dressed up warm tonight." You can't split from the movie because they have police right outside there and they take note of who comes and goes. So I waited till it was over, and I wasn't the first one out, but I was about the fifth one out. I really walked quickly.

At that time they weren't using Cottage Twenty-six. And so I walked over behind there and climbed over the fence. And oh, as I was climbing the fence, I had on this pair of sneakers that was a little bit too big for me, and I got up—oh, it's about a twelve-foot fence with three strands of barbed wire—and I had got up over the fence and very carefully over the barbed wire, and I was pulling my last foot up over, and my shoe fell off.

I wanted to die, I really did. I was going to say, Oh, the hell with it, and go on, but second thoughts told me that just wasn't practical, so back over the fence, inside, crawling around in all the leaves and crud, 'cause it was raining lightly, and scrub around for the shoe, finally I put it back on, retied the other one so it doesn't do a repeat number, and back up over the fence. I was worried 'cause that was like the most exposed part of the whole operation. If the car had happened to swing by and hit me with its headlights, that would have been it.

KW: When you finally got over the fence, what did you do?

Suzi: Then I walked on the railroad tracks for about twenty miles west. I had walked through a couple of little towns sort of holding my breath. But it was dark, and it was raining lightly most of the night. And I guess that damped out the dogs. There was one place where the tracks went through this tunnel, underneath a mountain. And it wasn't like a double tunnel, but it was two single ones, so there wasn't much room. And it was about a mile long. And oh, it was scary. There was just this single little red signal light at the end giving a faint pink gleam on the rails, and I had never been so scared in my life. So I ran through the tunnel.

Shortly after I got out of the tunnel the eastbound passenger train went zipping through. And every time a train came by, you know, you'd have to jump into the bushes. I finally got to Hinton, and see, Hinton has a number of roads. Before that point like there's only the one highway. It's pretty obvious what highway it is, and any woman seen on that would be suspicious. But Hinton is a much larger town, and there are a number of other highways going through there, so strange people would be much more likely. But I wasn't hitchhiking even from Hinton, because I couldn't think of any plausible reason why I would be out there at four-thirty in the morning.

So I just walked along, and I was walking up the mountain towards Beckley, and I got about four or five miles further, and some people that were going into town for a long trip, into Beckley, about fifty miles from Alderson, stopped and picked me up. They thought I had run away from home, see. And they came on all very sympathetic, and after the initial silence one of them said in a very fatherly type tone, "Did things get pretty bad that you had to run away?" I said, "Oh, yes." And he said, "Well, what was the problem?" And I said, "Well, uh, my boyfriend was in trouble and they wouldn't let me go see him." "They" being unspecified, but they thought I meant parents. And I kind of got into a rap, you know, "They were always telling me what to do," and "I didn't have much freedom." Every word was the truth. So they made sympathetic noises and I fell asleep. And then when I got to Beckley, one of the guys gave me a couple dimes. I made a couple phone calls and arranged some transportation. Then when I got business taken care of I went out.

KW: Did you get to New York City?

Suzi: Oh, yeah. I spent a couple weeks there and found out that my friend was all right.

KW: Did you get to see him?

Suzi: No, I didn't. But there was a preacher that got to see him. But there was a funny thing on that, too. My friend was in jail and I would be down there like every day, asking to see him; they'd say, No, you can't see him, blah, blah, blah, blah, blah. And then one day they said, Well, Reverend So-and-So is up there seeing him, you can wait till he comes down. So I waited and he came down, some guy who was a Quaker, and the warden at the jail. The reverend introduced me to the guy by my right name, and then the guy offered to drive us to the subway, which he did in his official bureau business car. I had walked by that car on the way into the jail and sort of shuddered at it, because it was just the same kind of official car they had at Alderson. After I knew my friend was all right, I went up to my brother's place in Vermont and figured they could come by and get me, 'cause with just a year's sentence it really isn't worthwhile to hide for the rest of your life for a short thing like that, even if you get more time tagged on for escaping. But yet and still, I'm not really geared to turning myself in, so I settled for something of a compromise. And they did come and pick me up.

KW: Did they just come by to see if you were there?

Suzi: Yeah.

KW: So how long had you been out?

Suzi: Oh, just three weeks. But when someone escapes from Alderson, they notify all of the police in the area immediately, and the radio stations and the newspapers in the area are notified immediately. Of course the first thing they do is they call the FBI and then all the local police types, and they send male guards to beat through the bushes around the perimeter, and to go to certain crossroads of small dirt roads, and to run up and down the small dirt roads and main roads to see if anybody's there, at crossroads and railroad tracks, and different places like that. And they will hunt for you usually twenty-four hours, except if you're somebody they want real bad; then they'll search for you longer.

KW: Do they pay the local people for catching someone who escapes?

Suzi: Fifty dollars a head, which is a lot of money in that part of West Virginia. I think one reason why I had such an easy time escaping, once I had got out of the very immediate area, was that except for the people that work at the prison, I think all the locals believe that we all have horns and a tail and are ten feet tall and smoke cigars regularly and wear hobnail boots. So that you know, I was at the time twenty years old, had a short haircut, and looked about sixteen.

It was funny, right after I was picked up, at my brother's place in southern Vermont, one FBI agent and one state trooper took me down first to the state police barracks, which was in the same town. And they sort of parked me in a back room while they were making phone calls and getting the stuff run through. And this off-duty trooper wandered in, just getting ready to go on the job, and he was charmed at the idea that they had a young girl in there as a prisoner. And he said, "Oh, what did they arrest you for, playing hooky?"

And I wasn't feeling real talkative and wasn't feeling real happy at the time and didn't want to get into a big rap with him, so I just said, "No." But then he persisted. Had I been arrested for shoplifting? I said, "No," wishing he would go away. And he finally said, "Well, what *were* you arrested for?" I said, "Escaping from a federal penitentiary." And his mouth dropped and he stuttered, "You don't look old enough to even have heard of a federal penitentiary. What were you charged with to be there?" And I said, "Destruction of government property, destruction of public records, interfering with the Military Selective Service Act of 1967, and conspiracy." He shut up and went away, which was the desired effect.

It's silly how that shuts people up. When I went to court in Charleston to be sentenced for the escape, there were six of us altogether, from Alderson escape cases, staying in the Charleston jail. We stayed there for about four days while the thing was being run through. We came into the jail with handcuffs and waist chains and all this hardware garbage, and the two older of the four of us were put in the second floor with the rest of the women. But then we created an overflow, so they took the four younger ones of us and put us on the third tier, and they put one of the local inmates up there to sort of tell us what the rules were and so forth and so on. She was what they call in that particular jail a kick-out girl, which is, I guess, trustee or something. And she was their kind of person. Everything we said, she ran and told the police about. Yeah, we didn't care for this. And so we sent word to the police that we wanted her off our tier, please. She was gone in five minutes. They were really afraid of us. They thought we were really going to do something to her. Of course a couple of the other people were making big bad threatening noises, you know, and they had seen us being brought in in the chains and handcuffs and maximum security, escapees from the penitentiary, and we didn't really give a shit, because we had all had time, and we were going to get more time, so we were just goofing off. I got six months added to my sentence for the escape, so it ended up to be eighteen months total, regular procedure.

Dora Grey

"Dora Grey" says the worst thirty-six days of her life were spent in a halfway house in Des Moines, Iowa.

"That halfway house was worse than I could believe," Dora said one night as she sat on her prison bed in the Iowa Reformatory for Women in Rockwell City. "I had to share an apartment with a woman I detested and vice versa. Everybody knew it. She ran off with my good suede coat as a last measure. I was out on bond to Model Cities, and they put me in the halfway house. I worked at a cleaner's for some really good people. But my probation officer was uptight, and one day my roommate escaped and she thought I had escaped, too. She figured I wasn't at work, so they called work and asked for me. My boss just said, no, I wasn't there. He didn't think it was anybody's business that I was out making deliveries, and they didn't tell him why they were asking. So I was sentenced for a probation violation on a thirty-day indictable misdemeanor. The probation officer had no right to violate my probation, unless I was convicted. I was found innocent of the violation but I got sentenced here anyway.

"If they don't give me parole in July, it's all over. I'm not gonna stay around here. I'm not gonna do no two and a half years on a ten-year sentence. I'll run."

Dora, little and wiry, speaks in a small voice, but her words are big and ferocious. When she's really talking angrily, she talks out of the side of her mouth, reminding me of Woody Allen doing a take-off on Humphrey Bogart. Her blond wispy hair also reminds me of Allen. But humor doesn't come quickly to Dora. A laugh is a long time coming from her, as are tears.

Dora's first husband was killed in Vietnam. Her second husband, Lee, "treated me like a queen and I treated him like a king," Dora said. "He was a bricklayer, and he always earned good money and took good care of me. I woke up one morning and he was laying there waiting for me to come back from the bathroom. He looked upset and he was sweating, and he told me about this dream he'd had a few nights before. He told me he had dreamt that I was pregnant but that he died.

"He told me he knew I was pregnant—he could tell. And that same morning I had realized I was pregnant. He was crying. I told him one part of the dream could be true without the other part being true. But he said it was all true. He made me promise to take care of myself and the baby. That same day he went to work and he was knocked off a scaffolding. He fell from seven stories in the air. They took him to intensive care in the hospital and called me. He held out six days even though the doctor said he wouldn't live overnight. I visited him every day and stayed with him every hour I could. On the seventh day, the bus didn't come on time and I was late to the hospital. When I got there, they told me he was dead. When I was leaving the hospital, I fell down the steps and had a miscarriage. I lost my baby and my husband on the same day.

"Lee had this cousin Darrell he'd told about his dream, too. He told Darrell to marry me and take care of the baby and me. So Darrell forced me to marry him. He threatened to kill my baby sister if I didn't. My baby sister is my heart; I raised her myself. He beat me so bad. I lived with him one and a half years, and then we were married for four and a half months. He used to come home and he would have been drinking and he'd beat me. He wouldn't let me go out of the house or go anywhere alone. If I wanted to buy a soda, he would go with me across the hall and put the dime in the machine himself. He never gave me a penny. He wouldn't even give me a dime for a soda.

"This one night he had been drinking as usual, and when he came home he started beating me with a glass ashtray. Then he passed out on the bed. I just flipped out; I couldn't take any more. I tied him up in the sheets with his legs tied to the bottom and his arms above his head and I beat him with a baseball bat. Then I went to the hospital to get my head and cuts checked from where he beat me. When I came back, he was still tied up. I got all his money and the keys to the car. He had never given me a thing. His one mistake was that the car was in my name because he had a record and he couldn't get it under his name. He woke up and said, 'Untie me.' I told him, 'Motherfucker, you got yourself in there, untie yourself.' He got himself loose. When he came through the door into the living room, I gave it to him with the baseball bat again. I knocked him out and kept beating him. Then I left and I haven't seen him since. I heard he was looking for me, but he'll never find me."

Dora got in the car and drove—first to Chicago, then to Iowa. She has one daughter by her first husband, but when she got busted and came to prison, she said for the prison record she had no children. "I have a little girl, but I'd never tell anybody here I had her. They give you so much hassle. My sister on the West Coast has her and is waiting till I get home. I don't want any child of mine in a foster home or in the courts, ever."

Dora continually referred to her daughter as her "heart" and talked about her youngest sister, also her "heart." She showed me pictures of both. She is used to raising children. She was the oldest of sixteen children, "twelve by my father and four by my stepfather.

"My mother's biggest disappointment was that I was a girl. She was only seventeen when she had me, so she couldn't understand. One time when I was sitting down by a chair where they couldn't see me, I heard her tell my father she would never forgive me for not being a boy. She forgave my brother for having one leg shorter than the other, but she never forgave me for being a girl. She didn't love me. I guess I knew it but I never admitted it. I guess I just wanted her to love me so bad that I just kept trying to win her love. And I kept trying to believe she loved me. The last time she ever hit me was when I was sixteen. I was in the front yard, and she lifted my dress up and beat me in front of the neighbors with a board. I was wearing one of those summer dresses with spaghetti straps. I'll never forget it. I was so ashamed. I was so embarrassed. That night I snuck up behind her, and she jumped when she heard my voice. I said, 'Don't you never touch me again, Mommy. Don't you never touch me again in front of the neighbors or no one.' She never hit me again."

Jeanette Spenser

Jeanette Spenser, a sturdy woman with deep brown skin and a subtle twinkle in her eyes, grew up in Harlem. When she was twelve she moved to the Bronx with her mother, who worked as a domestic, and her new stepfather, a factory worker.

"I was a scholarly kid, and even though my mother didn't make much money, she always dressed me nice," Jeanette said. "I always had a good coat to wear to school and I looked neat and clean. This made me unpopular to start with, besides being scholarly. I had to fight to defend myself. Most every fight I had was for being called a bastard. I'd seen my father, but I didn't know him. I was insecure. And I didn't like my stepfather. I didn't know how to tell my mother anything, either. It had been our own little world till he came in. I got married at nineteen to escape. The only way I saw to get out of my house was to get married. So I got married for all the wrong reasons.

"My husband loved to drink. I loved the taste, but not what it did to me. It got to be a necessity for me. The doctor told me, when I was twenty-one, I was a potential alcoholic. I was drinking too much, and it was interfering with my life, which on the whole was pretty ordinary except for my extra problem.

"I had the home and the daughter and the husband with a decent job. But as years passed, I was less able to function as a housewife or a mother, and eventually I was unemployable. I lost my husband and my home, and eventually my daughter was taken away. Then I had nothing. I was on the fringes with drug addicts, alcoholics, and people considered sick.

"Society has made a lot of people outcasts, and they have their own little bars they hang out in. I had become an outcast and I hung out in those bars. I cared about my child, but I knew I couldn't do anything about it. The people I was with didn't have the answers. It was like being in a rat race and wanting to get out but not knowing how to get out. My people had turned their backs, and I couldn't blame them. I was terrible.

"Then one time in this 'Bucket of Blood' bar, I met a guy who had just come out of jail. He took a liking to me and I liked him, I guess . . . but I don't know, I was so numb at the time. Anyway, we started hanging out together. All I was interested in was, did I have enough money to get my bottle. It didn't bother me, nothing else did.

"We committed a robbery of a laundry in the Bronx. I was in the back, drinking out of my bottle while he was taking the money. And I was wearing a purple coat. When we got the money we ran out, but somebody had called the police. Police cars came from every direction, and they caught us and handcuffed us. They couldn't miss me running in that coat.

"In the beginning it was like it was happening to someone else. It wasn't happening to me. I didn't feel I had done anything wrong. I'm very glad I didn't get away with it the first time. I'm glad I was caught, or I might have been dead today. I was taken into the precinct and charged with armed robbery, then to the old House of Detention.

"An old friend of mine came to visit me in the jail. He said, 'What's happened to you? You've gone crazy since your mother died. She's not even cold, and look at all the trouble you're in.' I had been deteriorating and destroying myself for fifteen years, and this was like the end of the line. I had sought help, but not in the right places. I didn't want to be a drunk. I didn't want to be the kind of person who doesn't care about someone else, but I was. I only cared about my kid, and I knew the best thing I could do for her was stay away from her. I don't think I knew what love meant, 'cause I didn't love me. You have to love yourself before you can love anybody else.

"I had laid aside my own sense of right and wrong a long time before to meet my own needs. I had to get rid of all the garbage and reevaluate my old set of standards. It's hard—and that's why most people don't want to go through the changes.

"Anyway, I never did understand what happened to me legally. Emotionally, I was given a sense of degradation from the time of arrest. On the one level, women aren't supposed to do anything wrong. If a man is arrested for drunk, he's still treated like a man. But the attitude of the arresting officer was one of disgust that he had to be bothered with me. His feeling was, 'If you don't respect yourself as a woman, we won't respect you either.' The pattern goes all the way through. Even the probation officer checking me out of the House of Detention assumed I was a prostitute, since I hadn't been working—in spite of the fact I was arrested for another crime. It's like you're automatically loose if you've been arrested. The laws are unfair—for a girl it's promiscuity, for boys it's natural experimenting. Like with prostitution—a man goes home and the girl gets sixty days.

"Anyway, I laid in the House of Detention for six months. When I went to court and they read four indictments, I was scared to death. I was thirty-three years old, and this was my first real brush with the law under these circumstances. I had a Legal Aid lawyer. He recommended that I take a guilty plea to robbery in the third degree. I was sentenced and served my time, and I still don't know what robbery in the third degree is—except that it's better than armed robbery, timewise. I was sentenced to one to ten years and they told me I was lucky.

"I didn't expect anything else. I had committed a crime, and punishment for committing a crime against society is prison. But the officers at the House of Detention were shocked at the time I got. And I couldn't even picture ten years. But one CO said I really was lucky—that yesterday the judge was giving out three to ten years. I did six months in the House of Detention before I was sentenced to Bedford Hills. I did fourteen months in Bedford Hills and did five and a half years of parole before they released me.

"When I was arrested, I felt I was some kind of moral leper, some kind of bad seed. I didn't know alcohol was a sickness. I actually had thought I was keeping myself alive drinking, 'cause if I stopped, I got so sick. But I came to the realization at the House of Detention that alcohol was the problem, and I began to deal with me.

"I was scared when I went to Bedford Hills. But I knew a few things by then. Like if you act quiet and hostile, people will consider you dangerous and won't bother you. So when I got out of isolation and women came up and talked to me, I said, 'I left my feelings outside the gate, and I'll pick 'em up on my way out.' I meant I wasn't going to take no junk from anyone. I made a promise if anybody hit me, I was gonna send 'em to the hospital.

"When you go in, if you have certain characteristics, you're classified a certain way. First of all, if you are aggressive, if you're not a dependent kind of woman, you're placed in a position where people think you have homosexual tendencies. If you're in that society long, you play the game if it makes it easier to survive. And it makes it easier if people think you're a stud broad. I played the game to make it easier so they would leave me alone. I didn't have money to use makeup, and I couldn't see going through any changes. You're in there and the women are looking for new faces. Since I was quiet and not too feminine-looking, I was placed in a certain box in other people's mind. I let them think that's what box I was in, 'cause it was a good way to survive. My good friends knew better. But I had three good friends, and they were considered 'my women,' so they in turn were safe, too. You have to find ways to survive. You cultivate ways to survive. It's an alien world, and it has nothing to do with functioning in society better. What I learned there was to survive there."

What Jeanette saw happen in prison—to herself and others—is what pushed her into working with other ex-cons at the Fortune Society, a self-help organization in New York City that offers support services to prisoners and advocates for changes in the criminal justice system. Jeanette also was motivated by seeing what happened to a sixteen-year-old sentenced to Bedford Hills. "I watched that kid when I was there and the changes she went through about herself and about sex and who she was," Jeanette said. "One day some of the women put makeup on her and she ran. She was frightened by what she saw. Her sex drives had been misdirected by women older than her. A lot of women are caught up in that process who come out thinking they are lesbians just because they've been institutionalized. I got angry one day and said, 'I don't think there are five true lesbians here!'

"I did hard labor at Bedford Hills. I unloaded trucks at the storehouse first and then sat down and did records work. I had to figure out mathematically how much coffee each kitchen needed and proper distribution of supplies. I was a bookkeeper, too. I was paid five cents a day and got a bonus each month of one pound of sugar, one pound of coffee, and one can of evaporated milk.

"When you're in prison, time stops. You come out with the same problems you go in with—and start all over again with their twelve extra rules of parole in addition. While you're there, you just learn to survive and manipulate any extra pleasure you can. A comparatively honest person who just committed a crime of passion would end up becoming a manipulator in prison. A girl who works in the kitchen takes extra slices of meat and gets cigarettes for them. Cigarettes are money in prison. There's nothing there to foster the qualities society wants. You become dishonest just to make it. All the qualities you're being sent there to get, they forget you won't have when you get back. You wind up doing all those little things just to make life more comfortable for yourself.

"Sixty percent of what you do is against some rule. If you have more than four slices of bread in your room, it's against the rules. An egg or rice, you get three days in punishment. I know a woman who got nineteen days in punishment for refusing two slices of burnt toast. They'd have raids on your room. But they'd only look where you hide things. So I'd leave whatever I had that was contraband out in open view. I never got busted.

"When I think back, the only reason my time wasn't wasted was because I had come to the end of the road before I went there and was looking for answers. When a weekly alcoholic program came in from the outside, I found a beginning. When I got out on parole, that's when people in the program really helped me out. The day I got home, people from the program picked me up. A woman who had spoken at the prison became a friend. I don't think she knew how much she helped me. I was on parole, and I was living with a sick aunt. This lady gave me keys to her apartment so I could go there after work or whenever I needed to get away from my aunt. She trusted me. I couldn't believe it. My references were all to jail then. She said, 'Listen, that's behind you.' And she told me to stop thinking about my past life and start living in my present life.

"My parole officer said, 'You aren't considered a criminal.' And I said, 'If I'm not, then why was I locked up? I wasn't violent. I might as well have been.' Anyway, I got a one-room apartment of my own finally. I told the landlady I was a parolee, and she was very nice. I stayed there almost two years, using the phone in the greeting card shop down the block. The man in the shop said I had a nice smile. But I'd use his phone and go out and look for work.

"When I was honest, I couldn't get a job. I'd been out about nine months then and the man in the greeting card shop told me to go to the hardware store, that they needed a bookkeeper. I went, and the man hired me. He told me not to worry about not being a bookkeeper, that I would learn through the work. My starting salary was eighty-five dollars a week. Can you imagine how good that was after a nickel a day? I felt so good making a decent salary.

"I worked five years for this man and his wife and finished my parole on that job. I worked a year before I told them I was a parolee. I was turning gray worrying about it. By that time I had hooked up with Fortune Society and was using a different name on speaking engagements because of the job. When I finally told him, he gave me a raise. He was very honest, though, and told me he didn't know if he would have hired me or not if he had known I was an ex-con.

"My daughter and I eased back into our relationship again. At first we went to the movies every Saturday or Sunday. Eventually she came back to live with me out of her own choice. It took about six months.

"I was tired. I was very tired. What I had for a life wasn't anything like I had pictured in my teens, where I wanted to be a schoolteacher, get married, and be a wife and mother. So it was like starting all over again.

"I was scared to death of decisions. All decisions had been taken away from me in prison, and coming home is so hard. The only thing you've been responsible for is being on the job when you're supposed to work. How can you come out and make a good decision? I was scared to make any at all. I finally had to say, I'll just make the decision and live with it—good, bad, or indifferent.

"After I'd been home awhile, I wondered if ex-cons were doing anything for ex-cons. I couldn't forget what I'd experienced—the sixteen-year-old kid, the inmate who was put into punishment behind two doors and wound up in a catatonic state because she couldn't stand it. She couldn't stand being in a steel cell with only a Bible and a book of rules, a toilet, and a bed, with a matron coming by three times a day with a cigarette. I couldn't forget the claustrophobia I'd experienced and what it was like to go to the library to look for a book and find that anything pertinent or relevant must have been printed in the 1800s.

"I had come to believe that people destroy themselves by committing crimes and going to jail. It's a way of self-destruction. And I didn't see anything in there to help. Prisons don't serve any purpose but removing women from society. Even though the physical facilities and surroundings where I was at are better than men's prisons, and there is less physical brutality unless a woman fights, all the demands made at Attica could fit very well into any women's prison.

"Well, I was struck by the honesty of the people at Fortune. And I found out that I cared, I cared a lot. I became committed then—both to dealing with myself and to maybe help other people avoid my mistakes and to expose what prisons really are.

"I have a new way of life now. I don't take ordinary things for granted anymore. Ordinary things are gifts to me. I enjoy food. I enjoy going to a good show. I enjoy people. I've had a lot of luck, a lot of good breaks."

Eva Dugan

They changed the hanging law way back when Eva Dugan was decapitated because they miscalculated her weight. She was executed February 21, 1930. The last hanging we had was August 21, 1931. The reason we went to lethal gas was basically Eva Dugan. Death by lethal gas was made elective October 28, 1933. Out of sixty-three executions, Eva Dugan was the only woman.

—A. E. "Bud" Gomez, Business Manager, Arizona State Prison

Eva Dugan, a convicted murderer, was hanged at 5:02 A.M., February 21, 1930, in Arizona State Prison's death house.

Ms. Dugan had been convicted of killing an elderly Tucson rancher named A. J. Mathis in January 1927. Mathis's skeleton, encrusted with lime and a gag still in its teeth, had been found almost a year after his death by a camper from Oklahoma who accidentally discovered the rancher's shallow grave while driving a tent stake into the ground. Police arrested Eva Dugan for the crime and said at her trial that after the slaying, she "fled with a mysterious drifter," a young man known only as "Jack," who never was arrested.

Eva maintained her innocence from the beginning.

In fact, right up to the time she left the women's cell block at Arizona State Prison for the death house, Eva was sure she would be spared because she was innocent. "The attorney general is probably on his way here now," she said.

But no pardon came to stay her execution.

The day and night before her execution, Eva Dugan visited with friends and newsmen. According to one newsman she made small jokes, "some of them a bit macabre," and from time to time glanced at the clock. She told a reporter for the *Arizona Republic:* "I am going to my Maker with a clear conscience. I am innocent of any murder and God knows I am."

According to newspaper reports at the time, a rumor on the prison grapevine spread shortly after midnight that Eva Dugan would "cheat the gallows"—or cheat the spectators—by taking her own life. Guards searched her cell and found a hidden bottle of raw ammonia. They searched her body and found three razor blades in the collar of her dress; they charged her friends in the women's cell block with attempting to aid Eva's wish to die privately.

When dawn broke on Eva's execution day, a veteran guard called "Daddy" Allen led Eva Dugan's small procession to the death house.

The tiny fifty-two-year-old woman was flanked by two other guards and followed by the prison chaplain, who in later years became chairman of the state parole board.

"Don't hold my arms so hard," she told the guards as she mounted the scaffold. "People will think I'm afraid."

The noose was placed around her neck, and she swayed slightly as she stood on the trap door. She closed her eyes and shook her head "no" when the warden asked her if she had any last words.

Seventy-five people, including seven women, had gathered to view the execution. They watched as Eva Dugan plunged through the trap door and hit the end of the rope with a bouncing jolt. Her head snapped off and rolled into a corner.

Spectators were horrified. Politicians, newspapermen, and the public immediately began to demand that a "more humane means of execution"—such as a gas chamber—be substituted for the "unreliable gallows."

The outcry was not for the abolition of the death penalty, but for a more reliable, more antiseptic execution—one that would not shock the sensibilities of the onlookers.

Eva Dugan was buried in a Florence cemetery in a beaded, jazz-age silk dress she had sewn by hand while awaiting execution. She paid for her own coffin by selling handkerchiefs she had embroidered in her cell.

When I visited Arizona State Prison, I found a single piece of paper documenting the prison numbers, names, race, and time of death for the sixty-three people executed since Arizona had become a state. Of the forty-seven whites listed, nineteen appear to have Spanish or Mexican names, which would make the list read: four Chinese Americans, twelve African Americans, nineteen Mexican Americans, and twenty-eight Anglo-Americans executed. This stark "fact sheet" has been so haunting to me that I felt others also should see it. Notice that the death penalty was abolished in Arizona on December 8, 1916, and restored on December 5, 1918.

The fact sheet states that an initiative measure effective December 8, 1916, deleted the provision for the death penalty as punishment for first degree murder.

The death penalty was restored December 5, 1918. The method of execution was by hanging.

Death by Lethal Gas instead of by hanging was made effective October 28, 1933.

Last execution by hanging was 8-21-1931. First execution by Lethal Gas was 7-6-1934, at which time two brothers, Manuel and Fred Hernandez, were executed.

Highest number executed in one day were four Chinese on June 22, 1928.
28 have been executed by hanging since statehood.
35 have been executed by Lethal Gas since statehood.
1 commutation of sentence by death to life imprisonment has been granted since 1934.

In June 1972 the U.S. Supreme Court banned the death penalty on the basis of erratic and arbitrary enforcement. [Since the reinstatement of capital punishment in 1976, thirty-eight states have reintroduced the death penalty. As of January 1995, 2,976 people in the United States were awaiting execution. Forty-eight of them were women, and thirty-seven were teenage boys, sixteen and seventeen years old.[3]

Since 1976, there have been 276 executions. One of them, Margie Velma Barfield, was fifty-one years old when she was executed on November 2, 1984, in Raleigh, North Carolina, for the 1978 poisoning of her fiancé.

Ms. Barfield, a grandmother, was the first woman in the United States to have been killed by state decree since 1963. She ate a last meal of Cheese Doodles and Coke, said her prayers, and was executed—poisoned to death—by lethal injection in North Carolina's Central Prison. In 1995, she had the distinction of having been the only woman in this country who had been executed in thirty-three years. Perhaps the spectators at Eva Dugan's beheading would have been impressed by the simple, sterile technology used for Velma Barfield's death; no doubt they would have approved of the fact that no one watching had to suffer.

In April 1987 the U.S. Supreme Court handed down an opinion stating it would not invalidate state capital punishment plans, even if those plans were not applied in an equal manner with regard to race, even if a defendant was at least four times more likely to be sentenced to death if the victim was white.

Premeditated executions by the state can be "reformed" to make them "cleaner" and more efficient, but whether executions are performed with the aid of an ax, a guillotine, gallows, electric chair, or gas chamber, the fact of death remains the same. By 1995, lethal injections had become the state-of-the-art choice for executing death row inmates in most states. Nearly every murderer picked for execution has a similar story: he or she is "someone who is worthless who killed someone who was of value."[4]

The death penalty is not now, nor has it ever been, about stopping mur-

3. These figures are as of June 1995; they come from the Death Penalty Information Center of the NAACP Legal Defense and Educational Fund.
4. Leigh Bienen, "No Savings in Lives or Money with Death Penalty," *New York Times,* August 7, 1988.

der or crime. It's about political power and popularity, winning votes, drawing crowds, selling newspapers, and boosting media ratings by appealing to unexamined fear, excitement, and blood lust. It's about race and class differences and the way we deal with anger and revenge. As a deterrent to the usually irrational crime of murder, it's useless. And as attorney Leigh Bienen, a death penalty expert, pointed out in 1988, "A rational murderer could well conclude that his chances of being executed are minimal. In the whole of the United States, there have been 100 executions since 1976, and more than 240,000 murders have been committed in that same period."[5]

DEATH PENALTY IN ARIZONA

Executions by Hanging, Arizona State Prison

3094	Jose Lopez	White	10:23 A.M.	1-5-1910
3327	Cesario Sanchez	White	10:30 A.M.	12-2-1910
3326	Rafael Barela	White	11:10 A.M.	12-2-1910
3497	Domingo Franco	White		7-7-1911
3582	Alejandro Galles	White	10:40 A.M.	7-28-1911
4436	Ramon Villalobo	White	3:20 P.M.	12-10-1915
3566	Francisco Rodriquez	White	5:10 P.M.	5-19-1916
3479	N. B. Chavez	White	3:20 P.M.	6-9-1916
3814	Miguel Peralta	White	3:20 P.M.	7-7-1916
5400	Sinplicio Torrez	White	10:10 A.M.	4-16-1920
5597	Pedro Dominguez	White	5:30 A.M.	1-14-1921
5565	Nichan Martin	White	5:01 A.M.	9-9-1921
5693	Ricardo Lauterio	White	5:00 A.M.	1-13-1922
5699	Thomas Roman	White	5:20 A.M.	1-13-1922
5826	Theodore West	White	5:00 A.M.	9-29-1922
5979	Paul V. Hadley	White	5:00 A.M.	4-13-1923
5981	Manuel Martinez	White	5:25 A.M.	8-10-1923
6367	William Ward	Negro	5:00 A.M.	6-20-1924
6193	Sam Flowers	Negro	5:00 A.M.	1-9-1925
6621	William Lawrence	White	5:20 A.M.	1-8-1926
6824	Charles J. Blackburn	White	5:09 A.M.	5-20-1927
7046	B. W. L. Sam	Chinese	5:16 A.M.	6-22-1928
7047	Shew Chin	Chinese	5:42 A.M.	6-22-1928
7048	Jew Har	Chinese	6:06 A.M.	6-22-1928
7049	Gee King Long	Chinese	6:33 A.M.	6-22-1928
7435	Eva Dugan	White	5:01 A.M.	2-21-1930
7748	Refugio Macias	White	5:11 A.M.	3-7-1930
8149	Herman Young	White	5:03 A.M.	8-21-1931

Executions by Lethal Gas

9299	Manuel Hernandez	White	5:00 A.M.	7-6-1934
9300	Fred Hernandez	White	5:00 A.M.	7-6-1934

5. Ibid.

9250	George Shaughnessy	White	5:00 A.M.	7-13-1934
9391	Louis Sprague Douglas	White	12:30 A.M.	8-31-1934
9924	Jack Sullivan	White	5:05 A.M.	5-15-1936
10021	Frank Rascon	White	5:10 A.M.	7-10-1936
9880	Roland H. Cochrane	White	5:00 A.M.	10-2-1936
10094	Frank Duarte	White	5:00 A.M.	1-8-1937
10540	Ernest Patten	Negro	4:00 A.M.	8-13-1937
10580	Burt Anderson	White	4:00 A.M.	8-13-1937
10252	David Benjamin Knight	White	4:00 A.M.	9-3-1937
10853	Elvin Jack Odom	White	4:15 A.M.	1-14-1938
11163	James Bailey	White	5:00 A.M.	4-28-1939
11253	Frank Conner	Negro	5:00 A.M.	9-22-1939
11506	Robert Burgunder	White	5:00 A.M.	8-9-1940
12409	J. C. Levice	Negro		1-8-1943
12410	Charles Sanders	Negro		1-8-1943
12411	Grady B. Cole	Negro		1-8-1943
12609	James C. Rawling	White	6:15 A.M.	2-19-1943
12334	Elisandro L. Macias	White	6:00 A.M.	4-27-1943
12964	John Earnest Ransom	Negro	6:00 A.M.	1-5-1945
12988	Lee Albert Smith	White	5:00 A.M.	4-6-1945
13306	U. L. Holley	Negro	5:05 A.M.	4-13-1945
14854	Angel B. Serna	White	4:05 A.M.	7-29-1950
16003	Harold Thomas Lantz	White	5:04 A.M.	7-18-1951
17659	Carl J. Folk	White	5:00 A.M.	3-4-1955
18392	Lester Edward Bartholomew	White	5:00 A.M.	8-31-1955
18320	Leonard Coey	White	5:00 A.M.	5-22-1957
17337	Arthur Thomas	Negro	5:05 A.M.	11-17-1958
19169	Richard Lewis Jordan	White	5:00 A.M.	11-22-1958
19795	Lonnie Craft	Negro	5:05 A.M.	3-7-1959
20414	Robert D. Fenton	White	5:06 A.M.	3-11-1960
21245	Honor Robinson	Negro		10-31-1961
21598	Patrick M. McGee	White	5:00 A.M.	3-8-1963
23773	Manuel E. Silva	White	5:00 A.M.	3-14-1963

Nellie Parker

When Nellie Parker was thirteen years old, a man killed her mother. "It was a sex murder," she said. "He split her head open with an ax. I didn't find out who did it until about a year later, when I heard the man had bragged to my aunt that he was the one who did it.

"I went and got a gun and shot him," she says in a matter-of-fact voice. "When police arrested me, they asked me to tell who I got the gun from and they would let me go. They also told me to tell them where the gun was. I told them I'd dropped it in the river. They told me they'd let me go, but I knew what was what. I never told them who I got the gun from. And twelve years later, when I got out, I went right to the place I had hid the gun and took it back to the man who had loaned it to me. He had forgotten about it by then.''

Nellie Parker is seventy-one years old now, and she lives in a housing project in South Philadelphia with her husband, William. Her years in prison have given her indelible scars, but you don't immediately see them on her soft old wizened brown face. A small woman, she moves slowly, painfully with arthritis. I met her at a prisoners' workshop preceding a production of *The Cage*, a play produced by members of the Barbwire Theatre from San Quentin Prison in California. Ms. Parker and her husband had taken a subway and two buses to get to the performance in northeast Philadelphia, a white section remote from the heart of the city.

"I knew why I was in prison," she recalls. "A man killed my mother, and I killed him. I still have no regrets. I never did have. Not even when I was in Clinton [the state prison for women in New Jersey]. When I was in Clinton, I worked in the laundry and milked cows two times a day.

"We used to get up at four A.M. to milk the cows. That was fun to us. I was always on punishment, so I was only fed bread and water. So on those cold mornings, I would wash off the cow's titty and put it in my mouth and drink warm milk directly from the udder.

"The first seven years, I just didn't care. I was always in punishment. Punishment was terrible. They would beat you and give you cold-water showers with fire hoses. Afterwards they'd give you the needle to keep you from getting pneumonia and throw you in the hole. Sometimes they'd strap you on a rotating table and raise it up and you'd go around. Five or six matrons would whip your naked body as you went past them until you fainted. Then they'd rub you down with salt and vinegar. They'd punish you like that for fighting or cussing or something like that. You don't have to do much to get punished. But I got used to it.

"I guess the worst thing is to be locked up on Saturday and Sunday. Those are the days you're locked in all day, and if you don't go to church on Sunday, you won't get out. I'd go to every church service they had on Sunday. I'd go to every faith just to get out of my cell."

Nellie Parker talked on—in present tense, occasionally slipping into past tense—about her adolescence in prison during the 1920s. She talked about her mother and her sixteen older brothers and sisters. She talked about her own son, who was born six months before she went to prison. She also has a daughter and twenty-three grandchildren. "My son has seventeen children, just like my mother had," she says proudly. "My daughter, she ain't worth a cent."

After twelve years in prison, Nellie Parker completed the remainder of her sentence—twelve years—on parole. She worked first as a live-in maid, later as a day maid. Six years after she had finished parole, the mistress of the house where she was working as a maid accused her of taking a check and pressed charges. Ms. Parker was locked up awaiting trial. Because of her prior record, she felt she didn't have "a chance in hell" to beat the charges. She pled guilty. And so in 1958, nearly thirty years after she had first been sentenced to prison, Nellie Parker went to prison again—this time to the Federal Reformatory for Women in Alderson, West Virginia, for nine months.

"It wasn't so bad at Alderson," she said. "They knew I had a heart condition, so they let me work in the garment factory. It was a pretty good job. In the House of Correction, you only got slop to eat. But in Alderson, there was good food, all you can eat."

When Nellie Parker got out of Alderson, she put in another eleven years on parole, which she successfully terminated in 1969. "You know, for years I been walking around with all this inside me. I never been able to talk about it to nobody before. Nobody would listen. But I know it's still the same. I just know if you're in there and your parents or your people don't come to see you, they just bury you like a dog."

None of Us

In the dining room at Marysville, right after lunch, I'm talking to the kitchen workers. All women that come to Marysville are assigned to work in the kitchen for ten to twelve weeks after they get out of orientation. The institution's rationale is that since no one likes working in the kitchen permanently, this way everyone takes a turn. But prisoners say some women should be exempt.

"You got ladies carrying garbage cans and huge trays, and it don't make sense for us to have to do it," says one woman. "I'm three months' pregnant," says another, who is just beginning to show, "and she's seven months' pregnant. There's another woman who's six months' pregnant who works in here. I work in the dish room and I have to carry the garbage cans out full. We take 'em out once a day, and they're so heavy it could really make me lose my baby. But the officers, they won't let anyone else do it. You gotta wash 'em out after you get them out there and empty 'em."

"This work we're doing is a man's work. I done got a hernia lifting jugs and coffee," says a small woman in her late forties. "It's wet and slippery and too heavy even for a woman not pregnant. But at least they should let us old ones and the pregnant ones not have to work here."

"Did you ever go to the state prison in Nashville, Tennessee?" asks another woman. "That place is something else. You should go there! I was there in '66, and they have the white girls on one side and the black girls on the other side. They got their coffee urn and we got our coffee urn. There it's a physical thing, here it's a mental thing, with all the petty rules.

"None of us don't like it here. We know if you play, you gotta pay, but we just want to be treated like human beings. Back a dog up in a corner and keep yappin' at 'em, eventually they're gonna bite you."

Although a caseworker and another staff member are standing nearby, about eight women sit at a table with me detailing complaints and grievances against the institution:

- "You gotta have a piece of paper everywhere you go, and if you don't, you get restricted."
- "You can take a shower at six P.M., but not when you want to."
- "You have to be sick at five-thirty P.M. the day before the clinic or you don't get to go to sick call because your name's not on the list."
- "Only one box can come to each prisoner from the outside in one year."
- "Men friends cannot come to visit." ("Some of us don't have family come up—we need a friend to come up.")
- "The matrons don't know how to respect us—they treat us like slaves."
- "Men get privileges at the penitentiary we at Marysville don't get. They get boxes with canned goods, visiting with friends, literature, and college courses . . . "

As we are talking, another inmate comes up to the table and wipes it off with a wet cloth. The strokes of the cloth on the table are large, determined, seemingly angry. We all have to move our arms and back up.

A few minutes later, the woman who has wiped the table leans on a mop and shouts from across the room: "Why are you talking to her? What good's it gonna do? She ain't gonna do nothing!"

The women at the table, and a few working across the room whom I talked to earlier, holler back that I'm working on a book and that I'm going to "tell it like it is."

"She's okay!" a large woman shouts back. "Leave her alone. Leave us alone."

"Well, even if she does write it like it is, people ain't gonna do nothing about it," she says, alternately shaking her head with anger and wiping sweat from her brow. "They'll just say, 'Ain't that a shame,' and nothing will change. It'll be just the same. It was the same twenty years ago as it is now. Twenty years from now it'll still be the same. We'll still be here. And it'll be just the same."

10 A LOOK AT THE HISTORY OF WOMEN'S PRISONS IN AMERICA

One Step Forward, Two Steps Back

Women's institutions have made notable contributions to penology. The personnel requirements have always been reasonably high, and well-trained young women have been attracted to live and work in these institutions. Several of them are rated as among the best institutions for either men or women in the country. Women superintendents like to experiment, to try out new methods, and to use new techniques. Women offenders do not as a rule commit acts of violence or present a threat to the public to the extent that men do. Public opinion has therefore not thwarted the superintendents who were bold and fear-less enough to try new ways with offenders.

—"Facilities and Programs for Women," *Manual of Correctional Standards,* the American Correctional Association, 1969

We get about seventy-five percent recidivist rates here. Most of the girls who come in here are about twenty-one to twenty-five years old and are addicts. So we see them back. No, there is no drug therapy or treatment here. There are some girls who get rehabilitated as they get older. When a girl begins to reach forty, she rehabilitates herself. Not the institution, she does it herself. She gets tired. About twenty-five percent rehabilitate themselves somehow—they get jobs or they stay out of here. We don't know how, but at least we don't see them back.

—Lieutenant Dorothy Zeno, Day Officer in Charge, Cook County Jail Women's Division

Captain Paul A. Strohman sat behind the chief administrator's desk at the Sybil Brand Institute for Women in Los Angeles. A short, stocky man with a round face and receding hairline, Captain Strohman joked with the female deputy sheriffs who sat with him. A fat papier-mâché manikin dressed in female officer's clothing was propped against the wall behind him. On his desk was a yellow-and-black sign: "Behind this desk sits the sexiest executive in the world."

He seemed jovial as he greeted me. "What's the best jail you've been to?" he asked. I told him I didn't think I had been to a "best jail" yet. "Well," he went on, "I think you're going to like this jail. We think we have a fine place here. We think it's the best. Probably the best in the country."

According to penal standards of architectural design, the Sybil Brand Institute for Women *is* state-of-the-art. It is mechanically perfect, faultless in terms of security. From the "heartbeat of the jail," the main control center, a deputy sheriff can keep her eye on the entire prison without difficulty. At her fingertips are electronic detectors to monitor elevators and all entrances and exits. Television cameras throughout the prison oversee all "inmate traffic."

A two-way intercom system allows administrators to make public addresses in addition to tuning in on conversations in any part of the prison. The possibility of escape is infinitesimal.

Unlike most county or city jails in other parts of the country, which are antiquated or where women prisoners are confined and forgotten in tiny cell blocks within the larger jails for men, this jail was built exclusively for women. No one in Los Angeles can complain that the thirty thousand women booked in annually have been "neglected" or forgotten by the county jail system because of per capita cost. The Sybil Brand Institute for Women was built with the sanction of a $6,315,000 bond issue approved by the voters in 1960.[1] Typical complaints about physical conditions and understaffing just don't apply.

"The rules and regulations and rights here will probably all be changed by the time your book comes out," Captain Strohman said. "There's lots of new Supreme Court rules and legislation. Also there's a lot of pressure groups lobbying for change.

"For instance, now we segregate or exclude active homosexuals from

1. The bond issue was promoted by Sybil Brand, "a very active lady in today's society," H. S. Creamer, chief of the County Jail Division, told me in an interview. "She's active in civic affairs and especially in the area of corrections for women. She was highly instrumental in the building of this jail. She was the one that got the bond issue before the public."

the rest of the population and group activity. If they come in dressed in drag or are obvious homosexuals, we call them 'Exclusions.' That will probably change because the Gay Liberation Front is getting stronger all the time.[2]

"But the jail will still be run the same way. The only difference might be some rule changes. So I guess the basic facts won't change. Jails will always be the same, so your book will still be valid, even ten years from now or as long as jails exist, I guess."

Originally, segregated jails and prisons for women were designed to protect them and improve their lot. They were established as a benevolent move on the part of reformists. Women in the American colonies had been detained in dungeons, almshouses, and jails with men and children since the mid-1600s. There was little segregation by age, gender, or other factors.

Women gave birth to children in the unsanitary jails, and as one inspector said, "The early death of children is inevitable." In 1838 men and women in Bellevue Prison in New York walked the treadmill together to grind grain for the almshouse and the city prison. The work was long and exhausting and the diet inadequate; they ate the grain they had ground in a porridge. But as one author noted, "Women stood the ordeal better than men." There was no respite at Bellevue Prison, he said. At night "convicts could not lie down without mingling their limbs in one solid mass."[3]

In those years, prisons and punishments were in a state of upheaval, and women suffered extreme neglect and abuse. They were exposed to sexual attacks, floggings, and severe punishments that often led to sickness and death. The 1787 Walnut Street Prison in Philadelphia had collapsed from overcrowding, corruption, and rebellions. Everyone was looking for new answers to crime and punishment, new ways to establish law and order. One new experiment was the Eastern State Penitentiary in Philadelphia, built on a design similar to that of the Auburn State Prison in New York, which had opened in 1820. Eastern opened in 1825 after concerned religious people, including Benjamin Franklin, Dr. Benjamin Rush, and

2. In the 1990s overcrowding is so severe that corrections agencies at all levels have scrambled to build, purchase, expand, and renovate their facilities to handle the growing population. This has affected many policies, including those regarding women referred to as "Exclusions." As one former prison superintendent of a woman's prison told me, "Today there's no such thing as the luxury of separating people or putting them in single cells. If a woman is a known sexual aggressor, she'll be isolated so she can't prey on other women, but today nobody asks, 'Are you a lesbian?' "

3. Clifford M. Young, *Women's Prisons Past and Present* (Elmira, N.Y.: Elmira Reformatory, 1932).

Bishop William White, developed a theory of penance for sins through separate and solitary confinement.

The penitentiary (place for penance) was considered a humane reform in comparison to the still-common practice of corporal punishment for petty thieves and criminals. Early Quaker idealists denounced the policies of cropping ears, tying people to whipping posts, and castrating or mutilating a criminal for adultery and other violations of the social order. They deemed public hangings of men and women suspected of stealing or treason intolerable and excessive. They also felt that other prisons had failed because they were so chaotic. Imprisonment, they believed, should be based on repentance, not retribution. This repentance could be established through strict order and constant silence.

Male and female prisoners were taken to Eastern's medieval, fortress-like structure, where they were made to undress, bathe (purify themselves), and put on rough hewn prison tunics that scratched their skin to remind them of their transgressions. Then black hoods were put over their heads so their eyes would not meet the eyes of any other criminal, and they were blindly led to solitary cells, where the hoods were removed. The entryway to their cells was extremely low so they would be forced to "stoop before the Lord" when they stepped inside. Locked behind two thick doors in their individual cells, they were then left alone for days, months, or years with only a Bible for reading. Each prisoner had a back door and a tiny walled-in courtyard where he or she could step out for a glimpse of the sun and fresh air. Prisoners never left their solitary areas or saw anyone other than a minister or selected lay visitor. Guards would push bread, water, or mush through the small opening under the bottom of the cell door once or twice a day.

Charles Dickens was one of many overseas visitors who toured the famous Eastern State Penitentiary in 1842. Dickens walked from cell to cell and talked with prisoners, including three women prisoners. Later he wrote:

> The system here is rigid, strict and hopeless solitary confinement. I believe it, in its effects, to be cruel and wrong. In its intentions, I am well convinced that it is kind, humane and meant for reformation; but I am persuaded that those who devised this system of prison discipline, and those benevolent gentlemen who carry it into execution, do not know what they are doing. I believe that very few men are capable of estimating the immense amount of torture and agony which this dreadful punishment, prolonged for years, inflicts upon the sufferers; and . . . I am only the more convinced that there is a depth of terrible endurance in it which none but the sufferers themselves can fathom, and which no man has a right to inflict upon his fellow creatures. I hold this slow and daily tampering with the mysteries of the brain to be

immeasurably worse than any torture of the body; because its ghastly signs are not so palpable to the eye . . . and it exhorts few cries, that human ears can hear; therefore I am the more to denounce it, as a secret punishment which slumbering humanity is not roused up to stay.[4]

Nevertheless, the "Pennsylvania Plan" flourished. Penitentiaries built on the same model were constructed in other states in America and also in Europe. Eventually, when people continued to die and go mad in large numbers as a result of this isolation, society was forced to admit that thorough separation did not work. So they began to let prisoners mingle again while they worked at jobs to keep them busy. Eventually, women prisoners at Eastern were supervised by a matron as they sewed buttons and repaired uniforms, and they also were allowed visits by Quaker ladies who read scripture to them and sometimes furnished lessons in reading, writing, and arithmetic.

Quaker women led the prison reform movement, and during the 1830s they made some progress in segregating women from men and providing them with a degree of protection from sexual assaults and brutality. By 1839 the Mount Pleasant Female Prison was opened on the grounds of the Sing Sing prison for men in Ossining, New York. Mount Pleasant represented a major turning point in the development of women's prisons because it was the first prison where women were housed in a separate building apart from men and supervised by a staff of women. Starting in 1844, when Eliza Farnham became the chief matron, it also became a model for later reformists who also would encourage their prisoners to reform through "education, example, sympathy." Farnham and her colleague Georgiana Bruce believed that women would change their ways if they were educated, and they set about teaching them geography, literature, astronomy, and physiology. Farnham modified the rules of total silence and tried to change the bleak "environment by introducing flowers, music, and visitors from the outside."[5]

Georgiana Bruce later reported that "the wayward creatures found by degrees that their prison was turned into a school, and they lost the inclination to make trouble."[6] Farnham was criticized for her humane progressiveness, however, and resigned in 1847. By 1865 the prison was overcrowded and soon was closed.

4. Charles Dickens, *American Notes* and *Pictures from Italy* (Geneva: Edito-Service, Heron Books, 1976).

5. Nicole Hahn Rafter, *Partial Justice: Women in State Prisons, 1800–1935*, pp. 20, 18. Rafter's intriguing book is a valuable resource for anyone wanting to delve more deeply into the history of women's prisons.

6. Georgiana Bruce Kirby, *Years of Experience: An Autobiographical Narrative*, as quoted in Rafter, *Partial Justice*, p. 18.

By the time of the 1870 National Congress on Penitentiary and Reformatory Discipline in Cincinnati, Ohio, agitation over the unconscionable idleness and reports of brutality in prisons had increased. Leading penologists wanted to improve conditions by focusing not just on retribution but also on reformation. Quakers and women reformists for some time had been applying pressure to separate women and children from hardened male prisoners. They felt that women "more nearly represent the residue of civilization's by-products than does the male group."[7] The harsh environment of a male prison also was considered unhealthy and corrupting for dependent, weak, and "morally degraded" women and their children.

The congress discussed poverty as a cause of crime and its effect on male and female immigrants, who at that time were disproportionately arrested and sentenced to prison. One member of the congress described the quandary and its effect on public attitudes about immigrants:

> The figures [of immigrants in prison] are so startling in their disproportions as to foster, and apparently justify, a strong prejudice against our foreign population. Foreigners crowd our almshouses and asylums, our jails and penitentiaries. . . . In the Albany penitentiary [alone], the aggregate number of prisoners during the last twenty years was 18,390, of whom 10,770 were foreign born. Formidable as such numbers are in their disproportions, we must not be hasty or harsh in taking up a reproach against "the stranger."[8]

Many people at the congress asserted that the figures did not indicate prejudice against immigrants because, in fact, immigrants were in prison mainly *because* they were unassimilated into mainstream production. It was pointed out that four fifths of their crimes were against property, one fifth against persons. Twenty-eight percent of the total prison population at the time could not read when they entered; 97 percent had never learned a legal trade; 3.33 percent were considered insane or feebleminded.

> It is noticeable that most of these causes of crime are negative. They are want of knowledge, want of trade, want of work, want of a home, want of friends, want of mind and want of parents. It is not strange that a population from whom most of the natural and moral defenses are taken away, should be tempted and fall. Such helplessness borders on hopelessness, and nothing remains for its heirs but starvation or crime. Crime is the last resort of the helpless honest, unless society provides a refuge.[9]

It was resolved at the 1870 conference that the goal of prison should be rehabilitation—the act of restoring a person to useful life through educa-

7. J. B. Bittinger, "Responsibility of Society for the Causes of Crime," in *Transactions of the National Congress on Penitentiary and Reformatory Discipline,* ed. E. C. Wines (Albany, N.Y.: Weed, Parsons, 1871).
8. Ibid.
9. Ibid.

tion and therapy. The ambition was to educate prisoners and use work as therapy so they could go back out into society with altered values and attitudes.

Women were in the vanguard of putting this resolution into practice.

And it was only three years after the congress, in 1873, that the first totally separate prison for women—and the first to be administered by an all-female staff—was opened: the Indiana Reformatory Institution for Women and Girls, in Indianapolis.[10] The Indiana prison embraced the revolutionary notion that women criminals should be rehabilitated rather than punished. Young girls from the age of sixteen who "habitually associate with dissolute persons" and older uneducated and indigent women were ushered into the model prison, apart from men and isolated from the "corruption and chaos" of the outside world. The essential ingredient of their rehabilitative treatment would be to bring discipline and regularity into their lives. Obedience and systematic religious education would, it was felt, help the women form orderly habits and moral values.

Four more institutions for women were opened during the next forty years: the Massachusetts Prison (now called the Massachusetts Correctional Institution for Women) in Framingham in 1877; the New York Reformatory for Women (Westfield Farm) in 1901; the District of Columbia's Reformatory for Women in 1910; and the New Jersey Reformatory for Women (now the Edna Mahon Correctional Facility for Women) in Clinton in 1913.

By 1917 fourteen states had established similar institutions. They were usually referred to as "reformatories" or "industrial homes" to distinguish them from penitentiaries. The reformists seemed to have the fervor and drive of pentecostal preachers, decrying evil, exalting the divine. At the Fifty-eighth Congress of the American Prison Association in 1928, reformists clearly expressed their conviction: "We must work for the regeneration, the cleansing of the evil mind, the quickening of the dead heart, the building up of fine ideals. In short, we must bring the poor sin-stained soul to feel the touch of the Divine Hand." They discussed the "moral turpitude" of the "poor creatures" and expressed the belief that in separate, homelike rural institutions surrounded by fresh air, women prisoners would have an opportunity, with as much time as they needed, to "mend their criminal ways" and learn to be good housewives, helpmates, and mothers.[11]

10. Mount Pleasant Female Prison and the Detroit House of Shelter, both instrumental in the reform movement, had both been connected to men's prisons geographically and administratively, according to Nicole Hahn Rafter.

11. Maud Ballington Booth, "The Shadow of Prison," *Proceedings of the 58th Congress of the American Prison Association,* 1928.

In 1972, as a result of their ardent efforts, there were thirty separate state institutions for women, including the Federal Reformatory built in 1927. In addition, there were twenty-four state facilities for women under the control of the warden of the male institution of the state, plus one federal prison on Terminal Island in California.[12] Five separate county or city jails had been built for women, and state statutes ordered that women imprisoned in some 3,300 local jails be segregated on separate cell blocks from male prisoners.

[In the 1990s rush to lock people up and throw away the key, legislators have been approving plans to build women's prisons at a staggering pace. Erected at enormous public expense, these prisons are not the result of thoughtful assessment of society's need for maximum incarceration or alternative treatment; they are the frightening result of slapdash policy focused on retribution, not common sense. The trend started in the 1970s, when seventeen new prisons for women were opened, and jumped dramatically in the 1980s, when thirty-four additional units or prisons for women were constructed throughout the country. In the past decade, new prisons have been constructed in California, Michigan, Minnesota, and Wyoming. Over three years' time, New York State doubled its capacity to imprison women at an initial cost of three million dollars.[13] According to the 1994 American Correctional Association Directory, we now have a total of seventy separately run and operated state prisons for women; twenty-nine women's prison units that often are referred to as "co-ed facilities" but are housed in state prisons for men; three federal women's prisons; and nine women's units in federal ("co-ed") prisons for men.]

Another innovative move by reformists was the concept of the indeterminate sentence. An important part of the pioneer penal thinking was that women should stay in prison for whatever period of time it took to achieve the desired level of rehabilitation or "cleansing." Reformists, who included the Women's Christian Temperance Union and many other women who had worked for abolition and women's suffrage, believed that prisoners who demonstrated a readiness to return to the community should be granted an earlier discharge than would be possible under a set amount of time predetermined by a trial judge.

The possibility of release based on individual considerations seemed not only humane but integral to the new concept of rehabilitation. To accomplish this, many states established special indeterminate sentencing

12. The American Correctional Association, *Manual of Correctional Standards*, 1969.
13. Russ Immarigeon and Meda Chesney-Lind, *Women's Prisons: Overcrowded and Overused.*

provisions that applied only to women. Legislation establishing the separate prisons for women contained these sentencing provisions, as well as the requirement that all women over sixteen convicted of any offense be sent to these reformatories.

In theory, their "ideal sentence" would have no limits at all on the minimum and maximum terms an inmate was forced to serve. But most states put some limit on the sentence, usually setting the maximum term prescribed by law for the particular offense, with no minimum. For example, robbery might carry a twenty-five-year maximum sentence; burglary, twenty years; and prostitution, three years. Minnesota was one of the few states that met the reformists' ideal and originally passed a law requiring women to be sent to the reformatory "without limit as to time."

Theoretically, as soon as women were rehabilitated they could leave, but in practice the statutes resulted in women getting longer sentences than men for the same crimes.[14] In Pennsylvania the legislature created the Muncy Act, which required judges to issue "general" sentences to women convicted of offenses punishable by more than one year in prison. If the maximum by law was three years, the woman would be given three years, for instance. The sentencing judge had no discretion to provide a minimum sentence with eligibility for parole or to set less than the maximum sentence.

In 1966 a Pennsylvania woman, Jane Daniel, was convicted of simple robbery, and the trial judge initially sentenced her to one to four years in the county jail. When a district attorney drew the judge's attention to the Muncy Act, the judge vacated his first sentence and gave Jane Daniel the maximum sentence of ten years in the state prison at Muncy, as the law provided. A public defender, Carolyn E. Temin, took an appeal to the Superior Court on grounds that the Muncy Act constituted a denial of equal protection of the laws under the Fourteenth Amendment. It was clear from the first sentence that the defendant would have gotten a much lower term if she had been sentenced under the provisions relating to men convicted of the same offense. The Superior Court found the act constitutional, passing their decision on similar challenges to the law in Kansas, Massachusetts, and Maine. But Ms. Temin appealed the decision and added another attack in the case of Daisy Douglas, which raised the same issue.

Daisy Douglas and her codefendant, Richard Johnson, were tried together and convicted jointly of robbing a man. Douglas, whose past record

14. Carolyn Engle Temin, "Discriminatory Sentencing of Women Offenders: The Argument for ERA in a Nutshell," *American Criminal Law Journal* (Spring 1973).

consisted of a number of arrests for prostitution, was duly sentenced to Muncy for the maximum term allowed by the law for aggravated robbery: twenty years. Johnson, whose past record consisted of six prior convictions for burglary, received a sentence of three to ten years in a state penitentiary for men. He would be eligible for parole after three years, whereas Daisy Douglas technically would be eligible for parole at any time. In practice, however, Richard Johnson was eventually paroled after four years. Daisy Douglas served six and one-half years before being paroled.

Pennsylvania's Supreme Court held on July 1, 1968, that the Muncy Act was unconstitutional because there was no rational basis for distinguishing between men and women in sentencing. A similar finding was reached by the U.S. District Court for Connecticut in the case of *Robinson v. York* on February 28, 1968, when they held that an indeterminate sentencing statute relating to the sentencing of women misdemeanants in that state was unconstitutional. Since both courts reached the same conclusion independently of one another, it seemed the constitutional issue of disparate sentencing statutes had been laid to rest.

But two weeks after the Supreme Court of Pennsylvania handed down its decision, the state legislature passed a new version of the Muncy Act. The amendment provided that in sentencing a woman for a crime punishable by more than one year, the court "shall not fix a minimum sentence, but shall fix such maximum sentence as the court shall deem appropriate." So the victory turned out to be short-lived. Although women would not receive a longer maximum sentence than men, they were still to be denied the right to have their minimum sentence set by a judge. Which was, basically, still a denial of equal treatment.[15]

[Today these disparate sentencing laws for women no longer exist, but indeterminate sentences still continue for both sexes in a number of states. Indeterminate sentences for "young adults" are most common. In New Jersey, for instance, any person, male or female, less than twenty-six years of age may be sentenced to an indeterminate term. A young-adult panel on the state parole board establishes a "time goal" for each young person that represents his or her first tentative release date.

In practice, discretion still creates disparate sentencing, but that seems inevitable. In the 1980s and 1990s, while there have been no indeterminate sentences for adult women, the trend has been to imprison more women more often than previously was the case. And while both men and women are being sentenced to prison more than ever before, the percentage of

15. Ibid.

women sentenced far outstrips men. As I've said before, sentences for women also tend to be much harsher now than they were in the past.]

Discrimination and bias in the setting of prison terms has never been unusual, but the forms it takes seem to vary with the times. At the California Institution for Women during 1967 and 1968, for instance, white women with no drug history served up to two months longer than black women with no drug history for manslaughter, robbery, and assault. But black women served from five days to eight months longer for forgery, burglary, and theft. The biggest differences in time served were for women with narcotics history, where black women served from two and a half months to one and a half years longer for the same offenses.[16]

Unfortunately, a theory of equality and justice does not always match the results produced once that theory is put into practice. It seems a bitter irony that the theories of well-intentioned women and humanitarians in the late nineteenth and early twentieth centuries ultimately resulted in a plan of imprisonment so inhumane and ineffective. Yet it is a sign of great devotion to those theories that more than one hundred years after the 1870 congress, the goals of imprisonment, rehabilitation, discipline, and control all remain intact.

The words of the critics and reformers of 1870 could easily be transposed to fit today's prison population with few changes. Poor people still go to prison. A disproportionate number of exiles from slavery have replaced the exiles from Europe and China. People in prison are without formal education. Less than 2.3 percent have professional or technical skills. Many can't read or write. More than four fifths of the crimes they commit are still against property.

In the 1970s it was popular to allege that prisoners were "ill" or "sick" and needed to be "cured." Although the talk of inherent evil and "moral turpitude" wasn't entirely left on library shelves, reformers talked about "treating" offenders, making women offenders "well" by "curing" them, as though they were diseased. Prison administrators experimented with behavior-modification models to help prisoners mend antisocial ways for the purpose of "more thorough rehabilitation."

These steps appeared to be positive and progressive, a further move away from punishment and retribution. But if we are to learn from history, we must be very careful about humane intentions. We see that in the past reformers with good intent often weren't able to anticipate the effect of their actions. Prison reforms and prison "progress" seem to have a cyclical and regressive nature.

16. Department of Corrections Memorandum, "Results of Study of Race and Time Served at California Institution for Women," June 17, 1971.

When California adopted the treatment model for both men and women in 1959, for instance, the state's new indeterminate sentencing statutes were considered a ''giant step forward'' in American penology. They were credited with ''pioneering'' the indeterminate sentence for felony offenders and initiating a program for rehabilitation that would include diagnosis, evaluation, classification, and treatment. Excellent programs of work, education, vocational training, medical services, group counseling, and therapy were part of the plan.[17] In fact, the concept was not new. It was based on the same theory as the model for women offenders established in the late 1800s.

And as before, the plan to grant earlier discharges based on individual treatment and rehabilitation backfired. Since California's ''advance,'' the median time served in that state increased from twenty-four to thirty-six months, the longest median sentence in the country. The number of persons incarcerated more than doubled during that same period of time. Thus during the period when the treatment model was maximized in that state, more than twice as many people served twice as much time.[18] The proportion of prisoners released who were convicted of new crimes remained unchanged, leading to the obvious conclusion that people were not being ''helped'' any more by three years in a rehabilitation-oriented prison than they were by approximately two years in a punitively oriented prison. The public apparently was not protected from crime by these new measures in prison, nor was the offender ''corrected.''

In the 1990s the swing of public policy seems to have shifted back toward the straightforward punishment and retribution of earlier times. Right-wing zealots such as House Speaker Newt Gingrich also have made an effort to reestablish the view of prisoners as moral degenerates and ''evil'' people. The direction of public policy is reflected in a new maximum security, ''noncontact,'' state-of-the-art prison in Pelican Bay, California—a prison that cost a quarter of a billion dollars to build and millions of dollars a year to operate. Eerily reminiscent of the Eastern State Penitentiary, even though steel and concrete have replaced wood and stone, Pelican Bay locks its inmates into their cells twenty-two and a half hours a day, five days a week, and twenty-four hours a day on weekends. They never see direct sunlight, breathe fresh air, see a tree or a child, or get to touch another human being. Food trays are slipped through slots in

17. Jessica Mitford, ''Kind and Usual Punishment in California,'' *Atlantic Monthly,* March 1971.

18. American Friends Service Committee, *Struggle for Justice: A Report on Crime and Punishment in America* (New York: Hill & Wang, 1971).

Welcome to jail: The number of women in prison has skyrocketed over the past twenty years, mainly because of harsher sentencing laws and a propensity to use imprisonment instead of probation—not because of any actual increase in violence or drug use among women. *Kitty Caparella*

Getting booked: Before being finger-printed and photographed, each woman is ordered to strip naked for inspection. She must bend over and spread her buttocks so officers can inspect her vagina and rec-tum for weapons and drugs. Then she is sprayed for lice. *Kitty Caparella*

At home on a cellblock: In June 1994 more than 48,000 women were in city and county jails and some 60,000 women were locked into state and federal prisons throughout the U.S. The vast majority of women in prison are incarcerated for nonvio-lent crimes. *Doug Hyun*

Life in a cell: Upon arrival, women clean their new ''homes,'' where they will live for years with one or more cellmates. Overcrowding is normal in American prisons; we imprison more people for longer periods than any other country in the world. *Emiko Tonooka*

Control central: Officers can open and shut cells and security gates without any personal contact with the prisoners. Each cell costs about $100,000 to build; to keep women locked in these cells, Americans pay operating costs of more than five and a half million dollars a day. *Doug Hyun*

Housecleaning: Scrubbing floors, an everyday matter for inmates, is second in importance only to security and control. *Kitty Caparella*

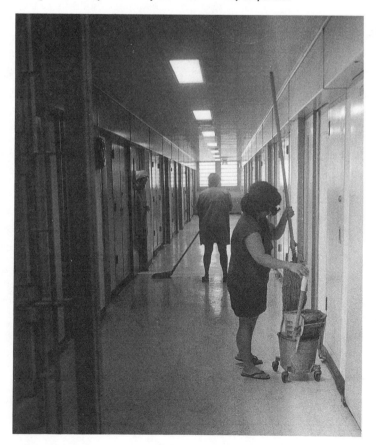

Hello, I love you: Even though women may spend as long as two years in a city or county jail, in most American jails they have to visit through a glass or screen with their loved ones. Often women are not allowed any visits at all with their own children. *Emiko Tonooka*

Waiting time: Prison life rarely is productive. Women wait in lines, wait for phones, wait for meals, wait for count. Prisoners have little or no access to rehabilitative programs, therapy, drug counselors or treatment, education, or job training. *Marjorie Berman*

Christmas interlude: Holidays come and go with sadness in prison. When women are locked up, their children usually stay with relatives or are sent to foster care. Men getting out of prison often go home to waiting mates and intact families; women leaving prison rarely are so lucky. *Marjorie Berman*

Pictures on the wall: Approximately one of ten mothers in prison in 1994 got to see her children only once every four to six months, while 54 percent *never* got to see their children while they were in prison—mostly because the distance between the child and the prison was so great. *Marjorie Berman*

Heartbreak: For a mother behind bars, sometimes the only way to hold a child close is to wear her picture. As of 1994, some 75 percent of American jails and two of every ten American prisons still didn't allow contact visits between prisoners and their children, spouses, or friends. *Emiko Tonooka*

See my kids? The greatest worries of prisoners revolve around the lives of their children. Eight of every ten women in prison are mothers—and most of the moms with children eighteen or younger had custody of those children before they were locked up. *Marjorie Berman*

No college campus: The Federal Reformatory for Women may *look* like a resort, but it's not. Most prisoners there are so far from their impoverished families that the cost of traveling to Alderson is prohibitive. Many women go for years without even one visitor. *Kitty Caparella*

Battered wives brigade: Nearly two-thirds of women in prison for violent crimes assaulted or killed male partners who had a history of abusing them. Nevertheless, these women generally serve much longer prison terms than do men who've killed their mates. *Kitty Caparella*

Bad girls: Prisoners get locked in maximum security—also referred to as punishment, solitary, reflection, peace and quiet, adjustment, the hole, or the rack—for infractions ranging from refusing a direct order to fighting to "silent insolence" for raising an eyebrow at a guard. *Kitty Caparella*

Long-term loneliness: Some women spend their lives in institutions. They're locked up as juveniles for noncriminal status offenses such as truancy or running away from home—often to escape abuse. Later they graduate to adult crime, adult prisons. *Kitty Caparella*

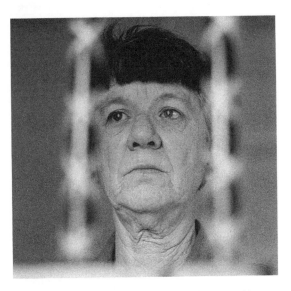

An aging population: The new trends of more and longer prison sentences, requirements to serve at least 85 percent of a sentence, and the "three-strikes-you're-out" laws may soon turn America's prisons into old-age homes. *Kitty Caparella*

Zonked on Zanex: More than half of the women in some jails receive Thorazine, Librium, or other drugs on a daily basis to keep them "manageable." Researchers have found that more psychotropic drugs are given to women than to men in prison. *Emiko Tonooka*

Mental illness: More and more women with serious mental health problems end up in prisons instead of hospitals. Severely disturbed prisoners often are kept in solitary confinement because proper or effective treatment simply is not available. *Emiko Tonooka*

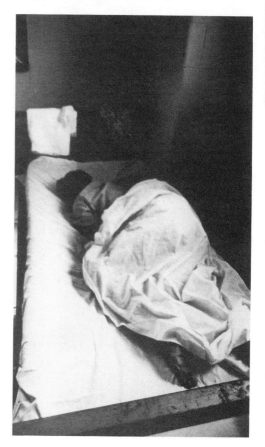

Prison industry: Many of the factories run by women in prison produce prison uniforms for male and female inmates, boxer shorts for men, uniforms for patients in state mental hospitals, sheets, towels, soap, and American and state flags. *Kitty Caparella*

A song breaks free: Above the hum of industrial sewing machines, a woman takes pleasure in her voice. Unfortunately, most of the jobs for which women are paid fifty cents to a dollar a day don't give them any skills that will be useful when they're released from prison. *Kitty Caparella*

Every woman in prison is someone's daughter, mother, sister, wife, or aunt. Up to 88 percent of the women in prison admit they have experienced physical violence or sexual abuse—or both—as children and adults. *Marjorie Berman*

Every kind of woman—rich, poor, black, white, educated, uneducated—is arrested, but the ones who end up in prison almost always are poor; on the average they are undereducated and have few marketable skills. Most earned less than poverty wages before their imprisonment. *Marjorie Berman*

The offenses for which most women go to jail or prison—disorderly conduct, vagrancy, drunkenness, drug addiction, drug possession, and drug- or alcohol-related crimes—could be deemed social or medical instead of criminal. Only a small percentage of women in prison are there for violent crimes. *Marjorie Berman*

Making connections: When women in prison are offered the all-too-rare chance to work through problems in support group sessions, they take advantage of the opportunity. "Just give us the tools and we'll fix our own engines," one woman said. *Marjorie Berman*

Reaching out: The strain and depression brought on by being arrested, indicted, tried, sentenced to prison, and separated from children and family can be understood by friends in prison, who offer solace and compassion in times of need. *Marjorie Berman*

Buddies behind bars: In prison, some friendships give women a chance to address old issues, make connections, and get comfort that helps to heal some of the abuse, emptiness, loneliness, and lack of support they've experienced in the past. *Marjorie Berman*

Time out: Prison friends often become the families women choose for themselves as the support necessary for surviving a hostile, abusive environment that can exacerbate the low self-esteem, lack of initiative, and poor decision-making skills that got women into prison in the first place. *Marjorie Berman*

Jitterbug break: Few people can imagine just how long even one year in prison is. ''In prison, time stops,'' one woman said. Prisoners find ways to relieve tension and monotony by having fun when they can.
Kitty Caparella

Dance to the music: Dancing, boogying, cutting up, singing, and playing let women laugh and enjoy themselves for a few short moments. *Marjorie Berman*

Women and AIDS: Prisoners at Bedford Hills held a walkathon to raise money for their AIDS Counseling and Education program (ACE). Today in New York state prisons, one of every five new women is HIV-positive, and AIDS is the leading cause of death. Inmates made this quilt to honor Bedford sisters who died of AIDS. *Marjorie Berman*

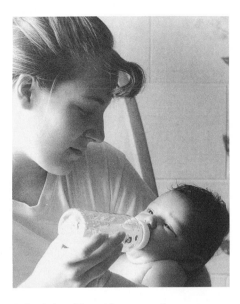

Baby, baby: About 10 percent of women entering prison are pregnant, but only three prisons in the country allow babies to stay with their mothers after they're born. At Bedford Hills, babies live with their mothers for up to eighteen months. Mothers take classes in parenting and child care. *Marjorie Berman*

Motherhood: Most new mothers in jail and prison—who often are handcuffed or shackled to hospital beds during labor for "security reasons"—are separated from their newborns soon after giving birth and sent right back to their prison cells under armed guard. *Marjorie Berman*

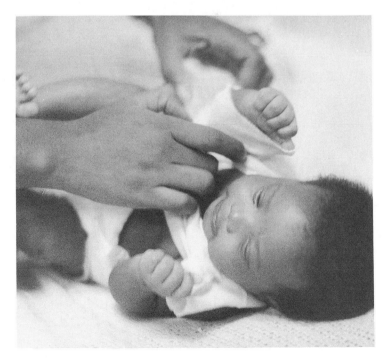

Mother love: Few prisons allow children to visit their mothers every day, overnight, or for weekends, but those that do so encourage parent-child bonding, which ultimately helps to forge a better sense of self-confidence and self-worth in these children. *Marjorie Berman*

Strong bonds: Women who see their children often are able to lower the risks of their children getting into trouble. The more frequently mothers and children can visit and stay in touch on the child's concerns, fears, and accomplishments, the more their connection is nurtured and reinforced. *Marjorie Berman*

Unconditional love: ''Mom is always Mom, and that doesn't stop just because we put mother in prison,'' says Elaine Lord, superintendent of Bedford Hills, which has had the most progressive programs in the country for mothers and children since 1980.
Marjorie Berman

Attachment and motivation: In a follow-up study of 530 women who had overnight visits with their children before getting out of prison in New York, only 4 percent had returned on new charges or as parole violators after three years, compared to the 66 percent who usually return during that time. *Marjorie Berman*

In prison, there's little space between laughter and tears.
Emiko Tonooka

Mother, daughter, and grandmother laugh and cry together during a visit to the mother in prison. *Marjorie Berman*

Welcome to the world: When a woman gets out of prison, she's given $40, a coat, and a dress and told to go out and see if she can make it. Most women will return; they do so because of stress, fear, and the fact that they haven't learned the skills needed for living more effectively outside while they've been locked up. *Kitty Caparella*

11 LOCKED OUT

The Concrete Wall between Women and Their Children

I Am a Woman

I am a woman.
I know.

I know every time I see,
   through the glass of this cage,
     a child, playing—laughing
  and my heart aches to see my own child.

I know every time I force my chin up,
  smile,
    and cry inside for home.

I know every time the hunger
  for male companionship
    overwhelms me,
  and I pull the covers over my head,
    hug my pillow,
      try to sleep.

I know every time I remember
  the sunrise
    or the stars
  and force myself to forget.

I know every time my soft and gentle spirit
  comes up against the steel,
    the barbed wire,
      of living in this place,
  and the tears flow from the pain
    from the frustration.

Yes, I am a woman.
I know.

—Joanne "Friday" Fry, California Institution for Women

Prisoners live in tremendous isolation from the rest of the world. Despite court rulings and administrative changes that allow them more access than they used to have to the courts, to mail, and to visitors, essentially they remain locked in publicly funded cities that most of us never see.

"When you're watch commander, it's like being mayor of a city," the control room officer tells me. "We don't travel around away from the city like Mayor Yorty does. We're here and we have to be responsible and take care of business. Everything that happens in the street—fires, accidents, fights, traffic tie-ups, emergencies—happens in here."

The interaction, the nuances inside these cities can never be fully known by outsiders. State inspection teams visit jails once or twice a year, if that. Their focus is mainly on physical conditions. Families and friends of prisoners, who often make long trips to get to the rural areas where women's prisons are located, never get beyond the visiting room; they don't see their loved one's cell or day-to-day life. Selected groups or individuals are sometimes allowed to come into approved areas of the institutions to conduct classes (religious instruction is the most common), and on occasion tours are conducted for the rare judicial authorities who request a visit. Prisoners usually don't have the opportunity to talk with visiting authorities; visitors are steered away from them. Visitors don't see the disciplinary cells or prisoners who are being punished. Whether or not the press is allowed in to talk to prisoners is, in most cases, up to the discretion of the administrators, who weigh the individual's interest against their interest in security.

And no matter the issue, security always wins. Security not only takes the major share of prison budgets, but it also takes precedence over any other concern. Captain Daisy McLendon at the House of Correction in Chicago put it succinctly when she was talking about count: "The most important thing is security," she said. "That's my problem in operating a jail, security. There's NOTHING that interrupts the count in a penal institution. It's the most important thing in a penal institution. It's the difference between going home and staying here. All activity stops during head counts; count has to be official. All counts have to balance with head counts."

Security is the charge the public gives to prison administrators. And because of that charge, the extent to which a prisoner is allowed contact with and connection to her children, family, and friends is governed first and foremost by security considerations. Using the mail, making telephone calls, and having personal visits are considered privileges to be maintained or lost depending on the prisoner's behaving in accordance with the regulations of the institution.

[Over the past twenty years, it has become easier for many mothers in prison to call their children on the telephone. Visiting rules also have been relaxed in some institutions to include more visits with children, but visits still remain extremely limited, especially in city and county jails. As of 1994, some 75 percent of American jails still didn't allow contact visits between prisoners and their children or other visitors. Only 25 percent of American jails permit contact visits, while 80 percent of state and federal prisons allow for contact visits between prisoners and their children, spouses, and friends.]

Even though women often spend as long as a year or two in a city or county jail, most of them have to visit through glass or a screen with their company—and often they're not allowed even that much with their own children. At the Sybil Brand Institute for Women, for instance, prisoners can have "visits" twice a week, for twenty minutes each. Even these visits—through glass—are isolating experiences. During these noncontact visits, women can't touch their men, mothers can't hold their babies. In fact, children under eighteen are not allowed to visit at all.

"We've found it's too traumatic for the child and the mother," said Lieutenant Audrey Lehre, a deputy sheriff who worked with Los Angeles County's women prisoners for twenty-four years, first at the Hall of Justice and then at Sybil Brand. "The child can't understand why they can't touch their mother. We're not unfeeling, but we can't bend for everyone. It's a problem thing for a nine-year-old to want to hug Mommy and can't get any closer than a glass window. We've had a couple of exceptions. One fourteen-year-old who was in trouble because she couldn't see her mother. Another was a little baby which was newborn. The court wanted the mother to be able to hold the child, and that couldn't cause any harm. But the regulation protects everyone from unnecessary traumas and problems."

Records are kept on every visitor that comes in to visit a prisoner, and many requests for visits are denied. "We wouldn't allow some people in here," Captain Strohman said. "It's not written in the rules. But we want to know who's coming in. We're not going to let just anyone into our jail. We search purses because a lot of people are trying to blow up jails these days. We only keep a record of visitors, not letters."

Visitors can bring in wool yarn for knitting, money, and three sets of panties, slips, and bras to the women inside. The money is put on the woman's "books," and she can use it for commissary items. Visitors cannot bring food or cigarettes. "Nothing else except eyeglasses or a hearing aid," said Captain Strohman. "We don't accept packages. There's too much possibility of contraband or bombs. They can buy what they need in the commissary: candy bars, cigarettes, magazines, toothpaste, papers, cosmetics . . . no douche bags or powders. I talked to our doctor and he said, if necessary, a douche can be prescribed in the medical department."[1]

For visitors, simply going through all the procedures to get inside can be traumatic. I experienced only a fraction of the stress visitors undergo when late one winter afternoon I sat in a tiny waiting room in Erie County Jail in Buffalo, New York. I was waiting to go into a knitting class in the women's section with Mara Siegel, a student working with the Buffalo Women's Prison Project, which runs knitting and art classes at the jail and helps women with bail, court, and family problems. The waiting room looked like a disaster area left over from a World War II movie: yellow paint peeling from the wall, exposed pipes, stuffy heat, and smoke-filled air.

Three black men sat on a thin wooden bench nearby, waiting for visits with their women. Two white guards in gray uniforms stood at attention. I was carrying only my purse, a notebook, and a paper bag with a sandwich in it. I hadn't eaten all day, and I was eager to take a bite of food. Mara and I signed our names, addresses, and occupations on the visitors' sheet. "Any medications?" the guard asked as he worked his way thoroughly through the contents of my purse. He pulled out a small bottle of Bufferin I had in my purse and put it in an envelope. He also took a bottle of eye drops and told me I could pick up both items on my way out. Then he looked in the paper bag. "A sandwich?" he nearly shouted. "A sandwich! You're not going to share that with anyone, are you? You can't take it in if any woman is getting any!"

As I went through the door with Mara, he reminded me again not to share the sandwich or he would confiscate it.

Inside another barren room, which would soon be used for the knitting class, I took a quick bite from my roast beef sandwich. A hefty black matron walked up and stood over me as I chewed the dry meat and bread. She scowled at me for a couple of minutes in silence and then said, "I

---

1. In some institutions visitors can bring food, but there are many restrictions on what kind of food, how much, and when it can be brought into the institution. Alternating weeks for receiving food packages may mean that inmates with last names beginning with *A* through *L* are eligible to receive packages during a week opposite the week for *M* through *Z* inmates. If a visitor brings a food package on the wrong week, it's not accepted.

won't let any women in until you have eaten your sandwich. Because if you're eating, you can't give them any food, and if they saw you, they would probably ask.'' I put the sandwich away in my purse and assured her I would eat it after class and not offer so much as one bite to anyone else.

Satisfied, she opened the door to let the prisoners in. As they slowly meandered into the room and began to gather up their yarn and needles from the week before, the matron sat down beside me again. ''Remember, there is to be no smoking while you knit or crochet, either,'' she said, looking at me. ''We don't want ashes on the floor.'' I knew that if I had come merely to visit an inmate, I wouldn't have been treated nearly as well as this.

At Sybil Brand, more than seven hundred women inmates take turns seeing their loved ones through glass visiting screens. There are only twenty stools for visiting. Visits here and at similar jails become sad circuses, with everyone shouting to be heard, talking through telephones to one another over the loud din of urgency and confusion. Visits are short, to allow each woman a chance to visit. The same amount of time is allotted to each inmate, whether she is ''innocent in the eyes of the law'' awaiting trial or already convicted and sentenced to as much as a year in jail.

This quarantine can have devastating effects, especially on mothers of young children. Most of them—if not all—are arrested unexpectedly. Although for some, arrest is an occupational hazard, they can't predict when it will happen. They are picked up at every time of day or night. It's not uncommon to talk to a woman who was waiting to meet her children after school at the time she was picked up by the police. Thus, her child comes home to an empty house and no mother.

In detention, a woman is allowed one telephone call to arrange for bail or a lawyer or a friend to take care of the children. In addition to the unpredictability and uncertainty of when she will have a hearing, when she will get bail, or when she will go to trial, a mother who is locked up faces an immediate and constant anxiety about her children—where they are, whether they're safe and are being well fed, whether they will be taken by the county and put into a children's shelter or a foster home. A mother also worries about her child's worries, knowing that her child is concerned and traumatized about her disappearance. Children who are kept in the dark about what has happened to their mother—where she is and why—often get no answers to their questions and feel responsible somehow for this separation and loss; they imagine that they are the cause of the problem and the pain.

[In 1973 most women in prison could not receive incoming calls or make calls out. In 1995 inmates still are prohibited from using institutional telephones, but most can make collect calls out of the prison on public telephones at least once a month. Prisoners have to sign up to use the telephone, and telephone privileges may be denied. Friends or family of inmates still are not able to call into the prison to speak to an inmate, nor are they able to leave any message for the inmate.]

As Lieutenant Merle Hess said, "If it's an emergency, they can receive messages through my office, like if it's a death or someone's dying, I will take a message and then let them call out. If she's trying to sell me a bill of goods, we'll listen in to try and keep her honest. But usually you can tell by listening to one end of the conversation."

"I'm worried that my sister has run out of cereal to feed the children," Judy Jacobs said as she sat in York County Jail in central Pennsylvania. "I don't even know what they'll have to eat today. My mother said she would take care of the children if I was sentenced to prison, but I'm afraid they'll take them away from her 'cause she's on welfare."

Judy, who had a newborn child, a one-year-old, and a two-year-old, is a small, pale woman with long, straight blond hair. She pulled at the skirt of her faded blue county prison dress and rubbed her hands, crying and looking as vulnerable as a four-year-old with the weight of a woman's responsibility. "I don't want my kids to end up in a home. I was in two foster homes before I got married, and it's really terrible. They put us there mainly because my father was drinking and they thought he couldn't take care of us. There were eleven of us; two of my sisters have been in foster homes since they were born. I wish I could just stay right here in York. The state penitentiary's so far away, I'll never get to see my kids. But then, I'm not allowed to see them here at all."

Probably the greatest source of tension in prison for women is the anxiety and concern they have about their children. Some 80 percent of the women in prison are mothers—and according to Bureau of Justice statistics in 1993, some 70 percent of those are single parents of children eighteen or under. Eighty-five percent of these women had custody of their children before they were locked in prison. (In comparison, only 47 percent of fathers had custody of their dependent children prior to their incarceration.)

"Mom is always Mom, and that doesn't stop just because we put Mother in prison," says Elaine Lord, superintendent of Bedford Hills, which has had the most progressive and supportive programs for mothers and children in the country since 1980. "If a kid gets hurt in school, the school will want to be on the phone to the mother. If a child needs surgery, the surgeon is going to call the mother. He'll say, 'I know there's a legal guardian, but I want to know what you think about this.' The people in charge still want the mother's input and connection—and the kids do, too.

"The kids feel guilty because their mother is in prison, and they wonder what they did wrong. If we keep them away from their mothers, we make the situation worse. I also want them to think that I'm an okay person; I represent authority and I want them to see me as fair. If we don't have that, we've lost the next generation too."

Some 8 to 10 percent of women are pregnant when they enter prisons, and another 15 percent are postpartum, according to Bureau of Justice statistics. But most prisons have no facilities for giving birth—and so women are transferred to nearby hospitals, and after giving birth, they are immediately separated from their babies and returned to prison. Only three prisons in the country have a program where babies and nursing mothers can be together for up to eighteen months: Bedford Hills, Taconic State, and the state prison for women in York, Nebraska. In those three institutions, mothers can be with their babies, nurse them, and bond with them before letting them go. In addition, California has a small but innovative program, the "Mother-Infant Care Program," which allows selected mothers to keep their infants and young children (up to six years old) with them while they serve their sentences in community-based treatment programs instead of state prisons.

But in all the other states in the union, mothers in jails and prisons have to give up their babies after they give birth to them. By and large their children are cared for by their parents, sisters, or other relatives—this is true for 45 percent of the children. Fathers assume responsibility for 22 percent of the children. (In contrast, when men are imprisoned, almost 90 percent of their children are cared for by the children's mothers.)[2] If mothers can't make arrangements for them to stay with their fathers, other family members, or court-approved friends, however, children under eighteen are placed in foster care—which involves the temporary transfer of the custody of a child from a parent to an authorized social service agency for either a set amount of time or an indefinite period.

When they're incarcerated, particularly for long periods of time, women face the risk of losing their children—both legally and emotionally. Sometimes family members want custody; other times the state takes steps to wrest custody from the mother. Often a mother feels totally helpless about being able to stay in contact with, let alone guide, her children. The bu-

2. "Women in Prison," National Women's Law Center, Washington, D.C., June 1993.

reaucracies surrounding her life and the lives of her children, through inefficiency and bumbling and sometimes outright lack of concern, leave her in the dark for days or weeks. Welfare departments are notorious for their inability to keep mothers informed about their children's placement.

When Pat got to prison, for instance, she didn't know the whereabouts of her three children: Johnny, seven; Heather, five; and Toni, eighteen months. On top of everything else, she said she was asked when she arrived at the prison if she wanted to make out a last will and testament. After two weeks in isolation, she was moved to a cottage and she asked to see a counselor about her children. Her counselor said she would write a letter, but Pat still didn't hear about what had happened to her kids.

All she could learn was that a family court judge had decided where her children should be placed. Nearly a month after her visit with the counselor, Pat found out from the county welfare department that Toni was in one foster home and Heather was in another. Johnny stayed with Heather for a while and then was transferred to a children's shelter. Pat had wanted the children to stay together with her two aunts, but the court did not grant her request. She was never given an explanation.

"My son began to have emotional problems in February," Pat said. "I was not notified of this until the following October. I was never asked about solving anything. I was merely informed of what they had done about it. Also, my son broke his arm in the spring, and I wasn't told until three weeks later.

"I haven't seen my children, and it seems like they're using 'not seeing mother' as a form of punishment for the kids. I resent being kept in total ignorance and not having any information about them.

"They haven't been able to visit me. It must be a welfare rule, because my counselor thought it would be all right for them to visit. She contacted the caseworker, who said she would have to think about it. That was in October 1971. Welfare says it wouldn't let Johnny come, but it should be all right to see Heather or Toni."

When Pat couldn't communicate directly with her children, she protested and received the right to correspond with Johnny and Heather. She still has to send letters to Toni through the welfare services.

"I keep asking about seeing my children, but I'm told to wait. I'm always stalled.

"It's the kids who suffer for our crimes.

"It's the children who are punished the worst."

Children who have been toilet trained for years often begin to wet the bed; they get into trouble at school and their self-confidence goes out the window. When they can't see their mothers, a big part of their identity and reassurance is missing. They no longer feel safe. More often than not, they don't have someone who can help them really understand why they feel the way they do. Without their mothers, they have to cope the best they can with their hollow, lonely feelings of being abandoned.

"My son Karim—he's the one who's twelve—he's so mad at me," "Leila Johnson" said. "He thinks I really let him down when I got busted. And you know what? He's right. I shouldn't have been doing dope. I was on a waiting list for program, but I slipped up. Slipped up bad. And now I got four years! That's a long time in a little boy's life. A *long* time. I wish I could go back and do it over again, but I can't. I'm so down I can hardly pick myself up.

"Karim, he used to be an A student, but since I got locked up, he's making C's and D's. I write him every couple of days, but he hasn't written me in over a month, and last week, when my mama was gonna bring him and my daughter up for visit? He didn't come. I gotta show him I can make it. I'm there for him. I am, but he don't know it. I don't want him or my daughter getting off track like I did. But it's hard from here, you know. It's hard."

Even in the state prisons where contact visits are allowed—usually in an open room where plastic chairs, and sometimes couches or comfortable chairs, are arranged in small groupings—the exposure still is controlled and communication is limited. Depending on the prison (where women usually are sentenced for at least two years), visits are allowed for one to two hours a week, sometimes more, sometimes less, if the children have a way to get to the prison—which most don't.

More often than not, it's extremely difficult for family or friends to get to the prisons. As I've said before, most women's prisons are located in rural areas, at great distances from urban centers and the homes and families of the average inmate. These prisons are rarely on public transportation lines, and since the families of most prisoners are extremely poor, this distance causes substantial transportation problems. Without someone to take them, the trip is impossible for the children of prisoners. As a result, many women prisoners and their children are deprived of contact with each other.

When a family does overcome all the difficulties and manages a trip to the prison—sometimes spending a lot of money and an entire day or more on travel—there's no guarantee that they will get to see the prisoner. If the inmate *or* the visitor is not dressed properly, they may not be allowed to see one another. If the inmate has broken a rule and is being punished in lockup, her visitors are turned away at the gate. Similarly, if the visitor got the wrong visit day by mistake—"It's a day for M through W's, not the A through the L's"—they can be told to come back on the right day. Security concerns come first, and visitors and children can be turned away for any number of reasons. If all conditions are favorable and a prisoner and her visitors are allowed to see one another, the visit can be terminated by staff at any time a child misbehaves or if the visit is not being conducted in an orderly and dignified fashion.

"When you're in that visiting room, you have to turn off so much," said Pearl Waters. "Your people, they say, 'What's the matter?' You can't show all your feelings because they're carrying that out with them and it eats them all the way home. You hurt, but that's your fault, and you shouldn't put it on them—especially not your children.

"When my children come I can hug them and hold them, but I can't fall apart and let them know how important it is they're there. You gotta give them strength to walk out with. You hurt, but you don't impose it on them; you don't force them through your ordeals about them coming and going. When they go they're not gonna cry and I'm not gonna cry—not until after they're gone, anyway. What crying I do, I do alone."

The events surrounding visits with children and family are fraught with trauma. Before a visit begins, an inmate knows that after she sees her child, she'll be subject to a strip-search before she returns to her cell. The words strip-search sound relatively innocuous, but the reality is that she knows before she begins that after seeing her children and family and perhaps feeling very good about herself, she will have to take off all her clothing and stand naked in front of the guards, who will check under her arms and breasts for contraband. She'll have to open her mouth and let them look under her tongue and in her cheeks. Then she has to squat, pull apart her buttocks and cough, so the guard in charge can check her vagina and anus for any hidden objects. In some states, even when rules provide otherwise, male guards are part of this strip search process. Sometimes prisoners' visitors—even children and grandmothers—are subjected to pat searches and, in some circumstances, to strip searches. Automatically what might be a positive, life-affirming contact is attached to a humiliating invasion of privacy.

Before the visit, the inmate has to consider carefully what she is wearing. If staff considers her inappropriately dressed, she can be returned to her housing unit and her visit can be canceled. [Inmates must wear bras and panties," one inmate handbook says. "Inmates are prohibited from wearing halters, shower shoes . . . excessively tight-fitting clothing." When Jean Harris was a prisoner at Bedford Hills, she described being turned away from one visit because a staff member said the blouse she was wearing was a turtleneck, when in fact it was not a turtleneck and she had worn it for many other visits.]

Women in state prisons usually are not allowed to greet or talk to anyone else's visitors, even if they know them from the outside. While they may be allowed to lightly kiss and hug hello and good-bye at the beginning and end of their visits, they are not allowed to hug or to hold on to their own mates when they talk.

"My old man got cut loose from San Quentin," Mary Vangie told me. "Two days later he came home and came to see me. We wanted to hug, kiss, and have that physical thing. He was told he couldn't visit me if we touched. We couldn't so much as hold hands. If you took away my clothes and gave me a county dress [jail uniform] and let me visit through the screen it would be easier. My man and I are sitting together on the couch and we can't touch. My daughter hugged me, and the staff said, 'You can't do that.' I told her to send me to lockup if I couldn't. Before my old man came to visit, I had to say into a tape recorder that if we are allowed to visit, we will not have any physical contact in the visiting room."

The inmate handbook from the Edna Mahon Correctional Facility for Women cautioned inmates in 1995: "All visits will be conducted in a quiet, orderly and dignified manner. Handshaking, embracing and kissing by the immediate family members and close friends are permitted within the bounds of good taste at the beginning and at the end of the visit only. Hand holding, in full view, is the only body contact allowed between a visitor and their inmate during a visit. Visitors and inmates must sit facing each other. Visiting children must remain under the inmate's supervision. Failure to properly supervise visiting children will be cause to terminate the visit."

Many of the rules and regulations add tension to encounters that often are fraught with the difficulty of reuniting and emotionally connecting after a long period. Visiting at the prison is often uncomfortable, cold, and intimidating for anyone, but most especially for children. As a result, personal visits, both in jails and in state prisons, often are excruciating experiences.

Because a number of prison administrators realize the importance of being supportive to mothers and their children, however, some of them try to create the best possible circumstances for visiting. They know the encounters can be difficult and upsetting under the best of circumstances, and they make an effort at least to soften the surroundings. In 1980, of three federal prisons, thirty-seven state prisons, and twenty-two jails that were surveyed, 60 percent said they had play areas for children visiting their mothers. Thirty-seven percent had special visiting hours for those who couldn't visit during regular time periods.[3] In the 1990s the trend toward child-centered visiting is reversing. Many of the programs that flourished in the 1980s have been discontinued owing to loss of state and federal funding.

Bedford Hills has maintained its efforts to support and nurture the relationships between children and their mothers in prison, and the results have been remarkable. It has parenting education programs that are run throughout the year, and a Children's Center where mothers can visit with their kids, many of whom get to Bedford by means of a program that transports them to the prison from their homes in New York City. The Children's Center is brightly painted and decorated, with children's furniture and toys. Mothers and their children can visit there, and inmates serve as day-care aides when the inmate mother has a private visit with only one of her children, or with other adult family members or friends.[4]

During the summers, Bedford runs a summer program for the children of inmates with the cooperation of the local community. Some two hundred children come to Westchester County from the cities where women live, and the children stay for a week with host families who keep the children in their homes and take them to the prison every day between 9:30 A.M. and 3:30 P.M. to spend uninterrupted time with their mothers. It's like summer camp for the children, and people in the community have been remarkably supportive and consistent. Some families have been keeping the same children every summer for years. Some of them also take the children on weekends during the school year.

When they meet the mothers of the children, people in the community often wonder why they're incarcerated. Elaine Lord, superintendent of Bedford, says that almost invariably, when families from the community get to know the mothers in prison, they say, "That woman shouldn't be here. Something is wrong that she's here."

"That's the connection we're missing," says Lord. "When people from the community have a chance to see the woman as an individual, it changes their view. Once a person interacts on an individual level, it breaks through the stereotypes."

But even with the support of the rarest of prison administrators, being a mother in prison is a painful experience, and the pain for her children is beyond measure.

At Bedford Hills, the writer Marie Ragghianti listened to an inmate

---

3. Marie Ragghianti, "Save the Innocent Victims of Prison," *Parade,* February 6, 1994.

4. V. Neto and L. Ranier, "Mother and Wife Locked Up: A Day with the Family," in Joycelyn Pollock-Byrne, ed., *Women, Prison, and Crime.*

describe what it had been like to see her eight-year-old son for the first time in years. "He wanted to measure her hand, her fingers, touch her face," Ragghianti wrote. "After a three-hour private visit, when the allotted time had expired, the little boy clung to his mother, his arms and legs wrapped tightly about her. Weeping hysterically, the child had to be wrenched away. He was taken to another state to live with relatives."[5]

Besides being isolated from their children, friends, and family, incarcerated women also are isolated from legal resources. At Sybil Brand in 1972 women had no opportunity to assist in their own defense because they had no law books, legal materials, or legal services. Captain Paul Strohman said, "We don't have a legal library. If a person is designated to act as their own attorney, they can have law books if the court decrees it. On rare occasions, they have the qualifications to act as their own attorney. But generally there's very little in regard to fighting their own case. They are entitled to law books. If they have money they can buy them. If they're acting as their own attorney, they can borrow law books from the central jail. But most of them aren't interested.

"We can't become involved in getting legal consultants or providing appeal papers or that sort of thing. We would not be doing our duty if we got involved with legal questions."

Administrators and officers in the prisons and jails I visited said that the women "aren't interested" in legal questions. "They wouldn't know how to read it, what to look for, or how to prepare a brief." An officer in Washington, D.C., pointing out meager library facilities for the more than one hundred women confined in the Women's Detention Center, said, "It wouldn't make sense to keep law books here—they abuse everything so badly." Another administrator, who was accepting a donation of law books for her state prison, said, "I would think when women take one look at the law books, they will go back to writing the boys in the penitentiary. I may be surprised—I often am—but I've never seen women who take to law books."

"It doesn't occur to anyone that since legal materials never have been available, they could be now," said one inmate. "If you ask any of the staff if they know how you can get a form for appealing your case, they look at you like you're crazy. They don't know any more about it than we do."

Although it has not been the prison's duty to provide legal forms, law books, advice, or assistance to inmates, some administrators do feel a duty

5. Ragghianti, "Save the Innocent Victims."

to provide police with legal assistance at the other end of the system's spectrum. They provide information to police agencies as a matter of course and have a developed relationship with state, local, and federal police agencies. The records kept on women in jails and prisons—including their work records, medical records, disciplinary procedures, and legal data from the court—are readily accessible to police and other law enforcement officers upon request.

"We keep a record of everything they do," Captain Strohman said. "Some are complete, some are not so complete. This has no bearing on their case, but their records can be subpoenaed by the court. The records are confidential, but if somebody asks—like the police, the FBI, or the probation department—we tell them undoubtedly. If I found out something bearing to a heinous crime committed outside or a planned escape, I'd call our detectives. We're law enforcement officers; it's our duty."

Strohman said that a woman's "jacket"—the file containing all her personal history and jailhouse records—is kept at the prison until she's released. After that, her records are sent to the archives of the central jail's record section. "Presently it's a manual thing," he said. "Ultimately all this information will be on computer tapes, and even at a station house they will be able to get all the information on somebody they arrest."

[Today courts have recognized women prisoners' rights to have access to the courts and to legal resources, but a study in 1982 found that women engage in less litigation than men do because they're less likely than men to have the legal resources they need. The survey found that although many prisons had law books and legal services, each system was consistently lacking in some important aspect of its resources, and prisoners often were unaware of what legal resources were available to them. "If institutions had sophisticated legal materials, no introductory or explanatory guides were available to facilitate their use. On the other hand, if institutions provided only introductory legal books inmates were unable to do in-depth research often necessary in pursuing cases."[6]]

In most jails and prisons, a woman is limited to writing only to approved correspondents. Names of these people, or those of visitors, are usually kept in her record. Theoretically, when all the information in her jacket is available at the time of a new arrest, all of her associates' names and family's names are available to the police. At Sybil Brand letters were not kept on file. "They can get an unlimited number of letters in here," said Captain Strohman. "It's the same for sentenced as unsentenced. We examine all the mail that comes and goes. A lot of the case law says we

6. K. Gabel, *Legal Issues of Female Inmates.*

can examine it. There's too much mail to read. We only skim it—but if we need to, we read it.

"If it's bad news, we can alert the inmate personnel so the woman doesn't go off. If it's a death or sickness in the family or one of her children is hurt or she gets a Dear John letter, she might get hysterical and start trouble in her dormitory or something. This way we can help her. We can take her aside and tell her the news and let her get out the tears in private.

"Also, there are certain things just not allowed in jail. If it's unacceptable coming in, if it's inflammatory or talking about the overthrow of the prison system, we just return it. If the mail going out is unacceptable, we destroy it. They can't discuss anyone else's case or prison business or be lewd. If letters coming in are too lewd we return them to the sender."

Now, in 1995, the amount of correspondence an inmate may receive is unlimited, but incoming correspondence is checked for contraband. It is not read unless it is "believed to contain disapproved content." Letters from inmates in other correctional facilities always are read to ensure that they do not contain any unacceptable references. "Disapproved content" includes any material detrimental to the security of the institution and also anything that "taken as a whole appeals to a prurient interest in sex, or depicts, in a patently offensive way, sexual conduct."

As one inmate at the California Institution for Women told me: "Once a friend of mine sent me one of those postcards with an artist's reproduction of a classic painting. There was a naked woman on it. The censor marked out the tits on the picture. I wouldn't have even noticed it except for it had a black magic marker bra." Another inmate, at the San Bruno County Jail, told me, "Once my boyfriend wrote me a fifteen-page letter. They sent it back to him, telling him it was too long. He sent it to me in sections, two pages at a time, twice a week, and got it in that way. You can't take any letters out with you when you go, but I'd like to keep that one, even though it took so long to get here."

Although the courts have recognized prisoners' rights to practice religion in ways that don't disrupt or endanger other prisoners or the security of the institution, many constitutional rights still don't apply to prisoners. In an opinion related to prisoners' rights regarding their correspondence, among other issues, U.S. District Court Judge J. Doyle wrote:

State governments have not undertaken to require members of the general adult population to rise at a certain hour, retire at a certain hour, eat at certain hours, live for periods with no companionship whatever, wear certain clothing, or submit to oral and anal searches after visiting hours, nor have state governments undertaken to prohibit members of the general adult population from speaking to one another, wearing beards, embracing their spouses, or corresponding with their lovers. There has been no occasion to test the constitutionality of such measures as applied to members of the general population. New ground must be broken, therefore, in deciding which, if any, of the individual interests affected by such requirements and prohibitions are to be characterized as fundamental [to prisoners].[7]

The reality of being locked in the self-contained world of prisons is that everything about your day-to-day life relates to security concerns and control on the inside. Everything is geared toward keeping the jail city and the prison city functioning efficiently and without disruption. Certainly day-to-day life has nothing to do with getting out, staying free of crime, or living in the real world.

It seems ironic that prisoners innocent in the eyes of the law—people awaiting trial—often live under some of the most punitive and physically primitive controls of all the people incarcerated in the country. More than thirty-five times as many people are locked into county and city jails in one year as are in state and federal prisons. More than half of them have not gone to trial. Over two million people are locked in local jails in one year just for drunkenness, and many of these people are women. Administrators frankly admit that the institutions they run are simply holding facilities that have little concern for the quality of a prisoner's life or for how a woman who is getting out will put her life back together with her children and family.

"We don't have time for rehabilitation here," said Captain Strohman. "We see our job as locking up those people society has decided should be out of the general population, and we're doing it as humanly as possible.

"These people awaiting trial aren't criminals. They're innocent within the eyes of the law. Sixty-five percent of the women here are unsentenced."

My memory focuses on the single-file line of two hundred women I saw earlier walking into the dining room to eat during their twenty-minute food shift. They wear blue uniforms. They are not allowed to talk on the way to the dining room, inside, or on the way back to their maximum security cell block. They work without pay. They are not allowed to see their children. They are punished for not obeying direct orders, for insolence, and for breaking other rules. Yet 65 percent of them are awaiting trial—innocent in the eyes of the law.

When Lewis Carroll wrote *Alice's Adventures in Wonderland,* he could

7. J. Doyle, *Morales v. Schmidt* (U.S. Dist. Ct. W. Dist. Wisconsin), opinion, 4/6/72.

have had no idea how his words would someday apply to America's jails: *"Let the jury consider their verdict," the King said, for about the twentieth time that day. "No, no!" said the Queen. "Sentence first—verdict afterwards." "Stuff and nonsense," said Alice loudly. "The idea of having the sentence first!"*

"We can't rehabilitate them when they haven't even been found guilty," Captain Strohman said. "With sentenced people we would like to rehabilitate them so they wouldn't do the same thing. But I couldn't point to any single individual or percentage of success we've had.

"Anybody that thinks they are rehabilitating these people are fooling themselves.

"We're responsible for their conduct, care, and safety. Of course, if they had learned to obey the rules of society, they wouldn't be here in the first place. But some functions we can't assume. We try to give them something in the way of vocational training, but we can't follow up on it. Once they leave the jail we're no longer responsible.

"Certainly I would like to rehabilitate these people, and I realize we'd save a lot of money to put them back on the street. If I were convinced we could rehabilitate them, I could be for it. But I'm not convinced. It becomes a problem of money. It's not my problem in operating a jail—it's all our problems. My chief problem is too few deputy sheriffs. I'm eighteen people short of what I'm authorized. If I still have to have security here, I need ten male deputies.

"Maybe we're trying to do too much rehabilitation here. Maybe we should strip them of everything and their human dignity when they come in and let them out sooner and they wouldn't want to come back. I've heard that in France the prisons are terrible and brutal but they don't keep anyone in them for long. Maybe that's what we should be doing. We only know what we're doing sure isn't working."

I wonder what the public would think if it really understood how our public funds are being spent on locking up people who are no threat to the community—and for what end. I think how programs could work with inmates and their families, help people learn saleable skills, ease out of jail and support strong connections with their families and life outside. I remember the words of Warden L. V. Roth, Jr., at the Montgomery County Jail in Jenkintown, Pennsylvania: "Work release is a positive thing, but you have to have facilities for it," Warden Roth said. "You have to have money for it. I've always dealt with people and with businesses, so I like this field. I would like to expand the work release program and also get rid of all untried prisoners. It will be a long time, though, before we could have any work release for the women. We have problems with some of the women banging on the walls and calling over to the men. It irritates the men a little bit. There's a lot of complications, but as long as you keep 'em fed—give them some milk and sugar and cigarettes—you usually don't have any problems.''

Sheriff Martin Segal at the Camden County Jail in Camden, New Jersey, had told me frankly: ''We have no room for counseling, attorneys, public defenders, no separate room for clergy. We don't even have one large room to run classes for rehabilitation purposes. We do the best we can, but it's impossible because of space. The jail was built for eighty-five people. There are a hundred and ninety-three here today. They have to meet with their attorneys in the washroom. You can see in conditions so crowded, communicable disease can spread quickly throughout the whole institution. We have to be careful of epidemics. The conditions are the same today as they were in 1958. The overcrowding is not in keeping with minimum standards. When they're brought in, we have to have space to process, classify, and keep.

''We don't want to put traffic violators in with hardened criminals, but we have no choice. It's very costly. A false economy.

''This jail reflects many of the disadvantages of jails built on top of courthouses or office buildings. If there was a catastrophe, an explosion or a fire or an airplane hitting the building, or even a bomb scare, I just wonder how we would get a hundred and ninety-three prisoners out. Where would we move them to?

''My purpose in my job is what they bring in with a warrant. I do what the law says. I keep 'em in custody. I keep 'em as human as possible with proper custody. I recommended a regional thing for female offenders a while back and never heard nothing about it. It would be a better way of dealing with females because it would be a savings to all three counties who kept the females in one place.''

John Walsh, of the Corrections Department at the New York City Correctional Institution for Women, explained why there's no rehabilitation for women in the new facilities for women, even though the space has been created: ''The vocational shops and the school are empty because there isn't enough staff to supervise the women going and coming from their dormitories or cells. These people have to be supervised—that's why correctional officers must accompany them wherever they go. What if they got into a fight? There could be a sociopath undiscovered, and then we would have a disrupted institution. If we weren't understaffed, the women would be freer to go to school and to programs. As it is, we don't have enough staff to accompany them.''

Ultimately, in these isolated, self-contained cities, the reality is bleak and the outlook is even more disheartening. As Lieutenant Audrey Lehre at the Sybil Brand Institute for Women said: "We're only teaching them how to live within an institution. We're not rehabilitating them. They can learn to get through here to do easy time, but this may not necessarily help them on the outside. It only helps them to know how to live in jail."

1 2   P R I S O N S

A Government Industry Fueled by Unpaid Labor

WORK

1. Every woman has a job to do which she is assigned. You are expected to do your work properly and to accept willingly and cooperatively the supervision of the person who is in charge of the work group.
2. If you have any question to raise about your assignment, take it up with your work supervisor first. If there is something further which you have to discuss, take it up with the assignment committee by putting in a pass to see your caseworker.
3. Remember that you are always in a better position to ask for a job transfer if you have a good record on the job you already have. Failure to do well on a job may result in demotion or punishment.
4. Each woman is paid four cents per hour for the assignment which she performs (except flat-timers who receive two cents per hour). Each assignment carries a pay scale based on the number of hours worked on that assignment during the month. One half of the pay is placed in a savings account and given to you when you leave the institution. The other half is placed in your commissary account and you may spend it, if you wish, while you are in the institution. In the case of flat-timers, all the pay is placed in the commissary account.

—From *Rule Book for Inmates,* Ohio Reformatory for Women, Marysville, Ohio

Prisons are big business.

Tremendous costs are involved in building and operating jails and prisons. We know that imprisoning a man, woman, or child in an institution costs from $20,000 per person per year in some states to more than

$60,000 in others for bare bones operations.[1] Even the total actual cost of imprisonment—$38 to $48 billion per year—does not include the costs of foster care and welfare for prisoners' children, court costs, or capital expenditures for new prison facilities.

And while the price of locking up one person per year in prison could easily cover the costs at such prestigious universities as Harvard and Princeton, education is a tiny, irrelevant, or nonexistent part of the prison package. Less than four cents out of every tax dollar spent on prisons (and usually less than one cent out of every dollar in county jails) goes for education, treatment, and vocational training within a prison.

What most of us do not realize is that aside from employee salaries and administrative costs that come from tax money, prisoners contribute undetermined sums to the state economy through their work in big prison businesses. The Federal Reformatory for Women at Alderson, West Virginia, for instance, runs a multimillion-dollar-a-year industry for the federal government. What the services would cost the government at minimum wage scales could make the expenses skyrocket.

Many of the "state goods" we use every day are made by prisoners who work six or seven days a week. They are "rewarded" for their work with only a pittance [two dollars a day is the going rate in 1995, but some states pay nothing at all] and the incentive of a good work record, which may contribute to an earlier release on parole. In some state prisons and in federal prisons, certain jobs earn inmates work credits and "good time" off their sentences.

Road signs; license plates; benches and tables in state parks; garments for patients in state hospitals and state schools; state and national flags; clothes for state children's schools; linens and pajamas for veteran's hospitals; mattresses, sheets, and blankets for state institutions—all these things are made by prisoners in state and federal institutions. In addition, prisoners make the cloth from which they sew their own uniforms; they make the shoes they and other prisoners wear; they sew uniforms for state troopers and prison guards. Women at Alderson make prison uniforms for all the male prisoners in other federal institutions.

Prisoners do printing and computer printouts for government agencies; they raise and harvest their own food and run canneries. They make soap for state and county jails and produce furniture that is used both within the prison and in the offices and homes of correctional personnel and government employees. The network of diversified industries is run by

1. These are 1994 figures. In 1973, when the first edition of this book appeared, the cost was said to be $3,500 to $7,400.

private corporations contracted to the various state departments of corrections and, for the federal government, Federal Prison Industries, Incorporated. The industrial goods are not sold in competitive trade because of labor laws restricting unfair competition. The goods and services contracted out from the prison to other parts of the state and federal government are considered interagency commerce.

State and federal agencies benefit greatly in costs saved from cheap prisoner labor. But we don't know how much the state actually makes or saves, because government agencies don't account for funds in terms of profit. Figures are additionally difficult to locate or analyze because prison commerce is such a murky undertaking and accounting procedures vary so widely that administrators themselves seem vague and uninformed about transactions. Apparently, when prison systems recover profits from their industries or from the sales of agricultural products or surplus land, these amounts seldom are reported or deducted from budget expenditures. [In the 1990s, some prisons and jails have started *charging* prisoners for room and board; it will be interesting to see how this income is reported.]

Even profits from commissary sales within the prison can be hard to understand. Some profits from commissary sales are supposed to go into welfare funds for the benefit of destitute inmates. But inmates, most of whom are destitute, say they rarely see any benefit other than candy, cookies, or free packs of state cigarettes handed out at Christmas parties. The inmates have no right to determine how the profits are spent. In New York City, the million-dollar commissary fund from combined jails somehow filters into the general fund for the city.

In San Francisco, Sheriff Richard Hongisto said that before he took office, "No one seemed to know where the money had gone to." Hongisto said the commissary profit from San Francisco jails alone totaled at least eighteen thousand dollars a year. [This would be much higher today.] Sheriff Hongisto planned to track down the money and start using it to improve direct services for inmates who live in what he called "outrageous and inhumane conditions." Hongisto said that he could only figure the money had been funneled off into private gain, because certainly it hadn't been used for inmate benefits.

During my research and travels to various prisons, I had been aware of the exchange of goods and of the "business traffic" from prison to prison, but it had always seemed an immense, impenetrable maze. Wardens had told me their institutions were "self-sustaining," and I had met foremen from penal industries in various prison factories who talked of their tremendous output and profit. But it wasn't until I visited Arizona State Prison and the Los Angeles County Jail Division that the reality of prison production cut through my resistance to economic details. It was in those two places that I first began to realize the extent to which prisoner labor is used and depended on by the state for much of the maintenance of state agencies and prisons and the control of prisoners.

In Arizona I was having one of those disastrous-before-it-even-begins-type interviews with the superintendent of the state prison, Frank Eyman. Eyman's word has been law at the old territorial prison for more than eighteen years.

When I came in and sat down opposite Superintendent Eyman, he was sitting at a large walnut desk in front of a wall of small framed photographs documenting his eighteen years of receiving awards and shaking hands with various Lions and Kiwanis Club presidents, state officials, military officers, and movie stars. He shuffled papers on his desk and snorted through his nose occasionally, not looking up once. His face was red and splotchy and the veins on his nose were swollen. He wore a yellow flannel shirt buttoned tight around his throat with a turquoise bolo tie made by Navajo Indians. He looked like he might have been an old cowboy from the O.K. Corral.

Finally, after nearly five minutes of uncomfortable silence punctuated only by his coughs and snorts, I introduced myself—even though I had already been introduced by the secretary when I first walked in the door.

Eyman glared at me for a minute and then demanded in a raspy voice: "What are you doing here?"

I handed him a copy of the letter he had sent granting me permission to visit the prison and told him, as I had said in my original letter, that I was doing research for a book on women in prison.

He looked at the letter and then wadded it up and threw it in the waste-basket by his desk.

"I was going to tell you you couldn't come in," he said.

"What changed your mind?"

"Nothing. Nothing at all. Nothing changed my mind."

I felt my initial anger dissipating and laughter erupting at the Alice-in-Wonderland statement, but the potential for getting thrown out of his office before I got my foot inside the women's division made me twist my face into seriousness and scramble through my brain to look for questions that might get me through the barricades.

"If you're doing more than one year, you have to be in prison, you can't be in county jail," he volunteered out of the blue. That was a contribution. Now it was my turn.

"We have one thousand two hundred and sixty-three men here and forty-five women," he confirmed in answer to my question, after making a telephone call to check the figures. "We've been up to as high as seventeen hundred men and seventy-some women. It fluctuates.

"There's more crime now than you ever had before.

"The reason my population is down is because of the conservation camp and the halfway houses for prerelease in Phoenix that have been taking people out.

"We have six or seven women up in Phoenix taking the drug cure.

"They belong to us, but they're up there for the drug cure.

"Women draw the same rations as men."

Each of these sentences was drawn out by questions, some of which I had to rephrase more than once. It was a painful process, like trying to draw water out of a cactus, but I kept going, trying to get somewhere.

"Hell, I don't know how many employees I have," he said when I asked about staffing.

It looked hopeless. But then I asked him about the prison industries, and he lit up. His response continued for nearly fifteen enthusiastic minutes.

"Hell, this is a big industry we have here. We just sell to state institutions and to the children's colony and university. Yes, this is a big business." He smiled! "A damn big business. We have four farms within a distance of seven miles, worked by male population. There are trustees living on ranches under the foreman. I don't know the number. We also manufacture innerspring mattresses and make all license plates for the state and all the street signs. We have a printing company, a cotton gin mill, a dairy farm, a swine farm, beef cattle, and a big chicken ranch. We also make the barbecue grills and big picnic tables they put in rest areas all over the state. We also have a cannery for fruits, vegetables, potatoes, and tomatoes. We feed 'em fresh seasonally and then can all the excess. We raise all our own food; everything they eat comes from here. Everything they wear comes from here. They even make the mattresses they sleep on.

"Hell, yes, running a prison is running a big business," he continued, bragging about how the prisoners at Arizona State did all the printing of documents, legislative reports, and studies for the state, as well as printing prison manuals and contracting for business with the state universities. He said the prison had its own draftsmen and construction crews and that prison labor had been used to build every building on the grounds, including the gas chamber, a minors' division, and the $275,000 women's division. Inmates had also built fifteen prison residences on the grounds for correctional administrators and officers and had completed a twenty-three-apartment housing project in Florence for correctional officers, paid for by state general funds. Prisoners pick cotton, process it through cotton gins, and make state garments with the cloth. Prisoners work as plumbers and electricians and masons, in addition to doing all repair work and upkeep of prison facilities.

The prison is more than self-sufficient. It's a moneymaking proposition. Yet the week I was there, of the 1,263 men and 45 women at the prison, only 107 were on the payroll under a "wage incentive pay plan" started six months earlier, in July 1971. Those 107 prisoners in "key positions" were paid twenty cents an hour. Six of the paying jobs were held by women inmates.

The majority of prisoners at Arizona State work only for time off their sentences. If prisoners have a "two-for-one" job, they get two days' credit for every day of labor served under state law. In addition, with a good work and behavior record, these men and women can get two months off their sentence after the first year and four months after the third year. Five months are cut from the sentence every year after the fifth year as long as their employment record is consistently "successful" and their behavior record "clean." Anyone in segregation or in the "adjustment center" cannot get two-for-one status and can lose time already earned. Inmates can try to earn money for commissary by selling crafts in the prison craft shop or by selling blood in the Cutter Blood Program. They get six dollars for each bleeding, and can do this once a week.

"There are no work furlough programs here and no work release for men or women," Eyman said. "I don't see that ever happening here. I wouldn't allow it. I just wouldn't be in favor of it. There's plenty of work to do right here. There won't be any work release from here. I just wouldn't like it. We don't have it, let's put it that way. And we don't expect to have it—not as long as I'm here." When I asked Eyman what he thought of conjugal visits, he said, "I'll never have 'em, I just don't want 'em. If they want that, they should have stayed in the free world. If they chose a criminal way of life, why should they enjoy the privileges of tax-paying citizens?"

The thought that prisoners pay more taxes in labor than any citizens in the "free world" was totally foreign to Eyman's thinking—just as the idea that sex and affection are "privileges of tax-paying citizens" was foreign to my thinking. He, like many others, openly disdains the concept of rehabilitation; rather, he believes that prisoners are in his prison to be punished and to pay for their crimes. And they do pay—not to victims of crime, but to the state general fund.

Under the Slave Emancipation Act of 1865, slavery and involuntary servitude were abolished for everyone except convicted criminals; it is thus perfectly within the law to force prisoners to work for no pay. Whether it is right or wise or just is an entirely different question.

Although it is legal to force a sentenced prisoner to work, it is illegal to force a detentioner, someone jailed while awaiting trial or sentence, into involuntary service. County and local jails therefore offer detentioners work as a privilege to pass the time. In many places the alternative to the privilege of having a job is being locked into a cell twenty-four hours a day. The difference between force or "incentive" becomes a very hazy question. Work by pretrial prisoners is also often encouraged by the privilege of getting "unlocked" an extra hour a day or being paid with a couple of packs of cigarettes a week. Also, it relieves boredom and makes day-to-day life more tolerable. Some jobs are in demand.

"I'm a hall girl," said Barbara, at the Cook County Jail. "That's supposed to mean I'm a trustee. Trustees get to stay out [in the dayroom] one hour later at night and get extra food. We work in the beauty shop, do the corridor, and sweep and mop. That extra hour means a lot to me; I don't like to be locked up. Usually the job is appointed to someone. Most ask the matron, but I got the job different. A girl got shipped to the penitentiary. So I just picked up her mop and started mopping, and I had the job."

At the Sybil Brand Institute for Women, no prisoner is paid for her daily labor, although more than 65 percent of them are awaiting trial. Legally, they can't be made to work. Yet nearly everyone confined there works, cleaning their living areas, working in a large garment factory, the laundry, or kitchen. Women do all the janitorial work, including trash collection and disposal. The garment factory makes shrouds for the coroner's office and gowns for the county hospitals.

Inmates, sentenced or unsentenced, get no pay for their work. "The inmates get no pay except at our camps," said Chief H. B. Creamer, chief of the Los Angeles County Jail Division, after telling me about the division's budget, the twenty-eight hundred acres of beef herds, a dairy, a produce farm, and a bakery run by inmates. "They work for reward. They get five days off their sentences for working and five days off for good conduct.

"Everybody who's sentenced is automatically figured at a twenty-day month. If they refuse to work, or have bad conduct, the time gets recomputed. It makes the time go much faster for them. I'm not saying we're rehabilitating them, but in many cases, they're adding a skill to a field of knowledge they can perhaps use someday.

"Constitutionally, we can't work unsentenced inmates unless they volunteer. We are merely a detaining agency until the court decision. Prisoners who are not sentenced are not getting time off. Once a person is sentenced, she starts earning her good time and her work.

"Reward is an excellent means for us to gain compliance to rules. If you want to gain time, you comply to our rules. That's the greatest reason why we've had so little trouble here."

A few women at Sybil Brand can earn some money for commissary items by washing or making blouses for officers, or washing cars on occasion after they have finished their regular industrial and maintenance jobs. Officers pay prisoners through their employee fund: three cents for washing and ironing a blouse. Two of the three cents are divided up between the laundress and the ironer, and one cent goes to the soap fund, since the officers aren't allowed to use county soap to wash their blouses.

Prisoners selected by officers to make blouses are also paid three cents per piece. The three cents are divided up between the cutter, the sewer, and the buttonholer. This means each woman would have to make nearly fifty blouses to buy one pack of cigarettes. The women don't make money individually for the things they make in craft shop programs. That money theoretically goes into the inmate welfare fund to pay for the various activities and to provide occasional cigarettes, soap, or toothpaste for destitute women who don't have anyone to bring them money from the outside.

Discussing work credits and good time as the best stimulus for inmate labor, Captain Paul A. Strohman said frankly, "The good time and the work time is a great help to custody. It gives us an incentive to get them to work. There's been a lot of talk about paying people in jail, but it gets back to the budget. There would be a taxpayer revolt to that."

Perhaps Captain Strohman is right; taxpayers might "revolt." But consider this. If prisoners earned fair wages for their labor, they would be able to support their families—and that alone would take thousands of people off welfare rolls. As it is now, dependent families are forced to go on welfare when their wage earner goes to prison. Children become dependents of the state, and the costs don't make sense—especially when prisoners are actually paying more than their share of taxes in terms of physical labor and profit to the state. In addition, if prisoners earned even minimum wages, they would be able to pay restitution. They would be able to save some small sums of money to help them get readjusted upon release. It seems more than reasonable that the profit they earn for the state should be returned to them rather than transferred to the state. But the fear that people would want to go to prison if they could earn a decent wage still seems to exist, irrational as it is.

One of the notions seemingly inherent in the concept of imprisonment in America is that prisoners should get no reward or sense of gratification during confinement. If they've done something bad, nothing good should happen to them. If they've harmed someone else, they should be harmed. We seem to feel that if prisoners are comfortable in any way—if they're able to have fun or recreation—then they're not being punished enough. In 1870 an Englishman named William Talleck argued that forced labor with no rewards would reduce people's temptation to go to prison for an easy life. Addressing the National Congress on Penitentiary and Reformatory Discipline, in Cincinnati, Ohio, Mr. Talleck sounded like a modern politician when he praised a model prison in the United States that was "at once punitory and reformatory":

> It makes the inmates pay handsomely, by their labor, for all the expenses of punishment, for their board and lodging, and for the salaries of the officers. In addition, they earn a new profit to the state of from $24,000 to $28,000 per annum (Upwards of £5,000). Thus, after all, an honest outsider is not likely to be very strongly tempted by the fish hash and corned-beef (diet of the prison), if he knows that for it he must be shut up for several years and "sweated" for the benefit of his chastisers to the extent of $220 (£40) per annum.[2]

It was also noted at the 1870 congress by a man from Pennsylvania that

> those prisons were best that paid best; therefore it would be necessary for every prison manager to make his prison pay, or else he would be pronounced a failure. It would also be necessary to introduce trades and manufactures, and in order to make these pay, it was necessary to employ all the modern machinery and improvements, so that they could get the same amount of labor and of the same kind, that private individuals, companies and firms did outside. . . . The result was that the inmates of our prisons were turned into machines.[3]

The evolution of prison labor, it seems, was a product of the Industrial Revolution, which created a need for cheap labor in economically expanding America. The view that labor was therapy was economically appealing and fit the Puritan moral heritage, which viewed idleness as the root of crime.[4] But even in 1870 there was a dispute as to whether "moral and religious improvement" was compatible with industry on the part of the prisoners and economy on the part of the prison officers. Several people were vehement that efforts to make prisons self-sustaining or

2. In Wines, ed., *Transactions of the National Congress on Penitentiary and Reformatory Discipline.*

3. Ibid.

4. American Friends Service Committee, *Struggle for Justice: A Report on Crime and Punishment in America.*

profitable never should be allowed to supersede the object of moral and religious improvement.

These beliefs led to great dispute over the labor contract system, under which prison labor was contracted out by state legislatures to private individuals and contractors. This practice, especially in the South, meant that slavery was perpetuated under a contract system. Free blacks virtually were kidnapped back into slavery in lieu of payment of fines or taxes or civil judgments. Vagrancy statutes were commonly used to enforce criminal sentences, with the result that, in spite of the recent abolition of slavery, thousands of black people who had committed no real criminal offenses were kept in involuntary servitude on farms or road gangs.

In urban areas, European immigrants also were rounded up for vagrancy and violation of drinking and "morals" laws. At the 1870 congress, a Mr. Cordier of Pennsylvania opposed the contract system. Two things, he said, were essential to a prisoner's reformation: "the will to live honestly and the power to earn an honest living." Both must be given him in prison, the one through moral agencies, the other through industrial training. Cordier argued that the contract system, which used prisoners for hard manual labor, failed to teach a trade.

Even in 1870, opponents to the contract system in general still considered all prisoners to be "criminals" in need of reformation, even though many clearly were innocent victims of discrimination. Only Judge Carter of Ohio said that if prisons were to continue to exist (he believed they should be abolished), there should be "some system of co-operative labor, by which the prisoners would receive the wages they earned just as if they were at work outside."

It was not until the 1920s that pressures from competitive businesses and unions curbed the "unfair competition" of the labor contract system, thus limiting prison production to an intragovernmental matter with products confined to use only by state and federal agencies.[5] The free labor was simply too much competition for union labor, because it could naturally underbid anyone and still make a profit. Today it's considered radical to suggest that as long as prisons still exist, prisoners should be able to join unions and make union-scale wages for their work. Administrators say there isn't enough money in the budget—but if outside unions were al-

---

5. The abuses of the contract system of leasing out prisoner labor were curbed with a series of restrictive federal laws, beginning with the Hawes-Cooper Act of 1929, effective in 1934. These laws practically put prison contract industries out of competitive business. Road gangs and work projects still continue (with men still wearing shackles and iron chains in some states), but not for private contractors.

lowed in or the profit was returned to the people who earned it, the wages wouldn't come from ''the budget.''

In 1870 the annual net earnings from prison labor at Ohio Penitentiary, where women and men were confined, were ''over and above ordinary expenses from $40,000 to $50,000 profit.'' During World War II prison industries boomed and produced war goods valued at over $138 million. Where does that excess go today? Who controls it? How is it distributed?

It is beyond the scope of this book to analyze the figures today, but it seems that if the profit-making trend has continued, then what was fifty thousand dollars in profit for one institution in 1870 would well be many millions of dollars in today's economy. Since the number of penal industries has dramatically increased, estimates may be multiplied even further. The real economy of prison business is an area worthy of detailed investigation. And if in fact there are hidden profits, then the figures should be made public, and taxpayers inside and outside prison should be able to evaluate them. [Another area worthy of investigation is the big business of building prisons; who is getting the contracts to build these billion-dollar facilities that cost millions to run? What political donations have led to the sites chosen for new prisons and to the many contracts made as part of the building process? Taxpayers should demand to know these facts, since public funds are being poured into prisons in such huge quantities for such unproductive results.]

At the Federal Reformatory for Women at Alderson, the women prisoners who work in the garment factory make clothing for other federal prisons—khakis and denims for the men prisoners and shirts for guard uniforms. They have other federal contracts as well, such as making linens and pajamas for veteran's hospitals throughout the country. They have a tremendous production output annually, even though the industrial sewing machines they work on are out of date for commercial use. (''Even if you wanted to get a job in a garment factory on the streets, you wouldn't know how to operate the machines,'' one woman at Alderson said. ''And your speed isn't up because you've been working on such old machines. It's a real sweatshop, and the superintendent of industries is a real ogre about production, production, production. All she cares about is production.'')

The smaller-scale automatic data-processing operation puts women with a certain level of education and manual dexterity to work at computer jobs for the Bureau of Prisons, army, navy, Veteran's Administration, and other federal agencies. They keep statistics for the Bureau of Prisons, with extensive personal backgrounds on all federal prisoners, which the women say include even the most lowly misconduct report form.

The majority of women working in these industries are paid nineteen cents an hour. [Twenty-five to fifty cents an hour in 1995.] A very few women make top-grade prison industry wages of up to fifty-two cents an hour. They all work eight hours a day, sometimes six and seven days a week. Most women who have no funds from the outside depend on the work for their essential commissary items, from toothpaste to cigarettes to underwear. The biggest advantage to working in industry, besides the commissary income, is the reward of work credits or "industrial good time."

In institutional jobs other than those under industries—such as dining room, maintenance jobs, office jobs, paint crew, landscape crew, laundry and hospital and storehouse—women at Alderson are eligible to receive a meritorious service award (MSA): after three months on the job, a woman is eligible to get ten dollars a month, and this amount can be increased. But according to prisoners, most people don't get it at all. They are also eligible for "meritorious good time" allotted to those who get it at the same rate as industrial good time. But meritorious good time and meritorious pay are not given to long-timers (those serving five years or more) until the last three years of their actual sentences.

"To get paid, you have to be really, really good at what you're doing," Suzi Williams said. "You can't goof off at all, and you have to put in a lot of overtime, particularly in the dining room, where they're very hard on people. And they will give you like two people's jobs to do on your shift. They'll make you be the beverage girl and at the same time carry trays from the dish room, when you're only supposed to be doing one of those. We ran into somebody who had been washing pots and pans seven days a week for over a year, because she just didn't want to do anything that would mess with her parole. She was basically a straight housewife type who was very easily intimidated and didn't know much about bucking bureaucracies or making a stink.

"In all of these things people who can buck bureaucracies or who are hustlers just have a much easier time. It's the people who aren't hustlers who have it so hard—and there are a whole lot of them there, because prisons are for people not who committed bad crimes, but who committed crimes badly. You know, the fuck-ups and the bumblers. And the people who could be led around by the nose by other people and influenced and then left to take the rap when the smarter people cut out or have enough money to buy their way out afterwards.

"It's hard to get paid, and most people just don't know how to get around it. And then once you're getting paid, then this is an excuse to load everything on you, call you up at five and say, 'Hey, report at six,' and all this kind of stuff. Or they'll threaten to take it away. Because you're getting paid, you should do thus and thus. And, 'Hey, wow, remember you're getting paid and we can stop that!' You have to earn your days in pay. And you're also subject to take away your days in pay for things that have nothing to do with your job. For instance, if you're messy around the cottage, or loud—'We don't consider you an exemplary person'—or untidy in your dress, they can say, 'We can't give you days in pay and you're not eligible for the next three months.' "

The *Manual of Correctional Standards,* issued by the American Correctional Association, outlines elements "essential to the successful operation" of vocational training:

> A realisitic vocational training program which is divorced from the maintenance needs of the institution and under qualified instructors; training should be in as many as practicable of the varied industrial, commercial and service occupations in which women are engaged today. A work program to provide upkeep of the institution will also provide an opportunity to teach good work habits which are essential.

The ACA manual specifies that vocational training should teach skills "salable in the community" but says: "Perhaps the largest number of inmates are placed on work assignments necessary for maintaining the institution; by-products of such placements are the development of improved work habits and attitudes."

When I first visited several county jails where women were confined, I was appalled at the rules that demanded "ladylike" conduct in the midst of meaningless make-work such as scrubbing floors an excessive number of times each day and scrubbing bars on cells. Mainly the women were locked in their cells or kept from being idle by "keeping the place clean."

Male prisoners were assigned to heavier work details that contributed to prison maintenance, while the women remained cramped in small, segregated areas of these jails. It was only after I visited more state prisons that I realized what heavy labor women at all-female institutions do for the prison economy. Among other jobs, women work as butchers, truck loaders, janitors, and "maintenance men."

"How many women do you know that work on garbage trucks or repair cars or lawn mowers or drive tractors or lift hundred-pound bags of potatoes and whatnot for a living?" asked Sheila "Terry" Dunnigan, an inmate at Frontera. "How many people do you know that make six dollars a month working at an eight-hour-a-day job five days a week? If you're lucky, you may make up to nine dollars a month—if you're lucky.

"How many women do you know on the outside who drive trucks, and how many women plumbers do you know on the streets? The women here are wasting time and energy on these type of jobs running the institution when they could be in some kind of training program and making something of themselves, but there are little or no training programs that would benefit these people when they get out.

"There is a cosmetology course that is sixteen hundred hours long—but after spending all this time, there is no guarantee that you will be able to get a license, because they don't give licenses to felons or ex-convicts. So here you have wasted sixteen hundred hours or a year that won't do you any good at all on the streets.

"Society talks about rehabilitating the criminal. I guess one of the things that impresses people the most when they come here is the grounds and our surroundings. The campus has trees, flowers, shrubs and looks really nice when it's green and the sun's out shining or when it's wintertime and it snows in the mountains and looks really pretty. But it could never make up for all the mental pressure that people undergo. There is no rehabilitation here. They offer nothing.

"And not only is there no rehabilitation, there's no communication. If you want anything, you have to fight for it, and even then you usually get nothing. You get a good runaround from people who can't give you even a few minutes to rap, and that's about it."

Besides the complaint that lifting and loading from trucks, acting as butchers, and performing other such jobs do not develop saleable skills for work on the outside, women complain that the heavy jobs "break them down." In addition, they say, the health standards and safety conditions in the factories and work areas are often hazardous.

When state prisoners at the Detroit House of Correction went on strike in the fall of 1971 in an attempt to get better conditions, chief among the women's complaints were the hazards of the laundry and the canning factory. Included in their list of grievances was a demand for a state health inspector.

They said the jobs in the laundry and the canning factory were the hardest jobs and pointed out that women:

- Use presses that are outdated and break down frequently.
- Lift 100- and 150-pound bags of soap chips and other cleansers to pour the contents into barrels.
- Load washers by lifting anywhere from twenty-five to one hundred pounds each into old machines that have dangerous washer doors.
- Unload and sort approximately one hundred bags, each weighing twenty-five to one hundred pounds, of laundry that comes to the institution from the general hospitals. The sheets "are stained with blood, feces and other forms of contagious germs. This institution provides no masks, head-

dress, gloves or protective clothing for these women to wear while doing this.''

"We as women would like to leave here still able to have babies and our bodies as healthy and productive as when we entered this institution,'' the protestors said. "Are we wrong to feel this way?''

Suzi Williams, who did time at Alderson for interfering with the Military Selective Service Act of 1967 and destroying draft records, said the keypunching program there was probably the "only worthwhile vocational training program'' useful on the outside. But she pointed out that not too many people qualify for the program because of educational requirements. Those who do can go only so far.

"I had a friend who was doing a ten-year sentence for bank robbery,'' Suzi said. "She was a very intelligent person and wanted to learn computer programming instead of just keypunching because it's more interesting, plus it pays better. So she begged and pleaded with them, but they were not at all interested in helping her learn programming. Finally she decided she was going to learn it whether they helped her or not. She had to fight with them a couple months for permission to even order the books and pay for them herself. They were quite expensive, but finally she got them paid for and ordered.

"But the people who censor books held them up for another couple of months, and then they were transferred to her boss. After another month or so she heard a rumor that there were these books sitting around and she squawked, and sure enough, they were hers, the ones she had paid her own personal money for. She studied them hard, but she suffered continuously because authorities threw stuff in her way. Neither her boss, the head of her department, her caseworker, nor the education department people who had a hand in it were helpful. Nobody was really helpful. So they talk about all this rehabilitation stuff, but when you get it together to do something, they will not help you. You have to do it in spite of them.''

Suzi said that despite the rhetoric, production always comes before individual considerations. I have also found this to be true, no matter how good the intentions of some administrators. Women have a hard time getting out of work for a dental appointment or educational programs when they are available. At Alderson most of the Spanish-speaking women work in the garment shop because most of them don't have any money and depend on the income for their commissary. Suzi said a lot of them would like to learn English, but they can't if they have to be in the garment shop all the time. "Most of the classes are during the day, and when there are night classes, they're too exhausted,'' she said. There are a few isolated cases where women with an incredible amount of will get certified as laboratory technicians or earn college credits through correspondence courses, but usually they have done it in spite of the prison, not because of it.

Even the most conservative corrections officials admit that jobs in prison don't have any significant relationship to rehabilitation. They admit the production methods are obsolete but necessary to keep the prisons functioning. Jobs also have a way of helping the prisoners forget about the immediate oppression they are experiencing and where they are.

Alice Evans has been at the Ohio Reformatory for Women since 1965. She will be eligible to meet the parole review board in 1977, although her actual release date is 1985. She's doing a natural life sentence of twenty years for being an accessory to first-degree murder. We met in the basement of one of the living units of Marysville when Alice was hauling a huge beef carcass across a table. At the institution, she's a butcher.

A small, pale-skinned woman, Alice doesn't look any more like she could be a butcher than Julie Nixon Eisenhower does. But she hauled around the beef carcass with skill and nonchalance. "We do lifting, but usually two or three of us help each other. We get five beefs in at a time," she said. "We unload truckfull after truckfull. I come to work at eight-fifteen A.M. and we have orders to fill and get on the cart for the truck girls to deliver to the central food and diet kitchen. If it's on milk day we sit around until nine or nine-fifteen and unload the milk truck, which comes from Marion. Then if we have beef, the chief butcher does the breaking down and I do the sawing on the power saw. I cut it in steaks and get it ready to go out. If we don't use it that day we put it in the freezer for later on.

"We get off at eleven-thirty and go to lunch. We sit up on the corridor after we get back (twenty minutes later) until twelve forty-five. They crowd fifty-some women in the corridor, and it's the source of real tension. We have to sit all crowded up on those benches and can't go to our rooms. All of the women are trying to yak after lunch and it's a lot of tension because you don't want a bunch of women sitting on you. Officers say this and that and don't do nothing—hush. A lot of fights—practically every one I can think of—has started from that corridor sitting. Even if it erupts later, you can know where it started. There was a bad fight last night that had started in the corridor in the noon period. Three women jumped another one and beat her bad. The staff knows who did the beatings, but they're not doing anything about it. You would think they should move the three who beat her up to the adjustment unit, but oh no, they moved her out. None of what goes on here makes much sense—but they keep us working.

"I'm confined to this building only. The only time I get out is for dinner or to go to the hospital for clinic—which doesn't do any good. I really get the feeling of being confined. I live in this building and I work here in the basement.

"The BVR [Bureau of Vocational Rehabilitation] thing don't help lifers, and about all vocational things run here are by BVR. They say they have just so much money and so far it only goes for short-timers. I think it only takes three years of butchering to get a license, and I started working here in 1965. But I don't have a license, and I doubt if I could get a job if I did.

"There are so many jive rules here and so many things to hold a person back. We go through hell and there's nothing we can do about it. I'm cottage rep for the corridor and elected rep to the communications group, but we have no power. Our suggestions are always just 'taken under consideration'—they don't move on them. I don't know whether the outside world don't believe this hell or whether they don't care.

"There are so many things we should change, I don't know where to start. You gotta do manual labor for six dollars a month—that ought to be changed. But it's really hard to get the women together. How can we get anything from congressmen when we can't even get our problems together here on the farm. There's all sorts of petty shit. Like we can't go into the TV room, for instance, unless two officers are there. And there are only two officers on duty at a time, so we can't go in. Or if you forget to turn in your food card or forget to pick it up, you get three nights' early bed. That means if you don't want to eat, you still have to walk over with your food card and check back in here. There's a hundred more things like that. So there are all these petty things forced on people's minds, and it's hard to get organized around bigger issues when these little ones keep you worrying all the time.

"We've talked to the administration about our pay, but they say, We can't do anything about it, not us or Miss Wheeler or Governor Gilligan, unless you get state senators to pass a bill."

When I was at Marysville, everyone I talked to, including administrators, said they thought the pay scale should be changed, something that could be done only through legislation. The top salary for inmates was ten dollars a month. Six dollars were put automatically into the woman's commissary fund and four dollars into her savings account, to be given her on release. That's five cents an hour: three cents for commissary and two cents for savings. The pay is purely a book transaction; women never see the cash or benefit from interest accrued on their savings. When they leave the prison, they leave with a minimum of twenty-five dollars and a maximum of three hundred. At the time they reach the maximum amount, they stop earning that extra two cents an hour; it stops going into their savings fund. From that point on they get only three cents an hour.

"The twenty-five-dollar floor and three-hundred-dollar ceiling is established by legislation and departmental directive," Superintendent Martha Wheeler confirmed. "We have no idea why or who decided. But it would have to be changed by the legislature. Back in 1966 we wrote a proposal for pay to be raised, but we never got any response on that. If the person has another source of income, the ceiling has nothing to do with that. Money that comes in from the outside is considered personal. If someone gets a pension, for instance, we'll open a savings account in a local bank for her and she accumulates the interest.

"Some people make less than ten dollars a month. People who are in school are not presumed to work full time, for instance, so they don't get full pay. They get four ninety-five to spend on their personal account a month and three thirty in savings. This is if they're not docked for absences."

When I talked to Bennett Cooper, the commissioner of corrections for the state of Ohio, he said that the department planned to raise the pay of inmates, that there was money in the budget to do that and it wouldn't take legislative action. When I asked him about the floor and the ceiling on inmates' savings, he said he had been told it would take legislation to change that. I told him I thought it just didn't make sense and requested to see the statute that set it up. It would take a woman nearly seven years to earn $300, and if she was there for twenty years, she theoretically should be able to take $960 home with her, at a savings rate of four dollars a month.

During the interview, he asked his assistant to check what legislation stipulated the floor and ceiling. Before I left, his assistant had returned with the information that the ceiling of three hundred dollars and floor of twenty-five dollars were set not by legislation but by an administrative directive from 1952. It would take only another administrative directive to change that condition. No bill had to pass through the legislature.

Cooper said, "It just shows what creatures of habit we are," and noted that many of the unquestioned rules and procedures were going to be thoroughly reexamined. Administrations have changed many times since 1952, and I have no reason to doubt the sincerity of any of the administrators who believed it would take legislation to change this situation. It just reaffirms my belief that the more these vague and hidden procedures are given light, the more changes can be made simply and easily through directives, which were originally made in the economic interest of jailers, not inmates.

What appears to me even more direct exploitation than the minuscule wages prisoners are paid for their labor is the use of prisoners in the personal service of prison administrators. Women prisoners often work as housemaids and cooks for the families of prison superintendents, and men work as cooks, in lawn crews, and as maintenance men at the homes of superintendents. Certainly most administrators don't see anything wrong or try to hide the fact that prisoners cook and clean, wash and iron for them. It is an accepted custom, and the household servants come hand in hand with the administrative position. I'm sure in the administrators' minds they are just providing more jobs for prisoners who otherwise would be idle. Still, my sensibilities are offended when I hear a woman tell me about the long hours she spends cooking for the warden or experiences she's had "serving" at a party or dinner in the superintendent's home. It may be that my indignation at such arrangements is excessive, since I have been a live-in maid in years gone by. But I can't hear about it without feeling that it is wrong. Nevertheless, it's a common practice.

"Leslie Simms" told me of a time when, after she had recovered from a miscarriage, she was working in the staff dining room at a detention center I am not at liberty to name. The superintendent of prisons, a man I'll call "Mr. X," needed a "house girl." Ms. Williams, a lieutenant, put Leslie's name up for the job: "He interviewed me and asked me about doing housework and what I was there for. I only told him, 'I'm here for homicide,' which he already knew—he was just asking.

"Close to September I went to work there. Their house is set off from the actual prison itself. They have two bedrooms on the third floor and four on the second floor with two bathrooms. Downstairs there's a real big L-shaped living room and dining room, a den, and recreation room, with a place behind that for an extra stove and refrigerator. In the basement was the actual kitchen and laundry room and storerooms and bathroom for the help.

"They had a girl, Carol, already working there as head house girl. She did the cooking, and I did the laundry and cleaning shit upstairs with another gig. They always got three black girls and one white houseman nobody would want to fuck. I went over and helped Carol with dinner one night and helped serve dinner. I guess he liked the way I served. He fired Carol as head house girl and shifted her upstairs to do housework and then later fired her because she was 'sloppy and incompetent.' I don't know about incompetent, but she was definitely sloppy in appearance. We wore our prison uniforms to work in.

"Then I was head house girl. I went in at eight-thirty in the morning and did the laundry—washing, drying, and ironing, every day. They had a lot of laundry—six people—Mr. and Mrs. X and their four children. The kids would leave their dirty laundry laying all around. Then I left around ten or eleven A.M. and went back to the jail for lunch and count and all. Then around five a car would pick me up to go and do dinner. I'd be there till around nine or ten every night, even weekends, yes. There was always somebody home for dinner, even if Mr. and Mrs. X went out, which was almost never.

"I'd fix supper in the basement and put it on the dummy and then go up and pull it up from downstairs, 'cause they ate upstairs. I'd have already set the table up before they sat down, and I would put the food on the table. He did all the carving and serving of the meat. Then I'd bring water and coffee, and during the meal they'd call down and tell me to bring up milk or juice, or somebody might want mayonnaise or mustard, so I'd take it up. Sometimes somebody might want tea, so I'd have to find a damn tea bag and heat water and up the stairs I'd go again.

"Mrs. X complained about everything. There was a houseman—he was white, get that—and he was supposed to do the breakfast dishes. When I got there I was supposed to go up and gather up all the laundry—wash, dry, iron it, and hang it up and put it away. One day she told me about the stove being greasy, and I told her it was from breakfast and was supposed to be for the houseman. We got into a big hassle. She also complained that on Thursday, when they got the new groceries, the refrigerators weren't straightened up properly—that I hadn't gotten rid of the old stuff first and washed them out well.

"I told her that I wasn't a black maid and furthermore I was going to ask for a change of jobs. She said that was fine because 'I wouldn't want anybody working here that didn't want to.' I told her, 'I'm only working here because I have to, not 'cause I want to.'

"That night I came back to prepare supper and she had told Mr. X what I said. So he waited till after I served dinner and cleaned up before he came downstairs to talk to me. He came down then and said he understood I had told his wife I wanted to change my job, so I said, Yes, this was very true. Then he went into his act. 'Nobody's irreplaceable,' he said. 'I can replace you in five minutes.' I said, 'That's what I want you to do—replace me.'

"He said he could confine me to the wing for refusing to work—which means I would be locked in my cell. He told me I had a homicide and I was bound to get some time on it—that I'd have at least two years and my behavior record would count. He told me to think about what he said, and that the only reason he wasn't gonna lock me then was 'cause he felt I was upset. Yeah, he didn't want me to quit; that's what he was saying in reality, but he didn't say it in words. But evidently he wasn't too keen about replacing me. He could have locked me in my room—I didn't care. So apparently my work wasn't as bad as she was pretending it was.

"Anyway, the next morning I refused to go to work. Mrs. Williams called the warden and he and the major came over. He talked to me for about an hour or more, with Mrs. Williams and the major present. What he did was talk me into going back over there. He couldn't go over the superintendent's head, he said, but he said he didn't feel I should be put in the hole—and that was the alternative to not going back to work. The warden said I should understand that Mrs. X was a sick woman—she has a heart condition—and evidently X didn't want to fire me. He said I should go over to avoid being put in the hole for 'extreme disobedience.'

"It was a whole dressed-up thing. I was refusing to work—that's disobedience. But I was disobeying the goddamned superintendent—and that's extreme disobedience. I was thumbing my nose at them all until I started digging what it would do to me mentally to go to the hole. I could have handled the concrete floor and one meal a day. What I couldn't dig was the solitude. I thought I'd better let well enough alone. I didn't feel that mentally I would be able to cope with the hole right then. In fact, I probably would have gone crazy at that point.

"So I went back to work after I talked to the warden. I got very upset, so they sent me upstairs to the dispensary for a tranquilizer before I went back over. It wasn't any good, but really I had no choice. Really an untried prisoner doesn't have to work unless they choose. I think that's the law. But I cooked supper that night and stayed on the job. They weren't going to listen to anything else."

Reliable sources from the same institution told me that two years later, at the same institution, another of Superintendent X's house girls had a more severe crisis. "Sonya," an inmate awaiting trial, was also working as a daily maid at X's home. When she became pregnant, five months after she had been admitted to the jail, a matron performed an abortion on her in the cell block. The incident was hidden even from the warden until Sonya developed complications from the abortion and had to be put into intensive care in a local hospital.

Records are kept in such a way that it is very difficult to find written substantiation of such events. But I was told by involved persons that the superintendent's eldest son was the man who impregnated Sonya. Details were arranged in such a way that if the truth ever came out, a guard would take responsibility for the pregnancy to take X's son off the hook.

Leslie's and Sonya's jobs were considered trustee status because the women had to be "trusted" to work in the superintendent's home. Many trustees have been taken advantage of in similar ways because of their lack of independence. They depend on their jobs for meager income but are unable to quit if they find the job distasteful, degrading, or worse.

Many trustee status jobs (message carriers, "count" assistants, staff helpers, and low security jobs on the grounds) are held by people charged or convicted of homicides. One warden told me, "They're our best people. They're the most stable. They flipped out and killed somebody after a long and pressured situation—usually their spouse—and they'd never commit another crime. They know they've got a lot of time to do, and they don't want trouble 'cause they've got to live with it."

Work at old-fashioned industrial sewing machines isn't much better. In summertime, women in these shops often pass out from heat asphyxiation and lack of air ventilation. More than one woman has told me of the tremendous production pressure put on them, broken only by two ten- or fifteen-minute cigarette breaks in the morning and afternoon. Silence rules are still rigidly enforced in some of the factories.

"I worked in the garment shop with all the hassles just because I wanted that twenty dollars a month to buy my coffee and cigarettes," said a woman who had been confined at Terminal Island, a federal division for women in California. "I did it even though I used to pass out from the heat. Just bonk—I'd pass out. They'd give me smelling salts and bring me some water and I'd go back to work. It's so insane when I look back on it, I just can't believe I did it. But it was some kind of need; I had to do some of those little extra nice things for myself since I didn't have no outside source of funds. Not many people did have any outside source of funds.

"The people there that really needed a trade or skill besides the streets, something useful, are the same ones who go into the garment shop to work because they don't have a source of funds. But they can't learn anything useful in there—it's just a way to survive inside. Then they go back out in the street and hustle some more.

"I had to hustle a lot at prison—you know, like do people's ironing or cleaning for them. For about two dollars' worth of commissary a week you can do their laundry and that kind of thing. Even though cigarettes are cheaper without federal taxes and all, you can't earn enough money to support even smoking, let alone all the other little things you want, like extra food or goodies. People do all sorts of things, like maybe you knit sweaters or blankets for people or you do their hair or that kind of thing. If they get money from the outside, that's the way they can share it and get helped out at the same time themselves. It's all like a constant hustle between the women. But there's a lot of cooperation, too.''

In the women's garment factory at the Ohio Reformatory for Women, as in other places I have mentioned, prisoners make dresses and undergarments for patients in the state mental hospitals, for children in agencies supported by public funds, and for ORW prisoners. They also make flags—United States flags and Ohio state flags. According to the superintendent, ORW got into the flag business in 1963, under what I would consider a male power play on a woman's prison. ''The old governor, James Rhodes, discovered that the wonderful world of Ohio didn't make state flags. We had to buy them from out of state,'' Ms. Wheeler said. ''He was quite upset by this state of things, so we found ourselves in the flag business.''

Both the flagmakers and dressmakers work in the same industrial building at the prison six to eight hours a day for ten dollars a month under the auspices of Ohio Penal Industries.

''They don't really teach you nothing in here,'' said Venartha Graham, a small, mature woman with a long Afro, deep brown skin, and a devil-may-care attitude about the supervisor watching her. ''If you don't know how to sew, they don't teach you. You just do one specific part of a job and that's it. You never get a sense of overall production or real training.

''They say the production we put out is for the overall payroll. Our work pays the whole institution's six-dollars-a-month salaries, but we're the only ones who get docked for being absent or taking a break. Like for talking to you, I'll probably get docked about four hours off my pay, even if we only talk for twenty minutes. But I don't give a damn anymore. The thing they hold over our head is that if we don't work, they [the other inmates] don't get paid. That's what we're told every time we begin to think about organizing or stopping work or anything. Everybody depends on that six dollars a month, so it puts added pressure on us.''

Venartha and several other women, including myself, were standing around a table where finished products were folded—flags put in plastic bags and dresses stacked in piles for packing and delivery. An open record book lay on the table in front of me. Two figures caught my attention from the orders completed that week: $1,260 in sales to Gallipolis State Hospital; and a total of $4,995.50 for 690 regular jumpers at $2.45 each, 360 regular jumpers for $3.65 each, and 1,050 white blouses at $1.90 each.

Thumbing through the pages and seeing orders for $1,739, $2,620, $2,162, $2,220, I found it even more amazing to think that the workers were earning four cents an hour.[6]

Anyone at ORW who refuses to go to work is locked in her room or in maximum security; the same is true in other state and federal prisons. When I have asked administrators about this, they have said frankly it's because people refusing to work are disruptive to the institution.

The many work strikes we have and haven't heard about in institutions throughout the country reflect an increasing awareness on the part of prisoners that their work is also their chance for a demonstration of power. Stopping work is one way to be heard, one channel to the authority usually blocked by red tape.

Most Americans have been conditioned to believe that a reasonable protest will bring a reasonable response and, despite the evidence of the Atticas past, many women and men in prison still believe that if they organize in a nonviolent and adult manner, they will be treated accordingly. But the needs for control and security as seen both by the public and by prison administrations don't always allow much room for a reasonable response to a reasonable protest. Even when the administration resists pressure to retaliate with physical violence or force, it still deems it necessary to punish "insurgents."

Some of the women at Marysville attempted a reasonable protest, as many have in other women's institutions too extensive to document. I first heard about it from the women working in industry, and later from Becky Careway. Becky, who had been at Marysville since 1968, was serving a one-to-twenty-year sentence on seven counts of forgery, breaking and entering, and grand larceny. She was supposed to meet the parole board, but figured her chances of getting parole were slim since earlier in the year she had walked off her job in the sewing industry with fifteen other women, including Venartha Graham, Annestine Roper, and Barbara Baker.

"The prison offers nothing," Becky said. "The schoolbooks are out of date, the IBM machines are outdated, and the teachers aren't there half the time. Where would a woman get a job on the outside as a trash collector? Or on a chicken farm? A lot of the women worry about what they're going to do when they get out and want to change the situation. We decided to try to do something about it before it became a whole blown-up thing; the tension was getting really bad.

"Sixteen of us women walked off our jobs in industry to see the superintendent. I led the walk. We had put in pass after pass to see her—but she

6. Again, these figures would be much higher in 1995 than they were in 1973.

does not call passes. So we walked to the administration building and demanded to see her. We got to see her, and we actually got some things accomplished, even though she avoided questions we asked her. Two immediate things we accomplished were getting to smoke when we were with our visitors and getting to visit for longer hours when our people come to see us once a month.

"But for walking off our jobs and going to the administration building to see her, we all got six months' probation and had two weeks of recreation time taken away from us. She threatened if she ever seen us with another group of women within a six-month period she would send us off the farm and we'd be given new charges for inciting a riot. We didn't disturb anybody, beat up nobody, or anything. We went as ladies and conducted ourselves as ladies—and then she called us renegades."

The sixteen women carried twenty-nine grievances to the superintendent and later to the "communications group" (the inmate council). They also carried a written explanation of their actions and initiative:

First of all we want it known that our overall grievance does not come before the Communications Group. Neither does it come against the way that the inmates are conducting our complaints. . . . We trust their representation of their fellow inmates, but we also know that they are not the solution to our problem, they can only serve as a source of relaying what our problem is. The solution to our problem lies in the hands of our staff members but mainly our superintendent. As we believe, it is under her jurisdiction to assist us and converse with us on a woman to woman basis and help us relieve unnecessary mental strain. We are not here to be discriminated against due to a staff member's personal evaluation of us, or to be discriminated against because of the nature of our crime, but to be helped! We are here not with our individual problems, but with our overall problems that affect us as an individual.

Surely it is no oddity that people protest a certain system, it is done every day and permitted if it is conducted in an orderly manner. The reason that it is done is to bring forth what a particular group feels is best for the general welfare of the people concerned, and to reach either a satisfactory compromise or solution to whatever the problem is.

We know that changes will be made. The newspapers tell us that, our outside communications with people tell us that. The system will be changed. We are not interested in the system right now, we are interested in the things that affect us just because there seems to be a lack of communication between the inmates and the staff, or a lack of concern for the inmate as another human being. . . .

We did not assemble to be disorderly or to be destructive. We are seeking help from the source that we know a solution can be derived from. We are presenting things that need to be solved in our community now TODAY in this institution. Not things that will come before the system sometime in the future. . . . We are only trying to solve our own problems in a conducive manner, as ladies. We are seeking "help," understanding, compassion. We do not want any trouble, this is not our purpose; we want to unite together with the superintendent and her staff to solve problems we are faced with NOW in this institution. Problems that we must live with and is important to each of us as individuals.

The administration sent copies of the following letter to each of the sixteen women who had walked off the job:

On Wednesday, September 22, 1971, you and fifteen others left your assignments without permission in order to confront the Superintendent with demands regarding institution programs and procedures. In so doing, you were in violation of institution rules by being out of place. You also interfered with the function of the Communications Group which was scheduled to meet that very afternoon. Subsequently, the Communications Group agreed to include you in their meeting so as to hear you out on your concerns. You were so included for three meetings including the final one in which the Superintendent responded. At the end of the third meeting, it was apparent that the one remaining matter to be decided was the penalty, if any, to be imposed upon the group of sixteen. The Communications Group felt it was not appropriate for them to make this decision but that it should be made by the institution Disciplinary Committee.

The Disciplinary Committee has reviewed the total situation and the following decision has been made:

1) No report will be placed in the permanent case folder.

2) You are suspended from all extra-curricular activities for two weeks. This does not include Catholic Mass, Protestant Services, Muslim Study Group or Church of Christ Communion Services, all of which take place on Sunday. These are the only exceptions.

. . . If there is anymore of this "Walking Off" behavior within the next six months and any of you are a part of it, you must know that you will be identified as leaders and will be promptly separated from the institution community. You can avoid this by being where you belong, carrying out your assignment at all times.

The women involved thought this response from the Disciplinary Committee was reasonable. Prisoners know administrators have the power to make their lives miserable by denying privileges or locking them in solitary for long periods of time. The power of the parole board is equally ominous. Without a good work record and clean behavior record, there's not much chance of early parole. Prisoners' attempts to gain more control over their own lives or to determine the course of their work and training within the institution are squelched, even though these efforts potentially could lead to education and job and leadership skills and that could transform their futures—and help them stay free from crime—when they're released from prison.

1995 Addendum to Chapter Twelve

The suspicion that prisons are a money-making proposition is well founded. In 1994 approximately two thousand of America's one million state and federal prisoners were living in prisons run not by state or federal governments but by private companies in the prison business.

If these private companies have their way, soon prisons all over America will be run for profit.

Private companies tout themselves as more efficient and more cost-effective. Entrepreneurs in this new industry collect a per diem fee from the state—currently an average of about forty dollars a day for each prisoner—and make a profit by spending less than that amount.

The largest of the private companies building and running many of today's for-profit prisons is a publicly held company called Corrections Corporation of America. Based in Nashville, Tennessee, the company has twenty-three prisons under contract in seven states, according to the *New York Times,* and its profits rose 57 percent to $4 million on revenues of $100 million in 1993. The company said they save money by offering a stock option plan, and by 1) not being unionized, 2) having no pension plan, and 3) reducing tension through "attention to detail and quality control in basic services like food, mail delivery and regular communication with inmates."[7]

In the first six months of 1994, Corrections Corporation's income reportedly rose 30 percent, and one Nashville analyst estimated that "over the next two years, the company's 13,000 beds under contract should increase by 85 percent and profits should more than double."[8]

How amazing that you can buy stock market shares in this company. How amazing that their profits are growing. They say they are able to cut costs and "offer ample prison services." I wonder: to what percentage of the prisoners? What services? What programs? They give an example of saving money by buying more expensive plastic chairs that can't be broken and giving prisoners a better breakfast to keep them happy, but the example of "marketable skills" "in the usual computer and 'culinary arts' classes," as well as training in the worker-garment industry making "disposable hazardous waste suits" sounds like the same old hype. This seems like a very dangerous route to go.

On the other hand, perhaps prisons for profit will help illuminate the fact that we already have a large prison lobby invested in keeping prisons

---

7. Anthony Ramirez, "Privatizing America's Prisons, Slowly," *New York Times,* August 14, 1994.
8. Ibid.

going and growing purely for the revenues. Perhaps corporations openly running prisons for stock market profits will demonstrate that the greater social good has nothing to do with the human costs of this harmful enterprise.

Theoretically at least, we have built prisons to serve society's interests—and it seems only logical that it would be in the best interests of our country to have prisons work in such a way that as many prisoners as possible could return to their homes with the skills, earning power, and self-respect that would allow them to live peaceful, crime-free lives as contributing members of the community. Funds for prisons, it would then seem, should be used to set up programs to facilitate education, vocational training, drug treatment, and other programs that help people get out and stay out of prison.

But prisons for profit are based on the numbers of inmates served—and so it's not in the interest of corporations or stockholders or others (congressmen, contractors, prison unions) to rehabilitate prisoners. On the contrary, the recycling of prisoners—keeping a constant flow of bodies in the institutions and increasing the numbers every year—increases revenues. This growth is what makes prisons such an appealing money-making venture in the first place.

Greater profits also can be made by spending as little as possible on the prisoners—just enough to keep order and promote the likelihood of return. The profit makers can insure the security of their investments by keeping the public in a state of fear from ''the criminal element.'' As we've seen from the recent growth of the prison-industrial complex—like the growth of the military-industrial complex before it—when the public is living in fear, it doesn't complain about the price tag, no matter how outrageous.

It's important to realize that the safety and well-being of the community is at odds with the interest of the profit makers. Think about it: if we could make genuine progress toward eliminating racism, healing our divisions, creating economic opportunities for the poor, solving the problems of crime, and thus making our communities safer and reducing the numbers of people in prison, how could the prison business make money?

The concept of profits from prisons clearly is counter to the best interests of our society. It seems that it's time we look clearly at both the monetary costs and the human costs of imprisonment. As an investment in our children's future, and the future of humanity, we must devise a plan that works toward reducing crime and putting prisons out of business rather than onto Wall Street.

13 MEDICAL TREATMENT

Band-Aids over Broken Bones

To tell the truth, I didn't mind too much being sent up to the hospital for punishment because I was in a lot of pain. The cops had kicked me in the head and handled me pretty rough putting me in the paddy wagon. Somebody else had kicked me in the side. I'm not sure who did it at the time, but I sure was sore for days. And in jail I figured out I was pregnant, too. I could feel it in my body. They didn't give me any tests, but I know my body pretty good and I can tell. So then I was worried about whether the kick in the stomach had hurt the baby.

Anyway, in the hospital, I was between two mental patients. One who laughed all night, and another who would scream if you touched her bed. It was hard not to brush against her sheets if you moved 'cause the beds are so close together and I had to be really careful. I was also across from a heroin addict who cried and screamed all night. She was going through cold turkey and she was really sick. She was shackled to the bed.

I was ready to flip out because of the pain and all the hassle. One day there was a big cockroach on the wall and a woman hit it with her shoe and it screamed. I swear it screamed. That was about it for me. It was really a mind fuck, [but] I think that was because of all the physical pain.

You can't expect decent medical treatment when everything else is so fucked up. They don't have time to be concerned about your health. You can't expect anything less than indifference and neglect. But it could have been worse, I guess.

If you're really sick or dying, they take you to Cook County Hospital from the jail for treatment. There you're shackled to the beds in the hospital prison ward and you can't move around. A woman died there of pneumonia while being treated for a bullet wound of the hand. You can't expect anything less than neglect, but you know, sometimes the neglect is like really criminal.

—Dee Peterson, prisoner at the Cook County Jail, Chicago

Getting reliable health care for prisoners is a big problem. Most of the women who wind up in prison didn't have healthy diets, good nutrition, or patterns of adequate rest, fresh air, and exercise even before they were incarcerated. For the most part, they lacked the training, the resources, and the self-esteem to have taken good care of themselves. They don't have medical insurance and haven't had regular checkups, Pap smears, mammograms, or necessary dental care. If they're pregnant, they most likely haven't had adequate nutrition or prenatal care, and if they've recently given birth, they probably are lacking the necessary vitamins and nutrients they need for postnatal recovery. A surprisingly large number never saw an obstetrician during their pregnancies, and many did not see a doctor after giving birth unless they had excessive bleeding or other severe problems that forced them into an emergency room.

Certainly, a huge number of the women arrested and convicted of drug- or alcohol-related offenses aren't in optimal health, nor are those weakened by diabetes, high blood pressure or other chronic illnesses, sexually transmitted diseases, cancer, or tuberculosis. Some women don't learn until they get to prison and have an AIDS test that they are HIV-positive or have AIDS. In New York state in 1994, one of every five women who entered prison was HIV-positive. The severe health problems of the women with active cases of AIDS demand extraordinary care that's overwhelming to the prison population. In addition, increasing numbers of women arrive at prison malnourished, with sexually transmitted diseases and unaddressed gynecological problems. Because of their poor health conditions—and the strain and anxiety brought on by being arrested, indicted, tried, and sentenced to prison, away from their children and their families—women are particularly susceptible to tuberculosis and other communicable diseases that run rampant in crowded, poorly ventilated prisons.

Many years ago, in December 1970, prisoners in the old Women's House of Detention in New York staged a protest over health and living conditions by refusing to lock themselves in their cells. They were sprayed with water hoses and forcibly locked in their cells for nearly two weeks as punishment.

Their grievances, still relevant in the 1990s, were reprinted and circulated to New York residents by the Women's Bail Fund, a group of politically active women who had been helping provide bail and legal support for women awaiting trial at the House of D. The inmates had addressed an open letter to "the concerned people of New York" in which they described the conditions that "breed mental degradation and physical deterioration."

"The majority of us are Black and Puerto Rican," the letter stated. "We cannot afford the ransom the courts call bail. It is apparent to us that you, the public, are not aware of the barbaric conditions that exist here." Their letter included the following grievances:

WE do not receive adequate medical attention. We do not have a doctor on duty twenty-four hours a day although there are seven hundred and fifty-four women in here. [Maximum capacity was 457.] The doctors we do have are old and senile.

• We ask for a doctor to be on duty twenty-four hours a day.

• We ask that it be a requirement that any inmate suffering from any medical problem be permitted to see a doctor at any time of the day or night, and that it not be left to the discretion of the officer on duty or the nurse in attendance.

• We ask for first rate medicine. That it be labeled properly and after it has lost its potency, it be thrown out.

WE do not receive an adequate diet. We do not get any fresh vegetables or any fresh fruits. Our diet consists of beans, rice, potatoes, and powdered milk. We get hot cereal twice a week, one boiled egg once a week. The rest of the days we get cold cereal and powdered milk. The meats that we eat are as old as the building we must live in.

• We ask for our meats to be inspected.

• We ask for at least one glass of fresh milk daily.

• We ask for fresh vegetables and at least one piece of fruit a day.

• We ask for citrus juices once a day.

THE House of Detention is infested with mice and roaches. They roam the building freely, carrying filth and disease. We are often bitten by these germ-carrying rodents. There is no extermination system.

• We ask that an exterminating company be allowed to come in twice a month to eliminate these health hazards.

THERE are four punishment strip cells where we are put if we receive an "infraction." The cells do not have any toilets, sinks, or mattresses. In them we are stripped of all our clothing. We do not receive any bedding for the cold tile floor. We are allowed to shower only every five days. We ask that these cells be shut down immediately.

WE are two in a cell. The cells are 5 feet by 9 feet. Out of a fifteen hour day, we are locked up eleven of these hours. We ask for longer recreation periods.

WE have been raided at five-thirty in the morning, made to strip off all our clothing and to squat down, our personal belongings being thrown on the floor. The adolescents have been made to go into the kitchen and strip off their clothing in front of everyone.

• We ask that the stripping of inmates be stopped immediately. . . .

WE the oppressed women of the New York House of Detention humbly seek your support and help. We who are your fellow human beings need you, the public, to help us in our struggle to eliminate these injustices.

Other grievances involving harassment by guards, court dates, commissary privileges, and segregation of juveniles were included in the prisoners' list of demands, but their greatest concern was the need for adequate medical attention.

The fear of death, natural to most people, is heightened considerably in confinement. Women are afraid for themselves, as well as being additionally burdened by the responsibility for other inmates in the prison who are not well. "Home remedies," smuggled vitamins, extra glasses of milk, and long hours are involved in women inmates' caring for one another. Women usually have to steal the remedies they use. When a prisoner is denied medical attention, ignored, or called a malingerer, other inmates try to nurse her to health with the only resources they have available. The women say they sometimes prefer not to go to the institution's medical staff because it can mean risking the wrong prescriptions or diagnosis. They're afraid that incompetent medical attention, more than the illness itself, will lead to death.

The many other pressures of prison life—such as anxiety about court dates or the outcomes of warrants or appeals, tension about not hearing from a lawyer, guilt and worry over children's well-being—add to the stresses that contribute to the breaking down of both physical and mental defenses.

The grievances and requests of the women at the House of Detention were never really rectified. Less than six months after the protest, prisoners in the House of D were transferred from Eighth Street and Avenue of the Americas in Greenwich Village to the new correctional facility for women on Riker's Island, and the old House of D was closed down for good. It had long been condemned as overcrowded, antiquated, and inhumane.

It is interesting to note that when the House of D, a twelve-story, H-shaped building, was opened in 1932, it was considered a "break-through in prison design." The 1931 *Annual Report* of the Department of Corrections said it was "undoubtedly the best institution of its kind in the United States, if not in the entire world." They considered it luxurious because each cell had an outside window from which the inmate had a "clear and unobstructed view of the sky, the street, the changes in the weather." Early observers praised the "clean, new sanitary glass block construction, good ventilation and light." Having hot and cold water in the cells seemed almost revolutionary. But somehow this "humane" and "best of institutions" had become a filthy, rat-infested warehouse for human beings. Sanitation could not change it. Friends and families calling to inmates at the windows from the streets below became an irritant to Village residents and to administrators.

The House of D had to be removed—as if removing the pain from sight would make it not hurt anymore. So detained women, sentenced inmates, guards, administrators, medical staff, psychiatric staff, social workers, and reams of paper documenting each woman's criminal record, background, and institutional behavior were transferred to a new red-brick institution called the New York City Correctional Institution for Women.

What had been cramped into a twelve-story building that cost $1.2 million to build on one third of an acre was relocated in an enormously spread-out two-story building costing $24.2 million on fifty-five acres of ground on Riker's Island. Corrections Commissioner George F. McGrath called it "New York's newest and perhaps best hotel." It was praised for its clean, new, sanitary red-brick construction, good ventilation, and light. A *New York Times* article quoted officials praising its single cells, brightly colored decor, and lack of obvious prison "hard-ware." It was built to house 679 women. The day I first went there, the population was 723. [Today it houses some 1800 inmates.] Instead of four punishment cells, there was an entire cell block for solitary confinement. The medical department had a section to itself on the second floor, as did the psychiatric and social work departments.

But it seemed that the transfer from an antiquated, overcrowded facility to a modern, overcrowded facility had just been a relocation of the same problems—especially the medical and psychiatric problems. In fact, some of the problems were worse. In a petition to the mayor in the early fall of 1971, correctional officers at the new institution voiced *their* grievances.

"The female officers at the House of Detention for Women waited in vain for your concern and promised alleviation of our poor working conditions. The Deputy Commissioner asked us to wait until we moved into the new institution before we actually looked for an alleviation of our burdensome situation. We have moved and our situation is 10-fold more cumbersome," said the petition in part.

The officers complained that because of the tremendous size of the physical plant, the only job they were accomplishing was custody, and that real care or control was impossible. They said the telephone was not being used because of a lack of personnel to make calls out to the inmates' mothers, husbands, children, or lawyers. They asked the mayor, "How would you feel if, after five or six days after you were arrested, you had been unable to contact your family?

"The medical services are under-staffed professionally as well as custodially,'' they wrote. ''As you know, sir, approximately 80 per cent of our inmate population are drug addicts.''

The officers asked the mayor to imagine that he had been arrested, had been in court all day and was put into a receiving room to await processing, and was now experiencing the pains of drug withdrawal. He should imagine getting sick ''and then being told you will be isolated, not examined,'' and that ''tomorrow after you give your medical history and are examined—then you will be given medication.''

The petition continued:

> You are then put in a large hospital-like room with the other women to await tomorrow. But in your sickness and pain you look around. There are 20 women in this room with you and one of them is having a seizure. You call, ''Officer.'' No response. You call again, this time joined by some other women. Still no response. You get up and start banging on the glass in the door. Finally the officer comes. You tell the officer, ''There's a woman having a seizure in here.'' The officer turns away saying, ''I'll be right back.'' You think the officer doesn't feel a thing? You are wrong. The reason she can't come right in is because she is alone and has been alone all night. That is also the reason she did not hear you before—she was on the other side of the hospital making rounds. She is responsible for the entire floor. She must open doors with 20 girls inside to allow one to go to the bathroom in another area that houses 15 to 20 other inmates. Before this officer can help this inmate, she must call her superior so she can provide another officer to assist her.
>
> . . . Finally after what seems an eternity, the woman with the seizure is helped. But not before you realize that if time was a factor, that woman could be dead! . . . You question [why inmates are] potentially hostile?
>
> We have worked under these conditions for too long. We are petitioning you, sir, Mayor Lindsay, the Board of Correction, and our union for immediate redress of these long-standing grievances. Must we have happen in 1971 what happened in October 1970? Is this the only way to get relief?[1]

During my second visit to the new institution at Riker's Island, an inmate told me, ''Beauty is only skin deep. Like what you see, baby, is not what we're getting.'' She pointed to the freshly painted walls and empty vocational shops. ''They used all their money to build this place. Now they don't have enough money to run it. It's so cold here. Everybody has colds and is sneezing and coughing. There's no heat and no water to bathe with half the time. There's no recreation, no training, and not even enough to eat. We get the same old diet—no fruits or vegetables, just starch and more starch.

''Pregnant women can't even get milk to drink, or vitamins. Girls come

1. ''Guards Petition Mayor,'' *Village Voice,* December 2, 1971.

in here four and five and six months' pregnant and conditions are so bad that they have miscarriages. We're treated by medical rejects here; they're so old they can hardly walk. They don't consider us human. To them we're human robots. If you want tranquilizers, you can get them—unless you're a junkie. Women walk around here like zombies from all the tranquilizing.

"I was injured on my job and I was in the bing for six days for refusing to sign a medical statement saying I was attended by a doctor. They wanted me to sign it to relieve the institution of any responsibility for the accident here because it hurt my back and was fairly serious. I hadn't been attended by a doctor and so I wouldn't sign it. In the bing, I was given nothing. No washcloth, hair comb, towel, soap, or item to help you keep good hygiene. Toilet tissue was rolled off and shoved under the door. The food was shoved under the door, too.

"During my six days there, I saw a girl attempt to kill herself. She set fire to her mattress and burned the bing and herself. The smell of human flesh is still in there. While I was in there, I didn't get nothing and I didn't ask for nothing because that's what they want—for you to beg. I just wanted to maintain my mental freedom."

I had seen the burned cell the first time I had been to Riker's Island, and I remembered the stench of it as she talked. This time I had come to the prison because there had been a rumor that two women had been badly beaten by male guards, and that one of the women may have died. I had called Jack Newfield from the *Village Voice* to come along. He brought his wife, a photographer, and a friend. John Walsh of the Corrections Department, a radio reporter, and my friend and photographer Kitty Caparella were waiting when we arrived. Both John Walsh and Superintendent Essie Murph assured us that the rumor was false. They said they knew nothing about any incident at all until they started receiving calls from families and reporters. They seemed frankly baffled by the report and produced one of the women allegedly hurt, who said, "Nothing happened to me." The other woman was unavailable for comment. We never received confirmation as to what had happened or what might have caused the rumor.

Since we were already there, however, we asked to tour the institution. Because of a New York law allowing access to the press by prisoners, we were able to speak with imprisoned women at random, but only briefly. Mr. Walsh instructed us not to be "personal" or "talk too long" with any one inmate.

As he ushered us through the long, shiny corridors, Walsh talked about the "excellent psychiatric and medical set-up" at Riker's. In fact, the medical department at Riker's Island did look better than most other prison or jail medical facilities I had seen. Most were antiquated and staffed mainly by registered nurses. Riker's seemed better because a medical department actually existed with nurses and doctors and hospital beds. The second-floor medical department had a ward for women sick or recovering from surgery and two large wards for addicts recently arrested and going through withdrawal. It also had a pharmacy for dispensing medication and methadone to heroin addicts, a real nurses' station, and a glassed-off section for women with communicable diseases.

I was thinking that this looked like a small, clean, white-tiled hospital when four elderly women wearing white jackets stormed into the nurses' station, where we were standing talking with a nurse. The leader of the group was a tiny woman who I guessed was in her late sixties or early seventies. She had silver hair, a white jacket over her dress, and a stethoscope around her neck that bobbed up and down with each step she took toward us. She came in shaking her finger at us and shouting, "I won't answer any questions. I work under Health Services Administration and I don't have to talk to you. I don't want to talk to no reporters."

She turned around threateningly to Kitty Caparella, shook her finger at her, and hollered, "You better not take any pictures. No pictures. No pictures. I'll sue! I'll sue!"

The three short women behind her also started hollering, "We'll sue, we'll sue! No pictures, no pictures!"

I still hadn't said anything; I was dumbfounded. I didn't even know who this woman was. "No tapes, no recordings," she continued. "I don't want anything!"

"Yes, we're always misquoted," one of the white-haired women standing behind her said.

Just as quickly as the women had appeared, they disappeared back out the door, still shouting. John Walsh followed, hurrying to catch up with them. Only after they had left did we find out that the angry woman in the front was the chief doctor and head of the medical department at Riker's Island. The others were her medical staff; all were certified doctors.

After they stormed out, I noticed a memorandum addressed to the staff from the "superintendent-in-command" that was posted on the nurses' bulletin board on the subject of sanitary napkins. It announced:

1. As of this date sanitary napkins are not to be issued indiscriminately due to the severe plumbing stoppages caused by dispensing sanitaries in the toilets.
2. All officers are required to instruct the inmates to use the trash cans for disposal of napkins.
3. If this problem cannot be resolved, it will become necessary to place

strict controls on the issue of sanitary napkins and take disciplinary action against any inmate who causes a toilet stoppage by disposing the sanitaries in the toilets.

By the time I finished copying down this communiqué and was thinking how terrible it would be to have to get *permission* for a Kotex—and not to be able to use tampons at all because of strip searches that involve inspecting the vagina—I learned that John Walsh had talked the doctors we had just seen into having an interview with us. We only had to agree not to quote any one of them by name.

We were ushered into a bare-walled conference room, where we sat down around a rectangular, linoleum-topped table. The four doctors pulled their chairs close together at the end of the table nearest the door.

The first question we asked was about drug addiction. More than 80 percent of the prisoners were said to be addicts, mainly heroin addicts, and we asked whether the heroin addicts were forced to use methadone when they came to the prison. We said that several women at Riker's had told us that they didn't want to take methadone because they thought it was more addictive and caused a more painful withdrawal than heroin. Nevertheless, they were refused any alternative to methadone but going cold turkey—an excruciatingly painful process.

"No one has ever forced a girl coming in here to take methadone," the chief doctor said. "They are only detoxified. We give them up to a total of eighty milligrams of methadone until they go to court, and no more. If addicts don't want methadone, we don't give them anything else.

"If you believe the inmates and don't believe us, then you don't believe us," she said. Pointing her finger at me she shouted, "Don't use my name. It's a violation of my rights." Her three staff members nodded and murmured in agreement.

There was a surreal quality to sitting at the table looking at the four white-haired women. The chief doctor had worked at the Women's House of Detention since 1940, and the other three said they had come to work there in 1957, 1960, and 1965, respectively. One of the oldest, an extremely thin woman, sat rocking back and forth with a strange, distant smile. Her eyes seemed somewhat glazed, and when she spoke, her thoughts came out in half phrases. Sometimes she repeated the same phrase several times and then sat and rocked, nodding her head in agreement with what someone else had said. I thought she looked as if she might fall out of her chair if she tipped to the side, like a pantomime in "Laugh-In."

The chief doctor punctuated the air with her fists as she stated, "In my experience with inmates over the past thirty years, a great many, I would say at least half, are malingerers. The first day they have a pain in the head. The second day they have a pain in the stomach. The third day they have a pain in the wrist. The fourth day it's a pain in the knees. They come on purpose to trick us. They want medicine, that's all. Some are legitimately ill. They're the ones we take care of.''

"How do you know the difference?" I asked.

"You can just tell,'' she said. "You get to know them. We just tell them, 'Nothing's wrong with you.' Some just do it for attention.''

As concerned as I felt about the horror of being treated by one of these women if I was sick—and the fright of what it must be like for sick women at Riker's—I was flabbergasted by what these doctors were saying, and great surges of hilarity kept sweeping through me. I kept thinking, This is real, these are *really* doctors! This isn't a scene from a Kurt Vonnegut Jr. novel or *Dr. Strangelove* or somewhere else in time or space.

At one point, when I was imagining these women to be four little girls with stethoscopes around their necks playing doctor, the chief doctor stated that they give the rectal and vaginal searches to all the women going and coming from court every day, in addition to seeing about a hundred women a day for sick call between 9 A.M. and 12 noon and again for one hour in the afternoon.

Women at the prison had complained that the vaginal searches given them on return from court—ostensibly to look for heroin, weapons, or other contraband—not only were humiliating and painful but also were administered so roughly that they often caused infections and bleeding later on. At the same time that these vaginal exams were given indiscriminately to all the women, they said, no Pap smear—a preventive test for cervical cancer—was given.

The chief doctor confirmed the charges with irritation: "We don't do Pap smears unless it is indicated,'' she said. "If we notice anything on the vaginal exam, like a lump or anything, then we do a Pap smear.''

I pointed out that there was a basic medical contradiction in what she said. A Pap smear is a precautionary, diagnostic measure women are urged to take every six months or at least once a year; the Pap smear should come long before there's any visible indication of a problem.

"I don't understand what you're saying,'' she said. The other doctors shook their heads in agreement. "If we need a gynecologist, we send them to Bellevue. If it's an acute disease, something inflamed or distended, we may not want to treat them.''

"I saw sixty-two women yesterday,'' another of the doctors volunteered. "Half of that was faking. But everyone who was really sick was taken care of.''

"Yes, yes, half of them are faking," the oldest doctor murmured several times, nodding her head up and down.

"We also give a venereal-disease test to every single woman who comes in," the chief doctor continued. "We've seen a sixty to seventy percent increase in syphilis."

When pinned down to specifics, she estimated that about twenty women had syphilis, out of more than seven hundred, which was in fact a startling increase compared to ten years before.

"Is it true that you don't give pregnancy tests here?" I asked.

"We don't have the frogs and all those other things, but of course we examine for pregnancy," the chief doctor said with irritation, lightly pounding her fists on the table. "We do it by a simple vaginal exam. By the old method, the simple, old-fashioned way. We look inside the way we used to do it before they had frog tests and all these things you don't need. If we examine them and if we don't think they're pregnant, we tell them to wait. If they still think they're pregnant in a couple of months, they can come back for another exam."

We started asking more questions, such as, Why couldn't they use the simple slide technique for testing pregnancy, which takes less than five minutes? But the tolerance level of the doctors was diminishing as they defended the "simple, old-fashioned method" of feeling or looking inside for pregnancy, and they abruptly ended the interview by getting up and leaving, saying, "This is enough. This is enough."

John Walsh also seemed in a hurry to leave the institution. I wondered how he was feeling about being a spokesperson for Riker's "excellent medical department."

In fact, I later realized that the medical conditions at Riker's probably were about equal to those at most state prisons, and actually better than some. Many county jails have no doctor available to prisoners, period; someone who is severely injured or dying is taken to the hospital or fends for herself.

Some administrators told me that it is almost impossible to get qualified medical staff into institutional work. Not only is the pay quite low in relationship to other medical positions, but state prisons are generally located in isolated, out-of-the-way places, and routine institutional work often is quite uninteresting to skilled physicians. Moreover, the physicians they do hire, like the Riker's doctors, become desensitized to their patients as human beings.

This means that administrators who care simply have to do the best they can with what they have. James Murphy, the superintendent of the Muncy prison in Pennsylvania, for instance, cut back on the custom of tranquilizing the majority of the population after he arrived at Muncy. Before he became superintendent, the majority of women in the general population were on high dosages of Thorazine. Now a relatively small number are medicated. With an overall change of environment that allows the women more personal freedom, there also is less of the intense repression and nervousness that women felt under the old punitively oriented administration.

Nevertheless, because of the insulation of most institutions, many practices regarding the medical health of women prisoners go unquestioned and unchecked. At the Ohio Reformatory for Women I also was told that young women are given Pap smears "where there's any suspicion or suspicious history." Older women are given Pap smears by a gynecologist, the nurse told me, but younger women have to show "indications."

One strange medical custom at Marysville was giving small white pills to newly admitted prisoners three times a day for ten days. When I was in the "reception and orientation" unit, the women taking the medication asked me if I knew what it was. I had no idea and neither did they, but they had to take it. Some said it was making them nauseated and dizzy.

A woman named Barbara Tennon told me she had just been "processed in" three days earlier and was still in shock from getting a ten-year sentence. She was worried about her husband trying to work, go to school, and take care of their three children. She said she had demanded to know what the pill was before she took it. "They told me it was an 'internal douche,'" she said. "Whoever heard of an internal douche? It doesn't make any sense at all."

When I tried to find out what was in the pill, I was sent from the officer in charge of the unit to the superintendent, to the floor caseworker, and then to the doctor. None of them knew; each one sent me to someone else. Finally the nurse in the Adjustment Unit told me it was Flagyl, a drug given to women who have trichomoniasis, a vaginal infection caused by a protozoan and resulting in inflammation and discomfort. (A doctor I asked about the medication said, "If this doesn't knock it out of you, nothing will. Flagyl is really strong, so don't be surprised if it makes you nauseated or light-headed—but it will get rid of the infection.")

When I asked the nurse why *all* of the women arriving at Marysville were given such a strong drug whether or not they had an infection, she said, "So many of the girls have trich when they come in that we automatically give it to all the girls rather than wait until all the slides and cultures come in. It does get rid of the organism. It would take a week before we got the slides and cultures back, and this is much easier, since the majority of them have it anyway."

In an environment where the priorities are containment and control, security naturally becomes more important than individual concerns. Staff members focus on potential danger and disruption instead of on the personal concerns of women who are sick or who need preventive health care. One day when I was at Marysville, I met three women who had been sent out of the clinic and told they couldn't come back until the next week to see the doctor. One was told she had to leave because her earrings were too big. The other two had been told their dresses were hemmed too short. Women say they often are banned from the hospital for violating the dress code or for whispering to a sick patient—events that wouldn't appear to have any relationship to health.

Becky Careway told me of an incident that demonstrates how clearly security issues take precedence over humane interactions in prison: "I had passed out in my room, and a guard carried me from here over to the hospital," Becky said. "I was unconscious over there, and one of the girls got scared when she seen I wasn't breathing. There wasn't no doctor on duty, so she picked up the phone and called Miss Arn [the assistant superintendent]. Miss Arn came over and pinched me.

"I had a big black-and-blue mark on me later. I didn't know where it came from. They told me it was from where Miss Arn pinched me. Anyway, they took me to Memorial Hospital and put me in intensive care. They fed me intravenously and gave me oxygen. The doctor said later if they hadn't gotten me there when they did I would have died. But, you know, the girl who picked up the phone and called Miss Arn got punished for it. She got room punishment for three days because inmates aren't allowed to use the telephone."

Becky, like many other women prisoners, said, "You almost have to be down on your hands and knees dying to get into the infirmary" on an average day. When women do get in, they often meet with the kind of neglectful treatment Becky got another time when she broke her foot at baseball practice.

"The doctor looked at it and said, 'You'll be all right, girlie, just take a couple APCs [aspirin],' " she said. "They never set it. I walked around on it that way for four months, and the only reason I had something done about it was because I contacted my parents and my father came up here to see Miss Wheeler. I was walking around with my foot turned in. My father saw my foot and went storming into the administration office. The officer tried to put him off and say, 'Make an appointment,' but he busted right through the visiting room and into her office.

"When it comes to one of his children, my father doesn't play around.

He means business. So four months after it had been broken, they broke it and set it. A doctor from town—a specialist from Columbus—was the one that set it. It's pretty good now, but it gets stiff easy, that's all—and sometimes it still pulls in a little."

Women at several prisons and jails told me that if they were sent out to a hospital for surgery or treatment of a serious injury or illness, they were under prison guard in the hospital and often released almost immediately back to the prison for recuperation as a cost-saving device. Because of neglect, lack of treatment, or the wrong treatment upon their return to jail or prison, complications set in—some that affect them permanently. In some cases, the wrong medication or wrong dosage was prescribed by the prison doctor. In other cases after a D and C or other gynecological work, they got vaginal infections because of the strip searches they experienced when coming back to the prison. Strip searches always involve inspection of the vagina and anus.

"Most of the trouble comes from when they send you back from the hospital and don't bother to follow the doctor's orders," said one twenty-nine-year-old woman in a county jail. "When they're going to do that, why send you over there in the first place?

"I've been here one and a half years approximately. I was eleven months waiting trial for forgery, but a lot of that was bedridden because I had to go to the general hospital for removal of bilateral ovarian cysts. Two days after surgery I started bleeding again. The first time I came here was in 1967—also for forgery. I got sick and had to have a partial hysterectomy. Later I got a blood clot in my lungs, and I've had a reoccurrence of blood clots ever since.

"The first time, after I got out of the general hospital, I had to go back due to the doctor here switching medications around. He gave me an overdose of Coumadin, an anticoagulant. It started internal bleeding. Another time he discontinued my medications and within a month I got another clot. I understand that the head of the hospital wrote a letter over here that was pretty threatening. Since the doctor from the hospital and my mother got on their case, the institution hasn't been giving me any trouble. I've been getting my medicine on time. I also go to the outpatient clinic periodically for checkups ordered by the outside hospital doctor.

"Another thing I think helps is that I told them here I was writing for hospital records to send to the judge. This messing with medication puts my life on the line."

Because of the inattention of some matrons and the prevalent attitude that most women are faking illness, many serious problems are not detected until too late. I've heard dozens of stories like the one an inmate told about a woman from Buffalo, New York, who died at Albion in December 1969. "She was kicking and couldn't get any medication," Geraldine Lucas said. "Nobody would believe her or help her. She committed suicide, and I'll never forget that day."

Geraldine told of another woman on her floor who had hepatitis. "She was put in lockup because she got too weak to work. They said she was just trying to get out of work. After the other women refused to go to work until she got attention, she got some attention. By then she was almost dying and so she was rushed to the hospital."

Prisoners who work in hospital wards of state prisons have told me of incidents they have witnessed that still haunt them. Although there is no way to confirm many of these stories, which are a strong indictment of medical and prison personnel, the pain and the tears that come with the telling have convinced me of the truth of the pattern.

"Mary had a kidney operation and she kept complaining of pain, but they didn't give her nothing," said a prisoner working as a nurse's aide at one state hospital. " 'You're a dope fiend—we're not giving you medication,' this one nurse told her. 'We're not giving you heroin to stop your pain. You'll just have to learn to live with it like the rest of us do.' Three days Mary asked for help. Then one day I stopped by her bed and asked her how she was feeling. She looked real calm and cool. She told me all the pain had stopped. By some miracle she didn't hurt any more. She was dead within an hour. What had happened was the abscess inside had ruptured and the poison had spread through her whole body."

Prisoners and staff alike say that the prisoners sometimes have to "literally fall out" before they get medical attention. "If you don't go off you don't get attention. There's no way to win," said one middle-aged woman. "It's really humiliating to try to prove you're not bullshitting. I have a slipped disk and a chronic bone disease, and the doctor she tells me, 'Learn to live with your pain.' "

Addicts say they have an especially difficult time getting proper medical attention. On the average, these women have been arrested more frequently, locked up more often, and given longer sentences than many other inmates. Often they're looked upon with contempt for their addiction.

"When I ask for something for nerves, they just say, 'You drug addicts always ask for something for your nerves,' " said Deloras Neely, at the House of Correction in Philadelphia. "They say, 'You just want to get high.'

"If you're on drugs, you get nothin', just nothin'. You're just physically sick, but they say, 'I can't help.' And they don't."

Mary Vangi, a small blond woman I met at the California Institute for

Women, said she had been nine months' pregnant when she was arrested for possession of narcotics. She started labor when she was in the Sybil Brand Institute for Women, a county jail, and was taken to the Los Angeles County Hospital for delivery. "When I woke up I was shackled to the delivery table," she recalled. "Then I was shackled to the stretcher and taken back to this locked ward where there were so many women they had two in a bed. I kid you not. I had just delivered my baby and I was put into the bed with another woman there from the jail."

"I didn't get to see my baby. I almost got out to see her at the hospital. You can see your baby on the way out only if a deputy sheriff will take you from your locked room down past the nursery to look in through the window.

"Three days after I had delivered I was in a wheelchair. They weren't sure whether I was to stay at the hospital prison ward or be returned to Sybil Brand, so I was going to be allowed to make one phone call. A deputy sheriff was wheeling me along and I told her, 'Hey, I haven't seen my baby. The nurse said I could see her if you would stop the elevator on the nursery floor, and if you call ahead, they'll hold her up to the window.'

"She said, 'If you wanted to see your baby you wouldn't have gotten arrested. What kind of mother are you?' We got on the elevator and went past the nursery floor straight to the thirteenth floor. So I was sitting there in the wheelchair on the thirteenth floor, waiting for the phone, and there was this little black dude on a stretcher, bleeding all over the place from bullet wounds. He was moaning and his face was all twisted up. When some people came by I said, 'What are you gonna do for this dude? He's bleeding to death.'

"This one cop said, 'So what. He's a nigger. He shot a deputy sheriff.' I went off and told him where his mother came from. I was hollering at them and cursing them out. I was crying by then.

"This little dude on the stretcher looked at me and said, 'It's okay, little sister.'

"Then they took my cigarettes, Kotex, and dime and put me in the prison ward again. I was taken back to the jail that night without having made a phone call—stitched from stem to stern. They searched me for contraband and put me in general population. Do you dig that? My baby wasn't three days old and they gave me a vaginal search for contraband. I got an infection and three and a half years later had to get a D and C from it.

"I never saw my baby until she was four months old, and that was Christmas Eve of 1968. The judge ordered the foster mother to bring her to Sybil Brand for one twenty-minute visit."

[Episodes of callous disregard shown to women prisoners who are pregnant or sick is not old news. Throughout the 1980s a number of lawsuits were filed on behalf of women prisoners who had been seen as "complainers" and denied adequate medical, dental, and psychiatric care. Many of these cases led to consent decrees mandating better medical treatment, but according to Attorney Ellen Barry, the director of Legal Services for Prisoners in California, a lack of adequate medical care remains one of the most serious problems of women prisoners throughout the country in the 1990s. Ms. Barry says that throughout her twenty years of work on behalf of women prisoners, she has been aware of "hundreds and hundreds of examples—from gynecological problems, to incorrectly set bones, to incorrect medications, to misdiagnosed fatal illnesses—where women in prison have received thoughtless, careless, deliberately malicious, and sometimes barbaric treatment."]

Some personnel, including nurses and doctors, are repulsed by the inhumanity they see and experience in prison. But to fight it means risk of losing not only their jobs but also what good effect they do have by being in the institution. Like so many of us, they feel powerless to change bureaucratic procedures that cripple our compassion and empathy.

One such staff member was a registered nurse I met in a state prison. I first met her when she was standing behind a table, pouring pills from a cup into each prisoner's mouth. The women were lined up behind the table with their hands behind their backs. "Ms. Bonnie Brown" stood behind the table and a matron sat on a stool next to her. As the inmate stepped to the front of the line with her hands still behind her back, Ms. Brown would find that particular woman's medication and pour the pills onto the back of her tongue, then pour a small cup of water into the woman's mouth, too. The guard would watch the inmate's mouth to make sure she swallowed the pills and didn't keep them under her tongue to give to someone else or get high on later. The inmate would then step away and the next inmate would step up, mouth open, for her medication. (This is the common procedure in most prisons, whether the pills are given whole or crushed into powder as an extra precaution against "saving" medication for a high.)

Several inmates had told me to find Ms. Brown; she would "tell it like it is," they assured me. The next day, after she had punched out on the time clock, Ms. Brown met with me in a private place. I felt like a spy keeping a visit, covering my tracks and her tracks so as to minimize the risk of her getting into any trouble.

"I'm frustrated," she said. "More than anything else, I'm frustrated.

I'm primarily a psychiatric nurse. I need to have a job where there is more communication, more involvement. Primarily now they have me working as a robot. I'm a robot. That's my frustration. I'm not being a nurse standing in that little place popping pills into people's mouths.

"Let's face it. It's a cold world out there, and the women need somebody to talk to in the first place. All the procedures you have to go through before you can accomplish anything . . . [She shakes her head.] My biggest problem is being tied down to a mechanical job and not being able to rap with the girls when I think it's needed. Any rapping I do is on my own time.

"I believe we need more staff with empathy. Everybody thinks I'm crazy because I say they need to hire more people for the girls to talk to. If a girl needs someone to rap with right now, she's in trouble. She has to break a window to get attention or get sent to jail [maximum security]. She has to throw a fit or have convulsions on the floor. If they tell me, 'I need to talk to you now,' I still have to distribute medicine first. I can tell them to wait until the end of the line. But most of the nurses don't feel that way. They say they don't get paid for it, plus they don't want to get involved.

"All the rules reinforce their not getting involved. The staff can't give their telephone number or address to the women here. We're not allowed to communicate with the girls after they get out. They can call or write us here, but we can't answer unless they get special permission from their parole officer. It's irritating to me because I know a lot of girls out there need help. The reason given for the rule is that if you get attached and then they come back, they would get preferential treatment. But by being able to communicate we might be able to prevent half of 'em from coming back.

"A lot of staff members like that rule because it lets them keep their distance with no questions. Just as in any staff, there are some that are very institutionalized, so if a narcotics addict complains of pain, the nurse says she's just looking for a fix. They won't give her the medication she should have—or she'll be steered away, deterred from getting to the doctor.

"As far as realistic nursing care—if you get surgery, you get damn good nursing care here. But with everyday things, because of a few, they categorize everybody as malingerers. If you come into arrival and orientation and state that you are an epileptic and state you are on medication, they take your medication and put you in the hospital for thirty days. It is true some do it to get out of work for thirty days, but a true epileptic has to have a couple of convulsions to be diagnosed through tests before she gets her proper medication. For a true epileptic, it's awful. For a malingerer, they just lay around and get chubbier; they don't realize they're really harming themselves. But for the epileptic, as soon as we find verification with a couple of seizures, we can give medication.''

Ms. Brown said that one of the biggest complaints is that sick call is at 6:30 A.M. and the women who are sick have to sign the slip the night before. This is a "routine" procedure at most institutions. If an inmate calls into the clinic at 2 P.M. and says she has a rip-roaring headache, she's told to get on the list for the next morning.

I told Ms. Brown that women in nearly every jail I'd visited had said, "Don't get sick at night. Whatever you do, don't have any sort of attack or seizure at night, because you'll die before you get any attention." I told her about Barbara, who had been awaiting trial on larceny charges in the Erie County Jail in Buffalo, New York, when she developed gallstones. She said she was in constant pain for nearly two months, but was given only Maalox and aspirin. She said that one night, "The pain was killing me and my body was beginning to swell with the poison from the gallstone infection. I started calling for the matron to get me some medicine and finally she came by my cell. She told me I was faking. 'Faking at three A.M.?' I told her. 'What the hell for? I'd like to be sleeping too!'" At her trial, Barbara was acquitted on all charges and released from jail. Right after that she had emergency surgery to remove the gallstones.

Ms. Brown wasn't surprised by Barbara's story. She said that night care at the institution she worked in was virtually nonexistent. "After five o'clock in the afternoon, there's only one nurse in the whole institution," she said. "She'll have about twenty patients in the hospital and three or four surgical patients she's taking care of, plus any psychiatric patients there—and there are usually three or so at a time. Then calls start coming in from the cottages, and she has to log them in and chart them and decide whether to send medication to the cottages. If she decides to send medication over to the cottage, she has to package it. She gets so busy she can't even get to the hospital patients; she hasn't been allowed to, really.

"I've suggested they get a two-to-ten P.M. nurse. If you get sick in the middle of the night, forget it! You have to stick a towel out the window. It used to be you were locked in your room during the day if you were sick, but that's changed now, at least here.

"I used to break the rule. If a girl was sick at night, I would leave her door open so at least she could stagger out in the hall so I could see her. And I would make hall visits every thirty minutes, but I'm sure many staff don't do that. They say they do, but many do homework and have no knowledge of what's going on.

"There's another rule that hangs over new staff's head—and I know I'd break this rule. I don't know if I'd get fired or what, but if a girl is hanging in her room or on fire after ten o'clock at night, a staff is not allowed to open the door unless another staff is there. This is allegedly to avoid a trap. But nobody can tell me—'cause I'm a nurse—I can't open a door or cut a girl down who may still have a chance to live. A new staff without medical background would think, Should I open that door or would it be my head? This rule has been broken twice I've heard of, where staff cut them down, but I don't know what happened to the staff.

"Since I've been here there have been attempted suicides, but no deaths. There are several slashed wrists or arms periodically, or overdoses from bluing from the laundry or cleaner. We get a lot of overdoses here.

"Some staff knock themselves out for the girls. They really do care. But like with any staff, you have good ones and bad ones. My question continues to be, Why do you still tolerate the bad ones? Their answer is, 'What are you going to do? You have to have somebody here.' I maintain we'd be better off with no one.

"The dentist here is an example of that. We'd be better off with no dentist. Once he gets around to it, he does a fair job. But he's pretty cruel and sadistic. If someone comes in with a toothache and he doesn't like her, he often tells her to go away or says he won't treat her. We are always treating his abscesses. And abscesses can be pretty dangerous, in addition to being miserable.

"There's a lot of sadism here, and it really does wear you down if you let yourself see it. I don't know how long I will stay here. It depends on what other offers I get—and also on whether I can really do something here without robot binders on me.

"I did work for a while with the psychiatric treatment staff here, but it was a lot of political games between staff. I got to do a lot with staff, but not much with the women. I was always being frustrated. They wanted me to be more assaultive towards the staff. In encounter sessions with staff, you're supposed to get out gripes—say, 'I feel like I don't like you,' and all that. I feel like if I don't like you, or something you do irritates me, I'll tell you personally. I don't believe you have to do it in a group in front of other staff. I don't feel it was a very good or successful program.

"I think all the women here have problems and could stand therapy. But the treatment unit played games with them out there. If you played games with them, you'd get out of prison. If you didn't, you got kicked out of the unit and would have a big confidential psychiatric report filed in your jacket. And what good is that?"

14 CRIME OR ILLNESS?

Shrinks, Drugs, and Therapy

ECHOES OF ROSA

One cold winter day in New York City, Jeanette Washington stood firm.
A black mother on welfare, she refused to pay thirty cents to ride the sub-
way. She got on, determined to ride, refusing to let bystanders pay
her fare.
"I wasn't going to be locked in the community any longer," she said. "I
was going to use public transportation, which should be free."
Police apparently thought she was crazy.
They called an ambulance and took her to see a psychiatrist.
"He asked me why I do what I do," she said. "I asked him to think about
why society does what it does to me."
Police charged Jeanette Washington with "criminal trespassing on public
property."
The judge set bail at fifteen hundred dollars, and Jeanette was locked, out
of the community, in jail.
Later she got a bill for the ambulance.[1]

In terms of public policy, it seems we have a lot of confusion about
whether we're treating people for illnesses or punishing them for crimes.
We punish people for being addicts by making possession of drugs a
crime. We treat them by locking them in prison for long periods of time.
We imprison many others for behavior caused by mental disorders, and
often we induce or exacerbate serious emotional and mental problems by
locking people into confinement where they receive no effective social,

1. This information was taken from a taped interview on "Radio Free People," broadcast on
WBAI, New York City.

educational, medical, or therapeutic intervention. At the same time, we slap psychiatric terms on prisoners for reasons that have to do more with social, economic, racial, or gender factors than anything remotely medical.

Since the early 1900s medical doctors have been called upon to identify mentally ill prisoners and to classify and treat other prisoners. Their diagnoses often have been used to justify discipline or punishment in the name of mental illness. In a letter to the State Board of Charities in 1918, Miss Helen A. Cobb, the superintendent at the New York State Reformatory for Women at Bedford Hills, wrote that she was eager for the assistant physician to begin making "mental examinations, which we appreciate are needed for classifying inmates."

The assistant physician, Dr. Orie M. Grover, testified that she had "no qualifications for such work." Dr. Grover also said that while she worked at the institution from January 1914 to March 1918 she had witnessed prisoners "strung up with handcuffs," with "toes barely touching the floor. Young women, many of them psychopaths, were handcuffed to cell gratings so that only their toes touched the floor . . . and then their faces were dipped into pails of water until subdued."

She wrote in her notes of August 14, 1916, that on one occasion she was "sent by Miss Cobb with Miss Julia A. Minogue (assistant superintendent) to Elizabeth Fry Hall to help discipline two girls . . . they were handcuffed to cot and spanked, one 25 blows, the other 20 . . . they were then gagged and hung up for one hour each . . . [a male guard] helped to hang them to the grating by the handcuffs, standing on their toes. They were also gagged. Miss Minogue and Dr. Grover present." Two months later the two girls were transferred to a state hospital for the criminally insane. Excessive treatment for mental patients was much the same.

Medical doctors employed by institutions still serve dual roles as medical healers who are put into the position of making custodial decisions in the interest of institutional security. And still today prisoners are classified and labeled with medical terms, both formally and informally. I've often been told by administrators, guards, or other staff that prisoner X is a "sociopath," a "psychopath," prepsychotic or psychotic, or that she behaved in such and such a way because she has a "personality disorder." When I have prodded the speaker for definition of these terms and the specifics of an individual's behavior, more often than not I've discovered that the prisoner in question has broken some rule, been assertive, or "talked back" to a staff member. Thoughtful professionals would be horrified at the careless use of terminology and the mystique surrounding these terms within the confines of prison.

We see medical jargon used in courtrooms as well. Judges often tell people, "I'm doing this for your own good. I'm sending you to prison for rehabilitation/drug therapy/psychiatric treatment." Although treatment programs rarely exist in prisons, judges who haven't been to the institution can imagine they are acting in a constructive or humane fashion. Similarly, they condemn prisoners by saying they are "psychopaths" who deserve to spend many years behind bars.

We also see medical and therapeutic terminology used in the current euphemisms for prisons, such as "correctional institutions." Staff members are called "correctional officers" and "correctional counselors." Prisoners are called "inmates," "residents," "patients," or "clients." Sections of cells used for solitary confinement and punishment are "psychiatric administration units" or "adjustment centers." Prisoners locked in solitary confinement are in "administrative" or "punitive segregation." Systems for control through rewards and punishment are called "behavior modification models."

In theory, rehabilitation, treatment, and therapy in prison would be a commendable thing because lawbreakers *are* human beings who have committed crimes symptomatic of deeper problems. Change is possible and desirable for many prisoners. But just as the establishment of the penitentiary seemed humane compared to public hangings and corporal punishments, therapeutic definitions attached to prisoners' lives can be equally insidious. Within a highly controlled setting, it's easy to equate nonconformity with mental illness and to call various nonharmful idiosyncracies "deviant." It also seems that if the knowledge of medicine, psychiatric terms, and sanctions are in fact used to legitimize actions designed for the security of the institution, not for the good of the individual, then it is not the practice of medicine as we normally regard it.

The role if prison psychiatrists is one fraught with contradictions. In the prison setting, psychiatrists are expected to be all things to all people, despite their obvious conflicts of interest. During a visit to Riker's Island, I asked to talk to the chief psychiatrist, who agreed to a meeting. When I walked into his small, barren office, he was sitting behind his desk, stiff and expressionless. I introduced myself and extended my hand to shake hands with him, but he pulled back, as if the gesture frightened him. He clasped his hands tightly together and pulled his shoulders together as if trying to protect his chest. He kept his hands pressed together so tightly that they turned a white-blue color, and he kept them clasped like that throughout our interview.

"You can't quote me by name," he said. Why not? "Well, if you did, I would get millions of telephone calls. Just refer to me as the chief psychiatrist, that's all.

"I work fifteen hours a week. I have to screen emergency problems as they come up," he said when asked about his work. "I've worked here fourteen years. I don't particularly do diagnosis. I mainly treat emergency cases that are 'acting out' and medicate them."

The chief psychiatrist said he had a staff of six, including one part-time psychiatrist, one intake worker, one social worker, and a psychologist for each "intake area"; these staff members do the initial background interviews of the women coming in each day. He said he and one other psychiatrist do all the "therapeutic" work with the more than seven hundred women incarcerated at Riker's. (Theoretically, if each of the psychiatrists devoted his entire attention to consultations all day long, each woman could have a three-and-a-half-minute psychiatric session once a week.) In addition to "therapy," however, the psychiatrists have administrative duties, staff coordinating, and reports to write.

"I've never had a suicide in the fourteen years I've been in this department," he said. "I think that's because they know they can see a psychiatrist if they have a problem. They know that help is available. I think it's also because this place is run like a family. The officers know them and they know us. The ones who don't come back we don't see, so we don't know what our success rate is."

The doctor said he "couldn't say" how many inmates he "did therapy" with each week, but he said he rarely saw more than fifteen at the most in a week's time. He said these were all "situational cases" of women "acting out."

"Besides seeing inmates, I see staff with administrative problems," he said. "Today I saw three inmates. They were 'situational cases.' For instance, one of the women was upset because she is facing seven and a half to fifteen years of prison. She was just sentenced. You don't tell her to face it, you just give her a feeling of sympathy. I medicated her."

He said there really wasn't any time to do follow-up work with cases; usually if there's more "acting out," the medication is just continued.

The chief psychiatrist at Riker's was not unlike other psychiatrists I'd met in other prisons. His time was chiefly spent as an administrator and distributor of "nerve medications." He didn't have the time to deal with the source of problems or the dynamic behind various psychiatric symptoms.

Certainly at some jails, women greatly in need of help are not given any psychotropic drugs such as antipsychotic, antianxiety, or antidepressant medications when they need them. I remembered Captain Daisy McLendon in Chicago's House of Correction saying in a matter-of-fact voice: "Emotionally disturbed women are locked in their cells twenty-four hours a day." I also had a memory I couldn't forget of a gaunt, bleary-eyed woman methodically banging her head against the wall between "argghhhh" sounds. "She's emotionally disturbed," Captain McLendon explained to me when I expressed concern. "She does that all the time."

A lack of tranquilizers—or "nerve medications," as prison doctors and staff often refer to them—does not seem to be a common problem, however. More often, it seems, both at Riker's and at other prisons, women inmates walk the halls in a dazed, zombielike state. Their words are slurred, their eyes glazed, their clothes disheveled. Some women I have seen on one day having to be supported by other inmates even to walk look like totally different people a day or two later, when they said they "got off the medication."

Some women complain that they are given Thorazine and Millaril against their will when they are upset about something; others complain they are unable to get medication when they feel they need it. Administrators estimate that between 50 and 80 percent of the population in most institutions are given some kind of tranquilizers on a daily basis. Only at the state reformatory in Iowa were a minority of women taking any tranquilizers—less than 10 percent of the population.[2]

"The psychiatrist here is an ex-inmate of a concentration camp," said "Jeanie," a prisoner at a state institution. "He's Jewish, and he should have a better understanding of us because of his own experience, but he prefers to operate as a Nazi in his attitude.

"He's very authoritarian and rigid on the outside. But underneath all that authority, he's a very frightened person. Really he's scared to even talk to a lot of women. Women put in slips to see him and he just avoids them. If they come up to him and ask for an appointment or say they've been trying to see him, he'll either tell them to go away or say, 'I'm busy. I'm busy. Can't you see I'm busy?' He'll tell them to send him a slip. He sometimes just runs away if he sees someone coming he doesn't want to talk to.

"He suggested to me he'd put me in the state mental hospital for a year. I told him he was crazy. He said I'd never get out of here until I learned to keep my mouth shut."

In prison, two views of medicine seem to merge. The first view is that good medicine is based on a voluntary contract where we willingly put

2. Women reported in a 1984 study that although medication they need is withheld when they are being punished, they still are excessively medicated with tranquilizers.

our lives in the hands of our doctor or therapist. We trust that the doctor will take care of us. When we are sick we voluntarily allow the doctor to say, "Take this pill," or, "Have this operation," or, "Follow this diet," or, "Change this specific action." We trust his judgment enough to willingly suspend our rights and know that as a doctor he will do his best to give us our rights back by making us well.

The other view sees medicine as compulsory treatment, where a patient's rights have been forcibly taken from her. Prisoner's lives are in someone else's hands, even though they have not made a voluntary contract. There is no choice of doctor or medicine; more often than not, there's no chance at a second opinion. In some circumstances, prisoners are "treated" against their will.

In the section on health and medical services in the American Correction Association's *Manual of Correctional Standards,* the authors write:

> There is a vital need to implement and enhance our knowledge in the field of deviated behavior. Toward this end, penal institutions offer unparalleled resources for research. For instance, the prison community is an excellent setting in which to test the thesis that deviated behavior results from underlying mental disorder. Studies of offenders can add to our knowledge about maladaption or failure in adaptive capacity. The practice of medicine in penal institutions affords unique opportunities to gain increased understanding of medical psychology; to improve administrative skills and to participate in behavioral research.

Over the years there have been many situations where prisoners have been a captive audience for experimentation. In the past, prisoners in Texas and other parts of the country were subjected to sterilization when scientists believed that a chromosome factor in criminals could be passed on to their offspring. Women were sterilized so they would not pass on "defective" genes. Other prisoners have been subjected to lobotomies and used as guinea pigs to see if the "aggressive impulse" is located in one part of the brain. A spokesman for the Food and Drug Administration said in 1972 that 90 percent of all initial drug testing had been done on prisoners. In 1995, this is no longer the case. Federal regulations stipulate experimental drugs cannot be used on prisoners. Ironically, this has become a problem for HIV-infected prisoners who want and need to use experimental drugs to treat AIDS.

While psychiatric experimentation on prisoners has been banned in most states, it's still true that in many states, prisoners can be transferred indefinitely to state mental hospitals or state prisons for the criminally insane by administrative order. All that is needed is the recommendation of the prison superintendent and a psychiatrist, with the approval of the department of corrections, and inmates have virtually no appeal. They have no opportunity to be heard or to challenge "scientific" conclusions about them, which are often based on no more than one interview. There is no hearing and no requirement for consultation with their families. It is considered an "administrative transfer." And it's possible because legal criteria have not been delineated for such transfers. The lack of established safeguards and the imprecise standards for commitment to psychiatric treatment leave open the possibility of excess and abuse, as well as misuse.

The lack of procedures that protect the rights of individuals being treated or transferred may be related to the absence of fear, when mental hospitals were established, that people not suffering from mental illnesses would be subject to forced or coerced psychiatric treatment. It was assumed that medical professionals would act without bias in the interest of the individual, honoring the contract between doctor and patient and safeguarding the patient's interests. The view of psychiatry as an established field with measurable medical definitions required no need for legal definitions to protect the rights of individuals.[3]

But the study of human behavior is ongoing, and standards used for defining mental health within an institutional setting too easily can be based on security judgments, not medical criteria. Leaders, for instance, often are labeled "aggressive," "hostile," and "sociopathic." When prisoners are transferred to "adjustment units" or psychiatric centers without opportunity to challenge the commitment, the criteria for transfer should be questioned. This is not to say that some of the women transferred might not be disturbed and in need of help; but just as a transfer can be used in the interest of an individual, it can be used against her and in violation of her rights. Procedures should and must be established to protect the rights of the individuals whose lives are in the total control of others. Imprecise standards and lack of safeguards often allow security considerations of the prison to dominate therapeutic considerations of the individual.

A case in point occurred at the Ohio Reformatory for Women, when five "difficult" women were transferred to Lima State Hospital. The five had tied up two officers and escaped from the isolation unit one cold November night. They all were captured within twelve hours and returned to the prison, where they were kept in solitary confinement for four months before being transferred to the state mental hospital in Lima.

The women said they were given no prior warning about their impend-

3. See Nicolas N. Kittrie, *The Right to Be Different* (Baltimore: Johns Hopkins University Press, 1971).

ing transfer. They had no hearing. One woman was transferred to Lima in December, and the other four remained in solitary confinement until February, when they were taken away in waist chains. (See Mary Lynne Wilkins' account in chapter 9.)

Martha Wheeler, the superintendent at ORW, said the staff had decided to prosecute the women for the assaults on staff and the escape. She said they were locked in solitary pending indictments from a grand jury. "They threw food and raised all kinds of hell in there," she said. "They had welded close together. They threw things at us and hated us, so we had to separate them from each other and separate them from us. We can make an administrative transfer to Lima as we did with the four women—it's the only facility available. Male prisoners would be more apt to be transferred to one of several other prisons in the state.

"They were transferred on the recommendation of the psychiatrist, the psychologist, and myself, with the approval of the Department of Corrections. Their sentences continued to run while they were there."

Ms. Wheeler said that the procedure has been used before and since. "Usually they recover and are returned here for the remainder of their sentence," she said. "The review is in Lima—they decide when to send them back."

All five women remained at Lima for more than a year. Then they were transferred to the Union County Jail and sentenced to six months in the Dayton Workhouse for their escape. Finally, four of the women were returned to ORW. The fifth was returned to Lima, "cleared," and returned to ORW about five weeks later for the remainder of her sentence.

"What they did at Lima was think that we sent them up together to be punished," Ms. Wheeler said. "They kept them as a group and sent them back to us. Since that time we have moved away from the close custody approach, so we moved them to a psychiatric adjustment unit. Lima has been less and less satisfactory. We figure we can do a better job here.

"The adjustment unit is not all for punishment. We started it as a psychiatric alternative to Lima. They can work out of there and then go out eventually to recreation and activities. They don't go out to eat. They are served their meals in there."

The possibility of compulsory psychiatry is ominous, especially in cases such as this one, where it seemed to be "the only alternative." It is also ominous when it is used for determining when a person will get out of prison. Under indeterminate sentencing laws, psychiatric "adjustment" is often the measuring stick for when a woman is or isn't released on parole.

In an effort to understand the role of psychiatry in an institutional setting, I asked some physicians and psychiatrists about it. They explained that psychiatry, the branch of medicine involved with matters of the mind, can be divided roughly into three categories:

1. Medical psychiatry, where the psychiatrist remains in the mode of a physician, a healer, whose basic interest and responsibility lie in the emotional area of his patients;

2. Academic psychiatry, where the emphasis is on the understanding of disease entities or clinical patterns as abstractions, not necessarily related to individual people, but rather to theses and theories;

3. Administrative psychiatry, where the emphasis is on the management of behavior, triage (the methods by which individual patients are referred to appropriate facilities for treatment, etc.), the business or financial affairs of psychiatric institutions, and management of such matters as staffing and personnel direction as might be found in any organization.

As far as we know today, effective psychiatric treatment or therapy can exist only where the patient makes a voluntary contract with her therapist that includes the patient's willingness and desire to change. People in prison are, by definition, imprisoned because it was so ordered. There is no voluntary contract, so a relationship between a prison doctor and a prisoner is by definition already administrative. And when a prisoner is remanded to psychiatric treatment, she is being handled by administrative psychiatrists—a situation that is contradictory to effective psychiatric treatment. Although it is true that tranquilizers, for instance, may be used as a part of psychiatric treatment when they are included in the voluntary contract between a patient and a therapist, their use in a prison situation can constitute a form of chemical straitjacket.

It is feasible, even within a prison, for a person to make a voluntary contract. If a prisoner says to a therapist that she has a problem and would like help, she is initiating a contract with him or her. She is willingly putting herself in the therapist's care. She may tell a psychiatrist or psychologist, "I'd like to do something about my temper; I don't like the way I go off. If you think learning about my motivations or taking a certain medication would help me, I'd like to do it." At that point, if the therapist acts in the patient's interest, he or she will do the best he or she can to help the prisoner.

But the therapist's part of this contract requires that his or her role cannot be dual. The situation where the prisoner approaches the therapist and they establish a trusting doctor-patient relationship requires the practitioner to be loyal to the individual patient. The therapist cannot recommend medication for any purpose other than the patient's best interest.

And it is essential that he or she protect the patient's confidences and honor the therapist's professional ethics of confidentiality.

Unfortunately, voluntary contracts are rarely found in prison. Public and penal emphasis on prison security and custody not only violates the ethical relationship that would allow growth and change to people who choose it, but in fact makes it nearly impossible. Medical records and therapeutic reports are accessible to the institutional staff and parole board. The use of the psychiatrist for recommendation for or against parole reduces genuine exchange and effective therapeutic interaction. Therapy for the good of the individual must always play second fiddle to security and detention considerations. Any effective process that prisoners might choose if given the opportunity is invalidated before it even begins by the dual nature of treatment within a custodial institution.

"Real treatment or therapy will never work in the traditional prison setting," the superintendent of the Iowa Reformatory for Women told me, "because whenever there's a choice between rehabilitation efforts or custody, custody wins out."

"We can't make people change unless they want to change," Lieutenant Shaw told me at the Women's Detention Center in Washington, D.C. "If it was [George Orwell's] *1984,* we could give pills and change them into robots. Until then, we can't change anyone unless they want to change. We can influence them, that's all."

There are some ways prison administrators can provide inmates with their own vehicles for change. For instance, when support is given for prisoners to form treatment groups of their own choosing and through their own initiative (whether they are "group therapy" sessions, sessions with volunteer or independent therapists, Alcoholics Anonymous, Narcotics Anonymous, drama workshops, poetry readings, or some other program), the administration has begun to provide the inmate with the option of forming a voluntary contract toward effective self-help, that is, psychiatric treatment. Such opportunities, however, are all too rare.

Some people in prison have no interest in changing—no desire to be any different or lead any kind of life different from what they know. But a greater number of the men and women in prison would like to change, would like to break their addictions, improve their lives, develop stable relationships, get good jobs, and stay out of prison. They want to develop; they want to grow. Long waiting lists for the very few drug treatment spots and educational training programs in prison are a testament to their interest. The successes of the women who do get into programs are evidence of their abilities to use what's offered. But all too often, when prisoners ask for the tools to help them change, they are denied them. Their initiative is stifled.

As one state prisoner put it: "If I ask you for a pair of shoes, don't give me an overcoat. If I'm ready to ask for something, don't try to force something else on me, don't tell me I'm spoiled. Give me the tools and I'll fix my own carburetor."

Most administrators set an oppressively high standard of security based on the need to control a very small group of truly dangerous prisoners. These security measures make life especially oppressive for the nonviolent majority. But what seems odd is that most of this same, very tiny group of dangerous prisoners with severe mental problems are virtually ignored by administrators on a day-to-day basis. These people are prone to psychosis, sometimes are dangerous to others or dangerous to themselves, and need intensive security and care. And ironically, it is the nonviolent majority who does the caretaking.

As Mary Vangi said, "We end up taking care of them and trying not to get hurt by them while the administration concentrates all its attention on women who break rules or refuse to work. They [the administration] deal with political women in a psychiatric way while women who really need psychiatric care are just given Band-Aid care, drugged up or left to rot."

Vangi's observation seems to reflect the reality of psychiatry in prison. It has everything to do with management and nothing to do with effective treatment.

One night when I was at the California Institution for Women, an institution considered one of the most progressive and treatment oriented in the country, a woman was taken to the Psychiatric Treatment Unit for "flipping out." The other inmates were accustomed to watching out for her, so they were not surprised when she "went off." Marguerite Ferrante, an inmate whom "Jane" trusted, was assigned to sit with her through the night as an "inmate sitter."

"Jane is very paranoid," Marguerite said. "And there are some cruel people who play on a person like her who has no controls, no defenses. They told her there were guns here—and there are, along with some saws for escape—but they're very well hidden. This one gal told Jane, though, that someone was going to come in and kill her. She couldn't handle it. She flipped out.

"I got into the quiet room to see her and sit with her. She had the windows toilet-papered so the man who was going to kill her couldn't see in. When I walked in she was down under the steel bunk pounding on the supports to see if a gun was there. The room's bare—the toilet's not covered. And there are bars across the front of the room, so she has to reach through to the sink. I was asked to go down and sit with her—I didn't volunteer. The whole thing really blew my mind.

"I was sitting in the open passage way from eleven P.M. to four-thirty A.M., and she'd say, 'A man just walked by you.' Then she'd tell me again and again, 'They put recorders behind the air vent.' It's so hard. I can relate better to someone functional.

"Then she wouldn't take medication unless she was taken out of the quiet room. So two guards and a regular rack staff and the surveillance were going to hold her down and give her a needle. She screamed and hollered when they came because the guards were men. I told them, 'Look, give me a chance.' I got her to put the sheets down and put the blankets on the bed. She calmed down and went sound asleep. After she had been asleep for quite a while, I went to get a cup of coffee. I had told her before she went to sleep that if she woke up and I was gone, I would be right back. That I would have just gone for a cup of coffee. But just as I started pouring the coffee, she woke up and started screaming again and shaking those bars. They came instantly, held her down, and gave her a needle.

"The whole thing puts me through so many changes. I think they should have qualified personnel instead of inmate sitters."

From Bedford Hills, Ida Mae Tassin wrote a poem about the whole process of being "classified" and labeled by the prison system. The poem is called "Lady, You Don't Know Me."

> "The Lady" is reading the paper
> My record is on,
> "And she say" she know all about me
> Right on, right on.
> "And she say" I'm one of the hardest
> criminals, that she has ever known.
> That I've almost been a criminal
> since the day I was born.
> Right on, right on.
> "And she say" my mother is tired of
> sticking by me,
> I be away too long,
> That it seem I've made this place
> my second home.
> Right on, right on.
> "Now I say" you don't know me
> No you could never guess
> for it's you and your kind
> That has kept me oppressed
> "Now I say" I have been forced to
> live in poverty, and never had an

equal chance,
To be a free thinker or to advance.
''Now I say'' my mom was a hustler
She had to survive
And all the things she wanted for me
She had to put aside.
''Now I say'' she sort of got used to
looking for herself
And she truly forgot about how I felt.
''Now I say'' you didn't know since
I was twelve
I've lived on my own
and been through hell
''Now I say'' you finally recognize
I was born in the slums?
And it's you and your kind
that has kept me a bum.
''Now I say'' all the things you don't know
about me,
would make a new world
so lets start again
and see if you said what I thought
I heard.

Reprinted with permission from *Proud Mary, Poems from a Black Sister in Prison* by Ida Mae Tassin, © 1971 by Buffalo Women's Prison Project.

15   RELATIONSHIPS

Prison Families, Friendships, and Sexuality

> There's a difference between what I feel like when I do something with a
> girl from what it felt like outside when I did something with a man.
> When I was with my man outside, I felt big and strong and, you know,
> aware of being a real woman. My man's loving me really makes me
> feel like a woman. Like soft and full. But inside this place, when I do
> something with a girl, usually I feel like someone's comforting me and
> just making me feel good. It's not really a sex thing, even when it's
> sex, because in here you feel so damn little and alone. And you don't
> feel like a woman, because when you feel that little, you don't know
> anything about sex. All you know is it feels good.
>
> —"Rose Elizabeth" at a state prison

It seems sex for prisoners is considered dessert in our culture—too special
and rare a treat for bad children.

When the topic of sex in prison comes up, some people are shocked and
curious, as if they've never considered what people do with their sexual
and emotional needs when they're confined behind bars. Others seem to
think that if you lose your liberty for breaking a law, you also ought to
lose your sexuality and your right to intimacy and sexual contact.

At public gatherings about prison conditions or prison reform, people
from the community often ask ex-prisoners, "What about homosexuality?
Is there homosexuality in women's prisons, too?"

When people are in a homosexual, unisexual world, heterosexuality
isn't easy to come by. Women restricted to a single-sex environment
month after month, year after year, still have the feelings, emotions, and
needs they had when they came in.

We forget how long people must live in that prison environment: one year, three years, ten years, twenty years. Americans sentence lawbreakers to longer terms in prison than any other nation on earth. But no matter the sentence and no matter the crime, the circumstances that dictated imprisonment do not turn people into automatons. It isn't realistic to expect human beings to survive without intimacy or affection for long, lonely months or years. If anything, inner life becomes more intense in this strange world. The need for warmth and identification and support is greater.

"Almost all the women who come to prison have husbands or children," said the superintendent of the California Institution for Women, Virginia Carlson. "It makes a tremendous impact on lifestyle. If a man goes to prison, the wife stays home and he usually has his family to return to. The household is there when he gets out. But women generally don't have family support from the outside.

"A woman who has a husband and children is in a different situation. Very few men are going to sit around and take care of the children and be there when she gets back. So to send a woman to prison means you are virtually going to disrupt her family. She knows that when she gets out she probably won't have a husband waiting for her. It will really mean starting her life over again."

A woman in prison knows she is limited in what she can do to keep her real family together or protect them. Whatever happens to them will happen, no matter what she wants or how she worries or how much she writes. A woman can know her husband is going through traumas on the outside, but she can do nothing to help. He may be having a new relationship; he may have lost his job; he may have broken his leg or been in a car accident. What can she do? Her oldest child may have run away from his foster home or be having problems in school. Her children may be lonely, upset, hurt, or sick, but she is unable to mother them or be there for them when they need her. Friends and loved ones die. Time moves on outside prison walls with all its usual chaos and disorder, but if she worries and concentrates on events she is unable to affect or change, she goes crazy doing hard time.

"You just can't afford to worry all the time," Shelley said. "You just have to tell yourself there's nothing you can do and then try to put your mind on other things. The old-timers tell me, 'Baby, you just gotta learn to do easy time. You're gonna kill yourself with the hard time you puttin' on yourself.' But I worry anyway. I can't seem to help it."

If you're going to remain sane in prison, you have to make adaptations—unless you choose to escape and face what that will mean. In a thousand little ways, prisoners have perfected the art of survival in a sterile environment where few outlets for self-expression exist. They make do with few resources. They make dressers for their clothes out of boxes. They decorate paper bags and use them for wastepaper baskets and make ashtrays from the tinfoil lining of cereal and cigarette boxes. Women in the Cook County Jail in Chicago charge batteries for their portable radios on the lights in the top of the jail cells and make their own tampons out of strips of Kotex. They make hangers for their clothes out of rolled-up newspaper and alter worn prison uniforms to fit.

Women accustomed to the life in prison try to help newcomers learn the ways of coping with the prison environment. They show them how to split a match into three sections to make it last. They show them by example workable methods of self-preservation. Games and humor are perhaps two of the greatest tactics for survival.

"If you don't got a sense of humor, you just can't make it, honey," said one woman who had just done a splendid imitation of police sniffing around to smell out homemade booze. She strutted and searched till she found the hooch, making everyone watching hoot with laughter at her pantomime. "Takin' things with a sense of humor is the best weapon we got to live through this shit."

"I find that even flat timers [who know when they're getting out] can't cope with all the pressures," said Alice Evans at Marysville. "I tell 'em, 'Hey, look, you can't always think about yourself. You gotta think about other people.' I sort of serve as a backbone for them—and here I am doing life."

It seems human beings have endless ways of making terrible circumstances seem more acceptable. When we live in destructive environments, whether with brutal parents or in concentration or refugee camps, we often adapt by creating worlds of our own, fantasy worlds that allow us to survive. These worlds don't necessarily have a connection to reality, but they usually do.

Women who face the emotional deprivation and cold environment of imprisonment find ingenious ways of accommodating to the world in which they live. One of the ways they seem to have devised is modeled on the real world of families—a supportive affiliation with mothers and fathers, children, sisters and brothers. In prison women often create a world that has been referred to as an extended "family system" or "kinship system."[1]

1. See Rose Giallombardo, *Society of Women: A Study of a Women's Prison* (New York: Wiley, 1966).

In prison families, some women play the parts of men: fathers, husbands, boyfriends, sons, grandfathers. A lot of these women model themselves after men, cutting their hair short, wearing slacks, walking and talking in a masculine way. Some of them show a lot of machismo, reflecting the sense of power, authority, and strength expected of a man in this society. Other women play the traditional role of mother or wife, roles that allow some degree of security and support.

The whole family system is characteristic of adult female institutions. Women don't consciously set out to build families. But after they arrive at prison, usually afraid and isolated, they either withdraw into themselves or begin forming relationships. As with any community, some relationships become exploitative or don't last, others deepen and gain meaning.

Prison families are much like friendships among people anywhere, like the kind of relationship where you guide and counsel a friend as though he or she were your own child, or relate to someone as if she were your sister or your mother. The difference in prison is that you openly call that friend your "child" or your "mother." They're part of your family—a family that allows a sense of belonging and eases the loneliness of feeling isolated and small. It creates a common bond that alleviates the pressures of doing hard time.

The world of the prison family not only gives women immediate contact with surrogate mothers, fathers, husbands, and wives, but also provides them with some degree of comfort, affiliation, and security. Some of the relationships are healthy, some are abusive, others are matters of convenience. And although it may sound peculiar, this world of prison families is extremely natural, somehow, in the unnatural world of prison.

In the context of prison society, it is not shocking to meet someone's institutional wife or grandfather. On several occasions while visiting prisons, I met a woman's entire prison "family" and saw the interweaving of wife, grandmother, son, daughter-in-law, daughter. The conventional interaction of these roles in general society often is reproduced in the prison family. For instance, a father looks out for his daughter's welfare, advising her with whom she should spend her time, warning her not to involve herself with so-and-so because it would be a bad relationship. The family actually becomes a substitute family, even though the relationships are formed by choice, not by birth.

It is easy to understand how the family system has evolved if you look at the intensity of loss for a woman separated so profoundly from her own children, siblings, and parents.

The history of women's prisons also plays a role. As described in chapter 10, women's prisons were created as a reform measure in the 1920s.

Women sent to prison were considered dishonored and disgraced creatures who had violated the moral and social code of their sex. Punishing them reinforced boundaries for "good" women and set a standard for the community. Architecture for state prisons for women and for the federal reformatory at Alderson followed the reformist philosophy that women prisoners need sexual morality and sobriety to resume eventually their predestined roles as homemakers, mothers, and wives—the roles that had been "perverted" or "sin-stained" through a life of crime.

Women weren't considered to be as dangerous or as violent as men. They weren't expected to rebel. The assumption was that they would accept imprisonment with less resistance than men. Being basically docile, dependent creatures, they could conform to a more open and less punitive environment with fewer difficulties. So rather than the mass penitentiary housing used for men—with high walls, guard towers, and armed guards—women's prisons were designed on a domestic model—as cottages, where each woman had a "room" of her own. Often no more than stretches of open fields or wire fences separated women prisoners and the "free world," and armed guards were rarely visible. Just like women outside, a woman prisoner would be confined to "the home."

The "home" planned for women was a cottage built to house twenty to thirty women, who would cook their own food in a "cottage kitchen." Several similar cottages would be arranged in quadrangles on green, tree-filled lawns. The cottages in most states were built to contain a living room, dining room, and one or two small reading rooms. The idea was that a domestic atmosphere would help the women learn the essential social skills of running a home and family.

The geographic isolation of the prisons in remote country areas reflected the belief that it would be good for the women to be close to the earth and growing things. The environment was designed to nurture the domestic instinct of a lady. Reformists theorized that on nice days women prisoners could do gardening or pick flowers to be close to the earth. They could grow their own vegetables and then cook and serve the food they had cultivated. This would give them a sense of satisfaction and completion.

Originally quarters for female matrons were provided in each cottage. The matrons who lived in the cottages and supervised the women were expected to instill moral values and the essentials of cooking, laundry, proper speech, and table manners. Local housewives were as well equipped as anyone else to be matrons under this requirement. They only needed to know the essentials of housekeeping to act as guardians of the moral status quo. They directed the work of women prisoners, who originally spent almost all of their time confined in their cottages sweeping and washing floors, doing laundry, ironing, and cooking. When they were allowed outside, it was for planting crops, milking cows, picking tomatoes. This is how individual state prisons came to be referred to as "the farm."

Further research has documented that this "benevolent enthusiasm for domesticating young women . . . slowly eroded." Reformatories became "simply places of punishment and incarceration for young women considered morally threatening to social stability." And matrons, "conservative social reformers who embraced the assigned role of 'woman as sexless guardian of the moral sphere,'" as Estelle B. Freedman says in *Their Sisters' Keepers*, had an "uncritical moral zeal that was unquestionably central to the development of the harsh and puritanical approach that has come to characterize much of the system's response to the female offender."[2]

Although many changes have taken place in staffing and running state and federal prisons, the same architecture still exists. In New York, Connecticut, Pennsylvania, Florida, Ohio, Texas, Oregon, Washington, and many other states, women still live in the old cottages or "residences" that house from twenty to sixty women each. Although industry has been introduced into most prisons and cooking has been transferred to a central dining room, women still "keep house" in their own cottages and dormitories. Outside of work or school hours, when they are allowed to walk across "campus," they are locked in their rooms or confined to the cottage. Some prisons have abandoned their farms, but in others, women still raise chickens and crops that provide the majority of the food they cook and eat.

In 1995 many of the old prisons for women have been remodeled to add maximum security units on the grounds; some now have guard towers, and most have armed guards. New prisons for women often are built on the male model; the new state prison for women in California, the Central California Women's Facility in Chowchilla, is a sprawling prison designed for two thousand women and currently holding four thousand. Chowchilla seems to embody the new, violent, no-holds-barred approach to women prisoners.

Even though women are locked in their cells at night, roughly treated, and locked in solitary as punishment for infractions, they still are told to act like ladies. The patriarchal goal still seems to be that fallen or erring women should conduct themselves in a ladylike manner, even though nothing about life in prison affords a woman prisoner the gentleness, grace, or respect theoretically afforded a lady.

2. Meda Chesney-Lind, "Women and Crime: The Female Offender."

The reality for incarcerated women is that no matter the ambiance, degradation, or lack of heat, this prison is "home"—a perfect setting for playing house. To play house, of course, you need all the players, including husbands and children. The architectural model is there, the emphasis is there. The only missing elements are the real relationships with men and children and blood relatives. So a family system has developed naturally, an evolution of the model for rehabilitation that reformers first conceived but failed to understand.

As Marguerite Ferrante said, "We are just like a small community except we don't have any men. So there are women who take the place of men."

"It just happens," one woman said. "Just like on the outside, you get close to certain people. It's the same in here—but we probably get even closer than a lot of families because of how lonely it is otherwise.

"It also becomes sort of a game between us and the staff. Because the staff places so much emphasis on our relationships, they're responsible for getting a lot of women interested. It gets back to the old game of cops and robbers—when they set down rules about relationships and contact, you're gonna try to break them."

"Families, at least in this penitentiary, come in all sizes, shapes, and colors, black, white, and brown," said Ruth Kelly, at the Ohio Reformatory for Women. "Some are a result of 'playing'—a form of homosexuality—and some are the result of having no one for a real family outside. For the remainder it's just a penitentiary thing. But just like in free families, there are sisters, mothers, grandmothers, fathers or 'pops,' brothers, and children—like 'my kid' or 'my child.' You'll notice I make no mention of aunts and uncles. I attribute this to the fact that aunts and uncles are not as close as immediate family.

"Women may not be old enough to really be mothers, but they're disciplinarians or they take care of their child. Grandmother goes for the elderly or older woman who fits the role. But when a woman of this age is not in your family, out of respect to her you refer to her as 'Miss' whatever her first name is, married or not.

"The father or brother's role is usually assumed by the stud broads, who take the part of the masculine role in an arrangement—like marriage, going steady, or that sort of thing. This is where the term 'players' or 'playing' comes in. The true homosexual doesn't fit totally into this category. He's different from a player. A player is usually a person who is married on the outside and has children, along with the annual visits from her husband and family. For some strange reason when they're in isolation in here, they put a hump in their backs [this is an expression for a type of masculine walk], get their hair cut, and assume the role of husband, father, brother. It's possible there may be some signs of latent homosexuality here, but it's usually a game, and they return to their proper roles at least once a month for visits and again when they're released.

"The true homosexual looks down on players like these with disdain and disgust," Kelly continued. "In this situation in prison, a gay person from the free world usually takes his or her time before getting involved with anyone, and once she takes a partner it's usually for a duration of time and only one woman. The player has many women, usually referred to as "wife-in-laws," who take their place in the harem—as first, second, or third wife. The player also uses an association for commissary reasons, which can become dangerous, because it's just one person taking advantage of another. But I suppose the most danger of the situation is the unrest in the harems. Everyone wants to be first wife, and this results in fights."

Some "men" take advantage of their macho position and act just like domineering men on the outside. They order their women around, demand to be waited on, have their laundry done and their rooms cleaned. The woman accepting this subservient role probably has been conditioned by previous relationships on the outside. For "love," she's willing to demean herself and do what she has to do to keep her man.

Women who act butch, who walk, dress, and behave like men, often appear to be so masculine that inmates constantly refer to them as "he" and "him." The habit is catching. I found myself relating to some of the very masculine women inmates as men, and referring to them as "he," even when I knew "he" was a woman.

Kelly said it's her feeling that only a small percentage of the women are "true homosexuals" in any penitentiary. "It just doesn't have that much to do with sex," she said. "And it's almost silly to call them homosexuals, especially here in this penitentiary anyway. The behavior of the players tags the true homosexual with much unhappiness and reflects poorly on people who are truly gay. The gay persons feel they are made to look worse than animals to the world at large from people who are just playing games.

"I've discussed this with both gay women and players quite thoroughly, and the gay women say, 'A woman likes a woman because she looks like a woman' and 'Nothing is prettier than two pretty women together.' They don't believe women need to dress up like men and act like men. They think that women who dress and act like men are sick. The player, on the other hand, says, 'Variety is the spice of life,' and she gets involved very quickly with people she's attracted to. A lot of it is just experimentation.

"The families here usually have a strong bond and find some pride in it. But I can't honestly say you can depend on your family. They are quite open with their family names and don't hesitate to use titles in front of the staff. But it makes me honestly believe that families are made up a lot out of defiance to the police because they strip us of so much. And since family means unity, it's a form of uniting against them—against the staff."

Ruth Kelly's observations seemed to hold true in most of the institutions I've been in or talked about with women. Women play the part of husband, lover, and protector, and women play the part of wife, mother, comforter. The term "playing the part" seems appropriate. Often we hear professional actors talk about becoming absorbed in their roles, merging to the extent that they feel the role has taken them over, that they are speaking as much for themselves as they are for the role and vice versa.

Some women who play the role in prison become equally absorbed in their part. They become what they pretend to be, and at least for a while the part is real, even though the degree to which people play the role varies. Many women say that some prison "couples" never consummate that relationship sexually, whereas others do. On occasion, a prison couple decides to have a marriage ceremony, which is sometimes comic, sometimes serious. [Prison marriages are usually very different in essence from marriages between committed gay or lesbian couples on the outside who have equal, freely chosen, and loving relationships. While prison relationships can be supportive, for the most part they have been born out of oppressive circumstances and are not expected to endure when the couple gets out of prison.]

While I was in one prison, a couple, B. and P., got married by another inmate in a small service they had planned in their dormitory. They had attendants, flowers, and rings. When it came time for count, the staff thought they had had an escape because the count turned up one person short. But B. and P. had managed to get themselves locked up in the same room for their honeymoon. After a search for the "escapee" was started and the honeymoon was discovered, both women were sent to individual cells in solitary confinement for two weeks. A number of women said they thought B. and P.'s ceremony was "silly" or "going a little too far with the game to justify what you're doing," but it provided some excitement in an otherwise monotonous routine.

Although emotional turmoil, confusion, and fighting sometimes are created by relationships that become destructive, the family system generally seems to provide a positive sense of belonging. It's a system that allows for a sharing of goods that come at a premium from the commissary. Cigarettes, supplementary food, clothes, and yearly "boxes" sent in from families on the outside are shared by family members. (A *Guide to Institutional Living* for Missouri inmates cautions against being used in this regard: "We like to see generosity among the women but we dislike having them use material things to buy favors or affections. Beware of the girl who says, 'I like you, can I borrow a cigarette?' Chumming too closely with any one person is strongly discouraged.")

But having a prison family means that when a woman is sick, she has someone to mother her. If a woman is being bullied or threatened by someone outside the family, she has brothers and a father to come to her defense. If she hears bad news from the outside, she has people to confide in. Women rely and depend on their family members to varying degrees.

Some women say the relationships provide role models—for instance, what a mother should be like, as opposed to what your own mother has been. For some women who have grown up emotionally isolated in institutions or orphanages, their prison mother becomes their first *real* mother—a mother who pays attention, guides, and helps set limits instead of being neglectful or withholding her love and comfort.

Women say that problems develop in the family system when wives become competitive with one another and when a woman changes relationships or "drops her belt"—in other words, goes from playing the male role back to her female role. There is a shortage of women acting as men. So when someone drops her belt, she not only reduces the number of available men but she also is considered fraudulent. Moreover, she is messing with the game—and this is threatening.

Although it might seem otherwise, a lesbian does not have an easier time of it in prison. Lesbians have just as difficult an adjustment in prison as do heterosexual women. It is no easier for a woman who is a lesbian to leave the person she is living with on the outside than it is for a woman who leaves her heterosexual partner. Sexual orientation has nothing to do with making any woman less lonely, frightened, and confused by facing years of prison life than anyone else. Some gay women, like some straight women who have close communication with a loved one on the outside, don't get involved sexually with anyone else while in prison.

"It's just like with anybody else," said "Roc." "Just because I'm gay doesn't mean I only like to be with women. I have friends that are men and women on the outside; in fact, several of my close friends are heterosexual couples."

Roc, a lively, attractive woman who works as a butcher in the penitentiary kitchen, doesn't play the masculine role or dress like a man. She is one of the women who cheers up other prisoners with her infectious laugh, lively spirit, and a humor that seems boundless. She's Italian and belongs to a club for Italian women in the prison where she's incarcerated. I met her "family"—her mother, who was black, her grandmother, also black, and one of her children, who was white. Another of her daughters was Chicana.

"I'm very comfortable being gay," Roc said. "And because I am, I have respect for myself. I wouldn't expect you to put your hands on me or my hands on you any more than you would anyone else. Relationships are meaningful to me and they're deep—based on a lot more than physical attraction.

"There are a lot of girls here who just want some cheap thrills or a quicky experiment, and then they go out and forget it. Or they drop their belt for a while and then curl up their hair again. To tell you the truth, I wouldn't have anything to do with any of them. No, I don't think being gay makes prison life any more bearable—especially when your woman is gone."

Prison administrators estimate that less than 5 percent of the women who come into their institutions have had lesbian relationships on the outside. Prisoners say the figure might be slightly higher, perhaps 10 percent of the total. Several administrators commented that women who had established lesbian relationships outside the prison either seemed to be very stable in a new relationship within the institution or remained loyal to their mate on the outside.

Nevertheless, women classified as homosexual when they enter jail often are discriminated against by staff—especially in county jails, where they are segregated from other women and not allowed to "mingle." At the Sybil Brand Institute in Los Angeles, for instance, a separate cell block for women who are considered gay is referred to by inmates as the "Daddy Tank." I was told that "obvious homosexuals" are put into the Daddy Tank. Authorities make the decision as to who is an "obvious homosexual." Women in the Daddy Tank are locked into solitary confinement cells twenty-four hours a day unless they are allowed out to work. They are rarely allowed to attend institutional functions, such as the monthly entertainment that comes into the prison. They are also barred from the few outside programs that come into the institution. [In the 1990s discrimination against women classified as homosexual is more informal and subtle, but prisoners say it still exists.]

Several of the women who had been in the Daddy Tank told me they had been mistreated by deputy sheriffs in charge of the area. Terry Dunningham told me she had spent three difficult months in the Daddy Tank at Sybil Brand before going to court. "One day when I came out of my cell they said, 'We're going to cut your fingernails,' " Terry said. "I said,

'Oh no, if anybody cuts them, I'm going to cut them.' I went to my work assignment, and when I came back, this police said, 'Come here, Terry.' I thought she was going to open my cell, but she took my wrist and proceeded to try to hold me down while she cut my fingernails. I proceeded to break her nose. They took me to court for it, but I won because I was in the right.''

Women in other parts of the country also related incidents of being labeled and segregated when they were booked into prison. ''When I got to Riker's Island, the guards asked me right off if I was a butch or a fem,'' said Guillermia, a short, stocky Cuban woman from New York. ''I didn't know what they were talking about. I had very long hair, down to here. But they took me down to the beauty shop and cut my hair and right away I was called a butch. People started calling me 'he' even though I have four children. It was a very confusing thing.''

When I met Guillermia after she had gotten out on bail awaiting trial, she still had her hair cropped short. She wore pants and shirts that gave her a masculine appearance. In restaurants, waitresses often called her ''sir.'' Although she had been in jail only three months, the experience seemed to have affected her sense of identity as a woman.

Prisoners say that matrons and staff members have an excessive focus on homosexual issues. For instance, they say that staff members often gossip about ''who is going with whom'' and make notes of relationships on their records of the prisoner's behavior. These records are put into the woman's prison file and become part of her ''personal history'' accessible to other staff members and the parole board. Prisoners claim that puritanical matrons who focus on sexual conduct often imagine false situations through their own prurient distortions.

''The first thing my counselor asks me when I see her is, 'Who are you going with? I know you are going with someone—you might as well tell me about it,' '' one woman in Pennsylvania says.

''They get disciplinaries and such if there's fighting between two women or if they're caught in a homosexual act,'' said Ms. ''Baum,'' a matron with her hair pulled neatly back from her face into curls at the back of her neck. She sat at a desk in the hallway of Cottage B on the first floor of a state prison and pointed toward the prisoners' rooms. ''They can't go into each other's rooms or that kind of thing—and they don't have much of an opportunity because we keep a close eye on them.''

In Iowa in the early 1960s, staff members at the state prison would single out anyone they thought to be a homosexual and make her wear a yellow uniform rather than the blue uniforms worn by other inmates. Inmates were not allowed in one another's cells for any reason. If two women were friends and one was found visiting another in her cell, the matron would slam and lock the door, and then each woman would be sent to solitary confinement. When they were released from solitary, they were given the yellow uniforms.

"You might as well have been going down on each other," said a woman who had been at the prison during that time. "The matrons were just looking for things to bust you for. Now, with the new administration, they don't bust you for homosexuality, and they're not as nosy as they were then. So there's not many serious problems any more, hardly any at all."

The warden at the Federal Reformatory for Women at Alderson, Virginia McLaughlin, also says that one of the biggest problems with homosexuality is the "staff's preoccupation with it."

"My personal attitude is that what goes on between two consenting, discreet adults is their own business," she said. "I like to think we're not moralistic about it. But some attitudes are difficult to change. I get quite a bit of criticism for my philosophy."

Ms. McLaughlin doesn't get upset at seeing two women walking around the prison grounds holding hands or sitting and talking quietly together in close proximity. But she doesn't approve of kissing in public; she expects the women at least to be discreet. Unlike many administrators, she isn't adamant about trying to keep women from wearing pants or walking with "a hump in their backs." She says rules against such behavior often only push people into breaking them.

She attributes many of the relationships between women to genuine friendship and says, "Who knows how much of it is real homosexuality? Or how much of what seems to be homosexuality is actually consummated? I would suppose that about eighty or ninety percent of the residents here are involved in some kind of boy-girl play. But in our culture, if you ain't got a man, you ain't got nothing. And that model from outside carries into this institution.

"People play roles, but a lot of it is just to fill out the public image the culture says women are supposed to project. And a lot of it just has to do with people needing to be close to another human being.

"I don't like jails. And I'm not going to defend them or everything that goes on here. There is no jail in the world that's any good. They're bad places, and you're in them against your will. If you're black, poor, or a woman in twentieth-century America, the dice are loaded against you. But I believe that you can learn and grow in any experience. In Nazi concentration camps, even, people survived and learned.

"I tell the women in here that they're each a unique individual. Every human being hurts. No one has a corner on that market. Every human being hurts and every human being dies, and we all end up in a pine box somewhere. But the important thing is to accept people as people and not for the role they're in. Life is lived by yourself, and there are some things no one shares with you, so it's important to live with yourself. I tell the women, 'You can spend all your time here fighting the cops and the system, or you can reach out for the things in this system which can be of benefit to you. I just want you to do your best here so you can go out and not spend the rest of your life in these joints.' ''

Ms. McLaughlin says she knows there's no way prison can be "good." Even if women had the finest conditions possible, there would still be the pain of incarceration, the pain of being separated from their children and the world and the people they love. So, she says, it doesn't make sense to her to guard against close relationships between women or struggle to control personal or physical interaction that doesn't cause friction. Relationships and friendships, she says, are only natural in the prison environment and indeed for a sense of identity anywhere. Besides that, "precautions just don't work, because women will manage to do what they want to do."

Ms. McLaughlin doesn't believe that role playing inside jail will carry over for most women when they leave prison. "If a woman comes into this joint heterosexual, she'll leave here heterosexual," she said. "She may play games here to make her time easier—and you've got to remember how much time women do—but darn few women who have developed real patterns on the outside get turned around permanently in here."

Women at Alderson are locked into solitary confinement for fighting or refusing to work, but they're not locked up for homosexuality unless they're caught in bed together. At many other institutions where there is more overt preoccupation with homosexuality, women are locked up for simply sitting in another woman's room or combing her hair. Before the new administration was installed at the state prison for women in Muncy, Pennsylvania, the institution used to send out letters to the families of women inside whenever a woman was sent to maximum confinement for homosexuality.

"Can you imagine what your family thinks when they get a letter stating that their daughter is a homosexual?" said one woman from Muncy. "How could I explain that one to them? Those disciplinaries had more to do with the staff's fantasies than with any reality. I mean, like two girls holding hands would get letters sent home to their mothers. And these are grown women!"

One of the long-termers at the California Institution for Women pointed out that although some women on the staff were involved in homosexual relationships, women prisoners were the ones who paid for the "crime" of homosexuality, real or imagined. "One of our CCs and another staff member have been living together for seven years and that's okay," she said. "They can meet in the snack bar and touch feet under the table, but oh no, not you. You're a convict. You have all that playing around with homosexuals on the staff, and then the married ones going with other staff members. And then they're the ones who tell us how to live our lives. Don't set standards for me when you're worse than half the women here.

"There's a couple now who been together for quite a while. Recently they got loaded and were in one of their rooms when they got busted for making it. So now the staff is saying their relationship is destructive. It's giving them more determination and strength to keep their relationship together. The staff says the one in Psychiatric Treatment Unit is doing all right. She's so doped up she has to be. They dope you up legally, you know. The other one is in the rack.

"There's just so much double standard. And there's a lot of discrimination against the stud broads here, especially. It would be hard for someone with T. or B.'s appearance to get a job up front in the administration building, for instance. Evidently they think no one in the free world has ever seen a gay woman. Last year if you had short hair and dressed masculine, they wouldn't give you minimum time."

Staff and administrative attitudes vary widely. Administrators like Ms. McLaughlin have a long view and an open mind. At other sites, a grim puritanism takes a strict and simplistic stand. "Ms. Westfield," a matron at Muncy who had been in charge of the "punishment cottage" for more than ten years, told me that she usually took care of twenty to twenty-five "disciplinary problems" at a time—usually sent to solitary confinement for fighting or homosexuality [referred to at Muncy then as "ducky" or "bulldagging"].

"A girl has to have friends," she said. "But when they get to a point of getting to be homosexuals, we try to separate them. You have a good idea when they've gone too far. Some are born that way and can't really help it, or maybe if they're not born that way they just acquire it at an early age."

Ms. Westfield believed it was appropriate for women to be punished for sexual "acting out" within the prison, and she was strongly opposed to the proposal for weekend passes and home furloughs, which were later instituted by the new prison administration under the auspices of a state law. "It might be all right for the men, but it's going to make a whole lot more work for the state nine months later if they allow women out," she said. "I worry about the dope involved and that the girls would get pregnant."

Some staff members see more trouble in women being allowed home on twenty-four- to forty-eight-hour furloughs than the advantages of their being able to maintain contact with their husbands and children on home territory. Staff members who feel that men are the source of women's problems often rebel against new administrative regulations that lift rigid mail restrictions or allow for home furloughs. They feel that furloughs are bad even though the women given furloughs usually have only a few months remaining before they are released from the institution.

Sometimes people who have worked in prisons for a long time have a difficult time changing old views in certain areas of their thinking, even when they are progressive in other ways. Some vehemently resist change. When the Ohio Department of Corrections put out an administrative order for open correspondence for all state prisoners in August 1971, for instance, staff at Marysville threatened a walk out. Open correspondence meant women could write to anyone anywhere, and anyone anywhere could write to them. Letters were no longer to be censored; incoming letters could only be inspected for contraband. ("If you're going to have open correspondence, that means no censorship," says Bennett Cooper, Ohio's commissioner of corrections. "Any limitations are naturally a form of censorship.")

This seemed like a good thing, but staff worried about its potentially negative effect on the women. "The open correspondence policy [means] the women can seal a letter and mail it, so she can encourage a man she wants on her visiting list and tell him what he should do to get it," said Martha Wheeler, the superintendent at Marysville. "We have always wanted the man to make the first move—a letter or a phone call saying, 'This is where I am, and I want to be involved with this woman.' He has to give his evidence. It's a pretty reliable way to find out what he feels about her.

"If she is free of impediments [another relationship or a marriage], we ask the parole authority to check the man out—his standing in the community, police record, and all. If they say, 'Yes, this is a relationship we approve,' we okay it. If they say, 'No, we wouldn't want them to associate,' we go along with that. So a man who genuinely cares about the woman and is her boyfriend can sometimes get permission to be on her visiting list. That is only if he is a community resource and not a drawback.

"If he goes out of his way and tells us he genuinely cares about her, then we explore the possibility. We have one pat rule: one husband to a customer. Our responsibility is to help a woman understand as long as she's married it's her responsibility. She has to get rid of one before she can get another.

"People are inclined to say we're keeping men out, on the assumption that men are lined up waiting to see the women. This isn't the case. It's just that we have a responsibility to these women, to help protect them.

"The psychiatrist is concerned about this open mail policy because these are quite dependent women so in need of an expression of concern. So many have been manipulated all of their lives by someone who tossed them a warm bone. With the open mail policy, they can get false encouragement, plus they can initiate the contact. It all reminds me of a card I saw: 'I'd climb the highest mountain, I'd swim the deepest river . . . I'll be over if it doesn't rain.' They have gotten empty promises, empty words.

"I feel that in the mental hospital at Lima they have a good policy. They feel the women need thirty days cut off from other people—without seeing the people who were part of their breakdown. The same is true here.

"But with this open correspondence policy we have a hot correspondence between the women here and the men in the state institutions. A good forty percent of the correspondence now is between the prisons. I didn't think it was a good idea to begin with.

"I'm well aware of the need for women to stand still and get acquainted with themselves. But they have such a need for acceptance that they want to please everyone. They don't distinguish between opinions that are important. They seek warmth and acceptance. We feel there are troubled people everywhere, so we need to decide who I am, what do I believe in, and if it pleases me, that's what's important. If the focus is changed, they are battered around and can't get direction. These women are frightened, lonely, and dependent. They'd hate me if they heard that. They think of themselves as tough, independent, and strong."

Ms. Wheeler doesn't think visiting policies or correspondence limitations have any real impact on homosexuality in prison. "The whole ramification of homosexual behavior is very difficult," she says. "There are some confirmed homosexuals, some confused as to whether they are boys or girls, and some experimental. They run the whole gamut.

"The most serious ramification is that the relationships give rise to fighting. There are very volatile emotional situations over jealousy and separation. Some idiots are like a moth to a flame—if they see a warm or close relationship forming, they have to get in between them and break it up.

"We deal with homosexuality in different ways, from counseling the women to punishment or separation if it's necessary. For instance, when someone gets parole, the women fall all over each other, and this is natu-ral—we don't do anything about it. But when we find people hiding behind bushes and French kissing, they get max.

"Some are seduced into relationships or bought for protection—like, I'll buy you commissary. A lot of the relationships are exploitive like that. But they are not attacked or raped. We have no problems with that. Sometimes there are mature adults who seem to care about each other, and if they're consenting adults and are discreet about it, there's no problem. I have the attitude that if you can handle it, fine—as far as we're con-cerned, they're good friends. But if one partner is terrified and not allowed to go here or there or not allowed to see this or that person or do this or that, it's not good. Then we like to intervene."

Ms. Wheeler's memo regarding additions to a prisoner's visiting list says, "The following kinds of questions are asked about the requested additional person or persons: name, address, age, sex, marital status, em-ployment, relationship, community adjustment, does your family know and approve of the person, will the Adult Parole Authority approve, in what way would visits from the person be of help in your future. The person may also be requested to complete a questionnaire. Your requests are forwarded in writing, by the caseworker to the superintendent for deci-sion."

Even when a woman can get permission for her husband or boyfriend to visit her, visits usually are difficult and infrequent because women's prisons are located in such remote areas. The Federal Reformatory for Women in Alderson, for instance, is more than a hundred miles from any urban center. No public transportation goes to Alderson; the closest bus or train stop is more than twenty miles away. The six hundred residents of the prison come from forty different states, and more than two dozen of the women are from South America or Europe, arrested usually at borders and convicted for smuggling drugs into this country. The vast majority of these women come from poor families, and few of them get to see their children during their incarceration, let alone the men who may have been important in their outside lives. The cost of travel is prohibitive if nothing else. Loved ones die, husbands drift away, children grow up without their mothers.

"The only way I can deal with it is just to cut myself off emotionally," one prisoner at Alderson said. "Like, I haven't seen my daughters for five years. I know I'm their mother, and I guess they know I'm their mother, but what kind of mother is that? It can't really be real to them.

"Thinking about it makes me feel dead inside. Sometimes I just want to forget everything and not have to feel anything else inside."

"The staff creates their own monsters," said Chatta Mercado at the California Institution for Women. "They worry about homosexuality and then they keep men away. We're only allowed one adult male on the visiting list. Mary had one man on her visiting list, and her eighteen-year-old nephew wanted to come and visit her on his leave from the air force. It was denied because he was a male, eighteen years or older, and single. And he's her nephew.

"My nephew brings my daughter down to visit, but he's not allowed in because he's twenty-two and single. He has to wait outside. It's really ridiculous. It tends to make you feel dirty and unclean, like you're a threat to anyone in pants."

"It's hard for people to understand how you get into what they call homosexual relationships," said Theresa Derry. "But they forget how powerless people feel, how alone they are in there." Terry said she had gone back to Muncy recently and was talking to James Murphy, the new superintendent—and the first male administrator of the prison.

"A lot of things have changed up there, and he has a pretty open attitude," she said. "But he was upset about the girls going together. I was telling him he has love, he has a wife and children to go home to every day. But I told him, 'Just imagine you were without them and isolated away from them with only people of the same sex. You still need that reassurance in the here and now of your own identity, your own emotions and worth that somebody cares about you.'

"Most of the girls in here don't have anybody that cares. Nobody. And even if you do, it doesn't help to know you have a mother a thousand miles away who loves you. You need somebody now.

"It doesn't start out as a big sex thing. Actually, it doesn't have anything to do with sex. People see girls holding hands and they just think sex. But it starts out as just a need to know someone cares about you now. I told him, 'You don't give any real alternative.'

"People need to be needed—just be warm—have somebody to care about you and recognize you as a person.

"It's a thing everybody needs—a thing of feeling and touching and reassuring you that you're somebody. And you are. You have human needs. I love my daughter, but I need to hug her, let her sit on my lap to let her feel my love. It's the same thing with homosexuality in prison."

"If you're friends with somebody, homosexuality is always suspect," said Janet, an inmate at Marysville. "There is so much emphasis on it. You have all those petty rules, and that ain't what it's all about. If you and another girl do something, you're gonna do it anyway.

"But as it is, their petty rules just create tension and resentfulness. You be combing somebody's hair or sitting in somebody's room filing your fingernails, and it's a maximum offense. Anything can be a maximum offense. We have two latrines on our floor, but only one person is allowed in at a time. We're supposed to be here for rehabilitation, not to see who's a homosexual. We couldn't possibly function in society as we're made to function in here. You're not going to go out there and be afraid to go into somebody else's room!

"So we did something—committed a crime, and the judge gave us time. We come here to do our time—not for more punishment, but for rehabilitation. And all we find is punishment and folks sneaking around looking for homosexuals. We leave here bitter and hostile, thinking when we're gonna get out we're gonna get even with society. It's not the right attitude. But it's a natural result of this place."

"There are a lot of homosexuals in prison," wrote Pat Singer, a former inmate at a state prison.

> It's only logical. A group of human beings placed into a given situation will act like human beings, with emotions, feelings, desires, and needs—the need for someone or something to relate to. And that's what I am doing—relating to someone. Have you ever really related to an animal? Sure. Why, then, do so many people get so uptight when one human being is relating to another human being? God, society is so fucked up. While I was relating to this woman, a whole bunch of people were uptight about it. What was a nice middle-class white college graduate girl doing relating to another woman? A total freak out. Some of the women were, of course, lesbians during their pre-jail days. Others, like myself, were not. I was never forced into anything. I guess there's a lot more of that in men's prisons. The whole thing in this case was my choice. I just kind of slid into it. I didn't sit down and think, Should I or shouldn't I? In fact, I try to stay away from that as much as possible—sitting down and trying to logically come upon some sort of decision about something. I just sort of slide with it. So I slid into this relationship. And I was really overcome—by beauty and dreams and good vibes and new awareness.

Pat said she went through many changes in jail, and participating in a lesbian relationship was just one of them: "We all grow every day," she said. "I grew in jail while others were growing in the 'free world.' A part of me grew that I never knew existed. Now I know that wonderful part of me exists.

"What many folks fail to realize is that one of the hardest things to deal with about jail is the sudden complete absence of males. In fact, it is rarely brought up. People ask me whether I ever got to eat ice cream, could I watch any television, could I get newspapers. But no one asks me, Did you have any sex? And the choice between ice cream and sex is a heavy one. Being taken away from sex like that for a said period of time is a heavy reason why I had relations with women. The first time I felt a love for a woman I realized that love can happen between me and any number of things: women, men, fathers, cats, dogs, trees, stars. . . .

"It was a beautiful sense of awareness. We are all capable of experiencing love feelings which we really never dreamed of. I knew that to love a man was beautiful, but now I know there are all different kinds of love. I loved two women in jail, both very differently, and I still love them. One of these women was my first female lover. It was beautiful. Sexually she turned me on like no one else had. It was a heavy mental thing because being in the situation we were in, we had few opportunities to physically make love. And those few opportunities always turned out to be sneak previews. But we did the best we could, as lovers do, and thrived on those sneak previews. I felt good about having a relationship with a woman. I was all wrapped up in it. Totally into it. A relationship between two human beings. A love relationship; a mental love and a physical love. Heavy. Light. Fun. Ugly. New. Old. All those things. I had no hang-ups about it at all—and I still don't. I love another human being.

"Many of the committed gay women would tell me that once I had sexual relations with a woman I'd never be able to go back to a man. As for my own experience, this has been proven false. I did go back to a man. Am I gay? Am I bisexual? What am I? I'll die not knowing the answer to that question. I'm a million things. I try not to think too much about the Whys of life. Deal with the facts; I went to jail for two years. While I was there I had homosexual relations with women. What the hell differences do the Whys make?"

"The staff is always asking you, 'Is homosexuality forced on you?' " said Alice Murray. "That's ridiculous. If you want to play the game, you do. Nobody forces anybody else. The only people who get any pressure are the stud broads.

"What happens is there are a lot of sick bitches here who are inmates. They see an aggressive-like woman come in and they're the ones head-hunting.

"You see a poor little pretty stud broad come in and everyone's after him. It's like everything—there's good and bad. But homosexual pressures are on the stud, not the bitches. Women look up to the masculine traits and want to identify with someone tough or strong. They feel like they're not right somehow unless they have somebody to walk around with.

"Some women do make homosexuality ugly—but that's all the staff looks at. Most of the women are just doing their time and it's no big deal. The staff really create their own monsters."

When women consider getting out of prison—integrating themselves back into a heterosexual world—they almost have to choose between worlds: the insular world they've lived in for months or years, or the world outside. Leaving any role or fantasy behind is a hard thing to do. But perhaps even more painful and confusing is figuring out what's real about yourself—what part is you and what part isn't. Often, masks have become a part of your face, and you don't know where the mask stops and you start. And a lot of times the role and the delusions are safer and more comfortable than painful reality.

Women who have adjusted to prison relationships often have no idea of the obstacles they're facing when they get out and try to establish new relationships. The complexity of motivations and the surfacing of old, unresolved issues in a woman's life only compound her problems. Fran's situation is a case in point:

The paisley-papered apartment is musty, dimly lit. Fran's lying in a narrow couch-bed that seems to crowd the tiny room. Her fever has reached 102° and she's crying and moaning with the despair of someone in mourning.

Both her wrists are wrapped with tape, and she has an old navy blue bandanna wrapped around her thin forehead to keep the sweat out of her eyes. Her stomach bulges slightly under the covers. She talks rapidly, then falls asleep. Her eyes glaze, but each time she begins to talk again she returns to the subject of the woman she left in prison.

"I love that girl, I really love her. I know it's wrong by society's standards, but I can't help it—I love her. I don't know why I ever did this to her. I don't know why I gave her up for him. Please tell her for me I love her; I want her back. Will you write her for me? If I was sick, she was there with me. She gave me strength. And now I've done this to her. Oh God . . ."

Fran, a thirty-two-year-old woman who has spent the better part of her life in jails and prisons for crimes of violence, was out of state prison four months before she met Hank. Hank had spent nearly twenty years in prison for a homicide. He had killed a man in a fight. Fran's last bit, eleven years long, was for manslaughter. She also had killed a man in a fight.

The night they met, Hank said to her: "You need a man, I need a woman. We can grow together. We can give each other the strength and support we need. We can understand each other; we both have done time and we both done hard time."

Five days later, Fran moved in with him. "Why not? We know marriages aren't made in heaven," she said. "They're made of hard work and commitment. We both need somebody. Neither one of us have nobody in this world." Within eight months, she was pregnant with his child.

This afternoon, Fran's face and eyes carry the look of an abused child. She has been sick a lot since she moved in with Hank, and he can't tolerate it. "You're not sick if you tell yourself you're not," he says. "It's all in your head. Sickness is a sign of weakness, and who the hell wants a weak woman?"

"I ought to be able to read what I want to read," she tells me in whispered tones when Hank is out of the room. "But he won't let me. If I want to read detective stories or murder novels or whatever, I have the right. I'm not ignorant. But he rips up the books if he doesn't approve of them. See my face? This didn't just happen yesterday. It happens once a day.

"I gotta get a place of my own. I hate him. I really hate him. But I loved him once. It's just I can't live with him this way. I killed a man once—I don't want to do it again . . . I just don't want to do it again. But I can't let him beat me."

Flat on her back and unable to move, Fran seems to have no alternatives. She seems totally helpless. She says she doesn't have the money to get an apartment by herself. She is on heavy medication because four days ago she tried to kill herself by slitting both wrists.

"I was so desperate. I just want to die. I just want to die. I don't want to live this way. It seems like it's been this way all my life.

"And now I've given up the only person who ever really loved me, and I don't know if it's too late to get her back. I am mentally ill, I know I am. I need help and there's no way to get it. I don't have money for a psychiatrist. But I'm sick. I've been spotting for three weeks, and I know I'm going to lose the baby."

After prison, the agony of trying to function in society again is more than many people can take. Hank's way was to imitate the power that had been used against him all his life. Twenty years in prison has made him copy the very things he hated behind prison walls. He is afraid of his smallness, his vulnerability. If he feels his authority is being challenged, he feels ashamed and enraged. He tries to make himself feel big by being a bully, by using his fists.

"In this house, I am the law," he said to me. "I will not have any outside propaganda brought into this house. If you're going to try to fill her head with that think-for-yourself shit, you are not allowed to talk to her. You'll corrupt her mind."

Fran, her face cut and bruised, her wrists and abdomen taped, looked like an accident victim. And she is, in a way. She was born into poverty, and she's never gotten past the abuse of her early years. She's still looking for the mother she never had—for the comfort she never had. The only kind of caretaker she's ever had has been powerful and abusive. She has grown accustomed to being powerless, to being helpless. While Hank chose one path, Fran chose another—both essential to the pattern, almost without conscious choice on the part of either of them.

As Fran spoke of death and her longing for her prison partner, she said, "This is the only dream I have left. I don't have any other dreams. I don't have any other hope." The only person she believed really understood her and cared for her in the loneliness of prison was the one she turned to again in a time of need. But her companion was behind bars and wouldn't be out for another two years. In the meantime, Fran wasn't allowed to write her or vice versa. The prison would let them correspond, but Hank wouldn't. He intercepted and censored all incoming mail. "I wish I could go to her," Fran said. "I'd do anything to be with her."

16   GETTING OUT

A Long and Frightening Road Home

> When you get out, it's like being all alone with no one around. You have all
>   these things on your mind with no one to talk to, not really, about all
>   the things on your mind.
> That's what pushes you to go back with the same crowd and the old drag,
>   because those people don't care what you are or aren't. You got deci-
>   sions and then you got your own identity to deal with. Whatever iden-
>   tity—artificial or not—you had before you came in here has been
>   stripped from you, and you just feel so small and exposed. You come
>   out feeling guilty and down and like nobody. Just a small nothing.
>   And everything was fucked up when you came in, but now it's really
>   fucked up.
> The hardest thing to face getting out is the decisions. For months, for years,
>   you haven't been able to decide anything for yourself. Then all of the
>   sudden, you're supposed to be able to decide everything, make every
>   kind of decision. It's just too much.
>
> —"Emma Green," parolee from the state prison
>   for women in Lansing, Kansas

"Would you believe—when I was in the county jail last time and found
out I had got bond, I cried. I fell back and grabbed hold of the bars,"
Cynthia Evans said. "I didn't want to go out in that street. It seems like a
big dark pit out there."

Cynthia Evans, a prisoner at the Ohio Reformatory for Women at
Marysville, was talking about going out again in a matter of weeks from
the prison she'd been confined in for more than two years. "I guess I'm a
little scared about going out again," she said. "It still seems like a big,

dark pit. On the one hand, I want to go out, and on the other hand, I'm scared. It's a big, cold world out there.

"I don't want to turn tricks no more. I want to go straight. I guess I'll live with my mother when I get out. But I can't talk to my mother about anything. My grandmother was the one who raised me till I was fourteen, and then I went to live with my mother. I couldn't talk to her about menstruation or pregnancy or anything. When I asked her about menstruating, she slapped me. So I tried to help myself. When I got pregnant, she was so angry, she kicked me out. So I did what I could. I didn't know anything, but I didn't quit school. I went to a home for unwed mothers. I was trying to do something halfway decent anyway.

"I just don't like to be around my mother. She leaves me alone and I leave her alone. It don't bother me. It's always been this way. She never wrote me while I was in the institution; she never came to call. In fact, sometimes I think she's glad I'm here. She's happy I'm here. I think she wants me to stay here. It's like this: I could be in a room with fifty other people and if she came in, I'd want to leave. I'd want to get out of there before she even knew I was there.

"I don't know. I don't know what I'm going to do. All I know is that when I get out I'm just going to try to raise my son and stay straight. I want to make it."

Cynthia didn't know at the time how she could support herself. She hadn't received any education or job training at Marysville that would help her find work or give her any future means of support. She didn't feel she had any alternative to living with her mother until she got herself together. She had no friends except her prison friends inside and the world of pimps and whores and people she was involved with on the outside when she was arrested—and she said she didn't want to see them again. Going back to Toledo promised nothing but loneliness and frustration.

"You're so sure you're not going back to the same crowd," Theresa Derry said. "But pretty soon you be hanging out with the same ol' crowd again, just to feel like you belong somewhere. And even though you can't get all the things off your mind, you're not quite so lonely.

"I know when I got out of there, after nearly four years away from civilization, I felt like I was walking around with a big tag on me: LOOK AT ME, I JUST CAME OUT OF PRISON. They take a city girl and put her in prison and she picks tomatoes for four years—it's oblivion—and then they send her back to the city as 'socially adjusted.' Even the bus ride back to Philadelphia scared the shit out of me—the noise and the people talking and moving around. I just shut my eyes and prayed to survive the trip.

"After I didn't see my family for so long, everything seemed so strange to me, and it was so hard to adjust. I really wanted to be a totally different person from when I had gone in. I had studied so hard. I had decided I wanted to be a registered nurse and I wanted to be a good mother. I had read so many books that I could tell you every bone in the body by name, and exactly how the circulatory system works. I came out with all these dreams and then started getting doors slammed in my face.

"Sometimes I just get so tired, I'd actually think about going back to prison. I guess I still do—just to rest, just to forget all the hassles out here. Like sometimes I just feel like I can't take the pressure any more. But I've been lucky. I have my daughter to think about and her future. She needs me. And I'm determined to do right by her."

Theresa did six years on parole and worked as a court-prison administrator for a release-on-recognizance program for women in Philadelphia jails. She still wants to enter nurse's training. But it hasn't been easy. It never is.

People getting out of prison, like soldiers returning from battle, often experience posttraumatic stress disorder. More than five hundred thousand people are released each year from state and federal penitentiaries, and most are filled with fear and the numbness of alienation, rage, guilt. Some people call it "impacted grief."

"You just come out *bam*," said Marian. "And you don't know how to deal with it. You don't have a family to go to, half the time. You don't have a home or a job. All this time you've been fantasizing about the way things are and the way things are going to be when you really have no way of knowing how they are. You can imagine the shock. A lot of times the only thing left for a person to do is commit a new crime.

"Besides that, prisons really help produce crime. You take away any human being and put them out of contact and take away all their responsibility and you're denying them an opportunity to grow. So to expect a person to leave here being grown and responsible, you're making an impossible demand, because all her sense of responsibility and her ability to interact has been brutalized.

"To deal with society you have to interact with society. We only know how to interact with one society—and that's prison society."

Ninety-eight percent of all the people sentenced to prison are eventually released. But the vast majority of these women return to prison or jail. In Los Angeles, officials say the recidivism rate exceeds 75 percent on the county jail level. At New York's Correctional Institution for Women, recidivism is 85 percent for misdemeanors. Some officials at state prisons for women say their rehabilitation programs are working for felons because recidivism rates are from 10 to 25 percent. But they are only counting the return to their particular institution from the same institution. They don't count the county jails or other state or federal prisons women have been in before or return to afterward.

There is no established method for prisons to keep track of what happens to women after they leave, unless they violate parole or return to the same prison on a new conviction. "We can't write to them, and they're not supposed to call us," said one officer. "I really worry about a lot of them. If they could just call us up when they feel like putting a needle in their arm, or if we could help them some way or just know somebody was helping them . . . But I know they're just out there in the middle of so much chaos, and they're just so alone."

Ninety percent of the women at the Federal Reformatory for Women at Alderson have histories of prior arrests. The majority have been incarcerated before. Little or no attention was paid them before when they got out of jail, nor is it paid them now when they get out of prison. Few services are provided in the community for the readjustment and reentry of prisoners, even though in the long run these services would pay for themselves in a reduction of crime and the cost of returning parolees to prison. Some ex-convicts have found that self-help groups can ease their reintegration into society by providing a supportive community. Groups such as the Fortune Society, Connections, Barbwire Society, and other ex-prisoners' organizations have made a great difference in the lives of many individuals.

But small community-based groups don't reach the great majority of prisoners released from prison. They can't begin to touch the lives of the thousands of people who are out of contact and basically alone when they leave prison gates with ten dollars—or twenty-five dollars or maybe even sixty-eight dollars—with nowhere to go and no one to go to.

For Cynthia and Theresa and a lot of other women facing release for the first time or second or fifth or tenth time, the fantasy of real freedom is tantalizing. And the fantasies are far from outrageous. They include talk of fat juicy cheeseburgers, milk shakes, pizzas, an abundance of milk and sugar, wine, comfort, a double bed and a lover, sleeping late, and doing what you want to do when you want to do it. After institutional food, starches, and food quotas as a steady diet, prisoners spend a lot of time stimulating taste buds with visions of delicious, well-prepared, and favorite foods. The idea of chitlins, beans and rice, tacos, and other home cooking can be scintillating. Also wonderful is the thought of opening your own mail, wearing what you want to wear, going where you want to go, and living each day without foghorns, bells, buzzers, and matrons giving you orders.

But the reality of being on your own and being thrown back into a big, hostile, and threatening existence where you are totally responsible is at the same time overwhelming. Taking a bus downtown can become a frightening thing. Walking into a store to buy something you need. Signing up at the unemployment bureau, looking for a job. Seeing your children again. Wondering if they've missed you as much as you've missed them, wondering if they will accept you again, forgive you for being gone. Wondering if your partner or husband will want to make things work again. Fear makes each event monstrous. Where will you live? What will you do with your freedom? Do you remember how to open a door? Being on your own should be easy—but it's not.

Getting free from prison regulations, prison life, prison food, prison lines is more liberating as a fantasy than as a reality. Disappointed expectations make reality just so much more painful, the experience more bitter.

People have come out of a prison environment in which they've been stripped of the autonomy of decisions, leadership, self-determination. Judges have sent them to that environment to be punished and "rehabilitated." Rehabilitation is by definition "to restore to the original state or form." It could be said that prison does reinforce the original state that has been normal to a person: the condition society alleges it doesn't want repeated. For many people that condition is one of real chaos and disorientation, where it is normal to be without marketable skills, education, economic resources, family support, and the habits of self-discipline, self-respect, and self-direction. It is normal to be abused, to be involved in petty crime, to get in trouble again. And it is normal to go back to jail. What's abnormal is finding a supportive and forgiving community, staying out, and making decisions based on a sense of self-worth, optimism, and the possibility of new opportunities.

At the Iowa Reformatory for Women, Superintendent Laurel Rans invited me to stay over in the cottages with the prisoners. During the time I spent at Iowa, locked into a room at night along with everyone else, I felt like a prisoner. Although Iowa's state prison was the most progressive institution I had visited, where more than half of the women are going out of the institution daily for work release or to school, I was able to experience for the first time the security of being taken care of in a cold place you don't even like. This *is* a concrete womb—and it's hard to break out, especially when you're trying to break out of a situation and a culture that have become normal to you.

"I don't know why I've been so depressed this week except maybe because I'm getting out so soon," Shirley Temple said the last night I shared her prison room in Rockwell City, Iowa. "I've been here so long—fourteen months now—and I keep wondering, How much have people changed and how will I act? Will I be able to get myself up for school, feed myself, and make it to work on time? I'm really afraid.

"I'm just so scared of going out there. I don't know. I'll have to wake myself up in the morning and get up and carry myself to work and make all my own decisions. I'll have an apartment of my own. I just don't know if I can make it. It's been so awful for the last two months. I've been thinking about things I never thought about before."

Looking at Shirley, a bouncy, smiling, black-haired woman with tattoos on her pale ivory skin—including a devil over her breast and on her arm a hummingbird perched over a rose and her name—you wouldn't think she could be so vulnerable, so afraid of being helpless. She would probably appear to the average person who saw her as fun-loving and carefree. But Shirley Temple was anxious as she contemplated living a new reality, a reality that involves responsibility and self-concern and thoughtful decisions. This new reality is not normal for her. It wasn't normal before she came to jail, and, naturally, it is not normal in jail. Her models in life, the people she loves and cares for, are part of the prison culture. Her mother is on parole, and her boyfriend and stepbrother are serving time at the men's prison in Newton, Iowa. Shirley has had a life that might seem devastating—but to her, it's what life is. Hearing her talk about old trips and highs and disastrously overlapping marriages made me cry, laugh, and experience the despair and joy of her turbulent existence.

"You talk about minorities—well, I'm a minority of one. Don't tell me about minorities," she had joked with Gloria Diggs, a close black friend, the day I met them both. You could tell it was a common topic between them. "Let me tell you, my people were suffering before your people even knew what continent they was on."

Shirley was the only Jewish woman at the prison. Her mother before her had been the only Jewish woman at the prison. She talked a lot about her mother, who ten years before had lived in the same cottage, on the same floor, in the same prison. "She ran around scrubbing floors, working on the farm. They all did farm work then. Now there's no farm. Then it was hard physically, but now it's hard mentally. She's on parole now. She'd send me anything, but she doesn't have any money herself. But I know if she had it, she would, and that's what counts."

Shirley was convicted of "receiving stolen property." "We'd broke into a factory and took the payroll," she said. "I was lucky for just getting the receiving property charge. It could have been for breaking and entering, forgery, and the whole *geshmir.*

"I know how to commit crimes badly—it's doing things straight and staying out of here that scares me. I want to be a beautician when I get out. That's what I'm in school for now. I guess I want to be one, but not really. It's just that that's what's available. What I would really like to do is just travel—travel everywhere.

"I was talking to the cottage supervisor the other day about getting my own apartment and being out on parole, and she said, 'Shirley, just remember that if things get too hard to handle, you can always call up the institution and come back until you get a hold on what you want to do.' I mean, it was like a mother saying to her daughter, 'Don't worry if things get too rough. You can always come home. This is your house.' That's what she was saying. I thought maybe she was saying she didn't think I could make it out there and that really upset me. I can always come back here, but this isn't my home! It's not! It's a prison. I gotta keep telling myself that. I really want to make it. But I really don't know what making it's all about."

In relation to many women getting out of prison in other states, Shirley was luckier than most. She was in a prison with a population of only fifty-seven women. The staff at Iowa actually spends a lot of relaxed, undirected time with prisoners. The administrator is young, friendly, and accessible to the inmates. Women are as involved with the community as possible, considering their remote location, and the disciplinary cells are used only for storage. Women can make telephone calls out from the prison on pay phones every night in order to maintain contact with their friends and families. Shirley herself was going into town daily—driven by another inmate in a state car—on a study release to learn a trade. Because she could continue her cosmetology studies at the same school when she got out, she had a link—somewhere to go and something to do that had a purpose. With the training and a license that was assured upon graduation, she'd be able to be self-supporting, self-sufficient.

But for Shirley, going into a new, unknown reality was frightening. The challenge of living with all that responsibility and self-empowerment—and staying away from the ever present temptation of a retreat into drugs—felt like facing a pit of hungry alligators with no visible way out.

I'm sure most people can make comparisons in their own lives: the decision to leave a marriage that is unhappy and unhealthy but that has somehow become comfortable; the decision to take a new job or move to a new community; the decision to begin to live a new way you know little about—all are frightening. And the biggest stumbling block to doing what you feel you want to do is fear.

For the majority of women in prison, the outside world has always represented hostility and chaos, disorganization that seems normal. Imagine yourself facing the possibility of finding a place to live and a way to earn money when you have only subway fare and all your worldly goods in a paper bag. You have no more money, no home, and nowhere to go, and you're let out of a bus in the middle of New York City at four o'clock in the afternoon. Or out of Rahway's city jail at ten past midnight. This is the reality for many women getting out of jail and prison.

Or imagine that you have been in prison in California or in Michigan or in Massachusetts for eight years. You haven't crossed a street or seen an escalator or driven a car in all the time you've been locked up. You've been unable to make small decisions about sleeping late, getting up early, taking a walk, singing out loud, or choosing your own job. You have been used to standing for count, obeying nonsense orders, being strip-searched after every time you've had a visit, eating food you may or may not like, sleeping on lumpy mattresses, being punished for trivial matters, being treated with contempt, being kept waiting for the smallest request.

Then you leave the prison with sixty-eight dollars to support yourself until you can find a place to settle again. If you're lucky, you might leave some penitentiaries after fifteen years with fifty dollars in savings to help you start your life again—and don't forget, you have neither marketable skills nor more than a tenth-grade education. In addition, you have a prison record. These are common realities to people getting out of prison—women and men alike.

Even with the rare blessing of financial security or the support of family and friends, adjusting to the outside again is no easy thing. One ex-inmate, Dorothy Day, described the experience:

> I had not expected that when I came out of jail I would feel so exhausted mentally, physically, and spiritually. The impact of the world and its problems is crushing, numbing and painful, at the same time. It is hard to rise in the morning to the "duties of one's state in life." . . .
>
> One comes out from jail into a world where everyone has problems, all but insoluble problems, and the first thing that strikes me is that the world today is almost worse than jail. Looking at newspapers, listening to the radio, even watching the activities of children, and fearfully thinking of what they have to look forward to in the way of education, work and war, I am appalled.
>
> If we who think are sensitive to this, the average ex-prisoner is sensitive in a different way. He comes out a marked man, with the eye of the law upon him.[1]

Three days after her release from the North County Holding Facility in Palo Alto, California, Angela Davis was drinking coffee in the home of a

1. "Thoughts after Prison," *Liberation,* September 1957.

friend in the Bay Area and feeling the exhausting effects of her release. "It's hard to believe how tired I am," she told me. "But I'm just physically exhausted from moving around in spaces bigger than a cell, let alone everything else. I really forgot what it's like. I guess it will take me a while to adjust to being able to move around freely—and even to get used to seeing the sunshine again.

"The last three days we've just been moving so fast . . . I can't take it all in at once. I really can't believe that it's all happening and that I'm really here."

Angela Davis had been in jails for sixteen and a half months awaiting trial on capital charges of murder, kidnapping, and criminal conspiracy in connection with the deaths of a judge and two prisoners in a Marin County courtroom. The state of California alleged that the guns used in the incident had been registered in her name. At her trial, she was found innocent of all charges. But the effect of her imprisonment without bail reflected a presumption of guilty until proven innocent.

During her long months of imprisonment, Angela had been transferred to different jails and usually confined to one cell during the day, where she had her books and legal materials. In Palo Alto, where I had met with her, there was barely room for me to sit down in her tiny cell. During the night she slept either in the same cell or in an adjoining one. She wasn't allowed to go outdoors for exercise or sunshine, nor was she allowed to "mingle freely" with other inmates in the institution. Only a court order won her the right not to be locked in solitary confinement under armed guard—even though she was innocent in the eyes of the law.

She shared with other detentioners throughout the country the anxiety and uncertainty of when she would go to trial, the jolt of unexpected transfers from one jail to another, and the lingering, unsettling possibility of not being released on bail.

The day before she finally got out on $102,500 bail, she sat in a gray sweater, pink prison smock, and warm woolen socks in her cramped, antiquated cell packed with her books, cartons of papers, and legal materials. The squalor of the physical conditions was in sharp contrast to her dignity and profound calm. The loneliness she had experienced in spite of so much overwhelming support from the outside seemed apparent.

"I don't want to get too excited about the possibility of getting bail," she said. "They say they're sure this time, but they've been sure before. I'm hoping, but it's too disappointing when it doesn't happen, so I can't afford to count on it." She was released the next day, February 28, 1972, five days after the California Supreme Court ruled the death penalty unconstitutional. Bail had been denied her up to that time on the grounds that persons accused of capital offenses are not entitled to bail.

Until Angela Davis's imprisonment, many people in the general society weren't even aware that women were jailed in this country. Many more people weren't aware that so many people accused of breaking a law are imprisoned while awaiting their trials. The support, and of course the counterreaction to the support, came in massive proportions.

Angela Davis knew, for instance, that literally thousands of letters were coming in for her every day from people in this country and from other countries throughout the world. "The mail I get overwhelms me," she said. "It's really moving. I want to answer each letter, but I can't." (She didn't receive most of the letters while she was in jail because officials said there were "too many letters for such a limited staff to sort and censor.")

But even with love, support, and understanding through sixteen and a half months, Angela Davis's sudden victory of being released on bail still entailed adjustment—physical, emotional, and mental. Lights, colors, space, conversation, interaction, friends, demands—all required reorientation. And the scars of those many nights, and many nightmares in shared human experiences and frailty, can never be erased by her acquittal.

Ericka Huggins, a close friend of Angela's, touched on many nuances of imprisonment so difficult to verbalize when she wrote from Niantic Prison in Connecticut in 1970:

> noises
> sounds
> unspoken words
> feelings repressed because
>   the prison walls are also
>   soul walls
>   barriers
> if only all barriers could be removed
>   and we could walk/talk/sing
>   be . . .
> free of all psychological, spiritual
>   political, economic
>   boundaries
> all of us all the freedom lovers of
>   the world but especially
>   right now—prisoners[2]

"Getting out isn't easy for anyone," said "Yvonne Williams," a woman I spent many hours talking with at the state prison for women in

2. Reprinted from Angela Y. Davis and Other Political Prisoners, *If They Come in the Morning,* © 1971 by Signet Books.

Iowa. She had served two sentences at the prison, and this time she was back on a parole violation for possession of narcotics. "But it's not just getting adjusted to the world again, it's getting adjusted to the people you care about. No matter how much understanding you have, two years later it's different. The stem of love might still be there, but it's branched off in different directions.

"Like with Ronnie and me, we loved each other deep for more than eighteen years now. He's a pimp and I'm a whore, but we love each other our own way and that counts. But to put it simple, we're victims of a system. If I'm ever gonna get out of here, I have to get a divorce from Ronnie to get out of here. The parole board they think he's a bad influence on me and if it wasn't for him I wouldn't have started using drugs in the first place. Before I got out the last time I filed for a divorce to satisfy the parole board. He's in Iowa City and he wanted to see me, naturally. But we had to sneak. I didn't think I should have to sneak to see my husband.

"They gave me a furlough once to see my kids and they asked, 'Is Ronnie going to be there?' Of course he was there. But we had to get a hotel room and sneak, 'cause I'd had to say I wouldn't be seeing him. Meanwhile the police had seen me get off the bus, and they called the institution to say Ronnie had been there to meet me—but I didn't know that until I got back. The police can do that; they know who we are.

"Anyway, I hadn't been to bed with any dude for fifteen months and I didn't know how to react. He didn't know how to react to my not reacting. We had got a hotel room and I had to go up after he did. We just sat there. We didn't know what to say. I wanted to make love to him and he wanted to make love to me, but we didn't know what to do. We finally did make love, but just did that. I could have done better with a trick. We talked about it afterward, but we couldn't figure it out. When I got out on parole, we still had to sneak to see each other. Imagine, having to sneak to see your own husband. So I got out there on parole, shot up, and forgot everything.

"It seems like if they cared, the institution would have involvement in relationships, like provide marriage counseling or home furloughs together—not like just split up the whole thing. I don't know how I'm going to keep from seeing him when I get out this time, unless I move to a different state. I guess that's what I'm going to have to do if I want to make it. I love the dude too much."

"Association" is one of the most noxious of restrictions placed on people released on parole. "Association" means that the parolee is not allowed to communicate with any person who also has a prison record, nor with any person specifically named "undesirable" under conditions of parole. A violation of the rule means return to prison on a parole violation for the duration of the sentence. For many people this restriction means that they are not able to associate with any of their old friends and buddies, even if the other ex-prisoner has a clean record.

This parole restriction, along with many others—such as the denial of the vote, curfews, restrictions on going into any establishment where alcohol is served—discourage newly released persons from participating in activities routinely performed by other people involved in the community around them. While it makes sense for prisoners not to hang out in bars or crack houses, many parole restrictions are counterproductive when they deny natural access to supportive friends and community members who can foster involvement and reintegration into the social structure of the community. People meet other people at political or community meetings, at parties, but these experiences usually are unavailable to the parolee. Parole officers, who are overburdened with cases, also are thrust into the dual and sometimes conflicting roles of counselor and policeman. If more support were offered for creative intervention on the part of parole officers, they would be able to maintain closer contact with parolees and manage to do more than only enforce violations, which is the case all too often. Enforcing violations without having the complete picture is a waste of resources and public funds.

I met many people in prison who were there for a parole violation based on "association" with another ex-convict on the outside—even when no criminal activity was involved. Perhaps the most ludicrous example was a man who had gotten married and started farming after he got out of prison. One day a horseman came by with a fine horse, and the man bought it. "I'd always wanted to have a horse, and it was a real dream come true," he told me. When his parole officer learned who had sold him the horse, however, he wrote a violation that sent the farmer back to prison for "association," because the seller also had a felony record. "The deal was aboveboard," Number 37846 said, shaking his head in the prison corridor. "I had no idea he'd ever been in the rack before. I don't suppose I had talked to him more than two or three times total." Records substantiated his story—also the stories of women returned to prison for living with a man they weren't married to, or "associating" with the "wrong" crowd or getting pregnant when they weren't legally married.

The conditions of parole leave a lot of room for subjective interpretation that may or may not have to do with public safety. Parole conditions for women leaving the Concord-Framingham Houses of Correction, in Massachusetts, specify:

1. I will remain at liberty without violating the law.

2. I will be honorable in all respects, work diligently at a lawful occupation and support my dependents, if any, to the best of my ability.

3. I will abstain from the use of intoxicating liquors and narcotics of all kinds and will not frequent places where they are dispensed. I will receive permission from my Parole Officer before working in a place where liquor is sold.

4. I will not associate with persons of questionable character, nor with anyone on parole, nor with any person having a criminal record.

5. I will not leave the State of Massachusetts without permission of the Parole Board.

6. I will not leave my employment nor change my place of residence without permission of the Parole Board.

7. I will make a full and truthful report to the Parole Board, State Office Building, Boston, Mass., once each week for the first month, and thereafter once each month until the expiration of my sentence.

8. I will submit to medical treatment if ordered to do so by the Parole Board.

9. I will not marry without the permission of the Parole Board, nor without informing my intended partner of my parole status.

10. I will not live with any person of the opposite sex to whom I am not lawfully married.

11. I will not make application for a license to hunt, or to drive a motor vehicle without the permission of the Parole Board.

12. I will not correspond with inmates confined in any Correctional Institutions without permission of the Parole Board.[3]

"Making it out there ain't no easy thing, honey," an older woman told me, her hands shaking slightly as she lit her cigarette with the burning stub of her last smoke. "We're as good as lepers out there. Tell somebody you just got out of the joint and they run like hell, 'fraid you'll grab their wad or something. Tell you the truth, tell you like it is—it's a hell of a lot easier in here. At least I know when I'm gonna eat. The most for-real people you gonna meet are right in here with me. That's the truth, that's the truth. They'll admit they're nobody. They'll admit they're scared, they're just what they are. And that makes 'em somebody in my books."

The onus of a criminal record can seem haunting, never ending. When Fran Blackwell asked to go to Florida on vacation from Pennsylvania, for instance, her parole officer required that she give him the exact time she would enter each state as she and her mother drove south. Parole stipula-

3. The Parole Board reserves the right to make exceptions to the above rules or to impose additional conditions in any case.

tions required that each state and city she passed through be informed of her entry. She had to carry papers showing her "criminal status" at all times. "It would be one thing if you could do your time and be finished with it," Fran said. "But they never let you out, it's never really over."

One of the most painful stigmas attached to being in and then getting out is that of having been a "bad" mother, if for nothing more than being separated from your children. In some cases, mothers pay a double penalty for their crimes, when they not only serve their time but also lose custody of their children. According to law professor Philip M. Genty at Columbia Law School, "Permanent loss of parental rights during imprisonment can occur when a child is in the custody of the state and the state brings a judicial proceeding to terminate the parent's rights permanently. Once a woman has lost her parental rights, she also loses all right to have contact with her child, and the child can be adopted without the parent's knowledge or consent." A mother who wants to retain her rights as a parent while she's in prison and to regain custody upon leaving prison must stay closely involved with her children and the social service agency responsible for them. But Genty points out that parents in prison face obstacles to maintaining contact—and they also lack access to court proceedings involving their children.

In New York City alone, nearly 250,000 children have mothers in jail or prison. While their mothers are incarcerated, the children have had to live with their grandparents or aunts and uncles or with other relatives or friends—or they have lived through the often stressful experience of staying in foster homes or juvenile shelters. Sometimes, but not as often, children have stayed with their father while their mother is in prison. But in most cases when a woman gets out, she doesn't have an intact family to which she can return. Among female and male inmates with children under eighteen, 25 percent of the women reported in a 1993 survey that their children were living with their other parent, as compared to nearly 90 percent of the men. Nearly half of the children of women in state and federal prisons live with their grandparents, according to a Bureau of Justice Statistics report in 1994. More than half of the children never get to see their mother while she's incarcerated. Twenty percent see their mother less than once a month, 18 percent see their mother once a month, and 8 percent see her once a week.

Going "home"—and going back to your children—means starting life together all over again, but with the burden of having been absent for crucial periods of your child's life. When mothers get out, they can't help carrying a lot of guilt and anxiety with them—sometimes because of the lack of emotional security they gave their children prior to their incarceration, and always because of not being able to "be there" for their children while they were in prison. Children, who can't help feeling angry, worried, and abandoned by their mother, have their own resentments and adjustments to deal with when their mother comes home. They've had to manage and struggle without her. And sometimes they're afraid of getting to know her again, afraid they'll feel secure again and that then she'll "disappear" again. The separation and the reunification cause deep strains and fears in both mothers and children.

"It really knocks me out to realize that I'm actually afraid of my own children," Victoria said. "I'm really afraid of them. I don't know what to do. I don't know how to act. I'm literally afraid of being a mother. Here I am, thirty-six years old with four beautiful children, and one day I realize I'm afraid of being a mother. I don't know what to say to them when I'm with them, what to do. I feel paralyzed and helpless. Really, sometimes I feel I don't even *like* them. Like I resent them being my children."

Little is done within most prisons or upon release to help women deal with motherhood—or with reacquainting them with their older children or their babies. In 1995 only three state prisons in the country allow newborn babies to stay with their mothers until they are one year old.[4] A couple of other prisons allow a stay of one month or allow a new mother to visit her baby before the baby is released to a relative or to a foster home, but most don't. Bedford Hills Correctional Institution and the Taconic Correctional Facility, both in New York, and the Nebraska State Prison for Women run these nursery facilities for infants born to imprisoned women. Their programs have prenatal education for the mothers, as well as units for thirty nursing mothers who can live with their children for up to eighteen months. Postnatal and parenting classes are held for these mothers, and the average stay for babies is one year. (Sometimes babies and moms get to leave prison together.)

Despite the well-established fact that the first year of life is critical to the bond between mother and child, no other prisons or jails in the entire United States allow incarcerated women to keep their newborns with them. This is true despite the fact that nearly one of every ten women who enter prison is pregnant. Most of these young mothers are separated from their babies within twenty-four to forty-eight hours after giving birth to

4. In Jean Harris's extraordinary books on her life in prison at Bedford Hills, New York's maximum security prison for women, she writes in moving detail about the Children's Center there, and about mothers' relationships with their children. Bedford Hills also has parenting classes and a summer program, which is extremely important for children and their mothers.

them. Instead of being able to hold their babies, nurse, and bond with them, most of these new mothers—who often are handcuffed or shackled to their hospital beds during labor for "security reasons"—are sent under guard right back to their prison cells. Some are given vaginal exams when they return to the prison—a cruel nod toward security.

Some supportive programs that facilitate the visits of children to their mothers in prison are currently being developed in other states, but the vast majority of mothers in prison get very little if any help with getting to see or staying in close contact with their children.

When a woman gets out of prison, she faces not only the trauma of finding a place to live and suitable work or economic support but also this trauma of being reunited with her children. It's what she's dreamed of, but it's terrifying. Some women who were in deep trouble before they went to prison neglected their children because of drugs, alcoholism, or prostitution. Some had their children stay with friends or relatives because they didn't want them exposed to what they were doing. Many never have had good mothering themselves, so they have no "mother model" to return with from jail, even though they love their children deeply and want to be effective, responsible mothers. The complications of bitter prison experience obviously don't help, nor do the uncertainties of what has been going on in the foster home or happening to the child while the mother is imprisoned.

For "Geraldine Johnson," who was at Muncy for more than two years after being in jail for a year awaiting trial, being with her children again was overwhelming. When she got out for a four-day furlough to visit her children, she was angry and afraid: angry at the foster parents she had met only once, after more than a year of trying to locate them; angry because it would be so hard for her to get her children back when she did get out; and afraid of how hard it would be to find a place to live and a job. She was afraid of what she would find, but she was excited to see her babies again. She loved them, carried their pictures around with her, and thought about them every day. Actually seeing them, however, was devastating.

"They didn't even know who I was," she told me. "The foster mother had them calling *her* Mother! She hadn't told them anything about me. When I got locked up Kathy was three months old and Linda was eighteen months old. My in-laws had kept the kids, but they didn't want Linda, so they had her staying with a friend and they kept Kathy. So while I was at the House of Correction, I had them removed from my in-laws and put into a foster home. Linda's my heart; I've been through some hard ups and downs, and my baby came through it all with me.

"I wrote letters to them through the DPW [Department of Public Welfare] caseworker. But I didn't find out where they lived for more than two years—and when I did it was only because my friend Terry started hooking things up for me to come home on furlough, and she traced down where they were.

"The woman in the foster family has tried to instill herself as a mother figure. But she can never be the true mother figure 'cause she's not their mother. I resent her because she lets 'em run around and call her 'Mommy.' She could say, 'I love you, but I'm not your mommy.' It's not fair to me.

"Nobody else could do the divine act of bringing Kathy and Linda into the world. There is no other Kathy and Linda and there is no other me. I'm their only mother. I can't tell you how much it tore me up for them not to know me when they saw me."

Geraldine ended her furlough of four days by slitting her wrists. The suicide attempt was unsuccessful, though, and she returned to the prison to face a staff and parole board who felt she was too unstable, after this incident, to be released on the date she previously had been given. At the present time, she is out of prison. She's had her share of troubles readjusting, but she was finally able to get a job, prove she was a "fit" mother, and get her children back. She has had custody of her children for more than a year. Often the mere fact that a woman has been arrested and sentenced to a jail or prison term in the first place, even when it's a first offense, has been the grounds for the court to declare her "unfit." Women say the legal processes they have to go through with the court to prove they are "fit" mothers again are as excruciating as their original trial.

The lack of counseling or concern available for prisoners rejoining their families is indicative of the low priority given by society to their struggles as individuals. Yet, without support, women will find going back to drugs or crime an obvious temptation. The onus of a criminal record makes it only that much more difficult for a person who's been imprisoned to find work or fit comfortably back into any legal and financially secure life.

Often when women come home, they learn about or witness major problems that their children have experienced because of their absence. The least of those problems can be that children of prisoners have been the target of teasing by schoolmates aware of their mother's background. The stigma of being a criminal is carried into every corner of society, no matter how normal going to prison is. "Your mother's a jailbird," or "Your mother's a you-know-what." Children have great fun "playing the dozens" on other children's mothers. The greatest problem, however, is that the child misses having his or her mother around. Anger and shame gets mixed up with the love the child feels because the child has to grow up without that parent. And for a child, even one year can seem like a lifetime.

Even if a child gets to visit his or her mother in prison, the visits are usually rare and far between. And even if a mother writes or calls often, it's not the same as having her home. The child may know his mother wants to be with him, but that hasn't put her at his bedside when he's crying himself to sleep or when he needs to talk to her about a problem. She's not there to provide the special understanding and care mothers reserve for their children. The reality is that the child's mother is gone, and the child has been left alone and "rejected"—no matter whose fault that is.

"I haven't seen my kids for six weeks," Joanne B. told interviewers for the National Council on Crime and Delinquency (NCCD) in 1993. "I write almost every day. But when I call, my mother-in-law won't let me talk to them. Sometimes she hangs up on me. I know my kids aren't happy. The oldest one (age six) is acting up at day care and throwing fits. The youngest (age four) cries at night because I'm not there."

Few prisons in the 1990s allow children to visit their mothers overnight or for a weekend, but those that do so are encouraging parent-child bonding and a family structure that ultimately may help forge a better sense of security and self-worth in these children. Also, women who have strong bonds with their children have more reason to stay out of prison once they get out. The more frequently mothers and children can visit in a child-oriented environment, the better.

As I mentioned previously, an extensive parenting and child-focused program at Bedford Hills, the maximum security prison for women in New York, allows children to visit their mothers on Saturdays or Sundays between 9:30 A.M. and 3:30 P.M. every weekend of the year, and every day during those hours for at least one week during the summer when the children live with host families in Westchester County. During these visits, mothers get to stay in touch with the day-to-day concerns of their children. They get to help their school-age kids with their homework and talk to them about their friends, their fears, their accomplishments. These relationships bloom because they have enough time to do so, and the visits nurture and reinforce close connections between mothers in prison and their children.

At the state prison for women in Nebraska a model child-care program allows a mother to have her children stay with her once a month for an eight-hour period, and once every three months for seventy-two consecutive hours. In the 1993 NCCD study, however, only one of ten of the women surveyed got to visit with her child at least once a week, whereas an equal number got to see their children every four to six months. This is not nearly enough time together to maintain a normal bond. Fifty-four percent of the mothers NCCD interviewed in eight states were *never* able to see their children while they were in prison—mostly because of the distance between the children and the correctional facility and also because of the reluctance of the children's caretaker to let the children visit.[5]

Perhaps one of the worst hurdles for a woman getting out of prison is her self-blame, her internalization of the disapproval and contempt she's experienced from others. She's disappointed in herself and afraid of failing. Leaving the harsh reality of prison to master her old environment and become self-sufficient and strong for her children sometimes seems impossible, especially when she feels deep inside that she's a misfit. The singer Billie Holiday described the burden of accumulated grief and anxiety that so many women leaving prison carry with them when they go:

> Things had happened to me that no amount of time could change or heal. I had gone to jail when I was ten because a forty-year-old man had tried to rape me. Sure, they had no more business putting me in that Catholic Institution than if I'd been hit by a damn truck. But they did. Sure, they had no business punishing me, but they did. For years I used to dream about it and wake up hollering and screaming. My God, it's terrible what something like this does to you. It takes years and years to get over it; it haunts you and haunts you.
>
> Getting booked and busted again didn't help, either. I might explain the first rap was a freak accident. But the second was tougher. For years it made me feel like a damn cripple. It changed the way I looked at everything and everybody. There was one chance I couldn't take. I couldn't stand any man who didn't know about the things that had happened to me when I was a kid. And I was leery of any man who could throw those things back at me in a quarrel. I could take almost anything, but My God, not that. I didn't want anyone around me who might ever hold this over me or even hint that on account of it he was a cut above me.[6]

In addition to taking responsibility for their crimes and the situations they've created for their children, women in prison often take responsibility for the harm done them as well. Theresa Derry said she's seen many women accept guilt for things they had never done, but rather had been done to them. "It's like, if they treat me this way, I must be bad, or there must be something wrong with me," she said. "They don't stop to wonder if there isn't something wrong with the people who are treating them this way!

"You'd be surprised how many of the women were raped by their fa-

---

5. Barbara Bloom and David Steinhart, "Why Punish the Children?" 1993.
6. Billie Holiday, *Lady Sings the Blues*, pp. 122–23.

thers, their mother's boyfriend, or their uncle when they were young,''
Theresa said. "I was shocked by how many had either been raped or got
vicious beatings a lot when they were young. It cut across all classes—
upper class, middle class, lower class. It wasn't just people from ghetto
areas, like some people might think. It was all classes. I had known from
friends of mine what happened to them, but this was across the board. I
kept interviewing women at the House of Correction and I kept being
shocked at the numbers.

"What's even more shocking is that they seem to accept the guilt for
what happened to them. Take 'Bodine'—you know her. She was raped by
her father when she was twelve. And look what she went straight to when
she got out of jail—a pimp. You'd think that would be the last person
she'd go to. But she's putting her daughter in the same situation she was
in, where the same thing could happen to her daughter as happened to her.
You'd think that's the last thing she'd do. But she assumes the guilt for
her father having raped her, and then she goes straight to a pimp.

"It doesn't make sense, but people seem to go back to the same thing
that messed them up in the first place. They seem to create the same
environment they came from—sort of like to keep themselves fucked up
so they'll be comfortable. I don't understand it. I just know it works that
way. They ought to want to change conditions, but they'll do their
damnedest to maintain it.''

I also saw many examples of these truths: women whose abusive parents
or grandparents raised them who were now giving their own children to
the same people to care for; drug addicts whose fathers or mothers had
been addicted to alcohol; people who were neglected and who now were
neglecting their own children. It seems a vicious cycle—a chain with few
broken links.

The American Correctional Association conducted a survey in 1990
that found that over half of the women in prison surveyed were victims of
physical abuse, and 36 percent had been sexually abused. These figures
are conservative. Rhea Schnaeman of the New York Correctional Association said she asked a drug counselor who worked daily with eighty women
how many he thought had been sexually abused. He told her he could tell
her how many had *not* been abused: there were five. His observation would
seem to be confirmed by a Massachusetts study, where researchers found
that when childhood physical and sexual abuse and adult rape and battery
were combined, fully 88 percent of the women in prison had experienced
at least one form of violent assault.[7]

7. Meda Chesney-Lind, "Patriarchy, Prisons, and Jails: A Critical Look at Trends in Women's
Incarceration."

"I think it's much easier for a man to get over the stigma of being a con than a woman when she gets out," said Fran Chrisman. "A man has broken a law—a social law. But a woman has violated both social and moral laws in the eyes of the public, and sometimes in herself, and the stigma is there. Granted, we have some advantages. Like when I filled out job application forms I could put 'housewife' to explain where I'd been for the last fifteen years, where a man can't get away with that. But that stigma, once people know, is always there. When we go out speaking, a man who is a former murderer or armed robber can get through to the audience, who accept him because now he's made it or it's part of his past he's overcome. But when I get up to speak, you can cut the hostility with a knife. They hear I was a prostitute and they project, 'There goes that tramp.' They just won't cut it loose. It's like I've committed a moral crime against them as well as a social crime."

Theresa Derry said, "When you forget all about the stigmas, it's still a hell of a thing to just plain come out of a prison, out of captivity, into society. Even if you had a model prison in every other way, you still have three basic elements that are destructive. You're in captivity, you have a laid-out system, and lack of freedom. These three things will destroy anyone, and you can't get around it. I've tried to imagine a model prison. But no prison can be made right. The only way is no prisons at all.

"You take the wildest beast in the jungle and put him in a cage and then take him out and put him back in the jungle, and he can't survive. You've destroyed his automatic defense."

A lot of ex-prisoners just never make it back. Like old prizefighters, they keep punching but never really get on their feet again. A lot of addicts never learn to love themselves or stop destroying themselves for what's been done to them. There's some kind of invisible line, though, where a person leaves the environment that so mutilated her and takes up the task herself. She has been victimized and then continues the process; it's true to some degree in all of us. Prison is another abusive parent, another suicide trip for some people who for so many reasons have given up their will to struggle for freedom.

But like anything and everything else, we don't look for alternatives when we don't know they exist. We all need to examine and explore other realities, especially other possibilities to get ourselves out of the bondage in which we find ourselves.

More than anything else, our prison system is America's vast wasteland. Besides being inhumane, racist, sexist, and destructive as a matter of public policy, it's a wasteland for human energy and creativity and growth. I only have to think of the life of one individual—and there are thousands—to know the enormity of the human tragedy we call the criminal justice system. Its effects made their fatal marks on Katie Haley, whose life was laced with the mutilating process of institutionalization from the time she was a young girl charged with a discriminatory status offense. Katie is one of many people who come to mind when I think of the futility of trying to solve social, economic, and medical problems through incarceration.

Katie and I met at the Sybil Brand Institute for Women in Los Angeles, just one month before her release from jail after a stay of one and a half years. She hoped this time would be the last. She had tried to make it on the outside before. She wanted this trip home to have a different ending.

"The first time I came in here was for eighteen months—November '67 to May '69," Katie said as she sat in a visiting booth across from me in the "attorney room." "When I was here I was schooled in work, the illegal kind. It was the first time I'd ever been to an adult jail. I was hearing all these stories . . . I learned about the streets and how to survive without legally working. I didn't have a trade and I couldn't get a job, so when I got out I couldn't seem to adjust after doing all that time. I didn't know the first thing to do when I got out.

"I didn't know I had to lie on questionnaires or anything like that. I was super naïve. I still had a little of the home training, and it never occurred to me to lie. The questionnaire would say, 'Have you ever been arrested?' 'Yes.' 'What for?' I'd write it down, and there went the job. So I started doing what I had learned in here to survive. This time they gave me one year for second-degree robbery."

Katie—a tall and attractive twenty-nine-year-old woman with deep brown skin and curly black hair held on top of her head by a bright yellow bow—studied my face and her hands for a while. "Now I'm getting PBX [telephone switchboard] training. I just want to go to work somewhere. The main thing, I don't want to go from place to place getting turned down. I'm afraid that if I go job hunting, the rejections will tear down the defenses I'm trying so hard to build up and I'll eventually just say to hell with it. It would be easier if the institution could get jobs for you so they'd know already you'd been in jail. Then I wouldn't have to be worrying about if they'll be running a check on me, or how long I can work before they find out."

More than just worrying about a job and financial future, Katie also had to worry about her five children. At the time, her sons, nine and ten years old, were staying with Katie's mother. Her three daughters—ages four, five, and six—were in a foster home together.

"In '67, they were all together. They found a home for all five of them in Altadena. That was the only way I'd have it. I wouldn't sign the papers for them to go to a foster home unless they guaranteed they would be in the same home. I didn't want them separated. It had just been me and the kids. All they had was each other. When I got out in '69, the first thing in my mind was I wanted my babies. So I go out and get 'em. Then I went down and applied for welfare.

"The welfare department said I would have to fill out an application and wait ninety days for the papers to be processed. I said, 'Hey, what will my babies eat for ninety days?' They said, 'Sorry, it's just a lot of red tape.' I said, 'Well, hey, my babies can't eat red tape.' So I called my mother and asked her if she could keep them. She said she could keep the boys, and then I called the foster home where they'd been and asked them could they keep my girls till I got on my feet. It kind of tore me up to have to get rid of 'em. I started tripping and all different forms of escape.

"This time I have definitely decided my kids are gonna stay where they are at least until next summer. I get out in March, and I'm not going to try to take all the responsibility at one time. I'll build up slowly. I'll have the kids once a week. Then I'll try to take them over the weekend and build up that way.

"The foster father has got awfully attached to my baby. She was only six months old when she went there. They wanted to adopt her. No. She's the last child I can have. Those are my babies, that's me. That's a part of me.

"I got a pretty good idea of what direction I want to go in, but I always had strict schedules to follow. Now I'm afraid I've built up so much resentment against having to do certain things at certain times in certain places that I won't want any routine. Sometimes I have mixed emotions about going home. At times I can hardly wait. Other times I'm a little scared. Plus I'm afraid to live with my mother. She pressures me too much, and I just go off. My mother's the kind, she's overpossessive. She stifles me. She's the 'I told you so' kind—always putting my past up to me.

"But I have to live with her. The county says so. If she wasn't here, the county would provide a place, but as long as you have a relative, there's some kind of rule that you have to live with them. It was when I was under that pressure before, with all those disappointments, that I started using dope. The main reason was to forget, to escape. I'm not worried about using it again, though. The thought of it makes me sick. I wasn't even aware I was addicted until I was busted, 'cause I was with people who was dealing, so it never entered my mind since I always had a supply. I really didn't know what was happening until I was in that jail cell getting sick.

For five days and nights I kicked cold turkey. It really turned me off. I don't think you could pay me to get down. When I listen to broads talk about highs I can only relate to the sickness. I can't stand pain. That's a funny thing about me. In 1960 I had a nervous breakdown and tried to kill myself. Yet I don't like pain.''

One of the things that haunted Katie was what kind of relationships she would have with women and men when she got out. In jail she found comfort with other women of a kind she hadn't found with male lovers on the outside. The only times she had been involved in lesbian relationships were when she was in all-female institutions, starting as a youngster.

"As a teenager I was in and out of Juvenile Hall," she said. "The first thing I wanted to do when I reached age was to get married—I didn't care to who—and have a baby. What this was—and I didn't figure it out until last year—was I was afraid I had homosexual tendencies. I didn't want to admit it. This wanting to have a baby was my way of saying, 'Look at me, world, I'm normal.'

"I had only had affairs with other women. Actually I didn't start having bisexual relations until I was nineteen, and then when I started having relations with men, that was only 'cause I wouldn't admit I dug women. So I was walking down the street pregnant, with a big belly, saying, 'See, I'm normal.'

"Now I completely accept my likes and dislikes, but I got my kids to consider. I've been married twice. The first time it was a big love thing, but it turned out later he was already married, so our marriage was annulled. The second time it was an older man. A forty-two-year-old disabled veteran. He loved my kids and he was one hundred percent government compensation. He was also supposed to be divorced. Would you believe, he was married, too. Time and time again I tried working out a marriage thing and it just didn't work.

"Then the guy I was going with before I came in here this time—Eddie. I had told him I knew he'd have to sleep with someone while I was gone, but please to go to her house or to a motel, not to my house. I didn't want them fucking in my bed or in my room or in my house. Well, he was coming up here every week and everything was just fine. Then one time for about four weeks he didn't come up or write. Then this broad came in who kept looking at me. Finally she said, 'Those pictures in Eddie's bedroom are yours, aren't they.' That was kind of a mindblower. She told everyone about how she had been living with Eddie, and I just about went off. What got me was that he lied to me, not so much he had done it. 'Cause when he had started coming up again, I had asked him if he had stayed away 'cause he was seeing someone else, and he had lied to me.

"This is another reason I have more feeling for women than I do for men. They're more understanding. They can hurt, too, but you can trust 'em more than men. Eddie still comes up and brings me money for cigarettes, but it's not the same. I really had thought I was in love with him.

"The most for-real people I have ever met are broads in here. They're not shallow, they're not surface. There are so few people that know where their head is and where they're coming from. When I'm in here I keep wondering, where they be hiding in the free world? I'd like to find their hiding place.

"There are good people here, but at the same time, jail can make a person so vicious and so violent. It's nauseating. Sometimes I lay in my bed and think about how I've changed. It's unbelievable. But it's mandatory to survive. It's dog eat dog. It's a true statement.

"If I could have any wish I wanted, I'd have money on my books and take off in an opposite direction from anybody I know. I wouldn't have my mother or Eddie come pick me up. I dread them being here when I get out. I'd leave by myself, if I had the money, and stay clear of them."

Katie realized that most of her problems started as a young girl. "I was mostly runaway and incorrigible," she said of herself. "Here the majority start getting in trouble when they're older.

"But I wouldn't really be running away. My mother was so strict on me, the only way I could get out was to crawl through the bathroom window. Naturally she'd call the police, and they'd pick me up and take me to Juvenile Hall. She used to gamble quite a bit. She'd leave the house, and I'd wake up and she wouldn't be there. At first I was scared. Then when I got older, I took advantage of it. I'd go to a football game or to my girlfriend's or to a party. She'd come home and if I wasn't there, she'd call the police."

It never ceases to amaze me how children accept the horrible, primitive things parents do as natural, as normal. And how so many of us live out our lives as adults never understanding or examining the total process, never looking at how we are affected today by what happened yesterday. It is horrifying that if a mother can't deal with her child or doesn't know how to relate to her, she would call the police. But to Katie's mother, I'm sure, it made perfect sense. It was as natural a response from her perspective as it was for the mother of another friend of mine who told me she feels safer when her son is in jail. "At least I don't have to worry about him," she says. "I don't have to wonder where he is or if he's all right. I know he's getting fed."

Katie wasn't criticizing her mother at all. She simply was relating what had happened, accepting the reality of it as part of life. Just like everyone's world—no matter how "different" it is.

As we talked, and as the hours went on, it seemed that somehow Katie and I were old friends, finally getting to talk after not seeing each other for the last five years, or maybe the last five weeks. Our time came abruptly to an end, though, when the deputy sheriff told us visiting hours were up.

"I wish we didn't have to stop," Katie said as we parted. "This is the first time since I've been here that I've been able to say what I feel and get so much out. Maybe it's the first time ever."

After I got back to Philadelphia, Katie and I exchanged correspondence a few times. Her letters were bright, brief. She said she wished we could get together—she didn't really have anyone to talk to. When I didn't hear from her for three or four months, I figured she had gotten swallowed by chaos again. But I hoped things were better for her, that somehow she could stabilize.

Then one hot August day I got a small envelope in the mail from East Eighty-eighth Street in Los Angeles. Before I opened it I knew Katie was dead. I pulled out a note from Katie's mother, along with a funeral program from Paradise Baptist Church, where Katie Haley's obsequies had been held on June 24, 1972. Katie was dead. I don't know how she died; someday maybe I'll hear the full story. I only know the rage I felt: the pain of "just another death" in another culture—as foreign a culture and as foreign a death to most Americans as if it had happened in some far-off land, not here at home.

I know that very few people knew or cared that Katie Haley was dead. And I know that her life was part of a process that kills millions of Americans emotionally and physically. Katie died a prisoner of herself and a prisoner of her world, never really knowing alternatives to the inner or outer tyrannies that shaped her reality.

17   PRISONS

A Paradigm of Failure

Jails are not conducive to women being good mothers. Mothers in jails are not conducive to bringing up good citizens. We have about seventy percent recidivism. Yes, they come back, and their daughters come back, and their daughters, and their daughters' daughters.

—Lieutenant Audrey Lehre, Assistant Warden, Sybil Brand Institute for Women

The man, more than fifty years old, is standing outside the front entrance of the Control Center at Riker's Island, New York City's penal colony. His eyes seem alert to movements and nuances in the scenery invisible to me. His brown face is full and gentle, and his neck bulges out above his tight-fitting military gray uniform, which looks like it has tried to mold his body but failed.

His name is Tim Davis, and he has worked on Riker's Island as a guard for more than twenty years.

"You see this over here," he says, waving his arm horizontally over the island. "That used to be a mountain, but we expanded so much they had to clear it away. Now we have buildings there, and there and there . . .

"We used to have farms here twenty years ago. This was a beautiful place to work those days.

"That's the new Women's House of Detention, where you want to go. There used to be trees there, and a mountain, but they chopped the mountain down and put in the Women's House of Detention.

"We used to call it a nursery out here because there were thousands and thousands of trees. But they took the trees one by one to plant along the highways. The Park Department took them.

"And see that over there?" he says as his hand goes up to shade his squinting eyes in the sun. "There used to be thousands and thousands of chicken coops, and the inmates used to take care of them. Now look at the place. It's fantastic. Just fantastic. Look at these jails. It used to be so beautiful here those days."

It would be impossible for me to say that imprisonment is worse for women than it is for men. Imprisonment is *different* for women because women are different from men. Men cope with prison differently than women do, but they too are treated as bad children who deserve harsh punishment. They too are forced into humiliating dependency. They suffer the same powerlessness, abuse, and mistreatment and then get out with no support, no new options. Plenty of male prisoners are gentle, tender, or frightened people. They are not the cold-hearted monsters and killers they are made out to be. The majority of men in prison are nonviolent people who have been sentenced to prison for nonviolent crimes; while they're there, they, like women in prison, are stripped of dignity and self-respect on a daily basis.

We are all fragile. Each of us is different; each has a separate reality, and everything we see, touch, feel, and hear is perceived slightly differently from the next person. We all have the potential to grow and change and contribute to life—even convicted murderers and armed robbers. But prison is a concrete womb for everyone. It is a place we send people for punishment, and while they're there, we surround them with concrete, force-feed regression, and then hurl them back into society expecting them to be self-sufficient. It doesn't make sense.

Nor does our extremely harsh treatment of impoverished mothers who have broken the law make sense. Since women generally are the primary caretakers of their children, their families disintegrate when they are imprisoned. When fathers are locked up, the family is disrupted, but when the mother is locked up, the children are lost. Substance and alcohol abuse are cycles that generations of families experience, and few people are more aware of those cycles being repeated than the women who are in prison.

For everyone—men, women, and children—prisons are a wasteland. No matter what politicians looking for favorable press might say, no prison is a country club. Crime in our country will not be alleviated by further imprisonment. It never has been and it never will be.

In 1870 a Judge Carter from Ohio said he favored the abolition of prisons. At the National Congress on Penitentiary and Reformatory Discipline, he said that any system of imprisonment or punishment was degradation and could not reform a person. He wanted to release all the people confined in prisons. The judge said he felt certain that prisons would be abolished once women had won the right to vote, hold office, and sit as judges and legislators. He maintained that women would correct the injustices men had mandated as law.

His view, not surprisingly, was as unpopular at the time as it would be today. Although congressmen condemned prisons as a failure, they wanted to reform them, not close them down. They were not willing to give up their belief that somehow prisons would work, nor were they willing to give up the assumption that intemperance and prostitution were the causes of crime. But Judge Carter and several congressmen argued that neither intemperance nor prostitution was the cause of crime. By bringing people into crime, these activities might be considered antecedents, but they were not the cause. Many spoke fervently in favor of establishing an equitable society that would prevent crime by eliminating poverty, discrimination, and hopelessness.

As I write this last chapter, I feel real despair. I feel bitter that people live in such oblivion to one another that books like this one must be written. Why don't people already know? Why are we as a society unwilling to seek the truth of how we are hurting ourselves?

For two hundred years, knowledgeable people in America have been saying that prisons don't work. They don't stop crime. They don't deter criminal behavior. Prisoners, who know better than anyone, have demonstrated what a destructive, sadistic, and bitter failure prisons have been. They have risked their lives to draw attention to the conditions they live in. Women and men in prisons across the country have responded to their environments by refusing to work, refusing to eat, or refusing to cooperate until conditions improve. In Kansas, inmates went so far as to cripple themselves by cutting their Achilles tendons to protest their living conditions.

The effect of experiences inside prison is perhaps most dramatically reflected in the fact that 80 percent of all new felonies are committed by people previously confined in these "correctional" institutions. Four fifths of all our major crimes solved are attributed to people already processed at least once through the criminal justice system.

In any other business, this rate of failure would not be tolerated. In any other business, investors would pull out if even half of the products failed and if no progress was made in achieving the company's goals. In any other business, the public would go wild over spending billions and billions of dollars in public funds with nothing to show for it but failure.

We are nearing the twenty-first century. We really don't have time to be so foolish. We have repeatedly heard prisoners and ex-prisoners, judges, attorneys general, and even presidents of the United States say that prisons are a blight on America: a reflection of our inhumanity and character. A former associate justice of the U.S. Supreme Court, Arthur J. Goldberg, said, "During my service as a justice of the United States Supreme Court, I had the unique opportunity to observe how self-defeating and destructive simplistic approaches to crime and punishment can be. Repressive measures and increased penalties are not the answer. These solutions will be no more successful in our own era than they have in times past."

I am troubled when I hear people calling for preventive detention, longer sentences, mandatory sentences, more severe punishment. They denounce the "coddling" of prisoners and cry for state-inflicted vengeance. These same people maintain that imprisonment will decrease crime on the streets and teach the offender a lesson. Like their forebears, they maintain that drugs, a replacement for alcohol, are the cause of crime, not the antecedent. These people don't understand what they're talking about. They do not realize that ultimately society suffers, in that we create more crime, from the continuation of an unworkable theory, founded only in blindness and maintained through rigid stubbornness. We are using precious resources and energy to hurt ourselves and our society.

In his book *Crime in America,* former attorney general Ramsey Clark points out that what we do in the field of penology has practically no relationship to what we say we do. He says that the effect of imprisonment—where the individual's integrity and personality have been totally abused—is to make prisoners come out of prison a threat to society.

"If we are to deal meaningfully with crime," Clark writes,

> what must be seen is the dehumanizing effect on the individual of slums, racism, ignorance and violence, of corruption and impotence to fulfill rights, of poverty and unemployment and idleness, of generations of malnutrition, of congenital brain damage and prenatal neglect, of sickness and disease, of pollution, of decrepit, dirty, ugly, unsafe, overcrowded housing, of alcoholism and narcotics addiction, of avarice, anxiety, fear, hatred, hopelessness and injustice. These are the fountainheads of crime. They can be controlled. As imprecise, distorted and prejudiced as our learning is, these sources of crime and their controllability clearly emerge to any who would see. (Pp. 17–18.)

Even the most conservative prison administrators assert that imprisonment doesn't work. Officials have told me frankly that the system is self-defeating; there is nothing they can do. Prisons don't rehabilitate anybody, they've said. If you want to stop crime, you need to start with preschoolers and programs where children have a healthy diet, safe environment, and a thorough education.

The National Council on Crime and Delinquency has taken the position that no new detention or penal institutions should be built before alternatives to imprisonment are fully explored. They have called for a halt on construction of all new prisons, jails, juvenile training schools, and detention homes until the funding, staffing, and implementation of noninstitutional corrections has been attained.

In formulating this policy statement, the council pointed to a three-year project in Saginaw, Michigan, that demonstrated that 80 percent of felony offenders can be placed on probation without danger to the community. They documented other research leading to the conclusion that of four hundred thousand [now more than one million] men, women, and children imprisoned in America on any given day, very few need to be locked up for the protection of society; that imprisonment is necessary only for the small minority of offenders so dangerous as to pose a serious threat to society if allowed at large. On that basis, the NCCD pointed out that we already have vastly more institutional space than is possibly needed.

Even a brief glimpse of history supports this position. But in November 1968 President Richard M. Nixon gave the U.S. attorney general a thirteen-point correction program that ignored all of these recommendations. He also called for further pretrial detention, a plan contradictory to the Constitution of the United States. Under the president's program, the Bureau of Prisons developed a ten-year plan calling for the construction of sixty-six new institutions at an estimated cost of $700 million, with annual operating costs projected at more than $150 million. In addition to the sixty-six new federal prisons, plans were developed by state and local authorities for the construction of more jails for sentenced offenders and for people awaiting trial and sentencing.

In Connecticut, where jails are operated by the state, the planning of replacements for local jails was financed by the Law Enforcement Assistance Administration—the same agency that financed the task force report *The Challenge of Crime in a Free Society,* which held that prisons don't deter crime or protect society.

The National Jail Census reported in 1970 that the total planned jail construction expenditures for that year were more than $170 million. According to the U.S. Bureau of Prisons, eight federal correctional centers for "guidance and detention" were being planned in metropolitan areas. Construction funds were appropriated for one center in New York City, and similar constructions were planned in Chicago, Philadelphia, San Diego, and San Francisco.

In 1995 federal, state, and city governments still are building new prisons and converting other buildings to accommodate increasing numbers of prisoners without having made comprehensive assessments of what level of security actually is required. Few states or municipal governments try to determine which women, men, and children could be safely cared for by using community resources instead of prison. No joint planning is being done by state, federal, or local authorities to determine the extent to which alternative measures would reduce the estimated numbers of people imprisoned.

In the first six months of 1994, the country's prison population grew by nearly forty thousand, equivalent to fifteen hundred new prisoners a week, according to Bureau of Justice Statistics. The *New York Times* reported that the growth in inmates is expected to accelerate as children of baby boomers enter their teen years and as the new federal crime bill, which includes a raft of federal crimes that require long mandatory sentences, takes effect. The bill encourages states to adopt tougher mandatory minimum sentences; additionally, some states have passed versions of the "three strikes and you're out" law, which imposes mandatory life sentences for anyone convicted of three felonies or, in some states, three violent crimes. "Even as the inmate population soars, politicians are vying to outdo each other in presenting an image of being tough on crime and willing to send more people to prison."[1]

Across the United States, spending on prisons is one of the fastest growing items in state and county budgets. Our costs are accelerating so rapidly that every year we have to redirect resources from other services to support imprisonment, because we are, after all, spending $100 million to $125 million a day just to keep people locked up so they can come back to our communities unchanged, commit more crimes, and be sent back to prison. And while we're spending all this money to keep people locked up, we're cutting back support services and leaving probation and parole caseworkers with unmanageable, overloaded caseloads.

Few of our political leaders seem to understand the implications of this alarming growth of prisons and prison budgets accompanied by the cutbacks of community services and opportunities. But it seems to me that if our Draconian public policies on crime continue to mandate more imprisonment—and if we don't soon reverse this trend—then it won't be long before we're spending double the money on prisons that we do on public schools for our children.

It seems clear that we're allowing the machinery of political expediency to roll on even though that machinery eventually will crush us all. None of us seems to feel we have the power to stop an unworkable and devastating system. Are we so locked into the prisons of the past that we are afraid

1. Steven A. Holmes, "Ranks of Inmates Reach One Million in a Two-Decade Rise."

to look into the future? Can't we see that this expensive trend is nothing but an illusion? We're spending our tax dollars to build prisons for the people who want revenge and who want to feel protected. But prisons nurture dangerousness and alienation; they don't keep us safe.

To reduce violence and to stop crime, we have to put our tax dollars into education and empowerment programs, provide training and education and programs that support people leaving prison so they are able to find meaningful work within the community. To have safer neighborhoods and prepare for the future, we must:

• Stop sending so many men and women and girls and boys to jail. Juvenile justice systems should divert youngsters from prisons. Incarcerating kids doesn't work; prisons reinforce aggressiveness, isolate the youngsters, and ensure that next time they'll commit real crimes. Kids need to learn how to handle anger without violence—they need to learn how to make positive decisions in the process of growing up. They need options. As it stands now, a lot of kids are constantly in danger; they're not violent, but they need support. As one teenager told a television interviewer: "A bullet is waiting for me with my name on it." Young people need programs and they need our attention. In 1991, more than ninety thousand kids were in institutions—which cost far more than what intensive education, job training, and counseling would cost.

• We must support services and programs for girls and boys who have been sexually and physically abused. We also need to provide after school and evening services for kids at risk. These programs aren't cheap, but they are inexpensive compared to the cost of incarcerating these children for years to come. Don't forget that nearly nine of ten women who fill our prisons have been victims of physical or sexual abuse; most of them wouldn't be where they are if they'd had intervention at a young age. (I suspect that researchers would also find that the vast majority of men in prison also have been physically or sexually abused.)

• We also need to provide support, education, and further resources to stop violence against women and children. Every day violence kills a parent—usually a mother. And witnessing violence has been found to be as traumatic for children as being abused themselves. We have more than three times as many animal shelters in America than we have shelters for battered women—which seems to imply that we care more about animals than we do about women and children.

We must be careful, however, to establish programs that are *alternatives to,* not additions to, the criminal justice system. We have to make sure that reforms do not extend imprisonment or add to an already unwieldy system. In the past, many well-intentioned reforms have expanded the system through sincere but piecemeal efforts to reform it. As I have pointed out, the concern of reformers for the neglect and mistreatment of women in prison at the turn of the century led to the establishment of separate prisons for women. Since that time more and more women have been funneled into the system and more prisons have been built to house them.

The establishment of the U.S. Bureau of Prisons was a reform measure of the 1930s, when seven federal prisons were funded by Congress and functioned autonomously. At that time, twelve thousand offenders were confined in those institutions, and an equal number of federal prisoners were held in state and local facilities. By 1972 the bureau operated thirty-eight institutions throughout the country, housing approximately twenty thousand people. More than thirty-six thousand people were under the supervision of the federal probation system—another reform. In 1994, 6,135 women and 78,768 men were serving time in federal prisons throughout the country, and more than that number were on federal probation.

Reformers' concerns about juveniles led to the establishment of a juvenile system of justice, with family courts, juvenile probation officers, and juvenile jails and prisons. This system has resulted in unnecessary, destructive imprisonment for hundreds of thousands of youngsters. Since most state institutions for women and children have been built without walls and have "nice" names, judges have been less hesitant about incarcerating them. Sending a mother or a child to a "home," a "reformatory," or a "center" doesn't sound nearly as distasteful as sending her to a prison.

The same semantic changes also are being used in correctional institutions for men. And yet it is plain to see that twisting language, using concertina wire instead of high walls and matrons instead of armed guards, does not change reality. It doesn't change the actuality or brutality of the depersonalized, degrading prison experience, nor does it eliminate coercion, neglect, or violence to the human spirit. Through reform, imprisonment has expanded.

And that's not all. When we realized that we had the longest prison sentences in the world, and that those sentences were unconscionably long, the parole system was established. Once parole was available, however, judges began to respond by giving offenders even longer sentences, on the theory that they would need more control over the person's behavior in the street.

We can see from history that when one small part of the system is changed, other parts often co-opt the effect of the reforms. For example, in Wisconsin it's now possible for an offender to have an attorney of her own if she is in danger of having her probation or parole revoked. This was a sound attempt to protect the civil liberties of the offender. But authorities in Wisconsin report that since the ruling, judges are now less willing to grant probation and parole boards are less willing to grant parole.

Today when I hear about community residential treatment centers being established, I am pleased that they are a step forward from security-oriented prisons. Plans for many centers include diagnostic services for courts to give judges more information to determine appropriate sentencing; intensive short-term treatment; and units for counseling and guidance of inmates being prepared to return to the community. A few existing centers also offer vocational and family counseling.

But I worry that the same errors of past reforms could be repeated with residential treatment centers if these residential centers are planned *in addition to* new prison construction. Instead, the plan should be to close down prisons and to *replace* them with community treatment centers, many of which could operate as public health facilities separate from the criminal justice system. Small treatment programs—residential and day-treatment—within communities should be encouraged. But large "residential centers" threaten to become only another appendage to a growing machine that is already out of whack: a justice system that could more correctly be termed an injustice system—one based on the belief that by locking up less than 2 percent of the lawbreakers reported, we will reduce crime in America.

It doesn't make sense.

Sometimes it seems to me that the efforts of the state are directed at further disrupting the black, brown, and white families who live in profound poverty. It seems society is punishing them for failing to have engaged properly with the precepts of production and a sound economy. Whatever the truth is, it seems that little of what we call criminology and penology has much to do with crime. It has more to do with economics, more to do with a failure to communicate and to connect with one another. Maybe the real questions we should be asking don't revolve around crime as much as they do around our fears, our values, and the quality of life. Maybe they have more to do with how we all fail to take care of each other and help each other grow.

Obviously we should experiment with new ways of preventing crime and supporting one another in life-affirming ways. The prison system has been maintained on a historical continuum. It's been a dud since its inception, but somehow it's become so imprinted into our consciousness, so lodged in our vengeful hearts, that we never have been willing to break away from it.

Fresh thinking is needed, and it is needed desperately. We must break with the past. The only obstacle is our own resistance—the inner prison—which stifles creative thinking and change. We have all the material, economic, technical, and intellectual tools necessary to realize a society that would allow equal education, income, opportunity, support, and self-realization for all citizens.

It is possible to abolish poverty and hunger. It is possible to make available life-giving work. It is possible to shut down prisons as we know them and share space and life with people now rejected, neglected, and abused. It is possible for us to care about ourselves and accept our racial, religious, and class differences, to accept our different realities and learn from the richness of all the ethnic cultures in this country.

All of us—in the general society and in the prison society—need to assert a sense of responsibility and determination over our own futures. We all have a need to be at peace with ourselves. We have a need for privacy, safety, and the opportunity to experience our lives without fear.

We need to create new channels for our energy that would prevent crime and destruction by placing value on human relationships, not on material gain. With clear intention and determination, we could change public policies, reorganize our institutions, and eliminate destructive theories and practices. We would have to stop placing blame for the immense problems of our society on a "criminal class." We would have to establish new priorities and models from which we could build fair, humane ways of dealing with problems between people in a direct, personal way. The criminal justice system today is a microcosm of our society. It is a good place to begin.

I know there is a group of people who are imprisoned unjustly and punished unfairly. They are held in jail for long periods of time awaiting trial. Or they are people who are being punished for drug abuse or small, desperate attempts to change their circumstances, usually by punishing themselves more than anyone else.

A second group of people—the vast majority of the general population—does not get punished because of an ability to manipulate the system or avoid detection. The discretion of the law protects these people, many of whom are successful businessmen, politicians, store owners, doctors, lawyers. They break laws—fornication, solicitation, traffic violations, drunk driving, drug possession and sales, business infractions, larceny, forgery, tax evasion, embezzlement—crimes other people *are* serving time for. The average urban resident is said to commit eighteen felonies a year, each punishable theoretically by a year or more of imprisonment. Some apparently "good citizens" also get away with even more severe crimes, including blackmail, domestic violence, assault and battery, robbery, and murder. When they're caught, they get psychiatric treatment or probation rather than prison sentences for their crimes. When they're caught, their crimes are considered symptoms of deeper problems, which should be addressed in order to help them back on their feet.

There is a third group of people—some of whom fall into the first category—to whom prison is essentially a normal part of life. These people are unprotected by the discretionary power of the law. They serve as the examples for the rest of us when they receive harsh public punishment for violating society's norms. Many of this group give lip service to such concepts as rehabilitation and getting out of the system, but essentially they lack the tools to do so. Some of this group resist all attempts to do what they say they want to do. They do not want to give up the immediate gratification of drugs or the minor moneymaking schemes of survival that involve hustling, stealing, living fast and dangerously. They need the electric edge, and they demonstrate this need by not giving it up, no matter how much punishment they suffer as a result.

But why should they change when society doesn't change? A strong analogy could be made between them and the public that gives lip service to providing rehabilitation without ever effectively offering it. We call our prisons "correctional facilities," but we build them for punishment, not for correction.

We expect poverty-stricken lawbreakers to change, but we are not willing to change. We reward the men who steal millions and punish the small-time losers. But are partners in securities firms who steal millions of dollars from investors really any more deserving of understanding than a numbers runner or shoplifter?

I know that a lot of people put themselves in bondage or keep themselves in bondage, both inside and outside prisons. There is a whole subculture in America that depends on being controlled and imprisoned—with drugs, with alcohol, or in jail. The concrete womb is security. The bottle is security. Heroin is security. It's artificial security—but it's a response to fear: fear of an overwhelming society, fear of powerlessness, fear of the unknown, and fear of the known. All these "places," prison included, contribute to escape, to abandonment of responsibility. For many, outside pressures and people are more frightening and more evil than imprisonment.

It is an ironic cycle: society has an exaggerated fear of crime because of the heinousness of certain murders and violent acts. These events seem to happen more often than they actually do because they are given such predominant coverage in our newspapers, on television, and in films (perhaps because we, too, are addicted to that electric edge?). Violent, psychotic killers and others who are extremely dangerous to the community are a tiny proportion of the people who go to prison. In fact, Allyn Sielaff, the former commissioner of the Pennsylvania Bureau of Corrections, estimated that less than 1 percent of all imprisoned felons need maximum security confinement.

But it is because of our fears of the most dangerous that we lock up huge numbers of people who pose no threat to the community. In prison, members of this nonviolent majority are depersonalized, isolated, and exposed to violence in many forms. As a result, the people society is afraid of—the people labeled "criminals"—become fearful of the people who are afraid of them, which ultimately makes them more of a threat.

The cycle must be broken if any of us are ever to go forward. Communication has to open up. The community must go into the prisons and see prisoners as human beings who must be accepted back into society—integrated and responsible, not alienated and isolated from responsibility.

We must stop new prison construction immediately and use diversionary programs *instead* of prisons. We should institute a permanent moratorium on the building of new prisons. Imprisonment is the most expensive and least effective way to deal with crime, and it should be our last resort, not our first. Certainly we must keep dangerous, violent people off the street; our children need to be protected and we need to feel safe. But we cannot achieve justice or a crime-free society through the simplistic approach we've taken to crime. The funds and the energy we've used to "lock 'em up and throw away the key" has more to do with political considerations than with any true intention to alleviate crime.

It is odd that no matter what spending cuts we propose—whether it's cutting funds for computer classes in public grade schools, teen intervention and sports programs, art therapy, summer jobs, or after-school care—we always have enough money to spend on prisons. Prisons destroy the lives of children whose parents are taken away from them. Their lives, already poverty-stricken, become more desperate. But our public policies pay only lip service to children while we neglect and ignore their needs. And when we approve of funds for building new prisons, we are condemning the future for all our children, who will inherit a legacy of prison-induced violence and despair unless we do something about it now.

If we really wanted to alleviate crime, we could use a fraction of the prison space we already have to house the truly psychotic, dangerous prisoners and to provide them with decent treatment. This would leave enormous amounts of money to work on eradicating the root causes of crime—drug and alcohol addiction, poverty, racism, illiteracy, and unemployment. If we stopped building prisons and instead provided alternatives, we would have the necessary funds for drug and alcohol treatment, literacy classes, job training and development, recreation and education for high-risk teenagers, and hands-on work in parenting skills. We could use our energies to build strong families, which would drastically reduce crime in America.

Alleviating crime and achieving justice for future generations should be our goal. And if justice is our goal, then for as long as prisons exist, inmates should be encouraged in every way possible to stay connected to their families and re-enter their communities as responsible participants. Inmates should be given the opportunity to learn real job skills and earn decent wages to support their families and to pay restitution to their victims. They should regain the right to vote. Their dignity should be encouraged; they should be able to see their children often, and furlough programs should be expanded. And although some people believe that criminals forfeit all their rights by breaking the law, we need to rethink this principle. While we may *feel* that a person who has broken the law should be harshly punished, punishment in a hostile environment won't reduce crime. People who have broken the law and who take responsibility for their actions, who feel connected to their families and to other people and issues within the community, will have motivation not to break the law again.

We also must change the mandatory sentencing laws. Judges need flexibility in sentencing that will allow them to choose less expensive and more productive punishments for offenders. Moreover, alternatives to imprisonment within the community should be developed—and be given urgent priority.

An immediate remedy for prison overcrowding—and a way to cut down on crime, violence, and the costs of imprisonment and crime—is to divert drug addicts from the criminal justice system. People who are drug addicted should be held responsible for their actions, but should receive medical treatment instead of a prison sentence. We acknowledge that alcoholism is a disease, but we continue to see drug addiction as *bad*. Drug addiction also is a disease. It's a public health problem and should be treated as such. Addicts need medical treatment, not incarceration.

It would benefit our communities to evaluate the safety risks of having addicts who are charged with criminal offenses in closely supervised programs that would cost a fraction of what jail space costs. We need to understand that by dealing with drug possession as a criminal offense, we're dealing with it in the most expensive and least effective way.

Billie Holiday, the blues singer who was sentenced to local jail and federal prison for her possession of narcotics, said it as well as anyone, nearly forty years ago:

> People on drugs are sick people. So now we end up with the government chasing sick people like they were criminals . . . prosecuting them because they had some stuff without paying the tax, and sending them to jail.
>
> Imagine if the government chased sick people with diabetes, put a tax on insulin and drove it into the black market . . . and then caught them, prosecuted them for not paying their taxes, and then sent them to jail. If we did that, everyone would know we were crazy. Yet we do practically the same thing every day in the week to sick people hooked on drugs. The jails are full and the problem is getting worse every day.[2]

Drug treatment works—and if we used daytime drug treatment and residential drug treatment programs for drug addicts instead of prisons, we could empty more than half of our jails in one fell swoop. Some of the alternatives that work and work well include drug residential treatment centers and small housing programs for women. Women in particular work well in small groups—and with drug counseling, they work best with small groups of women, not with confrontational, male-model programs.

One-on-one programs that work closely with women, juveniles, and men sound as if they would be unbelievably expensive, but in fact, they cost less than imprisonment and are much more effective. The idea of working one on one with people might not become a favorite, but it can change and save lives.

A project that seems to me to be a brilliant model has been going on in six cities—Austin, Texas; Bridgeport, Connecticut; Newark, New Jersey; Savannah, Georgia; Memphis, Tennessee, and Seattle, Washington—to intervene in the lives of impoverished young people. This project, called "Children at Risk," intervenes in the lives of juveniles who are drug users or in danger of using drugs, who have been suspended from school for violence, who have been in trouble with the law or have parents in trouble. A quarter of the kids in the program previously have been caught carrying weapons—have been in gang activity, been thieves or armed robbers, or been sexually abused by a relative. Others haven't been in serious trouble themselves, but have parents who are in prison or who deal drugs. (This program is overseen by the Center on Addiction and Substance Abuse at Columbia University and financed by the Justice Department and several foundations.)

The idea behind "Children at Risk" is to change a child's behavior by

2. Billie Holiday, with William Dufty, *Lady Sings the Blues,* pp. 157–58.

taking care of the child within the context of the family's problems. Case workers take on the role of being a friend and supervisor to the kid, and they're sometimes like fairy godmothers to family members.[3] They prod the parent to go to AA or Narcotics Anonymous meetings, help negotiate housing and job problems, negotiate family crises, even go in and wake up the child for school if necessary. The attention—which keeps kids in school and out of trouble—costs about $4,000 per child for a year's worth of services. This might be considered expensive, but it's only a fraction of the cost of imprisoning that child for one year—let alone for a lifetime of involvement with the criminal justice system. Preliminary results suggest that this kind of all-out support system has spectacular effects for the youngsters themselves and on juvenile crime in a particular neighborhood. (From 1991 to 1993, the project's second year, juvenile arrests in the target area rose at one third the rate of other poor sections of the city. The children in the project had only half the involvement with new crimes as did children in the control group.)[4]

Another effective alternative is to utilize drug courts independent of the criminal justice system to deal with addicts. Even if drugs remain illegal, drug possession should be treated as a noncriminal public health problem. Some drug courts in the 1990s are helping to reduce our prison population by providing options for people to change their lives at a fraction of the cost of imprisonment. These special drug courts are being held in thirty cities across the country; they make it possible for drug addicts to avoid criminal trials, convictions, and prison terms if they choose the option of going into an intensive drug-treatment program.

People charged with drug possession have a choice within hours of their arrest to go to jail for six months to a year *or* agree to closely monitored, court-supervised drug treatment, which may take twice as long as the jail time. This diversionary program involves "hard-nosed discipline and gritty work at every step, sometimes beginning with weeks of twenty-four-hour in-house supervision,"[5] and continuing with frequent mandatory urine tests to detect drug use. The program is working!

"If the drug court system is sufficiently financed to grow, it will not only save money committed to law enforcement," Mike Tidwell writes, "it will also save some—perhaps much—of the $166 billion a year in total

3. Isabel Wilkerson, "Doing Whatever It Takes To Save a Child," *New York Times,* December 30, 1994, p. 1.

4. Ibid.

5. Mike Tidwell, "Our Tax Dollars Have Promoted Drug Use and Violence," *Washington Spectator.*

costs, public and private, attributed to substance abuse by the Center on Addiction and Substance Abuse (CASA) at Columbia University.''[6]

For those women who aren't diverted, but who go through the regular courts, alternative sentencing to community treatment programs that address substance-abuse problems, educational, personal, and economic needs can make a life-changing difference. Judges in Philadelphia, for instance, have the option of sentencing a woman to a program called "New Directions" instead of the House of Detention or the state prison at Muncy. New Directions is a residential treatment program where the women go to school and to work while they deal with addiction issues and other personal problems.

"Many of these women are mothers," said Common Pleas Court Judge Lisa Richette in a recent interview. "How they survive their passage through the criminal justice system is a model to their children. Many of these women have no self-esteem. Many of them became sexually active at an early age and came to feel they had to have a man to be somebody. Job training and education is giving them a sense of autonomy and being able to control their lives independent of men.

"We also have the whole issue of addiction that's being treated—Narcotics Anonymous and Alcoholics Anonymous. It's taking them literally into new directions and showing them a new path.

"Prison is particularly destructive for women," says Richette. "It destroys whatever sense of self-esteem the women had, which was zilch when they started. There's also a stigma attached which is very destructive. They feel it. This is especially true of the women I have to send to Muncy [the state prison]. I do see them twice a year, and they worry about their children. Muncy is 175 miles away from Philadelphia—and then they go to a halfway house in Erie, which is even farther! Nobody seems to give a thought to the fact that it would be more therapeutic and conducive to rehabilitation for them to be closer to their families!"

Residential treatment or day-long outpatient community-based drug treatment programs that provide structure and supervision encourage offenders to learn drug-free habits in their own communities. These programs have demonstrated that drug treatment works, even when it takes long-term effort. The Pennsylvania Program for Women Offenders has been working on community-based programs to meet women's needs since the early 1970s, for instance. In 1988, the recidivism rate for women leaving their program was 17.7 percent, far below recidivism rates for women leaving jail or prison. In New York, the El Rio Drug Treatment

6. Ibid.

and Supportive Services run by the New York Correctional Association diverts hundreds of jail-bound defendants to treatment and rehabilitation each year. California's Mother-Infant Care Program, where sentenced women can keep their young children with them while they serve their sentences in residential homes, has been cost effective and highly successful at keeping women from going back to prison.

Another issue of great concern to the public has been the problem of pregnant women addicted to drugs or alcohol during their pregnancies. When judges feel compelled to sentence these women to jail or prison, they often don't realize they're sending them to institutions that lack adequate medical care and follow-up treatment for pregnant substance abusers withdrawing from drug and alcohol use. As a result, large numbers of these women suffer dramatic, late-term miscarriages. In contrast, some programs like Mandela House in Oakland and Houston House in Boston work directly with pregnant addicts with remarkable results. All these programs save hundreds of thousands of dollars per year and enhance public safety by reducing the number of drug abusers.

Programs such as these also save money by reducing the number of robberies and burglaries within communities. They allow people to take personal responsibility for their actions, make amends, and take care of their families in the meantime.

It also seems it would be wise to let more prisoners out on work-release programs. In times of crisis from disasters such as floods and hurricanes, prisoners have been let out of prisons to help clean up devastated areas. Their work has saved lives. They have volunteered to contribute to the community, and during these critical times the community has appreciated their work and their spirit. In some cases, bonds have been formed between townspeople and the inmates working with them. Normally, however, all avenues of growth or possibility for human contribution are closed off to people labeled "criminal."

Alternatives are essential and we must develop more of them. The number of alternatives we currently utilize is minuscule in relation to the total picture. Residential treatment programs, like work-release programs and prisoner support groups, make life better for the individuals who have those opportunities, but they are far too few in number. Basic prison conditions—and a lack of alternatives—remain the same for hundreds of thousands—now millions—of inmates during the time they're incarcerated and when they're released. The realities for people in prison today are very much what they were in 1840 and 1870 and 1940. The root causes of crime within our communities and our misguided response to the symptoms still exist despite changes. And if we don't deal with those issues, people may still be writing about this deepening crisis in 2070 and 2270, if our society survives that long.

Sometimes the horror of what I have seen happening to the human beings I've met in prisons gives me nightmares. The contradictions inside prison that erode the mind and spirit, the brutal punishment of people both guilty and innocent in the eyes of the law, the pain in the faces I've seen, the calls I have gotten in the middle of the night from women afraid of sticking a needle in their arms again or wondering what to do about their sick children—all overwhelms my senses. The agony and torture, the prolonged suffering and abuse prisoners experience are beyond what most people can fathom. It's beyond what I can fathom, and I've seen it. I live with the awareness that while I'm enjoying the freedom of choices in my life, other people are suffering behind prison walls, ignored and forgotten. It makes me so sad that I sometimes can't stand to think about it.

I retaliate by fantasizing new possibilities. I imagine taking my grandchildren by the hand and walking through the rubble of Holmesburg Prison and the House of Correction and Riker's Island. I imagine being an old white-haired woman feeling a sense of peace and quietness, telling them that these were terrible, hostile, and violent places where men and women and teenagers were locked up in small concrete cells year after year. I tell them that the ruins are here as a reminder for generations to come; they're a monument to the death of our inhumanity to one another.

I imagine telling my little grandchildren that people of my day realized that they didn't know what they were doing when they imprisoned each other—that they had an idea that was wrong, that was brutal, so they gave up thinking they were right and risked new possibilities.

"It's never too late to change," I tell them. "You just have to have the will to face your fear of being wrong and your fear of the unknown." I tell them about the days when hospitals and health centers were built in abundance and when clinics instead of criminal laws became available to people with problems they needed to solve. People who stole and threatened one another were remanded to groups of neighborhood people who scolded them, helped them work out their problems and repay their victims; community judges and juries started ordering good health care, exercise, and recreation for people who needed to learn how to play and laugh.

I tell them that although it's beyond their comprehension, "in my day, no one would have ever thought of a judge ordering a man who stole to pay back what he took and then to play Frisbee in the park with his neighbors. Can you imagine! No one ever thought of getting to know someone who stole something to find out what she needed and why she did what she did. No one ever thought of replacing bad habits and self-destructive environments with schools and music and art and theater in every neighborhood.

"It was all really very silly," I tell them, "but the silliness destroyed a lot of lives. People then actually locked people they didn't like away from society so they could adjust to society. They thought they could stop crime by locking people up in a hostile place. It didn't make any sense at all."

Realistically, I don't believe my fantasies will come true—or that prisons will be abolished during my lifetime. But I feel an urgency about the situation, perhaps more so than many people who have not been imprisoned, because of the places I have been and the people I have met who have taught me so much and made such a profound impact on my life. I remember the child's writing in the visitors' bathroom at the California Institution for Women: "I LOVE MY MOM." Each letter was scratched in large penciled marks, etching forever in my mind the loneliness we all share: the alienation, the fear, the sense of powerlessness and longing, the grief of not realizing our own potential.

And as I sit here at my desk, I think about a letter that reminds me of the concerns that have become part of my world. This letter began when a woman who had spent two years behind bars wrote to me and said she didn't want me to use her name in the book since her parents still didn't know she was in prison. She said they had suffered enough; she didn't want to worry them with additional burdens, so she wrote to them from a friend's address. (Her friend readdressed the envelopes for her.) I enlarged upon her letter to include the thoughts of other women behind bars who have communicated the clear emotional essence of prison life to me. I believe their perspective should make us all acutely aware of the need for new and creative thinking, followed by new paths of action:

July, sometime, 1972

Dear Kitsi,

I know you will write the book and I know some people will listen to you—but I just hope you can make them feel prison from the inside. I hope you can make them feel how the time ticks away on you here and how no matter how hard you try to maintain yourself and some degree of independence and self-respect, the daily process eats away your spirit. I have always thought of myself as a pretty strong and open woman, but this joint has taken some of my gentleness, some of my womanhood. Kitsi, I'm not the same warm person I remember myself to be. I find myself withdrawing from people in here—and even though I know it's a natural reaction, I know it will affect the way I relate to people, especially my own children, outside. I feel the walls around me all the time. And I'm afraid I'll carry them outside with me when I leave. Do you think I'll be able to be a good mother when I get my children back? I worry. I worry more than I should when I can't do anything about it.

I heard that state senator on the radio again yesterday, and he was knocking the furlough program because of one man's escape. He was saying it's a crime that these "dangerous criminals" are let out of a "correctional institution" for a weekend, that nobody should be let out on a furlough until a few months before they get out. There's a lot of pressure around here. (They're going to put armed guards around the perimeters, too.)

As I was listening to that senator, I was thinking, He's ignorant. He doesn't know what he's saying. He can't know what he's talking about. I'd like to get on the radio, too, and say that if you don't let people out, if you don't let them feel the world out there again slowly and let them be part of it, then you're making them dangerous. He's just asking for more trouble, more crime, because he's not recognizing us as human beings who have broken laws that don't even affect him. He doesn't know what a prison is. He doesn't know how it feels inside and what it does to a person. Isn't there some law about equal time? I'd like equal time to talk to people.

You know the truth, Kitsi, we are imprisoned in an idea, not just in a place. Prison doesn't work to change people except for the worse, so the idea must be wrong.

All people see is that they are safe from us because we are inside this concrete womb. This damn concrete womb. But I don't think there is any other place anywhere where people are expected to be so completely grown up and self-sufficient and sensible when they have been made for such a long time to feel so little and helpless and dependent. And this womb isn't even nourishing!

Something's got to change. And I guess the idea has to change before anything else. For now all I can hope is that I will be able to grow again when I get out . . . and get rid of the walls around me. I know it's gonna be hard leaving this womb and staying away. I just hope I have the strength to make it. I know it's a matter of will. But damn it, I want so much to feel big again, to feel like a whole woman again. I want to feel like a real, self-sufficient person again.

If you can, tell society to make some room for me and for the other men and women locked into their ideas, their prison camps. Tell people to keep their children out of these places, just to love and nourish them. Tell people we need them and they need us, even though they don't realize it yet. Tell them to claim us so we can claim them. It's overdue, but it's not too late.

Love, and power to you

1996

Epilogue for Women in Prison

We the living are now and throughout time responsible for what happens
    to the earth, to man, to life.
Shall we not learn from life its laws, dynamics, balances?
Learn to base our needs not on death, destruction, waste, but on renewal?
    —Ansel Adams and Nancy Newhall

After I wrote the first edition of *Women in Prison,* I had a number of
experiences that deepened my understanding of what it would mean to be
a woman in prison. The most important of those experiences was that I
became a mother. Two years after my son was born, I was pregnant with
a baby girl who died at birth. I also had two stepdaughters. While at first
glance this may not seem relevant, it gave me more common ground with
the eight of ten women in jails and prisons who are mothers—and reminded me that every woman prisoner is someone's daughter, someone's
granddaughter, someone's sister, someone's aunt. Although previously I
could empathize with the sadness of a mother and a child separated from
each other, the depth of that love and grief was beyond my comprehension.

"You're dealing with so much emotion here," said Sister Elaine Roulet,
director of the Children's Center and parenting programming at Bedford
Hills, who talked as some seventy children and their mothers chatted,
hugged, and played nearby. One woman was sitting in a chair alone crying.
Another sat doing homework with her little girl.

"You hear the laughing, but underneath, there's so much pain," Sister
Elaine said. "Before the mother was in prison, the mother was the central
figure in the child's life. When you remove the mother, the pain is unbelievable. Many children are angry that they're separated from their

3 5 5

mothers, and they're guilty—sometimes they feel responsible that she was taken away. They're juggling so many emotions. Growing up is such a difficult thing to do today anyway. But here, you have that anger to deal with as well. To see the children with their mothers is so moving. What are we doing to everybody?''

After talking to Sister Elaine, I remembered the shock of sadness I felt more than twenty years ago when I read the letters Ana Lou Coelho's children wrote to her in prison. Readers also responded to the grief of those children and their mother. Of all the questions I've been asked about this book over the past twenty years, the one I've been asked most often is, ''Whatever happened to Ana?'' The good news is: Ana won an ''early'' release after two years in prison (for a crime she didn't commit) and was reunited with her children. The last time I heard from Ana, she had just learned she would be on parole for fifteen years. ''Parole is not as bad as being in, but you live in fear of 'them' violating and sending you back,'' she wrote. ''Anyway I do, because I hated that place and still do.'' At the time, she was on her way to Oregon, where she hoped to go to college and set up a new life with her children.

I knew twenty years ago that as much as all of us hate crime—and hate feeling vulnerable to assaults or robberies or burglaries—prisons didn't make sense as a way to solve these problems. Now that I am a parent, it's even more obvious to me. And it's as parents, as grownups, in charge of the future for children on this planet, that I think we should reevaluate our city, state, and federal governments' helter-skelter, simplistic yet deadly rush into more prison construction, more imprisonment. It's in that light that we should think about positive alternatives to a prison system that accomplishes nothing but punishment, havoc, and hatred.

Good parents know that if you want to help a child change his or her behavior, punishment and abuse are not the way to do it. If your child hurts someone else or hurts himself, you don't help him understand what he has done or teach him new behavior by humiliating him or locking him in a closet. If he becomes addicted to drugs or alcohol, you don't help him by locking him up where he has no possibility of learning how to deal with the stresses that led him to drugs or alcohol in the first place. The same is true with adults. We are, after all, the children we once were—and we learn in basically the same manner.

That anyone survives years in prison is testimony to the resilience of the human spirit. Many people, of course, don't survive. Some of the women I interviewed for this book never got out, never had an opportunity to change the direction of their lives. They died in prison. Others got out and didn't make it. Many of them were released from jail with ten or twenty dollars to their name at a minute past midnight, with no ride and no public transportation available. Like my friend Katie Haley, some of those women went back to drugs and died on the street.

Others fared better. But it was never easy. For years I got telephone calls or a knock on the door—often at three and four A.M. from women who were struggling to manage their time during "normal" hours on the outside. Sometimes they were simply checking in to say hello. Others had questions about what to do with a sick baby, where to go about a pain in the side that wouldn't go away, where to find a new place to live, how to get a better job or to get into a drug treatment program.

Establishing a balanced, healthy life after prison—even with a lot of support, which most women don't have—is incredibly difficult. But it's surprising how many women getting out of prison thrive if they're given the slightest bit of encouragement and support. These women have had so few options that any opportunity for a new direction is eagerly embraced. I had the pleasure of seeing Louise Bezie, who was deaf, paroled to a small apartment where she lived, thrilled by her freedom and independence, until she died at the age of seventy-six. Terry Derry became a licensed practical nurse and then went back to school to get her degree as a registered nurse.

"If women get college degrees, they don't come back to prison," Elaine Lord said recently from her superintendent's office at Bedford Hills. "If you give them something that's real, they can get jobs. I don't remember any of those women who have good jobs coming back." At Bedford, the college program has been quite successful, as has the program by which women can become certified by the State Department of Health to do pre- and post-test counseling to HIV-positive people. A number of women certified as HIV counselors have been hired by outside agencies prior to their release. They don't go back to prison, either. But Bedford Hills' efforts are not typical of prisons in the rest of the nation.

And state cutbacks are dismantling the educational programs that help women get out and stay out of prison. They're cutting back education, job training, and drug treatment programs that work. They're cutting back aid to dependent children and programs that help women get out of poverty and give focus and meaning to the lives of high-risk kids who otherwise may end up in prison.

Recently, no matter where I go in the United States, I hear tough talk about crime and calls for harsher treatment of lawbreakers. In Phoenix, the local sheriff bragged that he had cut costs and overcrowding by putting prisoners into tents in the desert—where the temperature in summers reaches 115 degrees in the shade. He joked that he liked being hated by prisoners when he cut further costs by eliminating coffee and hot meals, substituting "corn dogs" for hot dogs. He didn't bother to mention that most of his prisoners are people *awaiting* trial. In Albuquerque, the city was planning to put up prefabricated housing near the city's landfill area as a way to provide space for more prisoners. In Alabama and Arizona, chain gangs are being resurrected for state prisoners.

It seems to me that many of today's politicians are leading 1990s witch hunts against poor people—especially against poor women and their children. And while the attacks often seem consciously aimed at poverty-stricken women and children who are for the most part African American and Hispanic, these policies affect our entire society—rich and poor, black, red, white, and brown. The three-strikes-you're-out laws, mandatory sentences, and longer sentences are condemning the futures of all our children—who will inherit a society even more divided between haves and have-nots, and who will pay the high price of imprisoning AIDS patients, poor people, and old people at the expense of life-affirming programs and education. Even as I write this, the governor of California has proposed a budget that will spend more on prisons than it does on its entire university system.[1]

We have to call the bluff of politicians and businessmen who attack the costs of welfare, special education programs, aid to dependent children, crime prevention programs, housing incentives, and job training, but who propose locking up more people and giving them longer sentences at exorbitant costs. We have to find out: who is profiting from these new prisons? Who benefits? Certainly it's not the public. We have to make our communities and our lawmakers realize that the price tags for increased corrections budgets are ten times what they would be for creating, expanding, and maintaining programs for the urban poor that would improve living conditions and decrease the level of crime in our urban communities.

Many well-meaning people seem to believe there are no alternatives to prison for lawbreakers, but they're wrong. Alternatives are available and, what's more, unlike prisons, they can work. Even more alternatives are needed that let people circumvent prison altogether—alternatives that let parents stay within the community near or together with their children.

We need to stop prison construction and determine that prison will be the last resort—not the first—in dealing with lawbreakers. Only when all other avenues have been eliminated or when a person has demonstrated he

1. In 1995, spending on prisons climbed to 9.9 percent of the California state budget, from 2 percent in 1980, while spending on higher education shrank to 9.5 percent of the budget, down from 12.6 percent in 1980.

or she cannot live in the community without being a danger to others should anyone be sent to prison. At the same time, we need to enforce gun control laws. When we have more gun dealers in America than we have gas stations, when our surgeon general has declared violence and handgun homicides are a national health epidemic among our young men, and when a thousand handguns are purchased every day in California, we have to start putting two and two together.

Changed behavior, responsibility for one's actions, restitution for one's crimes—not simply punishment—should be the goals when someone breaks the law. The public should realize that alternatives to imprisonment do not diminish individual responsibility. People given alternatives ultimately take greater responsibility for their crimes than do people in prison who get caught up in defending themselves against the abuses of the criminal justice system. A person working in the community can literally *pay* for his or her crimes by making amends, repaying victims, and becoming a productive member of society.

We must remember that people need to have something to say YES to—not just NO. Our current incarceration patterns rob hope from addicts and people arrested for petty crimes. We are breaking up families and hurting children in ways beyond our comprehension. We each need to work for the abolition of the prison system as we know it. We need to remember that prison administrators agree that 80 to 90 percent of the people in prison *should not be there* and could safely be treated within the communities where they live. They are no danger to the public and they should stay in their communities, get treatment for drug addiction, and learn skills that will allow them to contribute to the community and to their families.

I want everyone to understand the harm of prisons, but it's hard to find words that match the extent of the destruction imprisonment causes in the name of justice. The misery of our overused and ill-chosen remedy for crime is something too many people still don't understand. People who want more imprisonment should try being locked up themselves for a day or a week—and they might change their minds. One hundred and fifty years ago Charles Dickens, after his visit to the Eastern State Penitentiary, said that he debated whether, if he had the power to say yes or no, he would allow imprisonment to be used in certain cases, even if the terms of imprisonment were short. His conclusion was clear: ''I solemnly declare, that with no rewards or honours could I walk a happy man beneath the open sky by day, or lie me down upon my bed at night, with the consciousness that one human creature, for any length of time, no matter what, lay suffering in this unknown punishment in his silent cell, and I the cause, or I consenting to it in the least.''

We need to remember the children. We need to think about the one and a half million children in America who have parents in prison. If protecting our children has any importance, we have to do something about getting the mothers of these children out of prisons and back into their communities. These mothers in prison are not making us safer by being there—and their children—such as seven-year-old Lewis—are suffering from the separation. Like many children whose mothers are in prison, Lewis sees the world through the prism of his own losses. On his way up to Bedford Hills to see his mother for Mother's Day, for instance, Lewis's sister saw a dead deer on the highway and said, "Oh, look at the baby deer, Lewis!"

Lewis looked at the dead deer and put his hands up to his head. "Oh, no," he sobbed. "How awful on Mother's Day! How awful. The mother deer will be looking for her baby deer and she won't know where he is! How awful on Mother's Day!"

Dehlia, who is ten years old, is another child whose mother is in prison. Dehlia lives in a foster home in New York called "My Mother's Place." It's called that so when children who live there are asked, they can say they live "at My Mother's Place." Dehlia visits her mother every week at Bedford Hills in Westchester County—and her only complaint to Sister Elaine Roulet, who drives her home—is that visiting hours end at 3:30 and they have to leave at 3:20.

One recent Saturday, when Dehlia was doing her English homework with her mother at the Children's Center, she took time out to talk to me for a few minutes. She told me she'd written a story about her mother going to prison, and she'd also told Sister Elaine about how lucky she was compared to other kids. "I'm so lucky," Dehlia said, "I'm lucky because some kids have a wish tree with so many wishes on it. I'm lucky because I don't have a wish tree. I don't have all those wishes. I just have one wish. I wish my mom would come home!"

APPENDIX

I've included the following prison rules and regulations so readers can understand the nature of day-to-day controls within the prison environment. These lists are not complete, but they address various aspects of life as they're governed by prison authorities. Depending on the person enforcing the rules, they can be used in an evenhanded and fair way or can be used for abusive dominion and enforced capriciously and with cruelty by individual correctional officers.

In addition to sets of rules for inmates from three state prisons, I have included two sets of rules to illustrate typical regulations for prisoners in county jails throughout the country. Although inmates do not always receive written copies of these rules, they are expected to obey them. One section from regulations for guards is indicative of restrictions on personnel.

Over the past twenty years, most prison rules have not changed substantially—nor are they apt to change in the next twenty years or more, unless they become even more restrictive in an attempt to deal with overcrowding.

General Rules for Inmates, Cook County Jail, Chicago, Illinois

1. Address all correctional officers as "OFFICER."
2. DO NOT use slang in addressing an officer.
3. NEVER argue with an officer.
4. Obey all orders given to you by an officer or civilian personnel immediately. If you feel you have a legitimate complaint, you may put in a request to the person's superior only after you have done what you were ordered.
5. You cannot give anything to other inmates without permission.
6. Report all threats, acts of violence or pressures to an officer immediately.

7. Clothing, like everything else is County property. Take care of it. Destruction of ANY County property may get you more time.
8. You will not have cash in your possession at any time.
9. You cannot transfer money to another inmate at any time.
10. No gambling of any kind is permitted.
11. No food, tobacco, stamps, stamped envelopes, or medication can be brought in or sent to you.
12. Turn in all out going letters to officer in housing unit. Letters being written to Attorney, Judges, Court of legal nature may be given to the officer sealed by you.
13. Only books which have been approved are permitted.
14. When moving from one place to another, you will go straight to destination always with an officer or a runner.
15. When in a line, always move quietly, in an orderly manner.
16. Your family or friends may bring clothing 3 days before your out date.

Behavior:

1. Do not shout or yell at any time.
2. Do not change cells or bunks in dormitories.
3. Do not visit in other cells, dormitories, or housing units.
4. DO NOT FIGHT. No reason or excuse will be accepted.
5. Unnatural sex acts will not be tolerated. Anyone involved in such acts is subject to charges and prosecution.

Cleanliness:

1. You must keep yourself personally clean at all times.
2. You must keep your living area clean at all times.
3. You may obtain a razor to shave from an officer. When you have shaved you must return the razor to the officer.

Clothing:

1. You can have only 1 set of regular issue clothing at any time. No other clothing is permitted.
2. Do not wash clothing in housing unit. All clothing is washed in the Institution Laundry. Unless permitted by Superintendent Directive.

Smoking:

1. No smoking in bed or in sleeping area.
2. No smoking in any dining area.
3. No smoking in the hospital. Except by directive.

Medications:

1. You are not allowed to have any kind of medication without written permission.
2. All medication must be taken in the presence of a doctor, a nurse, or an officer.

Contraband:

1. You must turn in any contraband you find to an officer. No excuse will be accepted for having any contraband in your possession.

REMEMBER: ANYTHING NOT ISSUED BY THE INSTITUTION OR SOLD IN COMMISSARY IS CONSID-
ERED CONTRABAND!

In addition to the above, your housing unit may have some additional rules. If so, you will be told about them or they will be posted. Obey them. Violation of rules will subject you to a conduct report and the possible loss of privileges and/or Good Time. OBEY THE RULES! STAY OUT OF TROUBLE! DO YOUR TIME! LET US HELP YOU HELP YOURSELF!

Maximum Rules and Regulations

[i.e., for untried and unsentenced inmates], Sybil Brand Institute for Women, Los Angeles, California

THIS INSTITUTE IS A BRANCH OF THE LOS ANGELES COUNTY JAIL. IT IS KNOWN AS THE SYBIL BRAND INSTITUTE FOR WOMEN.

Time Schedules

Maximum—4:40 A.M.—Rising Time
5:00 A.M.—Breakfast
10:00 A.M.—Lunch
3:30 P.M.—Dinner
8:45 P.M.—Everyone in own bed area
9:00 P.M.—Lights out

Conduct Rules

Bed Areas. Bed assignments are made ONLY by an officer. Do not change your bed without permission from the officer. There are to be NO more than three inmates in a bed area or cell at the same time. Only two inmates are permitted on one bed at a time, and both are to be sitting up, with feet on the floor. When lying down on your bed, your shoes must be off. Do not hang towels, clothing or laundry in such a way that officers cannot see. Do not hang anything on the bars in cellblocks.

Bathroom Areas. Except for toilet facilities, not to be used prior to lights on. Personal underclothing is not to be washed in the wash basins. Dorm or cellblock trustees ONLY to wash and dry all personals including tennis shoes for entire area in Day Room. Showers are to be used only as scheduled. You must shower every day.

Smoking. In Dorms smoking is permitted in bed area ONLY. In cellblocks smoking is permitted inside a cell ONLY. You must not smoke in the cellblock corridors. Ashtrays must be kept empty and clean, and remain on the shelf of the locker or writing table. Never place on beds. Never smoke while lying down.

Talking. There is NO talking after lights out, during count, or when going from housing area to meals, work areas, visitation or Infirmary. There is no loitering outside of housing area. Inmates must walk by twos and close together in meal lines and when going to or from work areas. No talking is permitted in lines.

Red Lines. In Dorms a red line is painted on the floor at the grilled gate. In cellblocks it is painted on the floor between the showers and the first cell. Anytime a line is formed to leave the housing area, the formation is to begin behind this red line. If you are called from your housing area by an officer wait behind the red line until the door has been opened and the officer has instructed you to step out.

Count. Count is regularly taken after lights out. However, it may be called at any time. When count is called over the public address system, inmates in Dorms are to go to their own bed areas, inmates in Cellblocks are to go inside their own cells. When the officer enters the officer's station, inmates are to line up at the foot of their beds in Dorms and in front of their cell in cellblocks. Do not lean against the walls, beds, or bars. There is absolutely no talking while count is being taken. Remain standing until excused by the officer.

Meal Lines. Meal lines are called over the public address system. You must go to meals. There is no talking in meal lines or in the Dining Room.

Personal Contact. No personal contact is permitted. This includes playing, wrestling, massaging, plucking eyebrows, etc.

Borrowing, Lending, and Exchanging. You are not permitted to give, exchange, borrow or loan ANY personal items such as clothing, shoes, commissary, money, etc.

Disciplinary Actions. The BEST way to avoid disciplinary actions is to follow the Jail Rules and do as instructed by the officer. If you feel an order is unfair, the best policy is to do as told at the time and then write a request to see the Classification Board.

Identification Bands. Identification bands are not to be removed and if showing signs of wear or if cannot be read, report to your officer at once.

Clothing and Linens

Undergarments. Each inmate may have a maximum of five (5) sets of underclothing (bra, panties, slip). All personal items must be marked with your initials. Pettipants and girdles are counted as panties.

Street Clothing. You are permitted to receive one exchange of street clothing during your incarceration. If you receive a clothing exchange, the original clothing must be returned with visitor. No exchanges will be accepted on Saturdays, Sundays, or Holidays and may be made only between 8:00 A.M. and 4:00 P.M. and between 6:00 P.M. and 9:00 P.M. during the week. No socks are to be brought in.

Needlework. Permitted in reasonable quantities in Dorms only. You may work on one (1) needlework project at a time—knitting, crocheting, or embroidery. Visitors may bring you five (5) skeins of yarn at a time or enough thread to complete one embroidery or crocheting project.

You may knit or crochet the following items: sweaters, stoles, afghans, baby clothes, socks or hats. You may not knit or crochet pants, skirts, long coat sweaters, dresses or shorts. Visitors may bring you only those pattern books, plastic needles or crochet hooks to complete one project.

Completed articles must be turned in to the Officer (along with your authorization or sales slip) to be placed in your property.

If you wish to release articles to a visitor, you must inform the officer when you turn in your completed article. Excess yarn, thread, needles, and pattern books should be turned in at the time the article is completed.

You must retain your authorization or sales slip with your needlework at all times, or articles will be confiscated. You may not knit for another, nor may another inmate knit for you.

Appearance—Cleanliness—Neatness

Cells and Dormitories. Each inmate is required to keep her own cell or bed area and surrounding area neat and clean at all times.

Lockers. Only cup and ashtray on outside locker shelf in Dorms. There are to be no liners on the inside locker shelves. Locker contents must be orderly and not excessive. Any amount over five (5) of each cosmetic item is considered excessive and will NOT be returned to you. Dresses, etc. to be hung on rack inside locker. Do NOT hang anything on doors of locker.

Beds. Must be made prior to breakfast and kept neat during the day.

Floors and Walls. Nothing is to be left on the floor during the night except one (1) pair of shoes or thongs per person. Do NOT deface or paste pictures on walls or lockers. No blankets or pillows on floor.

Trash. All trash which will burn is to be placed in the trash can. There are to be NO individual trash receptacles (boxes, paper bags, etc.) in bed areas or lockers. Soiled napkins must be wrapped securely in newspaper and placed in trash cans. Glass and metal are to be turned in to the officer.

Personal Appearance. Each inmate is required to keep herself neat and clean at all times. You must be fully dressed and presentable when leaving your housing area for any reason; do NOT walk around in stocking feet or barefooted.

Showers. Shower is to be taken daily. You are allowed ten (10) minutes to shower. No showers one-half hour prior to any meal line or after lights out.

Headscarves or Pin Curls. Headscarves or pin curls are not permitted from 7:00 A.M. to 5:30 P.M. unless special permission is granted.

Nightcaps. May be worn after 5:30 P.M. only if hair is in curlers. May be worn from bedtime to 7:00 A.M. whether or not hair is in curlers. Are to be worn above eyebrows.

Money

Ways you may receive Money. Visitors may leave any amount at time of visit, to be deposited to your account. Visitors may leave up to $5.00 at time of visit, with the officer in the visiting room—to be given directly to you.

Mail. Cash received in the mail will be deposited to your account. A notation on the front of the envelope will show the amount. Checks and Money Orders will be placed in your property. Personal checks are NOT accepted.

Withdrawal of Money from Account. Money withdrawal slips will be issued in the housing area on Tuesday evenings. You may not draw more than eight dollars ($8.00) from your account per week. Slips will be processed and money issued to you the following Saturday morning. Special request for money withdrawal should be sent to Inmate Personnel Sergeant. You are not allowed to have more than $12.00 in your possession at any time. Bills of larger denomination than $5.00 will be confiscated.

Visiting—Mail

Visiting. Visiting hours are daily from 10:00 A.M. to 2:30 P.M. Monday through Saturday and holidays, and from 12:30 P.M. to 2:00 P.M. on Sunday. You are allowed two (2) visits per week. Each visit is limited to twenty (20) minutes. No children under eighteen (18) years of age will be permitted to visit. Ex-inmates are not allowed to visit. Visitors cannot visit more than one (1) inmate.

General Information about Mail. All mail is inspected. Letters may not contain institutional gossip or information about other inmates. Inmates without privileges may not send or receive personal mail. Mail pertaining to case is permitted. Incoming mail will be delivered when privileges are restored. There is no written communication permitted between inmates. No packages will be permitted.

Outgoing Mail. Each letter is limited to four (4) pages written on one side only. Do NOT write in margins. Top first page must have your NAME, BOOKING NUMBER and HOUSING AREA. The envelope must have the following return address:

NAME (as booked), BOOKING NUMBER
BOX 54320
Sybil Brand Institute for Women
Los Angeles, CA 90054

Leave envelope unsealed and drop in mail box on way to Dining Room. Letters will be returned to inmates if they are not prepared in accordance with these rules.

Photographs. You may receive small photographs through the mail, but may have no more than five (5) in your possession. Excess will be confiscated. You may not trade photographs and your name and booking number must be written on the back.

Other Information

Catholic Services. Confession at 8:00 A.M. on Fridays. Mass is held at 8:00 A.M. each Sunday in the Auditorium.

Protestant Services. Held at 9:00 A.M. every Sunday in the Auditorium.

AA Meetings. Held at 7:30 P.M. every Wednesday in the Minimum Dining Room. All persons booked on any drunk charge are automatically okayed to attend. Others wishing to attend must have special permission obtained from the Inmate Personnel Sergeant.

Sick Call. Nurses' Line will be called at 6:20 A.M. Monday through Friday for those who have illness complaints. No Nurses' Line on holidays.

Court. Items which may be taken to court are only the following: lipstick, compact, cake mascara, brush, cigarettes, matches, property slip, deposit slips, court papers, money, unpeeled fruit or eggs.

Rules and Regulations for the Direction of the Officers and Employees of the Massachusetts Correctional Institution, Framingham

Deportment and Conduct between Employee and Inmate

Your relations with the inmates may be of necessity dual in character. You may be both counselor and disciplinarian at one and the same time. This will enjoin your utmost tact and diplomacy. You should aim to be friendly not familiar, sympathetic not maudlin, firm not harsh, constant not obstinate, vigilant not unduly suspicious, strict not unjust.

Let the inmate feel the impact of your leadership. Do not discuss the discipline or management of this or other penal institutions, or the affairs of your fellow employees while in the presence or hearing of an inmate, nor inform her as to the nature of comments, entries, or reports regarding her made by another employee. Do not show or otherwise allow these rules to be made available to an inmate. Do not intercede personally for an inmate relative to release or outside employment, nor endorse a petition for granting parole, pardon or commutation without the permission of the Superintendent. You must not associate, accompany or consort with an inmate on parole or others permitted to be at liberty without specific written approval of the Superintendent and the Parole Board. Do not grant any inmate special privileges but treat all inmates impartially. Let your relations with inmates, or with their relatives or friends, at all times be such that you would have them known to any superior officer.

Rules, California Institution for Women,

Frontera, California

Section I. Campus Privileges[1]

1. Unless otherwise restricted, those who are off duty are permitted campus privileges between 8:00 A.M. and 5:00 P.M.
2. After the morning and noon meals, except in foggy weather, residents may remain in the Circle until scheduled for work or other appointments.
3. After the evening meal, residents off duty may visit in the Circle or in the areas directly

---

1. Rules governing behavior and dress are generally more relaxed in state and federal institutions than they are at the county level. Some of these rules may seem repetitious, but I have included them to emphasize the similarities of regulations throughout the country.

in front of the cottage recreation rooms until campus is cleared for the evening count or until dusk, whichever is sooner.

4. Residents may sit on the grass in the Circle, but not lie down or use the grass for a pathway. Sidewalks will be used in going from place to place.
5. Shift workers who are off duty from 8:00 A.M. to 4:00 P.M. Monday through Friday, may go to the Library but must have a pass issued by the Cottage Supervisor. Residents will present pass to the School Secretary.

Fog Procedure

1. When fog procedures are in effect, campus privileges are not authorized. Women will return to their cottages until time for work release or for regular authorized appointments.

Unauthorized Areas

1. The following areas are *out-of-bounds* at all times except to those on official business. . . .
   a. Adm. Building (including outside area)
   b. Bakery
   c. Clinic (including outside area)
   d. Canteen
   e. Commissary
   f. Counseling Center and outside areas
   g. Hospital and outside areas
   h. Industry
   i. Laundry
   j. Maintenance
   k. PTU and RGC
   l. School Building and outside areas
   m. Walker Detention and outside areas
   n. Vocation Sewing
   o. Areas behind Cottages
   p. Areas around CFF

Section III. Personal Appearance

A. Standards

1. Women in CIW will dress appropriately to the occasion and activity in which they are engaged. Each resident will be held fully responsible for her appearance.
2. Clothing will be neat, in good repair, and of proper fit.
   a. Dresses and skirts will be moderate without extreme of length or fit.
   b. No open or revealing patterns are permitted with regard to blouses.
3. Brassieres and panties will be worn at all times, unless the resident is alone in her room.
4. Knee socks may be worn as appropriate. Mid-calf or masculine sox are not permitted.

B. Clothing

1. General:
   a. Alteration of clothing, whether state issue or personal is not authorized except for shortening or lengthening of dresses and skirts.
   b. At no time will there be any cutting or restyling of wearing apparel.

2. Work Clothing:
    a. Dresses, skirts, blouses, sweaters and special uniforms issued for the particular assignment will be worn for work. Sweaters and blouses are not to be substituted for work uniform tops.
    b. Work uniforms will be worn for work only, and only for the assignment for which they are issued. They may not be worn on days off. Work uniforms will not be altered.
        (1) They may be worn to breakfast and the noon meal on work days but not the evening meal.
        (2) Work uniforms may be worn to school only if the person is going directly from work to school or vice versa.
3. Leisure Clothing:
    a. Dresses or skirts and blouses will be worn for:

Church	Special Programs	School
Movies	Receptions	Dance Nights
House Parties	Evening Meals	Adm.

    b. Leisure pants may be worn at the following times:
        (1) Breakfast and noon meals on days off.
        (2) After evening meals.
        (3) When attending athletic events; for individual sports; and for sunbathing.
        (4) To clinic or mail room appointments.
    c. Leisure pants may not be worn:
        (1) On house party or dance nights, whether participating or not.
        (2) For work or school.
        (3) To Adm. Building at anytime.
        (4) Any evening meal.
        (5) To entertainments, movies, church, or receptions.
4. Shoes:
    a. High heeled pumps or sling pumps may be worn during leisure hours, or for work except when safety or health requirements prevent. All high heeled shoes must have plastic or rubber capped heels. No steel caps or stiletto pointed heels are permitted.
    b. Rubber thongs may be worn during off duty hours only. They may not be worn for active recreational activities.
    c. Bedroom slippers and scuffies may be worn only in the house when off duty.
5. Sweaters:
    a. Only approved sweaters may be worn. Low neck, or loosely knit, revealing sweaters are not authorized.
    b. Sweaters may be substituted for blouses with skirts and leisure pants, but may not be substituted for work uniform tops.
    c. Sweaters may not be altered or restyled after being received or approved.
    d. Sweaters may be worn with uniforms.
    e. Sweaters knitted by residents while at CIW may be retained if:
        (1) Yarn was obtained legally.
        (2) Garments do not exceed the authorized allowance.
    f. Knitted shells will be counted separately—not exceeding 4.
6. Clothing Permitted in Medication Line:
    a. Gym suits may be worn to clinic only if a woman is coming directly from or going to any recreational activity where gym suits are authorized.
    b. Hospital aides may wear the hospital uniform to the clinic but not the white apron. Aprons are to be worn only when the aide is on duty.
    c. Kitchen uniforms may be worn to and from the clinic if a woman is on duty at the time she is due at the clinic. She may not linger on campus but must go directly to and from the clinic.

    d. Work uniforms may be worn on work days only.
    e. Leisure pants may be worn only when a person is off duty and is not scheduled for work or other appointments after clinic.
7. Gym Suits:
    a. Gym suits will be worn only:
        (1) While participating in athletic events.
        (2) Going to and from the athletic field or athletic activities.
        (3) While on athletic field or in the gym.
    b. Neither the shorts nor the blouse of the gym suit will be worn with any other outfit. Gym blouses and shorts may not be altered.

Missouri Inmate's Guide to Institutional Living
Social Rules

1. Be sure you are using acceptable language. No profanity or obscenities.
2. Keep yourself clean, well-groomed and attractive.
3. Always be considerate of those about you.
4. Be careful about telling tales and spreading gossip.
5. Do not appear off your Dorms unless you are suitably dressed. Reasonable modesty is expected on the Dorms.
6. On Sunday wear dresses until after 3 P.M.
7. No loud arguments which disturb others are permitted.
8. Improper personal behavior between two women is a segregation offense.

[Author's Note: Conventional notions of feminine propriety reveal themselves in the language of all such instructions. As the Missouri guide cautions, "We like to see generosity among the women but we dislike having them use material things to buy favors or affections. Beware of the girl who says, 'I like you, can I borrow a cigarette?' Chumming too closely with any one person is strongly discouraged."]

Inmate Handbook, State of New Jersey, Department of Corrections, Edna Mahan Correctional Facility for Women, Clinton, New Jersey
Rights and Privileges of Inmates

This last set of rules governs current (1995) procedures regarding mail and visitors. Under their Handbook on Discipline for Adults, *which follows these rules, female prisoners in New Jersey are now punished, as in many states, under the same standards set for male prisoners—a policy that seems to say, "They wanted equal treatment? Well, now they got it!"*

Correspondence, Publications and Mailed Packages

Inspection and Identification of Incoming Correspondence. Correspondence received will be opened and inspected for contraband and money. . . . Correspondence received without the inmate's name and number will be returned to the sender. If the sender's name and address do not appear on the outside of the correspondence, the correspondence may be delivered after [it] has been inspected for contraband [or may be] marked "refused" and returned unopened, to the United States Post Office. Incoming correspondence will not be read unless there is reason to believe that the correspondence contains disapproved content and then only upon authorization of the Superintendent.

Inspection of Outgoing Correspondence. If the inmate's name and number do not appear on the outside of the correspondence, the correspondence will be opened and examined to identify the sender and returned. If the inmate cannot be identified, the correspondence will be destroyed. . . . Correspondence sent by an inmate must be sealed with the stamp(s) properly placed in the upper right corner of the envelope. Tape applied over the stamp(s) or "washed" stamps are prohibited.

Outgoing correspondence will not be opened, read or censored unless there is a reason to believe that the correspondence contains disapproved content.

Outgoing correspondence to public officials, governmental agency officials and new media representatives, as listed below, will not be opened, read or censored. However, such correspondence may be held for 72 hours in order to verify that the addressee is genuine. . . .

Telegrams and Mailgrams. An inmate will be permitted to send telegrams and mailgrams in an emergency. An emergency may include: Death; Critical illness; Accident, or When the inmate is paroled and no one has picked up the inmate as arranged.

Cost of Mailing Correspondence by Indigent Inmates. If an inmate is judged indigent, the institution will provide letter writing materials and will assume the cost of mailing, excluding registered, certified or insured service, up to 12 letters per month. In the event funds are deposited into an inmate's account or the inmate earns some state wages, the amount owed to the institution for the cost of any postage will be recovered.

Correspondence Processing. Incoming correspondence will be distributed to inmates and outgoing properly identified correspondence will be sent to the post office within one day of receipt in the mail room, excluding weekends and holidays.

Postage Stamps. Inmates may purchase and retain a maximum of 40 postage stamps at any given time. Postage stamps must be purchased from the Inmate Commissary. Postage stamps cannot be mailed to an inmate, left on a visit or received in a package. Stamped envelopes, as identified in PERMISSIBLE GENERAL ITEMS, page 43 are included in the total number of postage stamps that may be retained by an inmate.

Inspection of Incoming Legal Correspondence. Incoming legal correspondence will not be read or copied, but will be opened, removed and inspected for contraband in the presence of the inmate to whom it is addressed. Upon receipt of the correspondence the inmate will sign an acknowledgment for delivery.

Publications

Publications to or from Other Inmates. All publications to or from inmates housed in other correctional facilities may be read to ensure that the publications do not contain disapproved content.

Inspection of Incoming Publications. Incoming publications will be opened and inspected for contraband, but will not be read unless there is reason to believe that the publication contains disapproved content and then only upon the authorization of the Superintendent.

Identification of Sender of Incoming Publications. The sender's name and address and the inmate's name and number must legibly appear on the outside of all incoming publications. If the sender's name and address do not appear on the outside of the publication, the publication will be opened and examined to determine the identity of the sender. If the sender cannot be identified, the publication will be destroyed.

Funds Received by Mail

Money orders and certified checks are the only funds received through the mail that can be accepted for deposit in an inmate's account. Personal checks and cash sent through the mail will not be accepted and will be returned to the sender. Inmates are issued receipts for all funds received through the mail that are accepted for deposit.

Disapproved Content in Correspondence and Publications

Disapproved Content. Any incoming correspondence or publication may be withheld in the mail room or taken from the inmate's possession if it falls within one of the following categories:

1. The correspondence contains material which is detrimental to the security and/or order of the correctional facility because it incites violence based upon race, religion, creed or nationality and a reasonable inference can be drawn, based upon the experience and professional expertise of correctional administrators, that it may result in the outbreak of violence within the facility;
2. The correspondence, or publications contains information regarding the manufacture of: i. Explosives; ii. Weapons; iii. Controlled dangerous substance; iv. Escape plans; v. Lock picking; or vi. Anything of a similar nature.
3. The correspondence, or publication contains information which appears to be written in code;
4. The correspondence, or publication contains information concerning the activities within or outside the correctional facility which would be subject to criminal prosecution under the law of New Jersey or the United States;
5. The correspondence or publication incites violence or destructive or disruptive behavior toward: i. Law enforcement officers; ii. Department of Corrections personnel; or iii. Correctional facility programs or procedures.
6. The correspondence, or publication contains material which, based upon the experience and professional expertise of correctional administrators and judged in the context of a correctional facility and its paramount interest in security, order and rehabilitation: i. Taken as a whole, appeals to a prurient interest in sex; ii. Lacks, as a whole, serious literary, artistic, political or scientific value; and iii. Depicts, in a patently offensive way, sexual conduct including patently offensive representations or descriptions of ultimate sexual acts, masturbation, excretory functions, lewd exhibition of the genitals, sadism or masochism.

Withheld/Seized Correspondence or Publications

Incoming correspondence that is withheld from an inmate will be returned to the sender with a notice that the material violates the Department's rules covering correspondence. Publications that are withheld from an inmate will be disposed of in a manner determined by the inmate and at her expense.

Rejected Items and Contraband Found in Correspondence, Publications, and Packages

Rejected items will be considered contraband for which the inmate will receive notice of the seizure. When a contraband notice is received, you will have five days to advise the Package House of how you wish to dispose of the rejected item(s). . . .

Inmates who have items withheld as contraband, who have not received a disciplinary charge and disagree with the decision to reject the item(s) will have 3 days from the receipt of contraband notice to send a written appeal to the Superintendent. The appeal must contain information why the rejected items should not be considered contraband. If a disciplinary charge has been issued, the inmate's appeal for the rejected item(s) is through the disciplinary process. If the Superintendent determines that the item or items are contraband, or the Disciplinary Hearing Officer upholds a contraband seizure, the inmate will have 2 working days, following receipt of the final determination, to indicate which of the following means will be used to dispose of the contraband: Mail to relative, or friend at the inmate's expense; Donate by the inmate to a charitable organization; or Destroy at the inmate's request.

Institutional Visit Program

Approval of Visitors

Visitors considered members of your immediate family, close friends, clergy and persons who may have a positive influence on you will usually receive approval to visit. . . .

Inmates who wish to receive visits from ex-offenders must secure approval from the Office of the Superintendent. Limitations that affect ex-offenders' visits at this institution are:

Requests for consideration will be limited to immediate family members . . . father, mother, husband, child, brother or sister.
Exceptions will be made for an individual's fiancée.
Ex-offenders applying for visitation privileges must be on parole status for a minimum of 6 months with a report of successful parole adjustment from the District Parole Officer.
Applications for consideration of ex-offender visits to this institution will be processed through the Internal Affairs Unit.

You will receive written confirmation of a visitor's approval or denial to visit. Please do not ask or invite your visitor to visit you until you receive notification that visitation privileges have been granted. When a proposed visitor is denied visit privileges, you will be advised of the reasons that support the rejection. You may appeal the decision to reject a visitor to the Superintendent.

Procedures for Individuals Visiting Inmates

Visitor Identification. All visitors 18 years and older must have in their possession 1 piece of current descriptive identification. Acceptable forms of identification include: Automobile driver's license; Welfare/Medicaid card; Employment photo ID card; Joint

Connection photo ID card; or Current validated passport and cards presented with another valid ID bearing a signature.

Social Security cards and birth certificates, as well as types of identification that expired are unacceptable forms of identification and cannot be used to admit an approved visitor.

Visitor Search and Metal Detector Processing. All visitors and their belongings are subject to search while on the premises of this institution. Additionally, a visitor may be required to submit to a pat frisk search. Should a visitor refuse to submit to a search, the opportunity to visit will be denied and the visitor will be directed to leave the grounds of the institution.

Before entering the institution, all visitors will walk through a metal detector and/or may be scanned with a hand-held trans-frisker.

Visitor Rules and Regulations

- Visitors are required to dress appropriately. Clothing that is revealing, or suggestive is prohibited.
- Visitors that appear to be intoxicated, under the influence of narcotics or display inappropriate behavior will be denied readmittance to the institution.
- Children accompanying an adult visitor must remain under the visitor's control. Failure of the visitor to properly supervise visiting children will be cause to terminate the visit.
- Children using any play area must be supervised by their parents or relatives. Use of play areas and play equipment is at the risk of the visitor.
- Kissing by immediate family members and close friends is permitted within the bounds of good taste at the beginning and at the end of the visit. Hand-holding, in full view, is the only body contact allowed between a visitor and their inmate during a visit.
- Visitors and inmates must sit facing each other.
- Visit area bathrooms are provided for visitor use only.
- Food and soft drinks purchased during the visit must be consumed in the visit area.
- Inmates are prohibited from handling money.
- Photographs taken during the visit can remain with the inmate or may be given to the visitor.
- Visitors are cautioned that State of New Jersey criminal laws regulate civilian conduct at a correctional facility.

Food Packages Received through the Visit Program

All food packages must be received at the Visit Center for processing on visit days no later than 10:00 A.M. for morning visits and 3:00 P.M. for afternoon visits. The visitor will be issued a receipt for any food package left for an inmate. The visitor may give the food package receipt to the inmate during the visit.

A schedule of alternating weeks has been established for receipt of food packages for inmates through the visit program. Inmates whose last names begin with the letters "A" through "L" are eligible to receive packages during a week opposite the week for packages of those inmates who's last names begin with the letter "M" through "Z." Food packages will not be accepted from any visitor if presented during a week the inmate is ineligible to receive packages.[2]

2. Some inmates have visitors only once or twice a year, since prisons are so difficult and costly to get to. Imagine how disappointing it would be to have someone go to the trouble of bringing you a gift package you couldn't receive because it wasn't "your" week.

Non-food items will not be accepted through the visit program. Non-food items must be sent to the inmate by mail or parcel service, this includes: all clothing, foot-wear, appliances (T.V.'s, radios, etc.) magazines, books, etc.

Rejected items or items removed from an over weight package may be picked up by the visitor after the visit. The institution provides a blackboard visible when leaving the Visit Center. If an item has been rejected from a package, the inmate's name will appear on the blackboard. Any rejected item that is not picked up by the visitor will be discarded.

Home cooked or prepared foods, for example meals, casseroles or cooked meats are permissible food items for inclusion in food packages left during the visit program. Meats may be fried, roasted, broiled or breaded. All meats must be sliced. Fowl must be in pieces with any stuffing to be separate from the food item. Home cooked foods are limited to 2 securely covered (lids) plastic containers per food package with each container no larger than 32 oz. in volume or 2 one gallon, clear "Zip-Lock" type bags.

For additional information affecting food packages, please refer to FOOD PACKAGES, GENERAL REGULATIONS, PROHIBITED FOOD ITEMS AND PERMISSIBLE SMOKED FOOD ITEMS pages 44 and 45.

Inmate Visit Rules and Regulations

The following rules and regulations are applicable to inmates and their visitors and insure that all participants in the visit program have an equal opportunity to enjoy the benefits of the program.

1. All visits will be conducted in a quiet, orderly and dignified manner. Handshak-ing, embracing and kissing by the immediate family members and close friends are permitted within the bounds of good taste at the beginning and at the end of the visit only. Prolonged or heated necking or petting is prohibited and violations may result in the loss of visitation privileges for both the inmate and/or the visitor. Hand-holding, in full view, is the only body contact allowed between an inmate and their visitor during a visit. Other forms or expressions of intimate contact are prohibited. Small children may sit on the inmate's lap, as contact restrictions, generally, do not apply to children.

2. Appropriate dress is required of all inmates attending visits. *Inmates determined to be inappropriately dressed to receive visitors will be returned to their housing unit* [my emphasis]. Inmates must wear bras and panties. Inmates are prohibited from wear-ing halters, shower shoes and curlers to a visit. Further, inmates are banned from wearing excessively tight fitting clothing, such as spandex or tights or any clothing which exposes large areas of skin. The wearing of hats is also prohibited at visits.

3. Inmates are not permitted to accept anything from, or give anything to a visitor with the exception of vending machine items, purchased for the inmate by their visitor. Inmates may not directly handle any money used to purchase vending items. Any vending items purchased during a visit must be consumed at the visit or taken out of the visit area by the visitor.

4. The items listed below may be carried into a visit by an inmate:

> 1 Wedding band;
> 1 Chain and/or religious medal;
> Comb/brush; and
> Voucher cards for concession items or pictures.

5. All visit areas are designated NO SMOKING.

6. Visiting children must remain under the inmate's supervision. Children disturb-ing other visitors in the visit area may provide sufficient cause to terminate the visit.

7. Inmates may not visit with another inmate's visitor(s).

8. Visits will terminate when the inmate is notified by the visit officer. Inmates are not to escort their visitor(s) to the exit door of the visit area.

9. Inmates must submit to a pat-frisk search when entering a visit and a strip search at the conclusion of the visit.

10. In the event a visitor is found to have contraband or appears to be under the influence of drugs or alcohol, their visiting privileges will be terminated. Restoration of visiting privileges for the offending visitor must be sought from the Superintendent.

11. Due to limitations of space, the duration of an inmate's visit may be shortened to provide visit opportunities to individuals who are waiting to enter the institution. If asked, the visitor(s) should promptly depart the visit area.

12. No one may return to the visit area, for any reason, once a visit has concluded.

Telephone Calls

Individuals who telephone the institution for inmates will be advised that any message left for an inmate will not be relayed.

Emergency Telephone Calls. An inmate will be permitted to make monitored telephone calls of reasonable length, as determined by the monitor, in emergencies when approved.

Whenever an emergency telephone call for an inmate is received at this institution, the telephone number, name of the caller and the nature of the emergency will be obtained. The validity of the emergency reported by the caller will be investigated and when confirmed, the information will be provided to the inmate.

New Jersey Department of Corrections Handbook on Discipline for Adults

Inmate Prohibited Acts

10A:4-4-1 Prohibited Acts.

(a) *.001 killing
   *.002 assaulting any person
   *.003 assaulting any person with a weapon
   *.004 fighting with another person
   *.005 threatening another with bodily harm or with any offense against his or her person or his or her property
   *.006 extortion, blackmail, protection; demanding or receiving favors, money or anything of value in return for protection against others, to avoid bodily harm, or under threat of informing
   *.007 hostage taking
   .008 abuse/cruelty to animals
   .051 engaging in sexual acts with others
   .052 making sexual proposals or threats to another
   .053 indecent exposure
   *.101 escape
   *.102 attempting or planning escape
   .103 wearing a disguise or mask
   .150 tampering with fire alarms, fire equipment or fire suppressant equipment

*.151 setting a fire

.152 destroying, altering or damaging government property, or the property of another person.[3]

*.153 stealing (theft)

.154 tampering with or blocking any locking device

*.155 adulteration of any food or drink

*.201 possession or introduction of an explosive, incendiary device or any ammunition

*.202 possession or introduction of a gun, firearm, weapon, sharpened instrument, knife or unauthorized tool

*.203 possession or introduction of any narcotic paraphernalia, drugs or intoxicants not prescribed for the individual by the medical or dental staff

*.204 use of any narcotic paraphernalia, drugs or intoxicants not prescribed for the individual by the medical or dental staff

*.205 misuse of authorized medication

*.206 possession of money or currency ($50.00 or less) unless specifically authorized

*.207 possession of money or currency (in excess of $50.00) unless specifically authorized

.208 possession of any property belonging to another person

.209 loaning of any property or anything of value

*.210 possession of anything not authorized for retention or receipt by an inmate or not issued to him or her through regular correctional facility channels

.211 possessing any staff member's clothing and/or equipment

.212 possessing unauthorized clothing

.213 mutilating or altering clothing issued by the government

*.214 possession of unauthorized keys or other security equipment

*.251 rioting

*.252 encouraging others to riot

*.253 engaging in, or encouraging, a group demonstration

*.254 refusing to work, or to accept a program assignment

*.255 encouraging others to refuse to work or to participate in work stoppage

.256 refusing to obey an order of any staff member

.257 violating a condition of any community release program

*.258 refusing to submit to urine analysis

.301 unexcused absence from work or any assignment; being late for work

.302 malingering, feigning an illness

.303 failing to perform work as instructed by a staff member

.304 using abusive or obscene language to a staff member

.305 lying, providing a false statement to a staff member

*.306 conduct which disrupts or interferes with the security or orderly running of the correctional facility

.351 counterfeiting, forging or unauthorized reproduction or use of any document not enumerated in prohibited act .352

*.352 counterfeiting, forging or unauthorized reproduction or use of any classification document, court document, psychiatric, psychological or medical report, money or any other official document

.401 participating in an unauthorized meeting or gathering

.402 being in an unauthorized area

.451 failure to follow safety or sanitation regulations

.452 using any equipment or machinery which is not specifically authorized

---

3. This rule is sometimes applied to the alteration of state-issued prison clothing.

.453 using any equipment or machinery contrary to instructions or posted safety standards

.501 failing to stand count

.502 interfering with the taking of count

*.551 making or possessing intoxicants or alcoholic beverages

*.552 being intoxicated

.553 smoking where prohibited

.601 gambling

.602 preparing or conducting a gambling pool

.603 possession of gambling paraphernalia

.651 being unsanitary or untidy; failing to keep one's person and one's quarters in accordance with posted standards

.652 tattooing or self-mutilation

.701 unauthorized use of mail or telephone

.702 unauthorized contacts with the public

.703 correspondence or conduct with a visitor in violation of regulations

*.704 perpetrating frauds, deceptions, confidence games, riots or escape plots

.705 commencing or operating a business or group for profit or commencing or operating a nonprofit enterprise without the approval of the Superintendent

*.706 soliciting funds and/or noncash contributions from donors within or without the correctional facility except where permitted by the Superintendent

.707 refusal to cooperate in following a prescribed course of treatment (that is, refusal to appear for or go to a scheduled exam—medical, dental, etc.)

*.708 refusal to submit to a search

.709 failure to comply with a written rule or regulation of the correctional facility

*.751 giving or offering any official or staff member a bribe or anything of value

.752 giving money or anything of value to, or accepting money or anything of value from, another inmate

.753 purchasing anything on credit

.754 giving money or anything of value to, or accepting money or anything of value from, a member of another inmate's family or another inmate's friend with an intent to circumvent any correctional facility or Departmental rule, regulation or policy or with an intent to further an illegal or improper purpose

.802 attempting to commit any of the above acts, aiding another person to commit any of the above acts or making plans to commit any of the above acts shall be considered the same as commission of the act itself

*.803 attempting to commit any of the above acts preceded by an asterisk, aiding another person to commit any such act or making plans to commit such acts shall be considered the same as a commission of the act itself.

(b) Only acts cited in (a) above preceded by an asterisk are considered to be of sufficient severity to warrant possible transfer to the Vroom Readjustment Unit. Transfer to the Vroom Readjustment Unit shall be effected only when specifically ordered by the Disciplinary Hearing Officers or Adjustment Committee and subsequently confirmed by the Inter-Institutional Classification Committee.

All prohibited acts which may constitute crimes of the first, second, third or fourth degree under the Criminal Code of the State of New Jersey shall be referred to the prosecutor of the county in which the correctional facility is located.

GLOSSARY

Prison and Prison-Related Terms

Some of these expressions may not be used in exactly the same manner throughout the country, but they were used in the various prisons and jails that I visited.

Acting out. Emotional or uncontrolled behavior on the part of a prisoner. The term, used by staff, covers a wide range of expression—from breaking a window to crying.

Adjustment center. Area of solitary confinement cells where prisoners are kept in maximum security confinement.

Administrative segregation. "Solitary confinement" that is administratively ordered as a result of classification or administrative decision instead of being "punitively" ordered through a disciplinary proceeding for violation of institutional rules. Emotionally disturbed women, for instance, are often kept in "administrative segregation" throughout their incarceration—as are women sentenced under the death penalty.

Appeal. A procedure whereby a person who has received an adverse decision in a lower court may have the decision reviewed by a higher court, usually known as an "appellate court." It is an "appeal" because the higher court may grant or deny the review.

Back time. The amount of unserved time remaining from a previous sentence that has to be served as a result of violating parole. When parole is revoked because a person has been convicted of committing a new crime, the new sentence imposed is known as "front time." For instance, if a woman who has been on parole for six years is convicted of a new crime, the judge may give her a new sentence and additionally demand she serve all her back time—the six years she was on parole.

Bags. Packets containing heroin or cocaine.

Beef. (*n*) Sentence or time. (*v*) To voice a complaint.

Behavior clinic. Disciplinary "court" that determines punishment for infractions of institutional rules.

Benny. An amphetamine pill.

Bing. Solitary confinement.

Black lock: Solitary confinement in either an isolation cell or one's own cell for a period of three days or more.

Blowing it. Losing the opportunity to do something desired; e.g., "blowing parole" means not making it, failing.

Blue room. Solitary confinement cell painted blue. (This euphemism is used at Cook County Jail in Chicago.)

Boosting. Shoplifting.

Bull dyke. Bull dagger. Woman who plays a masculine role in a lesbian relationship. Also a derogatory term used to describe any woman who looks masculine or tough.

Bust. A police raid or a raid from institutional staff. To "get busted" is to be arrested or, in prison, to get written up for an infraction of rules.

Campus. Prison grounds.

Cell block. A section of a prison or jail containing any number of cells, usually arranged perpendicular to a long, narrow walkway.

Clients. Prisoners.

Coke. Cocaine.

Con artist. A person skillful at convincing others of his or her good intentions while defrauding them. A good con artist can make almost anyone believe almost anything.

Continuance. A postponement. When a case is listed for a hearing in court on a particular date and the hearing is postponed for some reason, the case is said to have been "continued." The same term is used for a person who has been given another date for a parole hearing.

Contraband. Goods prohibited by law or regulation from being brought into or kept in the prison. Contraband can be anything so defined by the institution—from postage stamps to food products to personal items such as cosmetics or wedding rings.

Control center. The central point for prison surveillance, whether in a particular living area or in the whole institution. In modern institutions, guards at the center press buttons to slide cell doors open and lock them.

Cop. To steal or acquire.

Cop a plea. To plead guilty, by arrangement with the defense attorney and the prosecution, usually in exchange for a lesser sentence.

Cop out. To quit; to fail to keep a promise.

Correctional counselor. Prison employee whose job can include both counseling and surveillance.

Correctional institution. Prison. Technically, an institution that aims to ''correct faults.''

Correctional officer. Guard or matron.

Corrections. Terminology for the field of penology, which indicates an orientation toward treatment rather than toward mere custody. (Most state organizations previously called Bureaus of Prisons are now called Departments of Correction.)

Cottages. Residential houses containing cells or locked rooms for prisoners. The term is used primarily in women's and juvenile institutions that have housing in smaller units than those of the mass penitentiary.

Count. Population inventory, usually held from three to nine times a day in any prison. A security precaution against escape attempts.

Detainer. A writ authorizing further detention of a person in custody pending action.

Detention. Keeping a person, usually one awaiting trial, in custody or confinement.

Detention center. A jail used primarily for persons held awaiting trial.

Determinate sentence. *See* **Sentence.**

Discretionary power. The power exercised by the courts in placing a person on probation, suspending a sentence, or assigning a conviction. Also, the power exercised by administrative bodies in making decisions; e.g., parole boards usually have broad discretionary power to decide whether a prisoner should be placed on parole or kept in prison. Their decisions can be overturned in a court proceeding only if they can be shown to constitute an abuse of discretion.

Disciplinary board. Two or more staff members who determine punishment for infraction of institutional rules.

Discipline. Punishment.

Do time. To serve a prison sentence. A common expression is, ''Do your time, don't let your time do you.'' In other words, serve your sentence your own way, don't let it destroy you.

Dope. (*v*) To administer a narcotic or medication to someone; to drug them or ''dope them up.'' (*n*) An addictive drug or marijuana.

Dorm. Living area in a prison where beds are lined up in military fashion for multiple residence.

Drop her belt. To switch from playing the masculine role back to the feminine role. When a woman drops her belt she is often said to have ''curled up her hair'' again; the usual implication is that she has left a relationship in which she played the male role.

Feeding time. Official prison term for prisoner meal time. Meals are often referred to by jail administrators as ''feedings,'' like those given babies or animals.

Fix. An intravenous injection of heroin or another opiate.

Flat timer. A person serving a set amount of time or a fixed prison sentence without eligibility for parole, e.g., ''two years flat time.'' Flat timers are often envied because they have no uncertainty about when they will be getting out; they do not have to meet conditions of parole.

Fog procedure. Maximum security procedure followed in institution during fog, rain, or heavy storm to guard against escape.

Free world. The world outside prison; society at large.

Front time. *See* **Back time.**

Go off. To get angry, scream, or shout; to "blow your cool."

Guards. Custodial personnel assigned to prisoners; also referred to as matrons, staff, law officers, correctional officers, "the law," police, and "the heat."

H. Heroin.

Habit. Addiction to narcotics.

Heat. The police; the authorities; prison guards or staff members.

Hit the fence. Escape.

Hole. Solitary confinement.

Hooch. Homemade wine or alcoholic beverage illegal in prison, often made from potato peelings or sugar and fruit.

Hooked. Addicted to heroin or other narcotics.

Hooked up. Attached to a person or involved in a relationship.

Horse. Heroin.

Hot. Stolen or illegal.

House. Cell or room. Prisoners often refer to their individual cells as "my house."

Hustle. To obtain money in legally questionable ways that involve quick wit or movement; e.g., to solicit customers for or as a prostitute.

Hustler. A person who makes money in ways that involve quick thinking and/or deception. In some areas prostitutes are referred to as hustlers.

Hype. Drug addict.

Incorrigible. A term used by courts and prison officials to describe someone who will not be reformed, corrected, or tamed. The term is often synonymous with "uncontrollable"; many juveniles are imprisoned for being "incorrigible" when they have broken no criminal law.

Indeterminate sentence. A prison sentence that stipulates no maximum or minimum time; more commonly, a sentence that states the maximum term only, thus allowing the prisoner to be released at any time up to the maximum depending on her institutional record and parole approval. Prisoners traditionally serve longer terms under this sentencing procedure, although it was not intended to achieve this effect.

Inmate code. Unwritten rules of procedure and conduct for prisoners, which define loyalties and unity. To "break the code" means to go against the standards of behavior accepted by peers.

Institutionalization. Acceptance of prison values and standards; a loss of one's own spirit and focus.

Isolation. Solitary confinement.

Jacket. Institutional file on each prisoner, which includes data on her family history, education, past employment, and arrest record, as well as medical, psychiatric, and disciplinary reports, behavioral evaluations, and records of visitors and correspondents. The prisoner is not allowed to see what is in her jacket, although the information is accessible to police, federal agents, the institution, and the parole board.

Jag. A drug habit.

John. A prostitute's paying customer; also, toilet.

Joint. Prison or jail.

Jones. A strong desire for something or someone; a drug habit.

Junk. Heroin or other drugs.

Junkie. A person addicted to narcotics.

Juvie. Juvenile hall; reform school.

Kick the habit. To break or cure the addiction to narcotics.

Life (the). A culture separate from mainstream society that involves unconventional behavior and illegal moneymaking activities.

Mainline. To inject drugs directly into a major vein.

Minimum sentence. A term of imprisonment that in most states cannot be more than one half of the maximum sentence imposed. An offender is not usually eligible for parole before the expiration date of her minimum sentence. (*See* **Sentence.**)

Movement (as in inmate movement). Major inmate ''traffic'' or the actual physical motion of inmates walking or being transferred from one part of the institution to another for any purpose.

My heart. A favorite child or someone dear and close to the person speaking.

Nickel bags. Packets of heroin or another drug costing five dollars each. A dime bag costs ten dollars. ''Doing a nickel'' means serving a five-year sentence.

Old man. A woman's husband or lover; also used to refer to someone's father.

P & Q. ''Peace and Quiet'' unit for maximum security confinement; the same as the ''Adjustment Unit,'' primarily for women with mental problems or chronic disciplinary infractions.

Paperhanger. Person who writes bad checks.

Parole. Release from prison under the jurisdiction of the court until the maximum date of sentence expires. Most people sentenced to prison are released sometime before the maximum term of their sentence expires. They are usually under the jurisdiction of an administrative body most often known as a state parole board and must follow a certain code of behavior during the parole period. Failure to obey the rules of parole may result in the parolee's return to prison to serve not only the maximum sentence but also ''back time.''

Parole board. Administrative agency of the federal, state, or local criminal justice system. The board sends one or more representatives to interview inmates at ''parole hearings.'' A majority of the board determines whether the inmate will be released prior to expiration of sentence. The board sets its own rules and regulations immune from other governmental sanctions. The Federal Parole Board, for instance, has never announced the rules or principles guiding its determinations and gives no reasons for its decisions to approve, deny, or continue. Its discretion is unchecked by legal standards or judicial review. The nine members of the Federal Parole Board make about seventeen thousand decisions per year on individual prisoners—an average of seventy decisions a day.

Parole violation. A failure to obey the rules set down by the parole board that results in return to prison. A parolee also may be returned to prison if she is arrested for the commission of a new crime while on parole. If she is convicted, she will be made to serve not only the new sentence but also all the time remaining on the sentence for which she was paroled without any credit being given for that time she was on parole.

PBX training. Telephone switchboard training.

Penitentiary thing. Something that happens only in prison.

People. A person's family in the outside world. "My little people" are "my children."

Players. Heterosexual women involved in "playing a role," or homosexual "playing" in prison.

Playing the dozens. Playful and sometimes hostile exchange of rhymes in a certain pattern—usually aimed at being derogatory to either a person or the person's mother.

Police. Guards, matrons, or other prison staff members; also law enforcement officers.

Pop a door. Open a door by pressing an electronic control that triggers release of the lock.

Postconviction remedy. A procedure whereby a person who has been convicted of a criminal offense may have the proceedings reviewed in a supplemental proceeding. The best-known postconviction remedy is that of habeas corpus, which is initiated by the filing of a petition.

Presentence investigation. A report usually prepared by the probation department to provide information to the judge concerning the background and personality of the person to be sentenced. It also may contain many suggestions as to the disposition of the case. Unfortunately, only a small percentage of judges order these reports on people before sentencing them to prison.

Prisoners. Persons held in custody, captivity, or a condition of restraint. Women prisoners are also referred to as clients, residents, inmates, convicts, patients, girls, ladies, and students.

Probation. A legal directive that imposes criminal sanctions without imprisonment. Wherever a judge has the power to impose a term of imprisonment for conviction of a criminal offense, he also usually has the power to suspend the imposition of such a sentence and place the convict under the jurisdiction of a state or county administrative body to which she must report at regular intervals. Under mandatory sentencing laws, judges cannot exercise this power, even when it is perfectly safe, less expensive, and more effective than prison.

Probation revocation. Annulment of probation for failure to follow rules and regulations of probation. A person whose probation has been revoked may be sentenced to any period of time up to the maximum term for which the offense is punishable. She is not given credit for the time she served on probation.

Public defender. An attorney under contract to a city or a privately funded agency to represent indigent defendants. Because the majority of people going to trial are indigent, PDs or court-appointed lawyers represent the majority of people sentenced to prison.

Pulled out. To be taken out of the prison to go to court or to be transferred to another institution.

Pull my coat. Help me out; call my attention to something that's going on to keep me out of trouble.

Punitive segregation. Solitary confinement ordered as punishment.

Rack. Solitary confinement, as in "getting sent to the rack."

Rap. A conviction. A bad rap is a heavy sentence or a bad break. To take the rap means to take the conviction. Women prisoners often say that women "take the rap" for their men; men prisoners say that men "take the rap" for their women.

Rat. An informer or a snitch.

Red devils. Seconal.

Reform. (v) To correct an evil or an abuse; to improve by alteration; to cause a person to abandon irresponsible or "immoral" behavior. (n) An action that attempts to improve social or political institutions or conditions without radical change.

Reformatory. A prison usually designed for women or children; a place designated for the reformation of prisoners.

Rehabilitate. To restore a handicapped or delinquent person to useful life through education or therapy; to restore original rank, privilege, or rights.

Reintegration. The readjustment and reorientation of a person back into society. Work release programs, home furloughs, and halfway houses cushion the shock of reentry and aid in the reintegration of prisoners after the disabling effects of imprisonment.

Release on recognizance. To be released prior to trial on the condition of one's personal commitment to appear in court. The decision to release a person on her own recognizance is based on her perceived stability and the likelihood that she will not flee the jurisdiction; considerations include family status, history of employment, residence, and prior arrest record. Personal recognizance is ordered as a substitute for the posting of bail.

Residents. Prisoners.

Restitution. Compensation for loss, damage, or injury. A reparation.

Run a check/Run a make. To make a background check on a person's police record. Prosecutors usually "run a make" on a person they're prosecuting to see if she has any open or pending cases. If an employer runs a check and finds the person has a prison or arrest record she has not listed, he can dismiss her for "falsifying records."

Sentence. A legal directive made by a judge for a person convicted of a criminal offense. It can consist of either a fine or a prison term. A judge may also suspend a sentence completely, suspend imposition of a sentence and place a person on probation, or sentence a person to the jurisdiction of a private program. The laws of various states differ in the manner in which they direct the judge to impose sentences. In one type of sentencing, judges impose only the maximum term to be served. In another type, judges impose a minimum and a maximum term. The minimum term is that period of time which must be served before the person can be considered for parole. A sentence that states the maximum term only is referred to as an indeterminate sentence, and a sentence that states both a minimum and a maximum may be called a definite sentence. These terms are not used uniformly throughout the various jurisdictions, however; sometimes a sentence stating a minimum and a maximum is also called an "indefinite" sentence. Mandatory sentencing sets an absolute minimum sentence for certain crimes and cannot be altered to fit individual circumstances.

Shackle. A metal fastening that encircles and confines the ankles or wrists to hobble a person and restrict movement.

Shakedown. A thorough search of a prisoner's room or person for drugs, weapons, and other contraband. Also, extortion of money by blackmail or fraud.

Shank. To cut someone with a knife.

Shiv. A knife or razor used as a weapon. In prison, some women carry shivs made from various objects for self-defense or for use in fights.

Signify. Put someone down; use derogatory language about a person.

Snitch. An informer; a person who violates inmate code by telling police or prison staff about the activities or plans of other prisoners.

Solid. (*n*) An agreement or confirmation meaning "right" or true. (*adj*) Reliable. A "solid person" is trustworthy.

Solitary confinement. The isolation of a prisoner in a maximum security cell for the purpose of punishment or discipline. Solitary confinement usually means a loss of all prison privileges, such as mail, visitors, books, in addition to physical isolation. Solitary is also referred to as "the bing," "the rack," "the hole," "reflection," "the quiet room," "isolation," "lockup," "segregation," "punishment," and "adjustment."

Sprung (to get). To be released from jail on bail pending trial or appeal; to be released suddenly.

Square business. Anything that is "real," true, or factual.

Stable. A group of whores or prostitutes who belong to one pimp, who "protects" them and collects half or more of their earnings.

Stash. (*v*) To hide. (*n*) Anything saved or hidden. Usually any stash in prison is considered contraband.

Stone cop. A prison staff member who strictly enforces rules; a guard who makes life hard for inmates, searches for anything illegal, and reports violations to authorities. (Can also be applied to an inmate who is a snitch.)

Straight police. A guard who will not make exceptions, who follows rules as they are written. Often "straight police" are considered fair by prisoners because they are predictable and do not discriminate.

Street. The world outside prison. Also refers to low-income culture where people communicate primarily from the front stoop or on the street.

Street time. The period a person spends on parole or on probation.

Stud broad. A woman with a masculine appearance who plays the male role in a homosexual relationship.

Stuff. Narcotics, usually heroin.

Suspended sentence. A judge sometimes suspends a sentence for a period of time after which the defendant, if she has not been rearrested, has her case closed. The complete suspension of sentence is rare, except in cases where a judge, when sentencing a defendant on multiple bills of indictment, imposes a sentence on some of the bills and suspends sentence completely on others.

Trick. A male who pays a woman to give him some form of sexual gratification.

Trick baby. A child born to a woman prostitute from impregnation by a paying customer.

Tricked up. Confused, disoriented.

Turn a trick. To be paid by a male customer for sexual interaction.

Walk. To get out of prison. To walk free without restrictions of parole or probation.

Wire. Information or a message.

Write-up. A disciplinary report for violation of a rule; an infraction reported by a staff member.

BIBLIOGRAPHY

Consulted Works and Recommended Reading

Adams, Ansel, and Nancy Newhall. *This Is the American Earth*. San Francisco: Sierra Club, 1960.

"Alcoholism, Other Drug Addictions, and Related Problems among Women." Fact sheet. New York: National Council on Alcoholism and Drug Dependence, 1993.

American Correctional Association. *The Female Offender: What Does the Future Hold?* Washington, D.C.: St. Mary's Press, 1990.

———. *Manual of Correctional Standards*. Washington, D.C.: ACA, 1969.

———. *Volunteers Look at Corrections*. Washington, D.C.: ACA, 1969.

American Correctional Association, Joint Commission on Correctional Manpower and Training. *The Public Looks at Crime and Corrections*. Washington, D.C.: ACA, 1968.

American Foundation Institute of Corrections. *The County Jail and Related Criminal Justice Services, Polk County, Florida*. Philadelphia: AFIC, 1966.

———. *The County Prisons and Jails of Pennsylvania*. American Foundation Studies in Corrections. Philadelphia: AFIC, 1965.

American Friends Service Committee. *Struggle for Justice: A Report on Crime and Punishment in America*. New York: Hill & Wang, 1971.

American Prison Association, Committee on Classification and Case Work. *Handbook on Classification in Correctional Institutions.* Revised ed. Philadelphia: American Foundation Studies in Corrections, 1965.

Arnold, Regina. "Processes of Victimization and Criminalization of Black Women." In *Women of Color in American Society,* edited by Maxine Boca Zinn and Bonnie Thornton. Philadelphia: Temple University Press, 1991.

Artis, William, Jr. ". . . And Justice for All? An Interview with Haywood Burns, National Director of the National Conference of Black Lawyers." *CRJ Reporter,* September 1972.

Austin, James. *America's Growing Correctional-Industrial Complex.* San Francisco: National Council on Crime and Delinquency, 1990.

Austin, James, Barbara Bloom, and Trish Donahue. *Female Offenders in the Community: An Analysis of Innovative Strategies and Programs.* National Council on Crime and Delinquency. Washington, D.C.: National Institute of Corrections, 1992.

Austin, James, and Aaron McVey. *The 1989 Prison Population Forecast: The Impact of the War on Drugs.* San Francisco: National Council on Crime and Delinquency, 1989.

Balchen, Bess. "Prisons: The Changing Outside View of the Inside." *AIA Journal,* September 1971.

Barros, Colleen, Andrea Slavin, Virginia McArthur, and Stuart Adams. *Movement and Characteristics of Women's Detention Center Admissions, 1969.* Research Report no. 39. Washington, D.C.: District of Columbia Department of Corrections, 1971.

Barry, Ellen. "Imprisoned Mothers Face Extra Hardships," *Journal of the National Prison Project* (Winter 1987).

———. "Pregnant, Addicted and Sentenced," *ABA Criminal Justice Journal* (Winter 1991).

———. "Pregnant Prisoners," *Harvard Women's Law Journal* 12 (1989).

———. "Quality of Prenatal Care for Incarcerated Women Challenged," *Youth Law News* (November–December 1985).

———. "Reunification Difficult for Incarcerated Parents and Their Children," *Youth Law News* (July–August 1985).

———. "Women Prisoners and Health Care: Locked Up and Locked Out," in *Manmade Medicine: Women's Health, Public Policy and Reform,* edited by Kary Moss. Durham, N.C.: Duke University Press, 1995.

Barry, Ellen, with River Ginchild and Doreen Lee, "Legal Issues for Prisoners with Children," in *Children of Incarcerated Parents,* edited by Katherine Gabel and Denise Johnston. Lexington, Mass: Lexington Books, 1995.

Barry, Ellen, et al., "Women in Prison," in *Women and the Law,* edited by Carol Lefcourt et al. New York: Clark Boardman, 1993.

Bartlett, Donald L., and James B. Steele. "Crime and Injustice." *Philadelphia Inquirer,* February 1973.

Baunach, Phyllis Jo. *Mothers in Prison.* New Brunswick, N.J.: Transaction Books, 1985.

Beck, Robert. *The Naked Soul of Iceberg Slim.* Los Angeles: Holloway House, 1971.

Beckman, Lanny. "Psychology As a Social Problem: An Investigation into the Society for the Psychological Study of Social Issues." *Radical Therapist* 2, no. 6 (1972).

Benjamin, Harry, and R. E. L. Masters. *Prostitution and Morality: A Definitive Report on the Prostitute in Contemporary Society and an Analysis of the Causes and Effects of the Suppression of Prostitution.* New York: Julian Press, 1964.

Bienen, Leigh B. "A Good Murder." *Fordham Urban Law Journal* 20, no. 3 (1993).

————. "No Savings in Lives or Money with Death Penalty." *New York Times,* August 17, 1988.

————. "Of Race, Crime, and Punishment." *New York Times,* June 21, 1987.

"The Black Prisoner: Featuring the Writings of Black Prisoners." *The Black Scholar,* April–May 1971.

Bloom, Barbara, Meda Chesney-Lind, and Barbara Owen. *Women in California Prisons: Hidden Victims of the War on Drugs.* San Francisco: Center on Juvenile and Criminal Justice, 1994.

Bloom, Barbara, and David Steinhart. "Why Punish the Children? A Reappraisal of the Children of Incarcerated Mothers in America." San Francisco: National Council on Crime and Delinquency, January 1993.

Booth, Maud Ballington. "The Shadow of Prison." *Proceedings of the 58th Congress of the American Prison Association.* New York: National Prison Association, 1928.

Bowker, Lee H., ed. *Women and Crime in America.* New York: Macmillan, 1981.

Braithwaite, John. *Crime, Shame, and Reintegration.* Cambridge: Cambridge University Press, 1990.

Brown, Barbara A., Thomas I. Emerson, Gail Falk, and Ann E. Freedman. "The Equal Rights Amendment: A Constitutional Basis for Equal Rights for Women." *Yale Law Journal* 80 (1971).

Bullough, Vern L. *The History of Prostitution.* New Hyde Park, N.Y.: University Books, 1964.

Burke, Peggy, and Linda Adams. *Classification of Women Offenders in State Correctional Facilities: A Handbook for Practitioners.* Washington, D.C.: Cosmos Corp. for the National Institute of Corrections, 1991.

Byrnes, Inspector Thomas. *Professional Criminals of America.* 1866. Reprint, with an introduction by Arthur M. Schlesinger, Jr., and S. J. Perelman, New York: Chelsea House, 1969.

Carlen, Pat. *Alternatives to Women's Imprisonment.* Buckingham, England: Open University Press, 1990.

Carroll, Lewis. *Alice's Adventures in Wonderland.* New York: Harper & Brothers, 1901.

Case, John D., Warden, Bucks County Prison and Rehabilitation Center. Testimony at Philadelphia Hearings. In Pennsylvania Department of Corrections Report of the Legislative-Executive Task Force on Reorganization of Government, *Toward Reducing Crime in Pennsylvania,* vol. 2. Philadelphia: Citizens' Task Force, 1970.

Chapman, Jane Roberts. *Economic Realities and the Female Offender.* Lexington, Mass.: Lexington Books, 1980.

Chesney-Lind, Meda. "Chivalry Reexamined: Women and the Criminal Justice System." In *Women, Crime, and the Criminal Justice System,* edited by Lee H. Bowker and Meda Chesney-Lind. Lexington, Mass.: Lexington Books, 1978.

———. "Girls and Deinstitutionalization: Is Juvenile Justice Still Sexist?" *Journal of Criminal Justice Abstracts* 20 (1988).

———. "Girls, Delinquency, and Juvenile Justice: Toward a Feminist Theory of Young Women's Crime." In *The Criminal Justice System and Women,* edited by Barbara Raffel Price and Natalie Sokoloff. New York: McGraw-Hill, 1995.

———. "Patriarchy, Prisons, and Jails: A Critical Look at Trends in Women's Incarceration." *Prison Journal* 71, no. 1 (1991).

———. "Women and Crime: The Female Offender." *Signs* 12, no. 1 (1986).

———. "Women's Prison Reform in Hawaii: Trouble in Paradise." *Jericho* 43 (1987).

Chesney-Lind, Meda, and Noelie Rodriguez. "Women under Lock and Key: A View from the Inside." *Prison Journal* 63, no. 2 (Autumn–Winter 1983).

Chesney-Lind, Meda, and R. G. Shelden. *Girls, Delinquency, and the Juvenile Justice System.* Pacific Grove, Calif.: Brooks/Cole, 1992.

Chevigny, Paul. *Police Power.* New York: Pantheon, 1969.

Citizens Task Force. *Report on State Correctional Institution at Muncy, Pennsylvania.* Philadelphia: Citizens Task Force, 1970; distributed by Pennsylvania Program for Women and Girl Offenders, Inc.

The Clarion. Inmate publication at the California Institution for Women, bimonthly issues, October 1970 through December 1972.

Clark, Ramsey. *Crime in America: Observations on Its Nature, Causes, Prevention, and Control.* New York: Simon & Schuster, 1970.

Cleaver, Eldridge. *Soul on Ice.* New York: Dell, 1968.

"Coeducational Prison Is a Test in Rehabilitation." *New York Times,* July 8, 1972, p. M 27.

Cole, Larry, et al. *Street Kids.* New York: Grossman, 1970.

"The Costs of Preventative Detention." *Yale Law Journal* 79 (1972).

Crane, Richard. "Inmate Health Care." *Correctional Law Reporter,* December 1993.

Cray, Ed. *The Big Blue Line: Police Power versus Human Rights.* New York: Coward-McCann, 1967.

"Creation: The Arts in Prison." Supplement, *Penal Digest International* 1, no. 2 (July 1972).

Cunningham, Gloria. "Supervision of the Female Offender." *Federal Probation* 27 (December 1963).

Cyert, Margaret, Chairman of the Citizen Task Force to Propose a Community Treatment Center for Women Offenders. Testimony at Pittsburgh Hearing. In Pennsylvania Department of Corrections Report of the Legislative-Executive Task Force on Reorganization of Government, *Toward Reducing Crime in Pennsylvania,* vol. 2. Philadelphia: Citizens' Task Force, 1970.

Davis, Angela Y., et al. *If They Come in the Morning.* New York: Signet Books, 1971.

Dawson, Robert O. "The Decision to Grant or Deny Parole: A Study of Parole Criteria in Law and Practice." *Washington University Law Quarterly* (June 1966).

Day, Dorothy. "Thoughts after Prison." *Liberation,* September 1957.

Deans, Ralph C. "Racial Tensions in Prisons." *Editorial Research Reports,* October 20, 1971.

Death Penalty Information Center. "Facts about the Death Penalty." New York: NAACP Legal Defense and Education Fund, 1995.

Deming, Barbara. *Prison Notes.* New York: Grossman, 1966.

Diaz-Cotto, Juanita. "Women and Crime in the United States." In *Third World Women and the Politics of Feminism,* edited by Chandra Talpade Monaty, Ann Russo, and Lourdes Torres. Bloomington: Indiana University Press, 1991.

Dickens, Charles. *American Notes and Pictures from Italy.* 1867. Geneva, Switzerland: Edito-Service S.A., distributed by Heron Books, 1970.

District of Columbia Citizens Council for Criminal Justice. *The Treatment of Women Offenders in the District of Columbia.* Washington, D.C.: Citizens Council for Criminal Justice, 1972.

District of Columbia Department of Corrections. *Summary of Completed Research, 1967–1971.* Summary Report no. 1. Washington, D.C., 1971.

Dubler, Nancy Neveloff, ed. *Standards for Health Services in Correctional Institutions.* Washington, D.C.: American Public Health Association, 1986.

Duster, Troy. *The Legislation of Morality.* New York: Free Press, 1970.

Eastwood, Mary. "The Double Standard of Justice: Women's Rights under the Constitution." *Valparaiso University Law Review* 5, no. 2 (1971).

Eldridge, Stanley. *Return Me to My Mind.* New York: Fortune Society, 1970.

Erikson, Eric H. *Childhood and Society.* New York: Norton, 1964.

"Excerpts from Opinions on Death Penalty." *New York Times,* June 30, 1972.

Eyman, Joy S. *Prisons for Women: A Practical Guide to Administration Problems.* Springfield, Ill.: C. C. Thomas, 1971.

Faustini, Gino. "La delinquenza fra le adolescenti in Italia." *Esperiènza di rieducazione* 16 (1969).

Feinman, Clarice. *Women in the Criminal Justice System.* New York: Praeger, 1980.

Fernald, Mabel Ruth, May Hayes, and Almena Dawley. *A Study of Women Delinquents in New York State.* Patterson, N.J.: Smith, 1920.

Flynn, Elizabeth Gurley. *The Alderson Story: My Life As a Political Prisoner.* New York: International, 1963.

Forer, Lois G. *Criminals and Victims.* New York: Norton, 1980.

————. *No One Will Listen: How Our Legal System Brutalizes the Youthful Poor.* New York: Grosset, 1970.

————. *A Rage to Punish: The Unintended Consequences of Mandatory Sentencing.* New York: Norton, 1994.

————. "Youth and the Law." *YWCA Magazine,* February 1972.

Frankl, Viktor E. *From Death Camp to Existentialism.* Translated by Ilse Lasch. Boston: Beacon Press, 1959.

Gabel, Katherine. *Legal Issues of Female Inmates.* Washington, D.C.: National Institute of Corrections, U.S. Department of Justice, 1982.

Galbraith, Susan. "Women and Legal Drugs." In *Alcohol and Drugs Are Women's Issues,* vol. 1, edited by Paula Roth. Metuchen, N.J.: Women's Action Alliance and The Scarecrow Press, 1991.

Geller, William. "The Problems of Prisons: A Way Out?" *The Humanist,* May–June 1972.

Genty, Philip M. "Procedural Due Process Rights of Incarcerated Parents in Termination of Parental Rights Proceedings: A Fifty-State Analysis." *Journal of Family Law* 30, no. 4 (1991–92).

————. "Protecting the Parental Rights of Incarcerated Mothers Whose Children Are in Foster Care: Proposed Changes to New York's Termination of Parental Rights Law." *Fordham Urban Law Journal* 17, no. 1 (1989).

Giallombardo, Rose. *Society of Women: A Study of a Women's Prison.* New York: Wiley, 1966.

Gibbons, Don C. *Delinquent Behavior.* Englewood Cliffs, N.J.: Prentice-Hall, 1980.

Gilfus, Mary E. "Seasoned by Violence/Tempered by Law: A Qualitative Study of Women and Crime." Ph.D. dissertation, Brandeis University, 1988.

Gillan, John L. *Criminology and Penology.* New York: Appelton-Century, 1945.

Glaser, Daniel. "Societal Trends: From Revenge to Resocialization: Changing Perspectives in Combatting Crime." *American Scholar* 40, no. 4 (Autumn 1971).

Goffman, Erving. *Asylums.* Garden City, N.Y.: Doubleday, 1961.

Gold, Sally. "Equal Protection for Juvenile Girls in Need of Supervision in New York State." Unpublished paper available in Yale Law Library, 1970.

Goldman, Emma. *Living My Life.* New York: Dover, 1971.

Goodell, Charles, and Andrew Von Hirsch. Testimony before Subcommittee no. 3 of the House Judiciary Committee. "On H.R. 13118. The Parole Procedures and Improvement Act of 1972." In *Corrections, Part VII-A.* Washington, D.C.: U.S. Government Printing Office, 1972.

Graham, Fred P. "Criminal Statistics." *Crime and Delinquency,* August 1969.

Grant, Joanne, ed. *Black Protest: History, Documents, and Analysis, 1619 to the Present.* Greenwich, Conn.: Fawcett, 1970.

Greenberg, David. *The Problem of Prisons.* Philadelphia: American Friends Service Committee, 1970.

Haley, Alex. *The Autobiography of Malcolm X.* New York: Grove Press, 1965.

Halleck, Seymour. *The Politics of Therapy.* New York: Science House, 1971.

———. *Psychiatry and the Dilemmas Of Crime.* New York: Harper, 1967.

Harmon, Sasha. "Attitudes toward Women in the Criminal Process." Unpublished paper available in Yale Law Library, 1970.

Harris, Jean. *Marking Time: Letters from Jean Harris to Shana Alexander.* New York: Scribner's, 1991.

———. *Stranger in Two Worlds.* New York: Zebra Books, 1986.

———. *They Always Call Us Ladies: Stories from Prison.* New York: Scribner's, 1988.

Harris, Sara. *Hell Hole.* New York: Dutton, 1967.

Health Law Project Report. *Health Care and Conditions in Pennsylvania's Prisons.* Philadelphia: University of Pennsylvania Law School, 1972.

Hearings before Subcommittee no. 3 of the Committee on the Judiciary, House of Representatives. "Illinois: The Problems of the Ex-Offender." *Corrections, Part VI.* Washington, D.C.: U.S. Government Printing Office, 1972.

———. "Prisons, Prison Reform, and Prisoners' Rights: California." *Corrections, Part II.* Washington, D.C.: U.S. Government Printing Office, 1972.

———. "Prisons, Prison Reform, and Prisoners' Rights: Massachusetts." *Corrections, Part V.* Washington, D.C.: U.S. Government Printing Office, 1972.

———. "Prisons, Prison Reform, and Prisoners' Rights: Michigan." *Corrections, Part VIII.* Washington, D.C.: U.S. Government Printing Office, 1972.

———. "Prisons, Prison Reform, and Prisoners' Rights: Wisconsin." *Corrections, Part IV.* Washington, D.C.: U.S. Government Printing Office, 1971.

Hecht, Judith A. *Effects of Halfway Houses on Neighborhood Crime Rates and Property Values: A Preliminary Survey.* Research Report no. 37. Washington, D.C.: District of Columbia Department of Corrections, 1970.

Heidensohn, Frances. *Women and Crime: The Life of the Female Offender.* New York: New York University Press, 1983.

Helfer, Ray E., and Henry C. Kempe. *The Battered Child.* Chicago: University of Chicago Press, 1968.

Hendrix, Omar. *A Study in Neglect: A Report on Women Prisoners.* New York: Women's Prison Association, 1972.

Henry, Joan. *Women in Prison.* New York: Doubleday, 1952.

Herbert, Rachel Bluntzen. *Shadow on the Nueces: The Saga of Chepita Rodriguez.* Atlanta: Emory University, Banner, 1942.

Herman, Judith. *Trauma and Recovery.* New York: Basic Books, 1992.

Hickey, William L. "Strategies for Decreasing Jail Populations." *Crime and Delinquency* 3, no. 1 (March 1971).

Holder, Angela R. "Law and Medicine: The Prisoner's Right to Medical Treatment." *American Journal of Correction* 33, no. 4 (July–August 1971).

Holiday, Billie, with William Dufty. *Lady Sings the Blues.* New York: Lancer, 1969.

Holmes, Steven A. "Ranks of Inmates Reach One Million in a Two-Decade Rise." *New York Times,* October 28, 1994.

Holt, Norman. "Temporary Prison Release: California's Pre-release Furlough Program." *Crime and Delinquency* 17, no. 4 (1971).

Hurt, Harry, III. "Is the Justice System Biased against Women?" *Self,* January 1995.

Illinois Department of Corrections. *Women and Children Residential Program Feasibility Study.* Springfield, Ill.: Illinois Department of Corrections, 1990.

Immarigeon, Russ, and Meda Chesney-Lind. *Women's Prisons: Overcrowded and Overused.* San Francisco: National Council on Crime and Delinquency, 1992.

Iowa Central Community College and Iowa Women's Reformatory. *Special Needs Proposal: Educational Program in Corrections for Clients at the Iowa Women's Reformatory.* Presented to the Iowa State Department of Public Instruction. Des Moines, 1971.

Jackson, George. *Soledad Brother: The Prison Letters of George Jackson.* New York: Bantam Books, 1970.

Jackson, Lorraine A. *Impact of the Women's Detention Center on First Timers.* Research Report no. 41. Washington, D.C.: District of Columbia Department of Corrections, 1971.

James, Howard. *Children in Trouble: A National Scandal.* Boston: Christian Science Publications, 1969.

James, Jennifer. *The Prostitute As Victim: Criminal Justice System and Women.* New York: Clark Boardman, 1982.

Johnston, Norman, Leonard Savitz, and Marvin E. Wolfgang. *The Sociology of Punishment and Correction.* New York: Wiley, 1970.

Jones, Ann. *Women Who Kill.* New York: Fawcett, 1980.

Jones, Georgia. "Heritage: Three Women." *Off Our Backs: A Women's News Journal* 2, no. 8 (April 1972).

Jones, Rochelle. "Females without Freedom." Seven-part series. *Palm Beach Post-Times,* October 1970.

Kairys, David. "Juror Selection: The Law, A Mathematical Method of Analysis, and a Case Study." *American Criminal Law Review* 10, no. 4 (1972).

———. *The Politics of Law.* New York: Pantheon, 1990.

———. *With Liberty and Justice for Some,* New York: New Press, 1993.

Kanowitz, Leo. *Women and the Law.* Albuquerque: University of New Mexico Press, 1969.

Keely, Sara F. "The Organization and Discipline of the Indiana Women's Prison." In *Proceedings of the Annual Congress of the National Prison Association.* New York: National Prison Association, 1898.

Kittrie, Nicholas N. *The Right to Be Different.* Baltimore: Johns Hopkins University Press, 1971.

Klapmuts, Nora. "Children's Rights: The Legal Rights of Minors in Conflict with Law or Social Custom." *Crime and Delinquency* 4, no. 3 (September 1972).

Kline, Sue. *A Profile of Female Offenders in the Federal Bureau of Prisons.* Washington, D.C.: National Council on Alcoholism and Drug Dependence, 1992.

Kopkind, Andrew. "White on Black: The Riot Commission and the Rhetoric of Reform." *Hard Times,* no. 44 (September 1969).

Kratz, Althea Hallowell. *Prosecutions and Treatment of Women Offenders and the Economic Crisis: Philadelphia, 1925–1934.* Philadelphia: University of Pennsylvania Press, 1940.

Krauss, Clifford, "Women Doing Crime, Women Doing Time." *New York Times,* July 3, 1994, p. E 3.

Kruttschnitt, Candace. "Respectable Women and the Law." *Sociological Quarterly* 23, no. 2 (1982).

Lee, Henry. "The Ten Most Wanted Criminals of the Past Fifty Years." *Liberty,* Fall 1972.

Lekkerkerker, Eugenia C. *Reformatories for Women in the United States.* Batavia, Ill.: J. B. Wolters, 1931.

Lemmert, Edwin M. *The Juvenile Court: Quest and Realities.* Task Force Report: Juvenile Delinquency and Youth Crime. President's Commission on Law Enforcement and the Administration of Justice. Washington, D.C.: U.S. Government Printing Office, 1967.

Levine, Stephen. *Death Row: An Affirmation of Life.* New York: Grove Press, 1971.

Levy, Howard, and David Miller. *Going to Jail: The Political Prisoner.* New York: Grove Press, 1971.

Lindsey, Richard W. *Pennsylvania Board of Probation and Parole: Media Fact Sheet.* Philadelphia, 1971.

Lord, Elaine. "A Prison Superintendent's Perspective on Women in Prison." *Prison Journal* 75 no. 2 (June 1995).

Los Angeles County Jail Division. *Annual Report of the Los Angeles County Jail Division.* Los Angeles, 1971.

Lucey, D. J., III, and J. C. Keene. "Women in Prison: The Treatment Model: The Muncy Experience." *Social Welfare Law,* c.p. 735 (1972).

Lundberg, Emma O. *Unmarried Mothers in the Municipal Court of Philadelphia.* Philadelphia: Thomas Harrison, 1933.

McDonald, Douglas C. "The Cost of Corrections: In Search of the Bottom Line." *Research in Corrections* 2 (February 1989).

McGaha, "Health Care Issues of Incarcerated Women." *Journal of Offender Counseling, Services, and Rehabilitation* 12, no. 1 (1987).

McGowan, Brenda G., and Karen L. Blumenthal. "Why Punish the Children? A Study of Children of Women Prisoners." *Children's Rights Report* 3 (November 1978).

Menninger, Karl. *The Crime of Punishment.* New York: Viking Press, 1968.

Millett, Kate. *Sexual Politics*. New York: Doubleday, 1970.

Mitford, Jessica. "Experiments behind Bars." *Atlantic Monthly,* January 1973.

———. *Kind and Usual Punishment*. New York: Knopf, 1973.

———. "Kind and Usual Punishment in California." *Atlantic Monthly,* March 1971.

Moheb, Ghali, and Meda Chesney-Lind. "Gender Bias and the Criminal Justice System." *Sociology and Social Research* 70, no. 2 (1986).

Moyer, Imogene L. *The Changing Roles of Women in the Criminal Justice System: Offenders, Victims and Professionals*. Prospect Heights, Ill.: Waveland Press, 1992.

Mukherjee, Satyanshu K., and Jocelynne A. Scutt, eds. *Women and Crime*. Sydney: Australian Institute of Criminology, 1981.

Murphy, Jim, Nancy Johnson, and Wanda Edwards. *Addicted Mothers: Imprisonment and Alternatives*. Albany, N.Y.: Coalition for Criminal Justice/Center for Justice Education, 1992.

Murton, Tom. "Drugs Used to Control Inmates." *Freeworld Times* 1, no. 2 (February 1972).

Nagel, William G. *The New Red Barn: A Critical Look at the Modern American Prison*. New York: Walker, 1973.

"The National Committee for Prisoners' Rights." *Prisoners Rights Newsletter* 1, no. 1 (State University of New York at Buffalo, School of Law, September 1971).

National Council on Crime and Delinquency, Committee on the Model Act. *A Model Act for the Protection of the Rights of Prisoners*. Hackensack, N.J.: National Council on Crime and Delinquency, 1972.

New Jersey Law Enforcement Planning Agency. *1971 New Jersey Plan for Criminal Justice*. Trenton, N.J., 1971.

New York City Board of Correction. *Annual Report: Crisis in the Prisons: New York City Responds: A Commitment to Change*. New York: Department of Corrections, 1971.

Nussbaum, Albert F. "The Rehabilitation Myth." *American Scholar* 40, no. 4 (1971).

Office for Substance Abuse Prevention. "A Snapshot of Women and Substance Use." In *Impact: Prevention Resource Guide*. Minneapolis: OSAP, 1992.

Ohio Department of Mental Hygiene and Correction. *Annual Financial and Statistical Report, 1970–1971*. Columbus, Ohio: Bureau of Statistics, 1971.

Ohio Reformatory for Women. *Annual Report, July 1, 1970, to July 1, 1971*. Marysville, Ohio, 1971.

Owen, Barbara, and Barbara Bloom. "Profiling Women Prisoners: Findings from National Surveys and a California Sample." *Prison Journal* 75, no. 2 (June 1995).

Parker, Tony. *Women in Crime: Five Revealing Cases* (first published in Great Britain under the title *Five Women*). New York: Delta Books, 1968.

Pell, Eve. "The Soledad Brothers: How a Prison Picks Its Victims." *Ramparts,* August 1970.

Pennsylvania Association on Probation, Parole, and Correction. "Toward Social Justice: Bridging Idealism and Realism." Proceedings of the 18th National Institute on Crime and Delinquency. *The Quarterly* 28, nos. 2 and 3 (Autumn 1971).

Pennsylvania Department of Corrections. "Report of the Legislative-Executive Task Force on Reorganization of Government." In *Toward Reducing Crime in Pennsylvania,* vol. 2. Philadelphia: Citizens' Task Force, 1970.

Perez, Judy Ann. "The Effects of My Incarceration on My Loved Ones." In *Out of Silence,* vol. 1. New York City: Women in Jail and Prison Project, Correctional Association of New York, 1993.

Pollock, Otto. *The Criminality of Women.* Philadelphia: University of Pennsylvania Press, 1950.

Pollock-Byrne, Joycelyn, ed. *Women, Prison, and Crime.* Pacific Grove, Calif.: Brooks-Cole, 1990.

President's Commission on Law Enforcement and the Administration of Justice. *The Challenge of Crime in a Free Society.* Washington, D.C.: U.S. Government Printing Office, 1967.

Price, Barbara Raffel, and Natalie Sokoloff, eds. *The Criminal Justice System and Women.* New York: McGraw-Hill, 1995.

Rafter, Nicole Hahn. *Partial Justice: Women in State Prisons, 1800–1935.* Boston: Northeastern University Press, 1985.

Rafter, Nicole Hahn, and Elizabeth Stanko, eds. *Judge, Lawyer, Victim, Thief.* Boston: Northeastern University Press, 1982.

Ragghianti, Marie. "Save the Innocent Victims of Prison." *Parade Magazine.* February 6, 1994.

"Reading of Lawyer-Inmate Mail Barred." *Prison Law Reporter* 1, no. 12 (September 1972).

Reckless, Walter C., and Barbara Ann Kay. "The Female Offender." Unpublished paper submitted to the President's Commission on Law Enforcement and the Administration of Justice, 1967.

Reiss, Albert. "Police Brutality: Answers to Key Questions." *Transaction* (July–August 1968).

Resnick, Judith, and Nancy Shaw. "Prisoners of Their Sex: Health Problems of Incarcerated Women." *Prisoners' Rights Sourcebook* 2 (1980).

Richette, Lisa Aversa. *The Throwaway Children.* Philadelphia: Lippincott, 1969.

Richmond, Al. *Native Daughter: The Story of Anita Whitney.* San Francisco: Anita Whitney Seventy-fifth Anniversary Committee, 1942.

Rocawich, Linda. "Lock 'Em Up: America's All-Purpose Cure for Crime." *The Progressive,* August 1987.

Rogers, Helen W. "A Digest of Laws Establishing Reformatories for Women." *Journal of Criminal Law and Criminology* 13 (November 1922).

———. "A History of the Movement to Establish a State Reformatory for Women in Connecticut." *Journal of Criminal Law and Criminology* 19 (1929).

Rosenberg, Ethel. *Death House Letters.* New York: Jero, 1953.

Roth, Paula, ed. *Alcohol and Drugs Are Women's Issues.* Metuchen, N.J.: Women's Action Alliance and The Scarecrow Press, 1991.

Rothman, David J. *The Discovery of the Asylum.* Boston: Little, Brown, 1971.

———. "Of Prisons, Asylums, and Other Decaying Institutions." *Public Interest,* no. 26 (1972).

Rudovsky, David. *The Rights of Prisoners,* revised ed. Carbondale: Southern Illinois University Press, 1988.

Rudovsky, David, with Michael Avery. *Police Misconduct: Law and Litigation.* New York: Clark Boardman Callaghan, 1988.

Rundle, Frank. "Institution vs. Ethics: The Dilemma of a Prison Doctor." *The Humanist,* May–June 1972.

Ryan, T. A. *Adult Female Offenders and Institutional Programs: A State of the Art Analysis.* Washington, D.C.: U.S. Department of Justice/National Institute of Corrections, 1984.

Sarrazin, Albertine. *The Runaway.* New York: Grove, 1967.

Schulder, Diane B. "Does the Law Oppress Women?" *Sisterhood Is Powerful: An Anthology of Writings from the Women's Liberation Movement,* edited by Robin Morgan. New York: Vintage Books, 1970.

Schurr, Edwin. *Crimes without Victims.* Englewood Cliffs, N.J.: Prentice-Hall, 1965.

———. *Labeling Women Deviant.* New York: Random House, 1984.

Serge, Victor. *Men in Prison.* Garden City, N.Y.: Doubleday, 1969.

Slim, Iceberg. *Pimp: The Story of My Life.* Los Angeles: Holloway House, 1969.

Shaw, George Bernard. *The Crime of Imprisonment.* New York: Citadel, 1961.

Silberman, Charles E. *Criminal Violence, Criminal Justice.* New York: Random House, 1978.

Simon, Rita J., and Jean Landis. *The Crimes Women Commit, the Punishments They Receive.* Lexington, Mass.: Lexington Books, 1991.

Snell, Tracy L. "Women in Prison: Survey of State Prison Inmates, 1991." Washington, D.C.: U.S. Department of Justice, Bureau of Justice Statistics, 1991.

Sobel, Suzanne B. "Difficulties Experienced by Women in Prison." *Psychology of Women Quarterly* 7, no. 2 (Winter 1982).

Spaeth, Edmund B., Jr. "The Court's Responsibility for Prison Reform." *Villanova Law Review* 16, no. 6 (August 1971).

Spencer, Carol, and John E. Berechocea. *Vocational Training at the California Institution for Women: An Evaluation.* S. 8139. Sacramento: California Corrections Department, 1971.

Stanton, Ann M. *When Mothers Go to Jail.* Lexington, Mass.: Lexington Books, 1980.

Starobin, Robert S. *Industrial Slavery in the Old South.* New York: Oxford University Press, 1970.

Sterling, Dorothy. *Tear Down the Walls! A History of the Black Revolution in the United States.* New York: Signet Books, 1970.

Sutherland, Sidney. "The Mystery of the Puritan Girl: Did Lizzie Borden Kill Her Parents?" *Liberty,* March 1929. Reprint, *Liberty,* Fall 1972.

Szasz, Thomas Stephen. *Law, Liberty, and Psychiatry: An Inquiry into the Social Uses of Mental Health Practices.* New York: Macmillan, 1963.

———. *Psychiatric Justice.* New York: Macmillan, 1965.

Tassin, Ida Mae. *Proud Mary: Poems from a Black Sister in Prison.* Buffalo, N.Y.: Buffalo Women's Prison Project, 1971.

Taylor, Victor E. "The Correctional Institution as a Rehabilitation Center: A Former Inmate's View." *Villanova Law Review* 16, no. 6 (August 1971).

———. "Drug Abuse Control: Heroin and the Black Community." *American Scholar* 40, no. 4 (1971).

Temin, Carolyn E. "Criminal Sentencing Procedures: A Judicial Straitjacket." *The Shingle* 32, no. 7 (Philadelphia Bar Association, October 1969).

———. "Discriminatory Sentencing of Women Offenders: The Argument for ERA in a Nutshell." *American Criminal Law Journal* (Spring 1973).

Tidwell, Mike. *In the Shadow of the White House: Drugs, Death, and Redemption on the Streets of the Nation's Capital.* Rocklin, Calif.: Prima, 1992.

———. "Our Tax Dollars Have Promoted Drug Use and Violence." *Washington Spectator* 20, no. 16 (September 1, 1994).

Tyler, Gus, ed. *Organized Crime in America: A Book of Readings.* Ann Arbor: University of Michigan Press, 1962.

U.S. Department of Justice. *Drugs, Crime, and the Justice System.* Washington, D.C.: Bureau of Justice Statistics, 1992.

———. *Drug Use Forecasting: 1993 Annual Report on Adult Arrestees: Drugs and Crime in American Cities.* Washington, D.C.: National Institute of Justice, 1994.

———. *Fact Sheet: Drug Data Summary.* Washington, D.C.: Bureau of Justice Statistics, 1994.

———. *Fact Sheet: Drug Use Trends.* Washington, D.C.: Bureau of Justice Statistics, 1994.

———. *Women in Jail, 1989.* Washington, D.C.: Bureau of Justice Statistics, 1990.

U.S. National Commission on the Causes and Prevention of Violence. *Crimes of Violence,* vol. 13. Washington, D.C.: U.S. Government Printing Office, 1969.

"Use of Group Dynamics and Bibliotherapy in Total Institution Training for Human Development." Workshop on self-worth and self-development at the Iowa Women's Reformatory. 1972. Available from Library Consultant, Iowa Department of Social Services, Des Moines, Iowa.

Vandor, Maria, Patti Juliana, and Rose Leone. "Women and Illegal Drugs." In *Alcohol and Drugs Are Women's Issues,* vol. 1, edited by Paula Roth. Metuchen, N.J.: Women's Action Alliance and The Scarecrow Press, 1991.

Velimesis, Margery L. "Criminal Justice for the Female Offender." *Journal of the American Association of University Women* (October 1969).

———. *Report on the Survey of 41 Pennsylvania County Court and Correctional Services for Women and Girl Offenders, Jan. 1, 1965–Dec. 31, 1966.* Philadelphia: American Association of University Women, Pennsylvania Division, 1969.

Walker, Nigel. *Sentencing in a Rational Society.* London: Allen Lane, 1969.

Ward, David A., and Gene Kassebaum. ''Homosexuality: A Mode of Adaption in a Prison for Women.'' *Social Problems* (Fall 1964).

———. *Women's Prison: Sex and Social Structure.* Chicago: Aldine, 1965.

Weisberg, D. Kelly, ed. *Women and the Law.* Cambridge, Mass.: Schenkman Books, 1982.

West, Cornel. *Race Matters.* Boston: Beacon Press, 1992.

Wicker, Tom. *A Time to Die: The Attica Prison Revolt.* Lincoln: University of Nebraska Press, 1994.

Wines, E. C., ed. *Transactions of the National Congress on Penitentiary and Reformatory Discipline Held at Cincinnati, Ohio, 1870.* Albany, N.Y.: Weed, Parsons, 1871.

Wolfgang, Marvin E. *Crime and Justice.* New York: Basic Books, 1977.

———. ''Making the Criminal Justice System Accountable.'' *Crime and Delinquency* 18, no. 1 (January 1972).

Wolfgang, Marvin E., ed. *Studies in Homicide.* New York: Harper, 1967.

Wolfgang, Marvin E., and Bernard Cohen. *Crime and Race: Conceptions and Misconceptions.* New York: Institute of Human Relations Press, 1970.

Wolfgang, Marvin E., and Franco Ferracuti. *The Subculture of Violence: Towards an Integrated Theory in Criminology.* London: Tavistock, 1967.

Woods, Paul, J. *A Study of Anger in the Federal Reformatory for Women.* Alderson, W.V.: Federal Reformatory for Women, 1970.

Worth, Dooley. ''American Women and Polydrug Abuse.'' In *Alcohol and Drugs Are Women's Issues,* vol. 1, edited by Paula Roth. Metuchen, N.J.: Women's Action Alliance and The Scarecrow Press, 1991.

Yablonsky, Lewis. *The Violent Gang.* New York: Macmillan, 1962.

Young, Clifford M. *Women's Prisons Past and Present.* Elmira, N.Y.: Elmira Reformatory, 1932.